T0059935

awakening
Shakti

awakening
Shakti

The Transformative Power of the Goddesses of Yoga

sally kempton

SOUNDS TRUE
BOULDER, COLORADO

Sounds True, Inc.
Boulder, CO 80306

Published 2013

Cover design by Jennifer Miles

Interior design by Karen Polaski

Illustrations © Ekabhumi Charles Ellik

The lines on page 25 by Jnaneshwar Maharaj are excerpted from *The Nectar of Self-Awareness*
(SYDA Foundation, 1979), ch. 1, v. 1-2, 10. Reprinted with permission from the publisher.

The excerpts on page 55 are from *In Praise of the Goddess: The Devimahatmya and Its Meaning*.
Translated by Devadatta Kali. Nicolas-Hays, 2003. Reprinted with permission from the publisher.

The hymn on page 90, "The Secret Heart of Lakshmi," is from verse 88, *Invoking Lakshmi: The Goddess
of Wealth in Song and Ceremony* by Constantina Rhodes, the State University of New York Press © 2010,
State University of New York. All rights reserved. Reprinted with permission from the publisher.

The lines on page 147 are in the *Cittavisuddhiprakarana* and the excerpt on pages
171–172 is in the *Chandamaharoshana Tantra*. Both are excerpted from Miranda Shaw's
Passionate Enlightenment: Women in Tantric Buddhism, Princeton University Press, 1994,
pages 140 and 143 respectively. Reprinted with permission from the author.

The passage on page 201 is from "Sita" © Jason Schneiderman.
Reprinted with permission from the author.

The poem on page 259 by Lalla is from *Lalla: Naked Song Translations*, Maypop
Books, © 1992 Coleman Barks. Reprinted with permission from the translator.

The lines on page 301 by Lawrence Edwards are from *Kali's Bazaar*, published by Muse House
Press; Atlanta, GA; 2012. Reprinted by permission from the author; thesoulsjourney.com.

Printed in the United States of America

Library of Congress Cataloging-in-Publication Data
Kempton, Sally.
  Awakening Shakti : the transformative power of the goddesses of yoga / by Sally Kempton.
    p. cm.
  Includes bibliographical references.
  1. Hindu goddesses. I. Title.
  BL1216.K46 2013
  294.5'2114--dc23
                                        2012022833

Ebook ISBN: 978-1-60407-944-9

FSC
www.fsc.org
MIX
Paper | Supporting
responsible forestry
FSC® C103098

To my mother

Contents

CONTENTS

Illustrations

Acknowledgments

I offer profound appreciation to the students and friends who participated in my classes and teleconferences on the Goddess. Your attention, feedback, and friendship helped create this book.

Thanks to everyone at Sounds True who helped shepherd *Awakening Shakti* through the process, especially Tami Simon, Haven Iverson, Jennifer Holder, Elisabeth Rinaldi, Karen Polaski, Jennifer Miles, and Rachael Murray.

Andrea Ferretti, Haven Iverson, and Tami Simon read several of these chapters at an early stage, and made significant editorial suggestions. Kelly Notaras did a masterful job of editing the completed manuscript. My gratitude to them and to the others who gave important feedback: Karen Osborne, Marc Gafni, Constantina Rhodes, Rudy Wurlitzer, and Mark Schmanko.

This book is not a work of scholarship in the classical sense. As a Western devotee/practitioner, I stand with one foot inside the Indian tradition and another outside it. I've interpreted these traditional texts and practices through a contemporary lens, often in the light of my own meditative experience. I'm conscious that my interpretations are sometimes creative and often nontraditional. At the same time, I have tried to let the tradition live in me and speak through me, to let my story and the stories of the goddesses dance together. That said, *Awakening Shakti* could not have been written without the work of so many scholars, practitioners, and devotees whose writings and translations I have relied on to guide me through the thicket of Shakta literature and symbolism. I am especially grateful to the late David Kinsley, whose books *Hindu Goddesses* and

Tantric Visions of the Divine Feminine are foundational for anyone who studies the sacred feminine. I've also been influenced by the writing of master Indologist Heinrich Zimmer and by Andrew Harvey, whose wonderful book *Return of the Mother* carries the Goddess's passion better than any I know. My friends Douglas Brooks and Constantina Rhodes always inspire me with their insights into how the mythic realms interface with the personal psyche.

I offer special thanks to Christopher Wallis for providing correct transliterations of Sanskrit mantras, and for clarifying certain points of translation and Tantric history.

Deep bows to all the sages and scholars whose works are cited in this book. Any mistakes I've made through inattention or audacity are not your fault, but my own.

Special thanks to *Yoga Journal* and my editors there—Kaitlin Quistgaard, Andrea Ferretti, Charity Ferreira, Hillari Dowdle, Shannon Sexton, and Kathryn Arnold—for giving me such a privileged platform from which to write about issues of the inner life, for your editorial brilliance, and for publishing my first articles on the goddesses.

To Deb Buxton, my indispensible virtual assistant, for help on every front.

To my soul-sister, Ruthie Hunter, for her gifts of support and insight.

To my dear friend Marc Gafni, whose insight and precision help make everything I write better, and whose love and kindness always expands my heart.

My deepest gratitude to Swami Muktananda, who kindled the energy of the Goddess inside me and showed me how to revere her inner forms.

To Ramakrishna Paramahamsa and all the other lovers of the divine Mother, whose devotion helps reveal her to the world.

To the goddess Matangi, who translates the Goddess's subtle wisdom into the earthy language of daily experience, and whose shakti pervades this book.

Above all, to the most personal of all forms of the Goddess, my inner lover, guru, and guide, Chiti Kundalini—by whose grace we are, in the end, set free.

CHAPTER 1

A Crown of Feminine Design

The Goddess Incarnates

I am the sovereign queen, the treasury of all treasures,
whose breathing forth gives birth to all the worlds and yet
extends beyond them—so vast am I in greatness.

DEVI SUKTA (Praise Hymn of the Goddess)
from the Rg Veda

If there is to be a future, it will wear a crown of feminine design.

AUROBINDO GHOSE

One October night in rural India, I fell in love with the Goddess. It happened on the second night of a festival called Navaratri, which celebrates the divine feminine as the warrior Durga, slayer of the demons of ego and greed. Like so many festivals in India, Navaratri is both a big party and an occasion for mystical communion with the divine. Women put on their most gorgeous clothes; temples overflow with worshippers. Nights are filled with dancing and storytelling. People have heightened, even visionary, experiences of the energy that the festival invokes.

That night, several hundred of us had gathered amid a blaze of candles next to a huge statue of Durga, eighteen feet high in her red sari, seated on top of a white tiger, arms bristling with weapons. I was supposed to tell one of my favorite mythological tales, the story of the romance of the Goddess Sati.

I was thrilled by the opportunity to tell a story—something I love to do—in such a heightened atmosphere. But when I stood up to speak, I was seized by a feeling much bigger than excitement. It was a kind of ecstasy, a deep pulsing joy that nearly undid me while I tried to form the words of my tale. Later, I would learn to recognize this feeling as one of the characteristic signatures of the Goddess's presence. The divine feminine has a thousand names and a thousand moods, but when she chooses to show up for you, she very often shows up as ecstasy.

Ecstasy is a feeling that is hard to convey and impossible to ignore. Every few minutes, I had to stop talking because tears kept threatening to break through my voice. When it was over, I knew that something had just happened which would change my life.

It wasn't just the story that did it. But I'll tell you the story anyway.

Back at the dawn of time, the great Goddess, who creates the world and then lives as the world, is asked to incarnate as Sati (She-Who-Is) in order to make the sacred marriage with her eternal consort, Shiva. Without her presence, Shiva cannot act in the world. He sits on a mountain, lost in meditation, disdaining to perform his cosmic function. This creates havoc in the cosmos. So, the great deities Brahma the Creator and Vishnu the Sustainer approach the Goddess on their knees. They beg her, for the sake of the world, to take the form of a woman and lure Shiva out of his yogic trance. Daksha, a mind-born son of Brahma, will be her father.

The Goddess agrees, but only on one condition. She has seen that men and gods have begun to treat women as property, lesser creatures in the cosmic hierarchy. "If I agree to become your daughter," she tells Daksha, "you must promise to honor me as the Great Goddess. If you do not, I shall instantly leave my body, for I will know that the time is not yet right for me to act fully in the world."

Daksha humbly agrees, and Sati is born in his household. At the age of sixteen, she marries Shiva, drawing him out of meditation through the allure of her irresistible beauty and her power of creating bliss. Shiva is the primal outsider of the Hindu pantheon, the lord of thieves as well as yogis. The original shaman as well as the primal yogi, he resides in the deep forests and mountains, attended by ghosts and goblins. He refuses to change his homeless lifestyle just because he has a wife. So for eons, Shiva and Sati make passionate erotic love under trees and beside streams, in subtle realms beyond the clouds, and in secret mountain caves. They adore each other with cosmic passion.

Then the trouble starts. A few thousand millennia have passed. Daksha has worked his way into a position of power as the leading deity of religious orthodoxy. In the process, he has forgotten his promise to the Goddess—and forgotten his daughter's real nature. He disapproves of Shiva's rebel status and feels personally threatened by Shiva's obvious disdain for convention. Daksha plans a huge cosmic fire ritual, which will establish for all time the religious structures of the universe. He invites every god, titan, celestial musician, snake deity, and nymph in the universe. But in a fit of celestial malice, Daksha deliberately sends no invitation to his daughter and her consort.

Sati hears the news on the day of the sacrifice. She is stunned beyond measure. Daksha has done the unthinkable. Not only has he grievously insulted her beloved, he has dishonored the World-Mother, the power of life itself, without whom religion is meaningless. Sati knows she cannot remain in a world that does not recognize her. She sits in meditation, summons her inner yogic fire, and sends her life-force into the ether, leaving her body behind.

Shiva goes mad when he finds her. He takes himself to the ritual ground and destroys the sacrifice. He then takes Sati's body in his arms and begins to careen through the worlds. Wherever he carries her body, earthquakes and volcanoes, tidal waves and forest fires erupt. At last, the gods do the only thing they can do to save the universe. They send the great wanderer, Saturn, to cut Sati's body into pieces. As the parts of her body fall to Earth, they become physical pockets of sacred ecstasy, earth shrines. For eons, in hidden caves and beside trees, near bodies of water and at the heart of villages, people will find the goddess enshrined in the soil and rock itself. Her body is the sacrifice that infuses the divine feminine into the earth.[1]

The story, as I told it, comes from the Shakta tradition, the branch of Hinduism that worships the Goddess as the ultimate reality. In the more traditional version, Shiva is the main figure in the story, and Sati is depicted as a submissive Indian wife who leaps into the sacrificial fire because her husband has been insulted. (In fact, this version has a dark side. It became a model for Hindu widows, who were often encouraged to immolate themselves on their husband's funeral pyre in imitation of Sati.) The Shakta version reveals a far more interesting take on the story. As the great Goddess Herself, Sati has the power to choose life or to depart it. She doesn't leave her body because her husband is insulted. She leaves because, like so many fathers and the conventional world he represents, Daksha has failed to honor her power and independence. He embodies patriarchy's inability to see the primal divinity of the feminine. She leaves because she knows that if the dignity of the feminine is not recognized, true union of the masculine and the feminine is not possible. The story reveals, more clearly than any in Eastern mythology, that moment when the patriarchy removed goddess worship from conventional rituals, leaving the Goddess to hide in the secret places of the earth.

Because the Goddess understands deep time, she also knows that her death is not really an ending, because one day the time will be right for her to reincarnate and once again marry her consort. This time, perhaps, the world will be ready for her.

CONNECTING TO THE ENERGY IN THE MYTH

There is a form of myth that is subversive. This version of the Sati story speaks for a hidden voice within its traditional culture: the voice of primal feminine dignity. Such a powerful myth interacts with the psyche and connects us to the deep structures of the universe. Sati's gesture, her willingness to immolate herself to call attention to injustice, called out an answering recognition in me. It had something to do with romance, with the power of doomed love, with Shiva's grief, but it was more a recognition of the deep feminine capacity for passion, for feeling itself, for the kind of love that cares nothing for safety or conventional wisdom. That kind of love, I saw, is a quality of the universe itself, which is willing to destroy its own life-forms when the conditions of life become untenable. The divine feminine knows that a birth sometimes demands a death, and that the personal self sometimes has to die if the world is to be made sacred.

It wasn't only the content of the story that moved me. It was the energy itself, the pulsing, love-saturated, subtly sensual energy that rose in the atmosphere that night in India as we invoked the Goddess. That energy seemed to be telling me that there are secrets, ways of being in the universe such that only the divine feminine can reveal. After that night, I began to "see" her everywhere, almost as if she were pursuing me. I went about my normal existence, which was highly scheduled and mostly work centered. But every now and then, "she" would show up. Once as a palpable presence who seemed to hover in the air next to me emanating soft waves of, yes, maternal tenderness. More often, I would sense her as a subtle sensation of luminosity that would infuse the air, or as an inner feeling of joy, or a sensation of being surrounded by a soft, embracing awareness.

One effect of all this was to make me fall in love with the natural world. My new awareness of the Goddess spilled over as a new awareness of trees and landscapes, so that what had seemed matter of fact and dull now began to vibrate with sentience. I would find myself staring up at a eucalyptus tree as if it were a lover, or looking out over a landscape with a feeling that it was alive and breathing. I began to practice a meditation where I imagined that the trees and the air were "seeing" me, and when I did that, the borders of my skin-encapsulated sense of self would soften, and I would "know" that the world and I were part of the same fabric. Goddess awareness literally put me in touch with something that felt like the soul in the physical world.

It also made me start looking deeper into the myths of the Hindu goddesses and into the practices of sacred feminism. As others have before me, I intuited that we are in a time when Sati will definitely take her place in the world once more.

WHERE IS THE GODDESS?

The story of Sati's disappearance tells a mythic version of a historical process that kept the Goddess underground for several millennia. We know from Marija Gimbutas's archaeological studies that many Neolithic cultures in Europe and in the Indian subcontinent worshipped a mother goddess, and that the worship of the feminine was displaced in the Bronze Age, especially in Europe and Asia Minor. In Celtic lore, there's a story about a culture that lived in Ireland before the warrior tribes arrived. It's said that when their land was invaded, these folk—goddess worshippers, artisans, and craftspeople—dressed in their finest costumes and arrayed themselves in battle to meet the invading tribes. Then, when the opposing warriors rode down on them, these beings "turned sideways into the light" and disappeared.[2] Legend says that they entered into the cracks between the visible and invisible worlds, where it is thought that they still reside, in what is called the land of faery.

In a sense, the Goddess too turned sideways into the light. She immolated herself like Sati—surviving demurely in India as a consort of male deities. She was exiled like the Shekinah, the feminine divine of Judaism. In our time, the Goddess has come roaring out of her hiding places—for it is also the nature of the feminine to roar—and we are beginning to recognize uniquely feminine kinds of power. We sense that something profoundly important is missing from a world in which the power of the divine feminine is not understood and in which women themselves are out of touch with their own Shakti, the force of feminine strength and the flavors of feminine love.

Many contemporary writers—I think especially of Riane Eisler, Andrew Harvey, and Llewellyn Vaughan-Lee—have pointed out to us that our survival as a species may depend on our ability to reengage with the feminine.[3] The great evolutionary mystic Aurobindo concurred. He wrote, "If there is to be a future, it will wear a crown of feminine design."[4] Whether or not this is true, there is no doubt that at this point in time most postmodern, educated Westerners, women as well as men, are profoundly cut off from the feminine. Women, at least in the developed world, enjoy freedoms and dignities and opportunities that were possible at no other time in history. But very few of us live from our intrinsic feminine strength and intelligence.

MODERNITY AND THE FEMININE

With all its gifts and dignities, modernity has created conditions that weaken our bonds with the feminine. We're born, most of us, in sterile hospital environments, emerging out of the womb to be blinded by bright lights, handed over to large beings who spank us and cut the umbilical cord—and even our foreskin if we happen to be boys. If we are premature or seem weak or sick, we might be separated from our mother or even kept in incubators—in short, abandoned by the feminine. We're often mothered by women who were not mothered themselves and who don't have the deep capacity for relaxed nurturance that lets children trust their place in the world. We grow up into a culture where girls are treated as objects of sexual desire long before they have any true sense of self, and where the secret language of the feminine has been commodified into shared conversations about fashion and nail polish. We become mothers outside a system of social support, often juggling demanding jobs, economic shortfalls, and our own emotional difficulties. As we age, we turn invisible. My friend Penny came home from a trip to New York, where she remembered from twenty years before that every man she passed undressed her with his eyes. She told her husband, "Men in New York have become so much less sexually aggressive." Her husband gave her a puzzled look. "Honey," he said, "You're fifty." The realization sent her into an identity crisis that lasted for several years—during which she spent time observing elderly women she knew, realizing that, rather than becoming true elders, many of them simply devolved into passivity and depression.

To change all this requires a deep turning of the heart, a shift of consciousness that has to come from our connection to the source of life. The sacred technologies of Tantric culture offer us this possibility.

THE GODDESS AS EVERYTHING

The yogic sages—especially in the branch of yoga called Tantra, which we'll discuss more in chapter 2—anticipated quantum physics by pointing out that a subtle vibratory energy is the substratum of everything we know. Unlike physicists, however, yogic seers experienced this energy not simply as an abstract vibration but as the expression of the divine *feminine* power, called Shakti. The word *shakti* means "power." Shakti, the innate power in reality, has five "faces." It manifests as the power to be conscious, the power to feel ecstasy, the power of will or desire, the power to know, and the power to act. The tantras say that all of these powers come into play in the act of cosmic creativity, when divine intelligence spins a universe out of itself, much the way a human mind creates a dream or a fantasy on its own inner screen. The cosmic creation explodes in a big bang and then evolves over millions of years as suns, planets, increasingly sophisticated life forms, and, of course, human beings. All of reality, this tradition says, is Shakti's dance. Shakti takes form as the biological processes of our body. She acts through our thoughts and the play of our emotions. She becomes every atom and dust mote in the physical world. We are, in our essence, made of Shakti. Her powers of consciousness, ecstasy, will, knowing, and acting are constantly at play both in ourselves and the world. She is also the force that inescapably nudges us toward the evolution of our consciousness, with which we must align when we seek conscious transformation.

But the Tantric sages weren't content with a generalized vision of energy-as-Shakti. They personalized it in mythic language and in an additional leap of insight, created a science for transforming human energy—by working with the goddess figures of the Hindu pantheon.

MULTIPLE DEITY FORMS

The Hindu traditions are famously comfortable with the idea that the Absolute Reality, while formless and transcendent, is perfectly capable of manifesting in both divine and mundane forms. So Shakti, the formless source of everything, is understood to take forms—as gods and goddesses, personifications of the different energies that make up the multiple dimensions of existence and of our own consciousness.

The Hindu pantheon is complex; every village has its gods and goddesses, while the major deities—Vishnu, Shiva, and Devi, the Great Goddess—have hundreds of names apiece. The great Hindu trinity of Brahma, Vishnu, and Shiva dominate the cosmic hierarchy, along with their consorts Saraswati, Lakshmi, and Parvati. Behind them stands Mahadevi, the Great Goddess, who vitalizes all the other deities and gives them the power to perform their cosmic functions. In Tantra, the goddess-consorts are seen as embodying the *power*, the active energy of each of the male gods. In other words, it is the goddesses as energy, their Shakti, that activates the functions of the male god figures. Brahma's job is to bring worlds into manifestation, and he does it through his Shakti, Saraswati, who is also the energy behind creative speech. Vishnu sustains and protects the worlds, empowered by his Shakti, Lakshmi, the energy of nourishment and abundance. Shiva dissolves structures and also oversees the practice of yoga, by which seekers attempt to merge into the formless essence beyond all that is. His power is embodied in strong goddesses like Durga, Parvati, and Kali. All of these deities have their own mythology, their own temples, and their own cults. To complicate matters, Vishnu has a habit of sending avatars—incarnations of himself—into the world. The most important of these are the man-gods Rama—a warrior king and model of rectitude—and Krishna, cosmic lover and canny master of cunning and statecraft. As Rama, Vishnu is the beloved of Sita, who embodies faithful, wifely devotion. As Krishna, he has dozens of consorts, but most notably Radha, his youthful lover and the partner of his most erotic games.

The Goddess, Shakti, also appears in a multiplicity of forms. As an independent goddess, she is often given the generic name of Devi (Goddess), but she is also worshipped on her own as Durga, the demon-slayer and mother of warriors, and as Kali, the Black One, who matches Shiva in her power to dissolve forms into formlessness. All these names and attributes can be confusing to the linear mind, especially when you first discover the same goddess being described under different names. Yet that multiplicity is also what allows us to choose our own gateways into the luscious field of goddess energies. For this, we need to give ourselves permission to explore the different faces and energy signatures of these deities. That's what we will do in this book.

The best way to explain in modern terms what a deity is, is to understand deity as a unique vortex of energy. Sometimes that energy vortex takes recognizable anthropomorphic form (for instance, in meditation visions). Sometimes that energy is felt through the sound vibrations called *mantra*, or through the geometric pictures, called *yantras*, that map the way that energy looks in "blueprint" form. To learn to experience these distinct energies, with their distinct powers and qualities, is the invitation of this book. Recognizing and decoding the various "tastes" of the goddesses is a way of deepening your capacity for living with passion and depth. It's a practice for mining your soul's connection to the cosmos. It offers a powerful means of understanding the capacities of your own psyche. And it can reveal spheres of consciousness that are ordinarily beyond the range of human understanding.

LEVELS OF CONSCIOUSNESS

Our relationships to the sacred change as we develop. The form of the divine we conceive as five year olds will be different than the way we conceive of the divine in our twenties. The religious fundamentalist's view of God will not be the same as the vision of a scientist nor that of a mystic.

The same goddess may be worshipped by uneducated villagers in rural India as the focus of superstition and fear, and by educated middle-class urbanites as the focal point of conventional religious worship. A mystically minded devotee might invoke that same goddess as the mediatrix of her spiritual unfolding or as a source of inner blissfulness. A meditator might experience the Goddess as his kundalini, expanding his awareness through meditation, appearing in visions, ultimately dissolving all forms into light.

OF GODS AND HUMANS

So, when we invoke the Goddess, our view of her always depends on our own level of consciousness at a given moment. That said, there is a level at which gods and goddesses have an independent existence, apart from the way we conceive them.

Gods and goddesses are "real." They are actual beings who exist in eternal forms in the subtlest realms of consciousness. But within the human psyche, these cosmic beings also exist as psychological archetypes in the Jungian sense of the word. Jung and his followers looked at the Greek gods—Zeus, Aphrodite, and the others—as archetypes of universal psychological energies. An archetype is a subtle blueprint that both transcends individual personality and lives in it, connecting our personal minds to the cosmic or collective mind. The Hindu deities are just as much a part of our psychic structure. When we work with them as symbols, the Hindu deities represent—and in my experience actually can *uncover*—dynamic psychological forces. They personify energies that we feel but may never have thought to name or invoke, both in ourselves and in the world.

This was what I began to discover as I studied and contemplated the personalities of the specific goddesses in the Indian pantheon. I had always thought of them as purely symbolic, even metaphoric. But now I began to see them less as symbols than as actual entities in the psyche and the universe— elemental and very real beings who could be reached through visualization, through mantra, and through the powerful structures of their myths. Because they recognize the transformative potential of contemplating deity energies, both Hindu and Buddhist Tantrikas (practitioners of Tantra) have performed deity meditations since at least the eighth century CE.

Getting to know these different energies through deity meditation changed my relationship to my own energy sources. On the most immediate level, practicing with the goddesses showed me that there are sacred powers within me, aspects of my unique self that connect me to the elemental forces of the cosmos, that I can call on for insight and help.

This book came out of these contemplations, and I offer it as a user's manual for connecting to the sacred feminine through the great goddesses of the Hindu pantheon. The book's intention is to help you open the layers of your soul that are related to these particular energies and the practices that invoke them. That way, you can better receive their gifts. You can recognize and own their shadowy aspects. You can access their power to awaken and transform you. Above all, you can dance with their energies.

There are dozens of goddesses in the Hindu pantheon. We'll work with eleven:

Durga ("Hard to Conquer"): the warrior, cosmic protector, and empowering mother.

Lakshmi ("Fortune"): the goddess of good fortune, wealth, and inner and outer abundance.

Kali ("The Black One"): the mysterious, terrifying, fiercely loving goddess who brings radical change into your life and ultimately dissolves all forms into the void. Among her forms are Tara and Bhairavi.

Parvati ("Mountain Lady"): the goddess of the sacred marriage; the divine yogini, who embodies the power of creative will.

Saraswati ("The Flowing One"): the goddess of language, creative intuition, music, eloquence, and speech.

Sita ("Furrow"): the faithful wife, guardian of the womb, goddess of the earth and its mysteries.

Radha ("Golden Girl"): the goddess of erotic devotional love who carries the gift of divine longing and mystical surrender.

Dhumavati ("Lady of Smoke"): the crone goddess who teaches us how to turn disappointment into spiritual growth.

Chinnamasta ("The Severed-Headed One"): the goddess who presides over the sacrifice of the false self.

Lalita Tripura Sundari ("The Playful Beauty of the Three Worlds"): the queenly goddess of sacred sexuality as well as the highest form of mystical experience, whose blessing unites the energy of the body with the energy of spirit.

Bhuvaneshwari ("Lady of the World"): the goddess of sacred space who creates reality out of the infinite space and dissolves all limitations into herself.

Some of these goddesses are warriors. Others are lovers. Some have maternal energy, others are dedicated to opening you to mystical realms. Each one of them can be a guide into the deepest realms of the soul and a teacher of the skills of living as an empowered feminine lover of life.

SACRED FEMINISM

I like to think of goddess practice as a form of sacred feminism—not political feminism, but feminism of the soul. To my generation, feminism was not only a movement for woman's economic and political equality. It also involved a deep and fearless self-exploration, a commitment to looking beyond our conditioned assumptions about masculine and feminine. That exploration got lost in a kind of backlash in the 1980s and 1990s, but young women are again exploring those questions, even as neuroscience is coming to understand the differences between a male and female brain. One of the great questions that sacred feminism looks at is: what is true feminine power?

Sacred feminism aims to answer this question. It also takes us beyond the association of femininity with gender, and it shows us that the very life-force of the universe is the feminine face of spirit. To be a sacred feminist is to be a lover of the feminine face of God as she appears in the world, in culture, and also in our own psyche and soul—while also recognizing that the feminine can never be separated from her masculine other half.

The Tantric traditions of India and Tibet, especially, understood the divine feminine as the force within life that can act creatively or destructively with equal facility. The sacred feminine can be nurturing but also appropriately ruthless, chaotic, and orderly. Goddess powers endlessly weave the strands of our personal and planetary destiny through space and time, and into the timeless and spaceless. Sacred feminism sees and loves the world as a sacred dance. Sacred feminism wants to embrace everything that is beautiful in the feminine, as well as everything that is terrifying. It wants you, whether you're a man or a woman, to learn to see and embody all these qualities in yourself.

The most immediate and powerful way to unlock the energies of the sacred feminine is through the technologies of deity practice. In deity practice, we contemplate the forms and qualities of subtle beings. Advanced practitioners in the Hindu and Buddhist Tantric traditions have developed deity meditation into a living science for transforming consciousness. In these traditions, a teacher suggests that a student meditate on a particular deity in order to activate qualities in his or her own psyche. The deity becomes the focus of your meditation and acts as an inner guide, protector, and as the one addressed in petitionary prayer. At more advanced levels, you meditate on the subtle and secret energies within the deity. Gradually, through your meditation and through your inner conversation with the deity, you start to feel the subtle energy of Shiva or Kali or Lakshmi inside your own energy field.

Deity meditation has powerful psychological benefits. It unsnarls psychological knots—for instance, issues with power or love. As a spiritual practice, it opens up transpersonal forces within your mind and heart. It can become a powerful focus for devotional feelings, put you in touch with protective energies, and subtly clear your inner vision so that you see the world in a softer, more loving way.

Moreover, your inner relationship with the deity becomes a source of refuge, like an intimate friendship that gives you comfort and a sense of home. When you invoke deities through meditation, visualization, inner dialogues, and mantras, you bring their light and energy into your own body and mind. Deity practice helps us embody the subtlest powers of the universe. It affects us psychologically, spiritually, and even physically. It can protect us, empower us, teach us unconditional love, and even enlighten us.

THE FEMININE AS POWER

The Hindu goddess tradition offers a uniquely insightful window on the dynamic aspect of the divine feminine. To recognize power as feminine is game-changing. In the West, we are used to regarding the feminine as essentially receptive, even passive. The Tantric sages took the opposite view. Looking deeply into the energies at play in the world, they intuited the feminine as pure creative Eros, the life-force behind all evolution and all change, whether physical or psychological. In fact—and this is a big insight—the Tantric traditions tell us that all power comes from an essentially feminine inner source. The masculine in its purest, most essential form is the source of *consciousness,* of *awareness.* So when the masculine wants power, it must draw it from the feminine, just as when the feminine wants to be conscious, to reflect, she must draw that capacity from her inner masculine source.

From the Tantric perspective, all our biological activity is inherently feminine. The power behind breath is the expression of the feminine, not to mention our heartbeat, the energy that fires our muscles, and the impulse behind thoughts. Even more important, the Hindu view of the Goddess identifies her with the kundalini energy, the hidden power of spiritual awakening. So practicing with these goddesses gives us a direct connection to the inner force that can transform consciousness itself.

THE LIVING GODDESS

Deities come alive when they are invoked and worshipped. If you want to know them, you need to treat them not only as figures out of myth but as living beings, energies that are palpable, powerful, and *real*. The Hindu deities, whether we see them as internal archetypes or as personalities or as aspects of a universal power, are truly present in millions of people's inner lives. These goddesses give boons. They manifest insights. They dance inside meditators as the kundalini energy, the subtle power that transforms consciousness. Because human consciousness and human imagination are so powerfully creative, our attention to these forms has a powerful effect on our own life experience, and also affects collective consciousness. In other words, when a lot of people are invoking a particular cosmic energy, they create a channel that makes it easier for that energy to show up in the human world.

Neil Gaiman, in his mordant novel *American Gods*, depicts the ancient Western deities Wotan, Zeus, and Freya as disreputable hobos, forced to live on the highways and truck stops of the American Midwest because no one gives them offerings anymore. Among the gods who appear in the novel, only one deity is doing well: Kali, whom Gaiman names Mama Ji, and who appears plump and sleek, supported by the love of her millions of devotees.[5]

Gaiman, in his irreverent way, was onto something important: the Hindu deities are now very much a part of our globally influenced collective consciousness. Kali, Lakshmi, Durga, and Saraswati appear on T-shirts, wall hangings, coffee mugs, and even lunchboxes, brought to the modern globalized West not only through the Indian diaspora and the international yoga movement, but also through Western popular culture. Their images and mantras are constantly downloaded from the Internet. From one perspective this is a clear example of how consumer culture commodifies sacred imagery. From another perspective it's a sign of the Goddess's reach. A few years ago, I saw a *New Yorker* cartoon featuring Durga, complete with her crown and her eight arms, as a multitasking road warrior. She is driving a car. Two of her hands hold a latte and a cigarette. Another hand holds her cell phone, while yet another is giving the finger to a passing motorist. What made this funny, of course, was the fact that so many middle-class contemporary women live that way—juggling roles, doing five things at once—quick-tempered power goddesses in their own spheres. For many women I know, Kali, Durga, and Lakshmi have become icons, each embodying a particular flavor of feminine strength.

There are reasons for this that go beyond our fascination with exotic cultures and mythic symbols, and even beyond the obvious connection with the political and social empowerment of women. The goddesses of the Hindu pantheon cover a much wider and more radical spectrum of feminine possibility than many of us are normally willing to own. There are Hindu goddesses of exquisite beauty and gentleness. There are also goddesses with sharp teeth, fangs, and arms bristling with weapons. The very wildness of their diversity is part of what makes them so powerfully relevant for contemporary women and men. The Indian goddesses represent aspects of our fundamental life-energy that we need to get to know. In other words, they aren't just related to their native culture or to the images of women in Indian society. Their energies are at play in every one of us, men as well as women, and also in cultures, in politics, and in the natural world. When we engage with the personal aspects of these energies—with their mythic, symbolic forms—we activate hidden powers in our own psyche. Then, these powers transform us.

TRANSFORMATIVE SYMBOLS

We've known since Jung's time that myths and symbols have a lock-and-key relationship to energies in our personal consciousness, as well as in the collective. The ancient spiritual traditions understood very well the power of the imaginal realm. They knew how contemplating an enlightened quality (like compassion) or a divine archetype (like the Sacred Heart, the Tree of Life, or Krishna with his flute) will eventually bring what you're contemplating alive in you. Ancient seers, or *rishis*, "saw" these deity energies both as light bodies and as geometric patterns called yantras. They "heard" them as inner sounds, which they then articulated as mantras. Out of their experience came practices that let us touch these energies emotionally, mentally, and even physically.

THE PSYCHOLOGY OF DEITY MEDITATION

On a personal, psychological level, deity meditation gives us access to a power that works on a deeper level than is available through conventional psychology. The transformative power of the goddess energies can untangle psychic knots, calling forth specific transformative forces within the mind and heart. It can cleanse our mental and emotional bodies, put us in touch with the protective powers within us, and deeply change the way we see the world. More than that, it can shift the way we see ourselves, giving us the power to see the divine qualities we already hold. For women especially, tuning into the goddesses is a way of homing in on aspects of our own life-energy that we may never have understood or owned. Celebrating the goddesses has the potential not only to tune us to our own sacred capacities, but also to help us work with the hidden and secret forces at play in our lives. When we can do that, we can literally harness these forces for our own transformation.

A student of mine, Victoria, has spent years in a traditional marriage. It gave her, she told me, deep joy to support her husband's projects, bring up the children they had together, even pick up his socks from the bathroom floor. Yet her position of financial and emotional dependence worried her and came to annoy her husband. When she began contemplating goddess energies, she saw two things. First, she saw that she had a powerful and ecstatic inner pull toward the Shakti of Sita, the loving, self-sacrificing form of the goddess-as-wife. Recognizing this helped her see that her submission was not just dependence, but the expression of a particular quality of love. She also saw that, given the context of contemporary life, her submission placed a terrible burden on her husband. He, an ordinary man with his own needs and fears, felt required to play the role of masculine protector to her feminine supporter. She solved the problem by searching out the part of herself that embodied another consort goddess, Parvati, whose energy is independent and active, and who maintains a dynamic power balance in relationship to her husband, Shiva. Victoria, like Parvati, is a hard-core yoga practitioner. In yoga, she manifested a natural confidence and strength that was missing in her interactions with her husband. She began consciously identifying herself with the energy of Parvati, imagining the forceful presence of this goddess in her own body. Gradually, she became more challenging to her husband, and as she did, their relationship dynamic shifted radically.

Another woman, a doctor, got herself fired from two hospital positions because she repeatedly and explosively challenged the hospital authorities. When she recognized that something was off in the environment or discerned what she considered a lack of integrity among her colleagues, she would unleash self-righteous anger on the people in charge. At one point, I asked her to dialogue with the energy of Durga, the battle goddess, who comes into the world to right wrongs. She began to touch into the sinuous quality of Durga's strength, which knows exactly when to engage in battle and when to hold back. As she began to look past her embattled ego into the sacred warrior that lay underneath the egoic drive to be right, she was able to speak up in a much more balanced way and eventually got a place on a hospital regulatory commission, where her reformer's zeal led to some significant changes in local hospital protocols.

Danny, a rapper and musician, has learned that when he invokes the energy of Saraswati before he plays, it brings a precision to his music and makes it easier for him to improvise. More than that, contact with her seems to mitigate his self-consciousness, his egoic fear of failure, and his desire for approval. He has come to think of Saraswati as the real force behind his music—not only a muse, but also the one who makes his playing compelling.

GODDESS ENERGIES IN THE PERSONALITY

Most of us have more than one goddess energy flowing through our personalities. Some we are clearly born with, but others seem to arise through the different conditions of our lives. The goddesses we channel when we are young have different faces than the goddesses of maturity and old age. Often we experience these different expressions of the feminine as contradictory: How can you enjoy submitting to a lover yet adore the power you feel when you throw yourself wholeheartedly into a task? What does it mean to be a seductress, yet stand up like a warrior to defend a truth you believe in? How do you integrate your love for beauty and comfort with your instinct to overthrow the conventional structures that restrict your freedom?

One way to overcome these contradictions is to learn how to befriend the deities you sense in yourself, the ones you're drawn to, and also the ones who scare you. As you learn to recognize these energies, they start to act through you in a more flowing way. Energies that have been co-opted by the ego shed their neurotic, self-aggrandizing qualities and start to reveal an essential core. Qualities like impatience and irritability, when irradiated by contact with the Goddess Durga, manifest as an ability to cut through obstructions. An addiction to comfort, purified by being immersed in the energy of Lakshmi, becomes an ability to create lines of beauty in any surroundings. Deity practice can help us enlist these energies for guidance or help. Even more important, meditating with a deity can help you integrate and work with some of your elemental qualities—the problematic as well as the constructive.

Perhaps you come to realize that the emotional intensity that surfaces as anger or a strong drive to change something in the environment is actually an expression of a transpersonal Kali-like energy. Then you can be more fluid when Kali-like intensity bubbles to the surface, instead of letting it overwhelm you and come out as a sharp word or an impulsive action. You can more readily recognize aspects of Sita in a moment when you feel impelled to sacrifice your own self-interest for others, or when you feel unheard or unseen by a lover or a boss. Or, seeing the connection between your moments of brilliance and Saraswati's universal intelligence, you might simultaneously feel more confidence in your intuitions, and less egotistical about your intellectual gifts. By engaging Lalita Tripura Sundari, you could begin to see the divine purity that lives in your sexual desire, and by tuning into Parvati you can celebrate the qualities of sacred partnership in a marriage or a love affair.

THE GODDESS AS THE POWER OF SPIRIT

The goddesses embody transformative power, especially the power to kindle the spiritual energy in each of us, the soul-making energy that lets us awaken to our true Self. On a spiritual level, each of these goddess energies can awaken you in multiple ways. In India, men have traditionally related to the Goddess as a giver of worldly and spiritual boons, and worshipped her so that she would lend them her power. Women do the same, of course. But women have also tended to *identify* themselves with the goddesses, especially with the more recognizably auspicious ones. (Lakshmi, for example, is often invoked as an example for wives to follow in their household affairs.) As we become more able to recognize that men and women contain both masculine and feminine qualities, it changes the way we honor the Goddess. We can start to see her qualities as less gender specific, and more as qualities of consciousness itself.

Recognizing your Shakti as it expands and empowers your inner gifts lets you flow at your growing edge and can also give you profound confidence that you are supported from within, and even from the universe itself. When we engage these Shaktis, we touch into the deep structures of the cosmos and of ourselves. We touch the source code, the hard drive of consciousness itself.

PERSPECTIVES ON THE GODDESS

In this book we'll look at the goddesses from several perspectives.

First, we'll approach each goddess as a unique transpersonal energy with a signature energy frequency. We'll examine the core myths and stories and look at the classical depictions of the goddesses. We'll consider the goddesses as divine personalities, unique beings who live in bodies of light and can show up in meditation or even out of it. We'll look at the iconography and its symbolism. And we'll see the different ways we can experience the personal energy of a deity in nature and culture.

For example, the icon of Goddess Lakshmi shows her with hands that drip gold coins, signifying her power to bestow abundance. In the physical world, she shows up as money and precious metals, but also as every form of fertility and abundance. You might recognize her energy in a blossoming fruit tree, in a golden bracelet, a *Vogue* fashion spread, or in the glow of health on your own face. You might experience Lakshmi working through your outer life as the experience of prosperity and success.

Second, we'll consider how each goddess shows up in our psychological and spiritual lives, in both her light and shadow aspects. We'll look at how the goddesses operate through our minds and hearts. One of the important insights of the Tantric sages was that each goddess can appear in ways that are liberating and expansive, but she can also manifest in ways that are binding, entrapping, and confusing.

For instance, as a liberating energy, Lakshmi's Shakti might appear as a moment of wonder, an inner sense of abundance, or a feeling of love. Her shadow side might trap you through your addiction to shopping or sweets, your fear of failure, or your obsession with looking good.

As we said earlier, once you are in dialogue with the Goddess in yourself, you can work with her psychological manifestations in a way that will radically shift how these energies play in your psyche. Even her shadow sides can teach you (as we'll see in later chapters). Goddess energies are innately transformative. When we interact with them on any level, they change us.

Third, we'll look at the goddesses as aspects of our awakened spiritual energy—the kundalini Shakti, or coiled power. To awaken the Goddess as kundalini is to awaken the transformative intelligence of our innate divine power. It literally brings cosmic energy—the energy of the Goddess—alive within us. The resting, or sleeping, kundalini operates as our basic life force. It operates the breath, powers the heartbeat and the brain, constantly impelling our attention toward external experience. When kundalini is asleep, you experience a split between subject and object, between yourself and the world. According to the tantras, the awakening of kundalini is the awakening of the Goddess's power to reveal fundamental unity. In order to do this, her energy will subtly or dramatically transform your nervous system and the architecture of your brain so that you begin to be able to see with what some traditions call the "eye of the spirit" or the "eye of the heart." Kundalini has been called the evolutionary energy in the human body, and the force of evolutionary eros. In mythic terms, kundalini is the liberating face of the Goddess. So, as we examine and practice with the goddesses, we'll look at how each goddess reveals herself in us as the active force of kundalini.

Finally, throughout the book, we'll explore practices for connecting to the Goddess. We'll find out how to approach her as a personal deity, as a helper, a guide and teacher, as a giver of boons, and as a fierce transpersonal force that dissolves old paradigms and reveals new aspects of the self. We'll learn many methods for invoking the Goddess, and for consciously bringing her presence into our field. We'll discover how to recognize her presence and guidance in our lives.

Each chapter includes contemplations, mantras, personal exercises, and meditations to help you access the goddesses in different ways. Some of these exercises are psychological. However, many of them draw on traditional Tantric methods, like visualization and invocation, that aim to help us recognize the subtle in ourselves and the world. Practices like these have been the mainstay of mystical traditions—not just Hinduism, but also Tibetan Buddhism and Christianity (with meditation on Jesus and the saints standing in for the deities).

IMAGINATION AND DEITY PRACTICE

Though traditional deity practice often uses external ritual, Goddess practice is primarily an activity of intention and imagination. Mystics, like artists, discover truth through imagination. In our ordinary understanding of things, the imagination is considered unreal, made up. "You imagined it," we say—meaning, "It doesn't hold up empirically, so it isn't real." To the mystic, imagination is the faculty through which we perceive the numinous, the supra-real. The forms and qualities of our divine nature are hidden in consciousness: we bring them forth through the faculty of imagination. The Greek word *phantasia*, from which we derive the word *fantasy*, comes from a verb that means "to make visible." We make subtle energies visible by creating images in the mind. What we don't always understand is how these images can transform our inner landscape, and then our life.

The courage, compassion, wisdom, and beauty of the inner self are mostly invisible to us. Our conditioning, our relentless dependence on the egoic perception of our separateness, even our neural wiring predispose us to view ourselves only as the physical and personality self. As egoic beings, we often feel inherently disconnected from the world around us and from our true sources of power. At times, we assume that we are in charge of our lives and capable of building, creating, or manifesting anything we want. Alternatively, we may feel incompetent, incapable, lost. Most of us alternate between the two points of view, both of which are aspects of egoic consciousness.

One way to discover both the richness of our deeper self and the availability of invisible help is through active imagination. Visionary practices, working with archetypes, creating intentions for our future life are all methodologies that challenge our limiting assumptions about ourselves and ask us to open to what we are beyond the ordinary. All are based on a fundamental insight about the mind—a realization that what we think about profoundly affects not only our psyches, but also our physical lives. When we tell ourselves angry stories, we fill ourselves with angry energy. For that moment at least, we become angry people. When we use active imagination to envision positive outcomes for ourselves and others, we can create realities that will eventually manifest in our personhood and in our culture. Through imagination, we tap into our highest human potential and encounter that which is more than human in us: that which is divine.

What we can imagine, we will ultimately be asked to bring forth—whether it is positive or negative. As poet William Blake wrote, "Imagination is not a state: it is the human existence itself." That recognition has become a major force in the Western new thought movements. But this way of thinking actually has deep roots in the Tantric traditions of India. Tantric technologies teach us to divinize—yes, literally, make divine—our bodies and minds by entering deeply into imaginative communion with deity forms. As you read this book and do the practices here, you'll learn how to make visible certain numinous qualities in yourself, qualities that are embodied in these forms and the principles associated with them.

We need to do this not only for ourselves, but for each other and for the world itself. It's a truism that scientific materialism has tended to reduce all natural phenomena to mechanical processes, as postmodernism has tended to reduce metaphysics to an outworn cultural artifact. Unless we live in rural India or Bali, there are no roadside shrines to remind us to look beyond the surface of the land, to see the energies at play within the soil or the soulful presences that live in plants and weather patterns. So we move through the world with tunnel vision, using our technological skills to control the weather, to engineer crops and their DNA, and to force productivity from desert soil. For most people, it's only when earthquakes, hurricanes, and tsunamis disrupt our human infrastructures that we recognize the awesome natural powers that create our world.

It's not just the powers of wind and water that we fail to understand. We also ignore the subtle presences within human culture and pay the consequences without even realizing it. When you don't realize, for example, that language arises from an inner divine power, and that every sound is filled with creative Shakti, you'll tend to use words thoughtlessly and wonder why they so often appear empty or uninspired, or why they turn out to be hurtful. When we don't recognize the numinous presences in ourselves and our world, we attempt to control them by human means and—when we can't control them—feel helpless or hopeless.

As we learn to recognize divine forces in the world, when we *invoke* them, then we are able to interact with the natural world as well as with the powers within ourselves. I have an acquaintance who is a weather worker. I've seen him lift the fog on the California coast. His ability to relate to elemental weather systems has been recognized by an oil company, which once hired him to talk a storm system into bypassing a particularly vulnerable piece of the coast. He does it, he says, by simply tuning in to the energies in the elements and relating to them as he would to another person. From a Tantric perspective, he is dialoguing with goddesses as they manifest in wind and water.

You may not have that particular gift, or even any interest in it. What you do have, however—because we all have it—is the power to communicate with the energies of the goddesses in your inner world. As you do so, as you sense a goddess's presence inside and around you, you may recognize her qualities of strength, of beauty, of flexibility. You'll begin to tune into that subtle energy that in Sanskrit is called *shri*—best translated as "auspiciousness"—which is one of the gifts of the divine feminine. And that energy will come forth in your speech and actions.

HOW TO WORK WITH THIS BOOK

I suggest that you read *Awakening Shakti* with an exploratory attitude. Notice what comes up for you as you read, and also notice how your view of each goddess expands when you do the exercises that are layered into each chapter.

The exercises are doorways into deeper resonance with each goddess. So I recommend reading this book slowly, pausing to practice at least one or two of the contemplations and meditations in each chapter. Let your reading be an opportunity to open yourself to the energies that are playing through these pages.

The goddesses highlighted in this book are embedded in a rich cosmology and a profound philosophical tradition. To understand the individual expressions of the Goddess, it helps to be somewhat familiar with the basic world view of the Hindu tradition. It's also useful to have at least a rudimentary understanding of the core Tantric cosmological narrative and of how that undergirds the relationships between the human and divine. Chapter 2 provides that. It is meant to give you the mythic and conceptual framework for the rest of your exploration.

Each of the subsequent chapters explores one of the goddesses in depth. Some of the goddesses—notably Durga and Kali, Lakshmi, and Saraswati—are so archetypally significant, so prominent in mythology and in the psyche, that I couldn't resist writing about them at greater length. That's why the chapters dealing with these particularly large and multifaceted goddesses are longer than the chapters on some of the others. A few of the goddesses—Chinnamasta, for example—are primarily Shaktis of the inner worlds. They are less apparent in our external life and therefore less discussed in the literature. Some of the chapters on the more esoteric goddesses are relatively short. In fact, several of these esoteric goddesses are forms of more prominent goddesses, especially of Kali, Parvati, and Lakshmi. Though the chapters on Chinnamasta, Dhumavati, and Bhuvaneshwari are not as packed with detail and stories as some of the others, they are set up so that you can contact these goddesses through meditation. You should find that when you meditate on any of the goddesses, using the practices described in these chapters, they will unlock important facets of your consciousness, aspects of the psyche that are unique to them and to you.

One way to use the book is as a practice manual. You could keep it by your bed or your meditation cushion and work with one goddess every week. As you read each chapter, practice the contemplations and meditations, and repeat the mantras. You might write or journal about what arises. Then notice how the Goddess unveils herself through your dreams and meditations, and how she shows up in your life.

You may feel a natural affinity with one or more of these goddesses. This might be because you hold her archetype strongly in your personality. It could also mean that she carries qualities that you need to develop. Different Shaktis become important at different times in our lives. You might have been born with a tendency to express a particular goddess energy, and manifest it naturally. On the other hand, your culture or upbringing, the style of your family, or your social context could have made you uncomfortable with some aspect of the feminine. You might have hidden her energies in yourself, or simply left them unrecognized or undeveloped until some event in your life calls forth a goddess you didn't realize was within you. If you're a man, you may have projected those energies onto women in your life. Now might be the time to recognize that the feminine energies you are drawn to or repelled by are also within you. It's my hope that reading about the Goddess in her different manifestations will show you qualities in yourself that are familiar to you and also qualities that you have wished or suspected were present and never knew how to name.

Mythic doesn't mean unreal. The mythic realm interfaces with our psyche on several different levels. What that means is that the energies of the Goddess will show up through the human beings and animals in your life. They will reveal themselves in the natural world. You'll begin to see their footprints in culture.

You'll recognize them in your friends and coworkers, in your lovers and family members. There's always the possibility that as you practice these contemplations, they will lead you into the dimension of reality in which deities actually reveal themselves as distinct presences. The forms of the goddesses are discerned with the eye of spirit rather than the physical gaze. But they are no less real for being invisible to the naked eye.

In the teachings of the Tantras, the goddesses are said to have three forms through which they can be engaged: the image we see in paintings and statues, the mantra, and the geometric form, or yantra. Each of these forms, the Tantric sages say, fully contains the energy of the deity. As we tune into that unique energy signature, it will start to come alive within us. (For an in-depth discussion on mantra, see Appendix II: Calling Out the Power in Mantra.)

Then there are the stories. For most of us, it's the tales that carry the Goddess. There are layers of meaning in the Goddess stories. Some are beautiful, others totally bizarre, some seem to teach ethics, others are so startling that they stop your mind. If you pay attention, you'll find that each time you read or hear one of these stories, you can find something new in it. There's a good reason why mythic stories are told and retold. They are a path into the heart of sacred reality. They open us to grace. They reveal, for each of us, a unique pathway into the divine feminine. So when you read these tales, let each of them resonate inside you. Maybe the interpretive frame I've given will help crack the façade of the story and get into its heart. Maybe you'll need to let the truth of it emerge from within yourself.

That's the beauty of goddess practice. As you invoke the Goddess in each of these forms, she will show up for you in new ways, unveiling herself within you and outside you, surprising you, loving you up, giving you unexpected gifts, disturbing you, and showing you how the manifestation of her Shakti can awaken you to your own heart.

CHAPTER 2

The Grand Tantric Narrative

Gods, Goddesses, and Worlds

I offer salutations to the God and the Goddess: the infinite parents of the world.
The lover, out of boundless love, has become the beloved.
Because of Her, He exists
And without Him, She would not be.

JNANESHWAR MAHARAJ
The Nectar of Self-Awareness

Goddesses have been invoked, adored, and worshipped in India since the most ancient times. They appear in the Vedas—the oldest texts in the Indian tradition. Stories about the goddesses fill the Puranas, the mythological books that are the basis of popular Hinduism. However, it was the texts and practices of the yogic tradition called Tantra—which began appearing in India around the fifth century CE—that most fully recognized the primal place of the divine feminine.

Before we begin talking about the individual goddesses, I'd like to explain something about what Tantra is and how it views the world. The word *tantra* is usually defined etymologically from its two roots. *Tan* means "to expand or develop." *Tra* means "instrument," but it also means "to save, liberate, or redeem." (Sanskrit is a language with many layers of meaning!) Basically, Tantra is a series of practices and teachings that help us realize that the world is filled with divine energy, with Shakti. It is also a series of tools (the first meaning of *tra*) that we can use both to liberate ourselves from illusion and to make our worldly lives more beautiful, abundant, and skillful. It is fair to say that most goddess paths are fundamentally Tantric in nature, and that one of the earmarks of a Tantric path is its emphasis on the significance of the Goddess.

There are many schools of Tantra in both Hinduism and Buddhism, and also parallel teachings and practices of Taoism, Kabbalah, and Gnostic Christianity. In the Indian tradition, Tantric paths can be divided into "right handed" and "left handed." The right-handed schools, like the modern Shri Vidya tradition that flourishes in South India, focused on mantras, rituals, and meditative practices. The left-handed schools included all these, but also worked with the so-called "transgressive" practices, including the sexual ritual and the ritual use of meat, fish, and intoxicants. The tradition that most influenced me, Trika, originated around the Seventh Century CE in Western India, but had its greatest flowering in Kashmir, for which reason it is sometimes called Kashmir Shaivism. Trika was historically a left-handed path, though contemporary Kashmir Shaivism as taught in the West tends to be more right-handed. The sister schools of the Trika tradition—Kaula and Krama Tantra—were also left-handed. All these traditions, however, taught that reality is nondual—meaning that the physical world, the individual, and the transcendent Absolute are not separate from one another, and instead exist as a continuum. All three put the Goddess at the center of everything and held that the human body contains all possible levels of reality.

Tantric visionaries see the visible and invisible universe as infused with light and power. To the Tantrika the world is fundamentally light. Within this light is also power, energy, vibrating creative dynamism: Shakti. This may seem obvious to us now, understanding as we do that at a subatomic level even matter is really energy. Tantra sees this energy as sacred, divine, the expression of the feminine power within everything. In Tantra, moreover, human women are the earthly containers for the most intense form of sacred energy.

In India, the worship of reality as Shakti directly contrasted with the views of two influential philosophers: Buddha and Shankara. So, let me tell you the story of how one of these philosophers, Shankara, got to know the Shakti. It's mythic, to be sure. Like so many of the myths of the Goddess, it points tellingly to her place in our lives.

THE WORLD AS ILLUSION

Shankara was the founder of Advaita (nondual) Vedanta, arguably the most influential school of Indian philosophy. Though he lived in the eighth century in India, Shankara's vision of ultimate reality is still very much alive. It is a foundation of the modern Hindu movement that was brought to the West by teachers like Swami Vivekananda. Every time you pick up a book with a title like *Wake Up Now!* or *Awakening from the Dream* you are reading teachings that were likely influenced by Shankara. Shankara's teachings point out different methods for dis-identifying with the body and personality—and to realize the Absolute as a pure, boundless awareness, free of forms, which he called Brahman. He saw the physical and subtle universe as a dream, projection, a magic trick, endlessly alluring, ephemeral, and ultimately painful. Only by penetrating through the dream, he might say, can you recognize your true Self, which is pure awareness, free of content, free of forms, and identical with the formless absolute. It was Shankara who wrote, "The Absolute is real, the world is unreal, and the individual soul is the Absolute."

Shankara and his followers metaphorically described the physical and social universe as a burning ocean of endless suffering, no more real than a cloud-castle, yet always ready to delude and trap the unwary. In his view, the cosmic villainess behind the whole mistake was the feminine power known as Maya, mistress of illusion and trickery. Maya, he might say, is an incomprehensible cosmic power that veils the true nature of this world. Maya makes us think that the One is actually Many, and that the world is separate from our own consciousness. Because Maya is considered feminine, all women were seen as tainted with Maya's illusory power, and were therefore dangerous to anyone who sought truth.

Of course, Shankara had part of the story right. Awareness is indeed the ground of everything. The problem was that he only saw half the picture. His greatest misperception had to do with the role of the Shakti, not to mention the body itself. Instead of recognizing that the world is itself made of sacred energy, or Shakti, he saw it as a mirage superimposed on reality. Instead of recognizing the body as a sacred vessel, he saw it as impure. Instead of recognizing the feminine as the creative power of life, he saw her as the enemy of truth. Human women with their alluring bodies ("Woman, burdened with breasts and that hole below the navel" he sang in one famous hymn) trap men with sex, lure them into family life, and then fill their lives with so much activity that the poor guys have no space to recognize reality. Shankara and his followers, like the early followers of the Buddha, gave up home and family life to become wandering monks. They created a powerful tradition of world renunciation. Even today, some teachers of this form of nonduality still say that trying to improve your worldly life is like rearranging the deckchairs on the Titanic. Since it's all illusion anyway, why get upset about the destruction of the forests and the ocean or the suffering of homeless children? Though Shankara might not have gone that far. His teachings had a profoundly world-denying flavor.

Then he met the Goddess.

THE PHILOSOPHER AND THE GODDESS

It happened like this. One day, as Shankara wandered through South India, he found himself on the bank of a river in flood. Shankara was fearless—he had faced down tigers, he had seen through the world-illusion—so what was the problem with a flood? He waded into the river and soon found himself up to his chest in rushing water. Then a weird thing happened. His body stopped working. Standing on one leg in the middle of a swift-moving river, with the other leg lifted to find his next foothold, he froze. His strength gone, his will paralyzed, Shankara panicked. For the first time in his life, Shankara knew the terror of being completely powerless. He realized that if he didn't get moving, he could drown.

Then he heard a cackling laugh. An old forager woman, bent with the weight of her years of labor, stood on the opposite bank. Desperately, Shankara called to her, "Help! Get help!"

The crone raised her head and looked fully into his eyes. She laughed again, her laughter foaming over until it filled the sky. Then she dove into the river and in a few swift strokes swam to where he floundered. She seized him around the chest and pulled him to shore.

"Shankara," she said, "You preach that women are a trap. You say that this world is an illusion. You won't so much as look at a woman. But can't you see that your strength comes from Shakti? What happens when you lose your Shakti? Without Shakti you couldn't even move your limbs! So why do you insult Shakti? Why do you insult the Goddess? Don't you know that I am everything? Don't you know that you can't live without me?"

THE MOMENT OF RECOGNITION

In that moment, the story goes, Shankara realized that he had been denying the obvious. He had been insulting his own life-energy—without which he would not even exist! He bowed down to the Goddess—for indeed, the old woman was the Goddess herself.

Moreover, he became a closet Shakta Tantrika—a lover of the sacred feminine power within the world. He kept his conversion more or less secret—after all, he was an official world-renouncer. But today in South India, many officials of his orders of Indian monks worship the Goddess.

THE TANTRIC VISION

Tantra has often been a kind of underground sect in India, precisely because by sanctifying the body and its energies it subverts the classical yogic teaching that places spirit above and beyond the physical world. But Tantra is secretly practiced even among conventional religious people, partly because Tantric practices are famous for conferring special powers. There is even a saying, "In public be a worshipper of Vishnu (the deity of conventional religion and morality). In private, be a worshipper of Shiva (the deity of yoga). In secret, worship Shakti, (the feminine power behind everything)."

Tantra has many branches and many faces. Some are quite primitive, while others are among the most sublime enlightenment teachings in the world. But all approaches to Tantra have at least three points in common.

First, Tantra is uncompromising in its embrace of reality, in all its beauty and horror. A core feature of Tantra is the principle of nonrejection. In Tantra, nothing is considered to be outside of the divine tapestry. Shakti, the immanent aspect of "godness," has become everything that exists. Therefore everything is worthy of being worshipped as a form of goddess, or Shakti. This is not to say that Tantra ignores ethics or ethical principles. Core texts like the *Kularnava Tantra* stress that a strong ethical grounding is crucial for Tantric practice. However, Tantra insists that all bodies, all worlds, all ideas are made of Shakti, and are therefore divine *in their essence.*

To experience this as fact, to experience it as true within our own bodies and minds, is said to be the knowledge that liberates us from all suffering. As mentioned earlier, one of the two Sanskrit roots of the word *tantra* refers to its capacity for liberating you. *Tan* means to expand, while *tra* means to liberate. So Tantra describes itself as an *expansion* of the knowledge and practice that *liberates* us from suffering. Another meaning of the word *tantra* is "loom." We could say that Tantra sees the world as a weaving of energies—all of them aspects of the energy of the divine, and therefore, all of them sacred. The physical world is as sacred and numinous as the world of spirit. Tantric ethics are based on this recognition.

Second, a corollary of the initial insight is the recognition that physical and emotional pleasures can be doorways into the divine. Tantrikas believe that pleasure can be sacred. The taste of food, the moment of sexual touch, the transporting joy felt when hearing beautiful music, the blissful experience of losing ourselves in movement or in the sight of beauty—any of these can open us to the divine ecstasy at the heart of life.

It's this aspect of Tantra that makes it such a powerful practice for contemporary Westerners looking for a path that merges spirituality with life in the visible world. In the West Tantra is often associated with secret (and now, not so secret!) sexual practices. But these are a tiny part of the Tantric system. Even more radical and significant is the Tantric view that bliss and presence can be discovered in upheaval, in the play of destructive forces, in sorrow and sickness—precisely because there is no place where Shakti is not.

Third, the Tantric view sees the universal Shakti, the divine feminine power—the Goddess—as the source of power. This is a revolutionary idea, and when we get it, it changes our relationship to our own energy forever. So, consider the following.

THE FEMININE IS POWER

True power arises from an inner feminine source—from Shakti. This is true whether the power appears in the cosmos (as in the big bang and the thrust of evolution) or in a human being—as our powers of thought, feeling, and action. In the West, we are used to associating power with masculinity and thinking of the feminine as purely passive, nurturing, and receptive. Tantra tells us that it's the other way around. From a Tantric perspective, the inner masculine—Shiva— is the source of consciousness, awareness. But in order to act, to stir, he must take energy from the inner feminine. In ordinary life, this is exactly what many men do when they project their creative energy outward into a muse, a nurturing wife or assistant, who then pours her energy into him.

In turn, the feminine is grounded and focused by the masculine quality of awareness. Awareness allows the feminine to see herself and gives both containment and direction to her energy. Whether cosmically or individually, every genuinely creative project emerges out of a marriage of consciousness and power. For full creative empowerment, these masculine and feminine polarities need to come together. We need the stability of linear focus—the masculine quality—to merge with the feminine quality of energy, with its invitation to inspiration, Eros, and aliveness. Though we know now that these qualities are present in both men and women, these polarities still get projected onto the opposite gender. Thus, we would have the traditional marriage where the man was supposed to provide directionality and focus, while the woman was supposed to lend her creative energy and feeling to his projects. These gender roles prevail in many relationships, including same-sex couples, where one partner will often enact the masculine role while the other partner plays the feminine.

As we bring a truly Tantric perspective into our daily life, we learn how to marry the God and Goddess in every individual. In relationship, this means that when two people meet, they don't feel the need to project either their life-force (Shakti) or their consciousness (Shiva) onto the other. Instead, they can come together from a place where the masculine and the feminine, awareness and energy, are incarnated equally in men and in women. This allows both for deeper relationship, and for greater fullness in each individual.

That said, when the Tantric sages talk about the divine masculine and the divine feminine, they refer to eternal principles that are fundamentally beyond gender—though they may be expressed through gender. The masculine, Shiva, is understood to be the transcendent quality of godness—the knowing light beyond all forms. The feminine, Shakti, is the immanent aspect of the divine. She is the power that becomes the world.

THE DANCE OF KALI

Cosmically speaking, the Tantras say that without the dynamism of Shakti—the feminine—the masculine, Shiva, is inert. Yet, without the awareness and stability of Shiva, Shakti is uncontrollably wild. A dramatic image from Tantric iconography conveys this essential Tantric viewpoint about reality. The image shows the goddess Kali—naked but for an apron of hands and a necklace of skulls—dancing on the prone body of Shiva, her eternal consort. Shiva's corpse-like pose represents the fact that pure awareness is the static ground of being, comparable to the awareness that a meditator discovers as the unchanging witness of his own mental world. Kali's wild dance expresses the dynamism of the cosmic process—intense, endless, dramatic, arising from and supported by Shiva's ground of stillness, yet expressing itself through endlessly evolving universes.

In the external world, she is the force of evolution, the erotic thrust at the heart of life. She is the intrinsic creative drive that fueled the big bang and continues to unfold as stars, galaxies, planets, life-forms, species, and also as human societies, cultures, and individual consciousness itself. Within our inner world, Shakti plays as our thoughts, emotions, ideas, inspirations, as well as our ideas about who we are. In meditation, she manifests as our visions, our feelings of bliss, our insights, the inner blocks that arise, and the spaciousness that dissolves them. In the process of transformation, she takes form as a passionate urgency that inspires us to step beyond apparent limits and expand our consciousness.

Shiva remains outside and beyond all this, as the unchanging knower, the witness-awareness that both observes and contains the dance. I once had a vision of this dance as a kaleidoscopic vortex of ecstatic light—gorgeous in its radiance, overwhelming in its blissfulness, and terrifyingly endless. That was what most deeply struck me, after my initial awe: the fact that this dance is eternal.

To stay awake to it demands total presence. There is, literally, no rest from the cosmic dance of Shakti, except to ground yourself in being, in Shiva—pure witness-awareness.

At every level of consciousness, the masculine and the feminine, Shiva and Shakti, steadiness and dynamism, awareness and bliss, stability and transformation, being and becoming, complete and complement each other. I want to say this again: without the spacious ground that is the light of consciousness, steady and still, nothing could exist. Without the dynamic power of becoming, nothing could grow, evolve, or transform. Shiva and Shakti, being and becoming, are like two sides of a spinning coin, like water and its wetness or fire and its heat. They are beyond gender, yet when they evolve into physical form, their qualities live in us as aspects of consciousness and also as uniquely gender-related qualities of the human soul.[1]

That's because, in the Tantric universe, everything arises out of that original union, the embrace of Shiva and Shakti. Just as a human embryo is made of the genetic mix of its parents, the universe is made of Shiva and Shakti.

In the next few pages, we'll look briefly at how the Tantras describe the process by which all this comes into existence. I suggest you look at this description as a story, a narrative that can help you grasp how something as subtle as consciousness could become something as dense as the world we all experience. This section is useful because it explains the underlying vision that lies behind our understanding of the individual goddesses. But, if you prefer, you can skip the metaphysics for now, and go to page 39, where you'll find a detailed description of the different forms and faces of the gods and goddesses of the Indian pantheon.

THE TANTRIC CREATION: HOW DID WE GET HERE?

At the start of the grand Tantric creation narrative, there is only one unmanifest presence: a vast transcendent cosmic awareness, filled with bliss and power. This presence has many names, including Paramashiva (supreme goodness), Para Brahman (supreme ultimate), Hrdaya (the heart), and Chidananda (awareness/bliss). This presence experiences itself as "I Am"—in Sanskrit, *aham*. The *I* in "I am"—the eternal subject—is Shiva. The "am"—Shiva's power to experience itself—is Shakti. At this level, Shiva/Shakti are one, merged in indissoluble embrace. Blissfully reflecting on itself, this primal presence is unimaginably free, immeasurably aware, and perfectly blissful. It is empty, yet pregnant with potency. The supreme awareness/bliss is *utterly free* of all constraints and free to become anything. In Sanskrit, the experience of this pure subjectivity is described as *purno'ham*—I am perfect.

Meditation: Being Awareness

We can replicate the experience of the pure "I am" in meditation when we turn our awareness back on itself and allow awareness to expand.

Sitting quietly, be aware of your breath. Notice the sensations in your body. Listen to the sounds around you.

Now, gently turn your attention back on itself. The power of attention that can be aware of sensations and thoughts can also be aware of itself. So just for a moment, turn backward your capacity for being aware and feel that you are becoming aware of your own capacity for being aware. You might experience your awareness as the container for your experience in this moment or as the part of your mind that *knows* you are thinking.

For a moment, let yourself recognize your own awareness.

Even if you can be aware of your awareness for only a moment, in that moment you will touch the primal awareness/bliss at the core of yourself.

FIVE POWERS

This supreme awareness contains infinite powers. In Tantric metaphysics, five of these are important. As we will see, these powers are present at every level of manifestation. They are:

Chit Shakti—The power of being eternally and absolutely conscious and present. At a cosmic level, this power is pure unconditioned presence, aware of itself and the universes that unfold within it. At an individual level, we experience it as the awareness that allows us to experience both ourselves and the world around us. It is the fundamental experience of being sentient and is shared by all creatures.

Ananda Shakti—The power of feeling unconditional bliss or ecstasy. In us, *ananda* can be experienced as every kind of natural happiness, from the simple feeling of relaxation and contentment we feel on waking, to the satisfaction of eating or moving our bodies, to the ecstasy of orgasm, to the subtle joy of falling in love or of deep meditative blissfulness.

Iccha Shakti—The power of unimpeded will. Will is the essential impulse that precedes any form of action. Cosmically, the power of will expresses itself in the flow of life, where everything is part of an interconnected whole. In an individual, it is the fundamental will to live, to exist, as well as every form of desire. Our will, or desire, is the source of all creativity. As the Brihadaranyaka Upanishad says, "As is your will, so is your thought; as is your thought, so is your deed; as is your deed, so is your life."

Jnana Shakti—The power of intuitive knowing and self-organization. It's this capacity that gives natural order to the universe, and that allows life-forms to self-organize. The power of knowing exists within every cell—it's what allows a liver cell to know how to join with other cells to become a liver. In the human mind, it is the capacity to know, to plan, to discern, and to make judgments. It is also the flash of intuition that reveals new information, makes connections, and gives insight.

Kriya Shakti—The power to do anything. Cosmically, this power brings universes into form. In the natural world and in us, it manifests as the activity within our cells and our brains, as well as in the deliberate activities we perform.

FIVE ACTS

With these five powers, supreme consciousness performs five essential actions. These activities take place on a cosmic level and also physically within cells, bodies, and also within the human mind. These actions are:

Shrishti (Manifestation)—Bringing worlds into existence. According to the Tantras, everything arises within one field of energy, or Shakti. All individual forms—living creatures, species, landforms, cultures, civilizations, and our own mental creations—come into being, are maintained for a while, then dissolve. This happens on the level of cells, thoughts, ideas, developmental stages, stars, galaxies, and so forth.

Sthiti (Sustenance)—This is the natural tendency of consciousness to maintain the forms that have manifested.

Samhara (Dissolution)—All forms ultimately dissolve back into their fundamental energy. Everything changes, nothing is permanent except consciousness itself.

Tirodhana (Concealment)—When forms come into existence, they conceal the underlying energy, the Shakti, that is their source. Unity is disguised as multiplicity. In the same way, the universe conceals much more than it reveals. Seeds are concealed within the ground until they sprout. Memories are concealed in the brain. Thoughts and images dissolve into consciousness, are concealed, then arise again.

Anugraha (Revelation or Grace)—Awakens us to the underlying unity behind all things. Grace is also the fundamental tendency within consciousness to heal, to love, and to reveal the underlying goodness of life. We experience our essential capacity for graceful self-revelation not only in mystical experience, but in any moment of wonder or peace.

STARTING IN BLISSFUL AWARENESS

Tantra tells us that our original nature, like Paramashiva's, is pure awareness and unbroken joy. When we rest in our own heart, our own core of consciousness in meditation, we re-experience that original feeling of pure presence and being. Meditation is one way human beings enact the original self-reflection of God or Goddess. The Tantric sages tell us that our in-breath and out-breath actually mirror the divine creative gesture. With the inhalation, we draw into our own center, our own being. With the exhalation, we expand outward into the world. Only by withdrawing into the center does the Shakti get the power to manifest a world. In the same way, it is by withdrawing into our own being—through meditation or deep sleep—that we access the power with which we manifest creatively in our own life.

Meditation: Breathing the World into the Heart, Breathing Out the World from the Heart

Find a comfortable sitting position in a quiet place, and begin
to settle your mind by paying attention to the breath.

Imagine a stream of silvery blue light entering your heart with your inhalation,
bringing full awareness into the presence within the core of your being.

As you exhale, imagine that the light emerges from your heart and surges out into the world around you.

Now take it a step further. Inhale with the feeling that you draw the world into your own heart. Exhale with the feeling that the world spirals out from your heart.

From within the empty fullness of Shakti's heart flows a surge of ecstatic creative urgency. That primal presence feels an impulse to manifest, to create something. Its creative urge, arising inside the field of cosmic awareness/love, *is* Shakti, or cosmic energy. The sage Maheshwarananda writes, "Shakti, reveling in her own bliss, pours herself forth as the universe."[2] All that exists will express the essential qualities and nature of the Goddess, who is the source of everything and to which everything will return.

THE CREATIVE SURGE OF SHAKTI

Shakti now expands into a full-blown creative desire, filled with the contained power of her untamable bliss. A pre-Tantric mythic view of this creative surge uses the metaphor of the creator becoming lonely, then manifesting a universe for the sake of having company: "I am alone, let me become many!" Another view imagines the cosmic couple separating, as lovers do after sex, in order to regard one another, then manifesting a world out of their shared delight. Many teachers of the Indian tradition say that Shakti manifests universes as an act of play, or cosmic game (*lila*)—a creation for its own sake. In fact, they call it an act of cosmic imagination.

Just as you or I would imagine a room in our mind or dream a scene peopled with complex characters and places, Shakti imagines a world. Her cosmic imagining flows through many subtle layers of spirit, gradually condensing and becoming more dense and specific. This process, an outflowing of her power of action (kriya Shakti) is known as involution, or contraction. It is a spontaneous explosion from formlessness into form, all held within the one cosmic awareness. But in this process, Shakti *hides* her full unity and power. In order to fully become each form, she limits her experience of being all the others, so that each morsel of subtle and material existence now experiences itself as unique, separate, and cut off from the whole. It is a process comparable to how, when you choose a particular partner, career, or path, you inevitably limit your experience to that one partner or path, cutting off your experience of the other possibilities. Shakti cannot individuate without simultaneously disguising her wholeness. Yet in limiting herself, she never loses her intrinsic fullness. To use a theological term, she remains transcendent as well as immanent.

The Tantric sages often say that Shakti has two faces: one of absolute unity, and the other consisting of billions of diverse realities. In involution, she hides the first face in order to reveal the second. Later, in our meditation, she will dissolve all these forms back into herself and reveal her face of unity. But now, stage by stage, she takes on increasingly dense forms.

The first forms she manifests are extremely subtle. They are worlds consisting of light and awareness, populated by beings with bodies far too subtle to be seen with human eyes. At this stage, the veils that hide the creation from its source are nearly transparent. By the time Shakti has condensed herself into the various universes of physical energy and matter, the illusion of separation has become so thick that it is impossible to penetrate with the naked eye.

At this point, the physical world explodes outward as the cosmic blast we call the big bang. Shakti "em-bodies" herself in that cosmic explosion. Her natural bliss becomes an ecstatic urgency to evolve, then transforms itself into physical energy and matter, becoming stars and planets, black holes and galaxies, quarks, atoms, molecules, and eventually creatures with complex brains.

The eco-cosmologist Brian Swimme likes to point out that the universe story is our story, that our bodies are made of split-off particles of star stuff, that the breath we breathe has been breathed by every being that has ever lived.[3] A Tantrika goes even further. Our awareness is not only connected to the power of awareness in other creatures, but it is also a miniature version of the great awareness that is the source of all that is. The subtle worlds that lie between the transcendent vastness and the physical universe are also *inside our own subtle bodies,* ready to be experienced by anyone who has the stamina and grace to enter into the inner world of the heart.

THE COSMIC VEILING

Of course, none of this is apparent to the naked eye. That's because, in the process of becoming all this, Shakti has completely disguised herself by disappearing into the tapestry. To add to the impenetrability of her disguise, she shrinks the great awareness—Shiva—so that instead of encompassing everything, consciousness experiences itself as a single, separated ego. She veils her blissfulness so that each individual consciousness believes that joy and satisfaction have to be brought from outside itself, by joining with or acquiring another atom of consciousness.

When Shakti separates from Shiva and pours herself into these billions of forms, she gets the name Maya (Measurer)—the cosmic enchantress who deludes us into feeling small, separate, and powerless. In this sense, Shankara was right. When Shakti is manifesting as the deluding force of Maya, it's difficult to see the hidden connections between ourselves and the rest of the physical world. It's even harder to recognize the invisible forms of the cosmic powers, even though they live inside us and around us.

That said, beings since the beginning of time have intuited the existence of the subtle worlds and have sensed that powerful, invisible forces operate through the physical universe. They've interpreted these forces according to their level of consciousness: a Neolithic animist, living in a cave surrounded by large animals and unpredictable weather, will tend to understand divine forces through a radically different prism than an educated middle-class person living in a European city. Deities change as human consciousness evolves—and so do the maps through which we understand the world.

At the same time, certain recognitions are timeless. Among these are the maps of the subtle worlds that the Tantric traditions offer.

MAPPING THE UPPER WORLDS

Of course, a map, especially a map of the nonmaterial worlds, is not the territory. It's a pointer to a level of nonlinear reality that may be invisible to the physical eye, but can be revealed by the eye of meditation and contemplation.

Still, having a map is useful when we want to enter the rich and complex world of Indian cosmology. To attempt a dive into the mythic world of the goddesses quickly becomes confusing unless we have a sense of how these divine feminine presences relate to each other. We need to have a clear picture of the relationship between the universal Shakti we've been speaking of and the individual goddesses. Otherwise, we wonder: how exactly do these individual gods and goddesses fit into the overarching unity of all-that-is? How do deities like Shiva and Shakti relate to other well-known gods like Vishnu, Krishna, and Hanuman? How are we supposed to understand the existence of so many gods? Are they all equal? Are some more "real" than others? Do they really look the way the statues and paintings depict them?

In the next few pages, I'll explain some of the basics of the cosmic hierarchy. We'll look at who the major and minor deities are and how they relate to each other. I've included a chart that shows the different levels or layers of reality, from the very subtlest at the top to the dense physical universe we know.

THE THREE WORLDS AND THE REALM BEYOND

The cosmos of Indian myth is divided into several levels of being, each accessible only in certain states. Though there are different ways of dividing the cosmos, virtually all Hindu and Buddhist systems share an underlying view of the three worlds and the three states. The three worlds are:

1) The gross world of physical human life, accessible in our normal waking state
2) The subtle world, accessible in dreams, meditation, and the after-death state
3) The formless void, accessible during deep sleep

Beyond these worlds are the realms of oneness, accessible in deep meditation and culminating in the state of union or self-realization. Within these are the extremely subtle worlds where the great gods reside along with enlightened sages like Buddha, Christ, and many less celebrated teachers, who are said to exist in subtle forms to confer blessings on the worlds. All the worlds and all states of consciousness exist together within the one light of consciousness. All of them are permeated with the aliveness that is Shakti and illuminated by the awareness that is Shiva.

This description and the chart on pages 42 and 43 draw from Tantric cosmology, while incorporating some different aspects of the Hindu pantheon.

THE HIERARCHY OF GODS AND GODDESSES

At the top of the chain, Shiva/Shakti exist in eternal union. They transcend, yet include, everything else in the cosmic hierarchy. Just below them, presiding as cosmic governors of the worlds, sit the cosmic trinities of Devatas. These are the male gods Brahma, Vishnu, and Shiva, with their consort-goddesses Saraswati, Lakshmi, and Durga/Parvati. (Although they go by the same name, the Shiva of the Trinity is actually an involuted—in other words, a "lower"—form of the absolute Shiva. He is the formless, attributeless absolute in *form*—an extremely subtle form, but a form nonetheless.) The gods of the Trinity are *aspects* of the absolute, of Shiva/Shakti. In its ultimate state, the absolute is *nishkala*—attributeless. At the level of the Trinity, the divine takes on qualities. In Sanskrit, this is called its *sakala* aspect: the absolute with qualities. These are the personal forms of the God and Goddess: the ones we can invoke and with whom we can have personal, devotional relationships.

Brahma: The Grandfather

Five-faced Brahma, with his Saraswati, is the deity in charge of the processes of creation. He embodies the first act of the cosmic five-fold act: *Shrishti,* or manifestation. Brahma is the grandfather figure of the worlds, much like the grandfather spirit of Native Americans. He appears mostly during the cosmic beginning time, when he is "assigned" the task of shaping worlds out of his mind. Because the worlds are born out of vibrational energy, they are said to arise as the notes of music or as the mantric sounds of the Sanskrit language. The Shakti of creation, Saraswati, is also known as *vach,* or speech, because it is her energy that inspires the creative sound forms out of which all this comes. That word, by the way, is *om.* (It is interesting to note here that in the 1960s, some scientists at Bell Labs discovered microwaves emanating a cosmic hum throughout the universe. Current scientific theory holds that this hum is the reverberation of the original big bang)

Through his empowered, Shakti-generated speech, Brahma gives birth to the early Vedic deities and sages, who are called his "mind-born sons." Then, he populates the worlds with beings of all species and classes. At that point, Brahma more or less retires from active participation in the cosmic play, except to give boons to petitioners at crucial points in the evolution of the world. Saraswati, as we shall see, continues to generate creative intuition, speech, mantra, and music through the spheres and within the human mind.

Vishnu: The Cosmic King

In the ongoing life of the cosmos, it is Vishnu who runs things. Vishnu, four-armed, kingly, and alluringly attractive, is the cosmic principle of *sthiti,* or maintenance. He embodies the cosmic function of harmony, stability, and sustenance. Vishnu also represents cosmic law, and he has a propensity for intervening in the world when things go wrong. If there is a really big crisis, he takes animal or human form and appears on Earth as an avatar.

Vishnu maintains the worlds and upholds the *dharma,* or universal law, but he is also the deity of statecraft, rulership, and politics. That means he is a master of expediency. One of his gifts is the discernment to know when a righteous end justifies unusual means. His Shakti consort is Lakshmi, goddess of abundance, fertility, and wealth. She is the power of attraction that holds life together. Powered by Lakshmi's Shakti, Vishnu represents both the love that upholds the worlds and the social mores that resonate with divine law. He is a deity of the enlightened public sphere, embodying classical virtues like detachment, generosity, and forbearance as well as the powers of governance, royal authority, and strategy.

Just as Christ is considered by Christians to embody divinity in human form, Vishnu's avatars, Rama and Krishna, are considered to be concentrated embodiments of divine qualities. Each of them has a consort: Sita for Rama and Radha for Krishna. Just as Rama and Krishna are unique expressions of Vishnu, Sita and Radha are unique expressions of Lakshmi. Each in her own ways, Lakshmi, Sita, and Radha are goddesses of fertility, prosperity, and nurturing love.

Shiva: The Naked Yogi-God

The absolute Shiva gives his own name to the deity of dissolution, who is his lower level, individual (sakala) form. In his sakala form, Shiva is depicted as the naked yogi wearing a snake around his neck, who acts as the cosmic destroyer of worldly forms. But Shiva is also the cosmic guru, who transmits the wisdom of hatha yoga and Tantric yoga. While Vishnu offers grace and help in worldly affairs, Shiva gives the knowledge and grace that opens the wisdom eye of the spirit. His Shaktis are the powers that liberate us not only from difficulties, but from illusion itself. Shiva's grace, powered by his Shakti, is the cosmic force that removes the veils. One of Shiva's divine functions is to dissolve forms so that we can know the truth that lies behind them. He is also that impulse within us that seeks freedom and detachment from the world, and that appears in the course of any radical transformation process. Shiva's consort is variously known as Durga, Kali, Parvati, Lalita, Devi, and the Yogini.

Mahadevi: The Great Goddess

Shakti, besides infusing herself into the seams of the universe, also embodies herself as these luscious consort goddesses. Through them, she lends Brahma, Vishnu, and Shiva the power to perform their cosmic tasks. She also retains her own personal form as an independent feminine power. As such, she is called Devi (Goddess), Mahadevi (Great Goddess), Maheshwari (Great Lady), or Durga. (Yes, Durga is both a name for Shiva's consort and a name for the eternally free cosmic Shakti!) Durga is one of the most popular forms of the Goddess in India. She is the subject of an important praise hymn, the *Devi Mahatmya (Triumph of the Goddess)* which sings of her world-saving battles with demons.

The Nurturing and Transformational Goddesses

To recapitulate, Lakshmi, Sita, and Radha—the Shaktis associated with Vishnu—are the energies who hold together the life of the world. They embody the nurturing, yin qualities of the divine feminine. These goddesses are the powers

FIGURE 1: CHART OF THE COSMIC HIERARCHY

Levels of Reality According to Nondual Shaiva Tantra	Corresponding Human State
1. PARAMASHIVA/PARASHAKTI Absolute Consciousness and Power, the perfect fusion of Shiva and Shakti, possessing absolute bliss and freedom	TURIYATITA STATE Fully Enlightened Awareness
2. SHIVA/SHAKTI Awareness/Love—Shiva is within all as the pure witness—Shakti becomes everything that exists pervading all forms and holding them within herself	

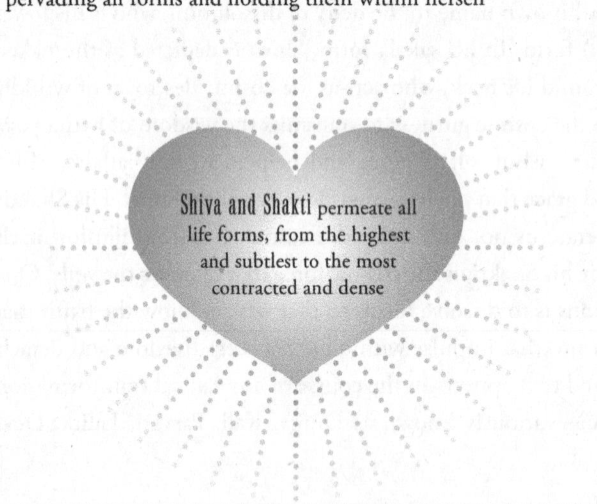

Shiva and Shakti permeate all life forms, from the highest and subtlest to the most contracted and dense

3. SADASHIVA/MAHADEVI Creative will to manifest	SUPRACAUSAL BODY Turiya, state of awakened awareness
4. ISHWARA Cosmic Lordship—Cosmic Trinity of high gods and goddesses	

Masculine Deities	Feminine Deities
Brahma—Creator	Saraswati
Vishnu—Sustainer of Worlds and Upholder of Dharma	Lakshmi
	Sita
Rama	Radha
Krishna	Durga
Shiva—Cosmic Yogi and Destroyer of Worlds	Parvati (Gauri, Uma, Girija)
	Kali (Shyama, Chandi)
	Amba (Ten Wisdom Goddesses: Lalita Tripura Sundari, Tara, Chinnamasta, Bhuvaneshwari, etc.)

5. SHUDDHA VIDYA/TATTVA The level from which mantras arise. Here the subtle form of the universe appears, not yet separated from the mind of the Absolute	

FIGURE 1: CHART OF THE COSMIC HIERARCHY *cont.*

Levels of Reality According to Nondual Shaiva Tantra		Corresponding Human State
6. MAYA Veils the Creation from Its Source, produces differentiation		CAUSAL BODY Deep sleep state
7. PURUSHA Pure consciousness without form or agency, manifesting as individual soul		
8. CREATIVE MATRIX Prakriti—Subtle source of all form and energy		
9. SUBTLE WORLDS AND THEIR INHABITANTS		SUBTLE BODY Dream state
9a. *Devas—Elemental deities with their Shaktis* Indra (Thunder) Chandra (Moon) Surya (Sun) Ashwin twins (Medicine) Vayu (Wind) Varuna (Waters) Agni (Fire) Prithvi (Earth) Yamaraj (Death and Dharma) Ganesha (Lord of Obstacles) Hanumān (Courage, Devotion, and Strength) Skanda (Cosmic commander)	*Asuras—Power gods* Bali Hiranya Kashipu Prahlada and others *Rakshasas—Demons* Ravana Shumbha/Nishumbha Chanda, Munda, and others	
9b. *Upper Astral Worlds* Celestial nymphs Gandharvas (musicians) Snake deities Forms of the goddesses worshipped as local deities and deities of places		
9c. *Lower Astral Worlds* Ghosts, spirits		
10. EARTH PLANE Human beings Animals, birds, fish, insects, and other terrestrial creatures The Physical Universe Made of the five elements in combination: earth, water, fire, air, and space		WAKING STATE

that sustain the human community. Their sphere is the social world: family, relationship, livelihood, business, wealth, government, politics, and law.

On the other hand, the goddesses who oversee the processes of awakening and transformation—Durga, Kali, and Lalita—are all associated with Shiva. They embody the assertive, transformative feminine. These goddesses tend to be mysterious and are sometimes dark, ambiguous, and even scary. They are powerful in their own right—and many of them show up as independent queenly warriors. Durga and Kali, like Shiva himself, are goddesses of the margins and warriors of the spirit. Their sphere is the disruptive and the extraordinary: battlefields, mountain caves, storms, and revolutions both internal and external. They are also powerful protectors. Parvati and Lalita are love goddesses, who mate with Shiva in the esoteric union of sacred sex. They are also yoginis, independent and unbounded in a way that the Vishnu Shaktis are not.

Taken together, these individual goddess energies form a kind of mandala, a power grid of energies that appears at every level of existence. In human consciousness, they embody worldly and spiritual energies that everyone has access to, but that are most visible and accessible to us in states of altered awareness, like ritual, meditation, or prayer. As forces in the cosmos, they act through natural occurrences, weather patterns, and movements in culture.

GODS AND ELEMENTS

Besides the major deities, the worlds of Hindu cosmology teem with lesser deities and other subtle beings: devas, titans, nymphs, snake-demons, and angelic and demonic presences. The second-level deity figures—known in Sanskrit as *devas,* or shining ones—wear bodies of light and exercise powers far greater and subtler than anything possible in the human world. Many of them are connected with the elements of the physical world. Indra, king of the gods, rules the relationships between the higher worlds and the physical universe; in a human being, he appears as our executive function. Prithvi, goddess of the earth, supports physical life. Chandra is the deity of the moon; Surya is lord of the sun; Varuna is lord of waters; Vayu is the wind god; Agni is lord of fire. These deities, and many others (including deities of the planets), can actually be invoked through rituals, visualizations, and mantras.

The ancient Vedic science of ritual, still practiced in India, aims at honoring these elemental deities and inviting their blessing for the earth. The rituals, when practiced with full awareness, can reveal the subtle elements behind the physical world. Through ritual, we can feel the presence of these elemental deities as energies that live in nature and that subtly affect our inner and outer lives. Through meditation, we can tune into them as the elemental processes within our subtle and physical bodies.

For instance, you might experience Vayu, the wind, as your breath and as the gases in your body. Surya rules the visible world as the sun and also gives us the power of vision both subtle and physical. Varuna, god of waters, appears as the fluids in our bodies as well as in the oceans and rivers. Prithvi, the earth goddess, appears as the physical world of rocks, plants, and soil, and also in our bones and flesh. Agni, fire, is both the power that cooks our food and the power that illumines our altars and ceremonies. Agni also exists as the heat in the body and, according to the ancient view of things, as the acids that digest our food and the electrical energies that fire our neurons.

UNITY IN PLURALITY

These deity energies are both internal forces and external, subtle presences. From an ultimate point of view, however, they are simply waves in the ocean of one cosmic mind. Despite all appearances, the Tantrika understands that all individual energies—whether vast or tiny—are simply forms of the primal Shiva/Shakti, the nondual presence that both includes and transcends everything. Shakti shapes all these deity forms, and then lives *as* them. Shiva is the aware ground of all that exists, the primal being behind all forms.

Shakti, the feminine aspect, is constantly creating and destroying forms. Externally, she acts through the elemental deities. She appears as the processes of nature and as the activities of your body and brain. In meditation, she manifests as our visionary experience, our inner intuition, as mantra, and as the guiding force behind the journey itself. Shiva is the witness of the great game. Shakti is the actress who plays all the parts. Our human consciousness contains both polarities: each one of us is both witness and player. But our lived experience is almost entirely an experience of Shakti. Shiva is the subtle field within which Shakti plays, but she is the power that *lives* you. As the sage Shankara discovered, your very life-force is Shakti. Quite literally, whatever you see, feel, and sense, both inside and outside, is made of her.

One very immediate and dramatic way to look at your body and the world is to imagine that whatever you see, feel, and sense, both inside and outside, is made of Shakti, made of the Goddess. In other words, your lungs are made of the Goddess's energy and so is the air you breathe. Your mind is a dance of tiny particles of goddess energy. Your limbic brain pulses to the rhythm of the goddess. Every atom in your body is made of the Goddess. Your inner and outer universe is a world of goddesses, and each of these goddesses is an aspect of the great Goddess, Mahadevi or Maheshwari—the one Goddess whose body is the world, whose mind is space, whose being encompasses universes within universes.

This understanding is the basis of the Tantric attitude that nothing is to be rejected. So, as we prepare to enter into the worlds of the individual goddesses, I invite you to invoke and meditate on MahaShakti, the goddess who lives as the world and as your own body.

MEDITATING ON THE GODDESS AS YOUR OWN BODY

In the Tantric tradition, there is a meditation that identifies every single physical function with a Shakti, or goddess energy. In some ways, this is not far from the understanding of Chinese medicine or some of the modern energy-medicine systems. Modern and traditional energy-medicine recognize that there are subtle energies associated with the organs, though few of them go so far as to identify them with deity forms. An exception is in Ayurveda, the traditional Vedic system of medicine, where these energies are associated with elemental god energies, which are invoked through herbs and light-filtering precious stones to help bring consciousness and healing to the physical body and the mind.

The Tantrika, however, aims above all to teach the body its own divinity. Therefore, most Tantric rituals begin with a conscious "placing" of the goddesses within every part of the body. So, as we begin to practice with the individual goddess energies, let's begin by holding this expansive, and ultimately loving, recognition that the Shakti, the Goddess, is living *as* your physical body as well as the external world. We'll do this in four stages.

1) First, we'll recognize that Shakti, in the form of the life-force, is breathing us.
2) Then, we'll tune into the elements of the body as particles of Shakti, aspects of the Goddess. We'll recognize that our bodies and the elements of the physical world are made of the same stuff.
3) We'll recognize our thoughts and feelings as goddess-energies.
4) Again, we'll allow ourselves to be breathed by the Goddess, who manifests as the vital force of the universe.

Meditation: The Goddess as Your Own Body

This meditation is a way to recognize the omnipresent sacredness of the body by connecting it to the Goddess who is its source. With this, and all the meditations in the book, you might want to read through it completely, then practice it. Or, you can record yourself reading it and play it back.

Find a place where you can sit quietly, without being disturbed, for at least fifteen minutes. Sit in a comfortable position, with your spine erect but not rigid. You may also practice this meditation lying on your back, perhaps on a mat on the floor, supporting your neck with a small pillow, and placing a pillow under your knees.

Close your eyes, and bring your awareness to your breath. Have the understanding that your breath is being breathed by a vast and loving presence, the Shakti of the life-force. Let yourself be breathed. This is the Goddess as the power of breath, the life-force of the universe, who breathes through every living thing.

Be aware now of the flesh and bones of your physical body. Consider that your skin is made of vibrating energy particles and that these energies are the goddess herself, vibrating as the skin of your body. Think of leaves, of bark, of the outer coverings of seeds, of the topsoil of the earth. Consider that all these are forms of skin and that they are made of energy—energy that is the essence of the Goddess.

Consider your bones. Consider how the solidity of your bones mirrors the solidity of rock, of earth. Consider the other fleshy elements in your body, the organs and fat, and recognize that they too are filled with energy, made of energy, made of particles of Shakti, which is the Goddess.

Consider your blood and the other fluids in your body. Consider the fact that three-fourths of your body is fluid. Consider also the rivers and oceans of the world. Realize that the fluids in your body and the waters of the world are made of energy and that this energy is the Goddess.

Consider the air you breathe, the air inside your lungs. Realize that the air is filled with particles of energy, particles of the Goddess. Be aware of the space inside your body, inside your cells, the space around you, the space within every object in your environment. Realize that space is energy and that energy is the transformation of the Goddess in the physical world.

With your eyes closed, imaginitively recognize that your body is made of goddess energies. Look into your mind, and sense the thoughts and emotions rising and subsiding in your inner space. Realize that these too are subtle energy—fluid, ever-changing aspects of Shakti. Shakti has become your body and your mind. Shakti has become the world.

Meditate with the thought that the Goddess has become your body and mind. Meditate on the Goddess as the world. Recognize that all the movements, changes, and shifts in this universe are movements of Shakti. Let yourself feel the rhythm of the breath. Allow yourself to be breathed by the energy, the Shakti in the atmosphere. Recognize that the energy that breathes you, the air that you breathe, the body and its energy, the thoughts that pass through your mind—all these are Shakti. Shakti is living your life.

Rest in this recognition.

THE TWO FACES OF THE GODDESS

We said in the beginning of this chapter that the path of the Goddess—Tantra—is a path of nonrejection. It's a path that sees everything—dark as well as light, matter as well as spirit—as aspects of the Goddess. Tantra explains this by pointing out that the Goddess has two faces: two apparently opposite tendencies that we could call her two gestures or the two sides of her dance.

The Face of Separation

On the one hand, Shakti creates the experience of radical separation. Manifesting as the compelling diversity of our inner and outer world, she blinds us to the basic unity of life. Did you ever wonder why it's so hard to get the mind to quiet down in meditation? Or why the world seems so oppositional, so filled with contradictions, conflicts, alienation? One reason is that your brain—powered by Shakti—is wired to show you that the world is outside you. It's this feeling of separation from the world that makes everyone and everything we meet seem potentially desirable or threatening, an object to be conquered, swallowed, or retreated from. From birth until death, the brain endlessly throws up images, thoughts, ideas, and—especially—projections, convincing us that the things and people we love and hate are outside us and that our welfare depends on getting these outside forces to give us what we want. We become fully convinced that the pictures we see in our brain and interpret as reality are the final reality.

This basic skew toward separation, the veiling of our fundamental oneness, is the work of Shakti as Mahamaya—the great illusion. In that guise, she conceals her presence and the fundamental identity between you and the world. She conceals it so skillfully that without some form of grace, we simply can't recognize her.

The Face of Grace

Here is where her other face comes to help us. Because it is Shakti that has created the illusion of separation, Shakti has to free us from it. It doesn't matter how much we understand intellectually that the world is made of a single energy. To experience it directly, to know it for certain, we need the grace of the one from whose energy it is made. Any experience of awakening arrives spontaneously, on its own—no matter how much we have worked for it, it comes when it will. That's because all true awakenings come from the world-energy herself. The same Shakti who binds us by trapping us in the delusion of separation also liberates us from it. At moments she will wake us up, and once we know how to dance with her awakening force, the moments of awakening become more and more frequent. Eventually we learn to stay awake to the unity behind the diversity. That's when we can begin to recognize the truth about the oneness of the physical world and the world of spirit.

Without recognizing that the Goddess is in everything, we will tend to get trapped in one side or another of the spirit/matter duality. Either we favor spirit at the expense of the physical world or we get caught up in the struggles and satisfactions of daily life without recognizing them as expressions of spirit. To wake up to reality is the gift of the Goddess. When we begin to contemplate the Goddess and invoke her through meditation, visualization, and prayer, what we are really asking is that she awaken us to our own blazing beauty and wisdom, which is also her beauty and the beauty of the world itself. We follow the path of nonrejection not for the sake of indulgence, or even for the sake of compassion. We follow it as an exercise in enlightenment so that the Goddess will, in time, show us that indeed she is fully present in every particle of our bodies and the world. The experience of compassion is the natural result of this recognition.

MahaShakti Meditation: The Goddess's Cosmic Form

Before starting this exercise, find a place where you can be undisturbed for a few minutes. Either sit or lie down on your back as suggested in the previous meditation exercise.

Focus for a few minutes on the flow of your breath, noticing how it touches your nostrils: somewhat cool on the inhalation, slightly warm with the exhalation.

Imagine yourself lying on a tropical beach, gazing up at a midnight-blue sky filled with stars.

See in the sky the form of the Goddess. Her body is made of sky, pale blue in color. Her eyes are large, lustrous, and dark, with long eyelashes. Her hair falls over her shoulders, and on her head is a golden crown.

Her torso is bare except for a diaphanous scarf that wraps her breasts, and she wears a red cloth around her waist.

She is dancing. Her arms reach out across the sky. Her feet touch the waters of the ocean and dance over the waves.

She looks at you with an indescribably tender and mischievous smile.

As you watch, you realize that from her fingers, stars are being born. Her hands send galaxies whirling out across the cosmos. As she dances, her body seems to grow, until it is as large as space. Inside it, you see galaxies, suns, and universes.

With every breath, you sense the unfolding majesty of the Goddess as she dances. Sometimes she is in the form of a woman. Sometimes her body opens up to become the universe.

Ask her to speak to you, to tell you something of her nature.

Listen and wait for the answer to arise.

Now, ask her to give you her grace so that you can know the real nature of this universe and of her unfolding play.

Ask her, "Let me know you."

MahaShakti

mah-hah-shuhk-tee—The Goddess Who Is All-That-Is
   Goddess of Universal Power

Other Names for MahaShakti:
   Maheshwari (*mah-heysh-war-ee*)—Great Goddess
   Mahadevi (*mah-hah-dey-vee*)—Great Goddess
   Mahamaya (*mah-hah-mah-yah*)—Great Illusion, referring to her
   power to manifest worlds that hide their fundamental unity

Mahavidya (*mah-hah-vid-yah*)—Great Wisdom
Jagaddhatri (*jahg-uhd-dah-tree*)—She Who Supports the World
Parashakti (*pah-rah-shuhk-tee*)—Supreme Power
Chiti (*chit-ee*)—Consciousness
Mahadurga (*mah-hah-door-gah*)—Great Unconquerable One

Recognize MahaShakti as:

- the force of life in all things
- the swirl of your thoughts and emotions (a particularly skillful way to work with emotions is to see them as the expressions of the Goddess)
- the power behind the breath
- the energy that makes the heart beat and makes cells divide, works through your mind and body to allow you to function in the world
- the power that draws you toward spirituality and the energy that draws you into meditation
- kundalini
- all goddesses and energies

Invoke MahaShakti for:

- unifying your body with the cosmos
- experiencing the world, your body, and its energies as divine
- recognizing the oneness of all things; recognizing that all is within you
- healing
- raising kundalini and integrating Shakti throughout your body
- receiving power and love from the divine feminine
- liberation from suffering and delusion
- dealing with unpleasant experiences by recognizing them as aspects of the divine
- working with stress by recognizing the energy within it
- bringing more energy into any situation
- your own spiritual evolution and that of another person
- experiencing blissfulness

Bija Mantra

Hrim (*hreem*)
Seed of all manifestation

Invocational Mantras
(Like many of the mantras throughout this book, the following uses seed syllables, short Sanskrit sounds that are said to contain concentrated forms of Shakti.)

> Hrim shrim klim parameshwari svaha
> *hreem shreem kleem puh-rah-mey-shwar-ee swah-hah*
> Hrim: seed mantra for MahaShakti as the power of manifestation
> Shrim: seed mantra for the energy of auspiciousness
> Klim: seed mantra containing the energy of attraction or allurement
> Param: supreme
> Eshwari: divine feminine principle
> Swaha: I offer salutations, or I invoke

Mantra of Praise for MahaShakti
> (Repeat three, five, or nine times)
> Ya devi sarva bhuteshu
> Shakti rupena samsthita
> Namastasyai namastasyai namastasyai namo namaha
> Ya devi sarva bhuteshu
> Chetanetyabhidhiyate
> Namastasyai namastasyai namastasyai namo namaha

> *yah dey-vee sahr-va bhoo-tey-shoo*
> *shuhk-tee roo-pey-na sam-sti-tah*
> *na-ma-sta-syai na-ma-stah-syai na-mah-sta-syai na-mo na-mah*
> *yah dey-vee sahr-va bhoo-tey-shoo*
> *chey-ta-ney-tya-bhee-dhee-ya-tey*
> *na-ma-stah-syai na-ma-stah-syai na-mah-sta-syai na-mo na-mah*

> O Goddess, who lives within everything in the form of power,
> Salutations to you, salutations to you, salutations to you
> O Goddess, whom we name with the word *awareness*,
> Salutations to you, salutations to you.

> MahaShakti's colors: red, gold, yellow
> MahaShakti's flower: hibiscus

GRACE
Awakening us to the
fundamental oneness
within multiplicity

CONCEALMENT
Disguising oneness
and revealing only
multiplicity

FIGURE 2: TWO FACES OF THE GODDESS

MahaShakti's festival: Navaratri (Nine Nights) in September–October
and in March–April
MahaShakti's mount: lion
MahaShakti's consort: Mahadev (Shiva)

CHAPTER 3

Durga

Warrior Goddess of Protection and Inner Strength

Dawn and dusk became her eyebrows, the wind god's splendor shaped her ears,
and all else born of the other gods' light shone too as the auspicious Devi.

DEVI MAHATMYA

We bow to her who is auspicious beauty. We make salutations again
and again to her who is prosperity and attainment. Salutations again
and again to her who is the fortune and misfortune of kings.

Salutations always to Durga who takes us through difficulties, who is the
creator and indwelling essence of all . . . who is right knowledge. . . .

We bow down to her who is at once most gentle and most fierce.

DEVI MAHATMYA

The Devi laughed thunderously and defiantly, again and again.

She filled the entire sky with her terrible roar, and from the immeasurable din
a great echo resounded. All the worlds shook, and the oceans churned.

(The demon) beheld the Devi, who pervaded the three worlds with her radiance,
bending the earth under her tread, scraping the sky with her diadem.

DEVI MAHATMYA

In Mahabalipuram, in South India, there is a stone bas-relief of the Goddess Durga. The goddess is captured in the act of pulling her bow. Round-breasted, she rides a roaring lion whose mane foams like ocean waves. Every sinew, every line of the sculpture carries the purposeful strength of a goddess who embodies the active power of the feminine. Even the stone seems to pulsate with energy.

Durga is both an Amazonian warrior and a mother goddess. One of the most popular goddesses in India, she has become, for young Indian women especially, an icon of contemporary liberation and power. One contemporary Mumbai artist painted Durga's body with the artist's own face, sitting in meditation and surrounded by flames. When you bring Durga into your inner world, the painting seems to say, she can empower your most radical aspirations and guide you through your most conflict-ridden life dramas.

Myths about Durga usually start with a demon slaying. But while Durga was the deity invoked by kings for victory in battle, she is not just a battle goddess. She is also the power behind spiritual awakening, the inner force that unleashes spiritual power within the human body in the form of kundalini. And she is a guardian: beautiful, queenly, and fierce. Paintings of Durga show her with flowing hair, a red sari, bangles, necklaces, a crown—and eight arms bristling with weapons.

Durga carries a spear, a mace, a discus, a bow, and a sword—as well as a conch (representing creative sound), a lotus (symbolizing fertility), and a rosary (symbolizing prayer). In one version of her origin, she appears as a divine female warrior, brought into manifestation by the male gods to save them from the buffalo demon, Mahisha. The assembled gods, furious and powerless over a demon who couldn't be conquered, sent forth their anger as a mass of light and power. Their combined strength coalesced into the form of a radiantly beautiful woman who filled every direction with her light. Her face was formed by Shiva; her hair came from Yama, the god of death; her arms were given by Vishnu. Shiva gave her his trident, Vishnu his discus, Vayu—the wind god—offered his bow and arrow. The mountain god, Himalaya, gave her the lion for her mount. Durga set forth to battle the demon for the sake of the world, armed and protected by all the powers of the divine masculine.[1]

As a world protector, Durga's fierceness arises out of her uniquely potent compassion. She is the deity to call on when you're in deep trouble. In the *Devi Mahatmya* (Greatness of the Goddess), a medieval song-cycle about Durga that is still recited all over India, we are reminded again and again that the goddess will always appear when we need her to protect our world. She invites us to turn to her in crisis, and she promises to move mountains to rescue us from every form of evil—including the evil we ourselves create!

SOME BACKGROUND ABOUT GODS AND DEMONS

The *Devi Mahatmya* revolves around three encounters—including two battles—with demonic forces. The most interesting of all is the tale of Durga's encounter with two demon brothers, *asuras*, named Shumbha and Nishumbha.

Before we explore the tale of Durga's encounter with these demons, a bit of background on the mythology will be helpful. In Indian mythology, the battle between the light force and the dark side is personified as an eternal struggle between two races of elemental beings. The forces of light are known as devas (shining ones) or power gods. Their ancient enemies are the asuras (anti-gods), sometimes translated as "titans" in a bow to the Greek pantheon. Both sides wear bodies made of light and thought. They use weapons powered by the force of their secret mantras, invocations that can turn a blade of grass into a deadly missile. The devas live in pleasure realms with jeweled streets and houses that they can renovate with just a flick of desire. Their women-folk are dancers and singers, whose gift for changing form is legion and whose beauty has infinite varieties.

The devas show up in your life in three ways. First, they arise as elemental presences in the universe—powers within the wind, the ocean, and the earth. Second, they represent inner qualities of consciousness—the powers and qualities of your higher self. Your generosity, your humility, your capacity for patience, your fearlessness, your vigor, your compassion, and your inner steadiness are all qualities of your inner devic energy. Finally, individual devas represent specific aspects of the mind. For example, Indra, king of the gods, represents the mind's executive function. He is your power of discernment, the one who can weigh the subtle balance of things, find the right course of action, and judge the implications and ethics at play in the situations of your life. In brain science terms, Indra is your neocortex. Even when he gets confused, or flooded with desires, Indra knows how to subject himself to the guiding power of higher authority.

He and the other devas regard themselves as keepers of the dharma, the rules of law that maintain balance in the cosmos. Above them in the cosmic hierarchy is the Trinity of great gods, Brahma, Vishnu, and Shiva. Unlike the devas, the deities of the Trinity are the three faces of what Judeo-Christian traditions would call the Godhead, and Indian tradition calls Ishwara. They have the power to step beyond law and custom and inject saving grace into even the direst situation. The devas, at their best, recognize that they are subject to these higher powers.

Dark Force Warriors

The *asuras* are the robber barons, tyrants, and corporate raiders of the cosmos. Gifted fighters with magical powers, they have subtle bodies like the devas, but very different characters. The asuras are obsessed with accumulation and conquest; they are exemplars of ego inflated beyond any reasonable bounds. Their offspring rule our contemporary global culture as kleptocratic dictators, corrupt corporate actors, terrorists, financial manipulators with armies of lobbyists and big checks.

Just as we carry devic energy in the higher Self, we also hold our own asuric energy. The inner asura is our power-shadow—our egoic pride, arrogance, cut-throat ambition, loveless lust, selfishness, and hard-heartedness. As the devas use power for the protection of the good, the asuras are obsessed with power for its own sake. They know as many spells and mantras for worshipping the Trinity as the gods do, and they also have the strength and patience for hard-core practice, especially when it benefits their aims.

THE FATAL BOON

Shumbha and Nishumbha, the story goes, have amassed an army of fighters with magical superpowers. Before undertaking their campaign of world conquest, they begin a long, intense course of yogic austerities, practices designed to impel the creator god, Brahma, to reward their efforts by giving them a boon.[2] Standing on one leg between five fires, arms raised heavenward, holding their breath for a thousand years at a time, the brothers petition Brahma for the power to be invincible in battle. By the cosmic laws of karma, so much effort has to be rewarded. (Besides, the heat generated by the demon brothers is starting to affect the weather in the higher worlds.) Brahma agrees to grant the brothers a guarantee from above that no man or god can defeat them in battle.

The boon, however, contains a loophole: no mention has been made of women or goddesses. That hardly seems to matter. There are no women warriors on the earth, and the Goddess has chosen to channel her skills at war and king-ship through male bodies, right up and down the great chain of being. Taking form as the consorts to the male gods, she lends them her powers, ruling from behind the curtain (as they used to say of powerful concubines in Asian royal courts), never showing her hand.

Now that they are more or less invincible, the demon brothers conquer the earth. They declare themselves rulers of the upper and lower worlds, and in one final putsch, expel the devas from their abodes. Now the heaven of Indra is filled with the palaces and pleasure gardens of Shumbha and Nishumbha and their minions, which sprawl like small cities over jeweled lawns. The brothers, having conquered everything worth conquering, devote themselves to collecting art and women, to building houses, and to commissioning songs of praise. Over sev-eral thousand years, they pursue the refined pleasures of upper-world aristocrats, study the arts of astrology and lovemaking, capture scholars and spiritual teachers to supervise their meditation and to perfect their knowledge of esoteric texts.

Meanwhile, the gods wander the sub-celestial worlds, plotting revenge without success.

Then one day, a friendly sage visits Indra to point out the loophole in the brothers' protection guarantee. No man or god can defeat the asura brothers, he tells the desperate king of the devas. But nobody said anything about a goddess.

APPROACH THE GODDESS

"Go to the abode of Durga, the Mahadevi, the supreme goddess," the sage advises Indra. "Beg her to appear in the world. She is waiting for you to ask."

So Indra and the other gods travel to the Vindhya Mountains, where the Mahadevi resides. It is not an easy trip. To find her abode they have to rely on intuition and guesswork. For a celestial century—twenty thousand years in human time—the gods petition her. They sing her praises. "O goddess, shining one, who lives within everything in the form of power, praise to you, praise to you, praise to you. O goddess, who lives within everything in the form of consciousness, praise to you, praise to you." Between prayers, the gods contemplate their own hubris, their forgetfulness. "Why did we think we were in charge?" they ask themselves ruefully. They invent new hymns, addressing her as sovereign, as queen, as mother. Especially as mother. "Bad sons we may be," they sing, with jeweled tears glistening in their eyes, "but there could never be a bad mother. Help us, help us. We are your children."

ASK FOR HELP

This part of the myth tells us something crucial about the goddess, something that is going to make a difference in the way we see our relationship to the force of grace in our life.

Because she is hidden, in order to act in the world, the great goddess needs us to ask for help. The grace of the goddess is a two-way stream. There's the movement from the subtle—the movement of grace descending into the human world. But it can't land unless there is a calling from below. That calling can take different forms: mantra repetition, meditation, petitionary prayer—but the calling has to be there.

Aurobindo Ghose, one of the great spiritual visionaries of the twentieth century, wrote passionately about his vision of a radical transformation in humanity. He believed that the crises of his time—the rise of totalitarian movements as well as the freedom movements that ended colonialism—were the external forms of an upheaval in consciousness that would eventually give birth to a new order. When demonic forces are unleashed in the world, the forces of evolution become highly accessible, and not just in human minds and hearts. Aurobindo believed that the force of the Shakti is yearning to evolve our awareness, to help us create a world in which we live in balance with each other and the earth, and with our own sacred masculine and feminine natures. His teaching, contained in his book *The Mother*, articulates one of the underlying meanings of the Durga myth: to access her transformative power, we have to call it, ask for it, pray for it.[3]

It's as if the protective, transformative power of the divine waits, just out of reach, unable to intervene until we summon the courage or the desperation to throw ourselves at her feet, literally or metaphorically, and ask for her help. In asking for her, we bring her forth.

This is true not only in our battles against external enemies or desperate illness. Our spiritual journey and the evolution of consciousness in society as a whole are impossible without help from the subtle realms. Inner awakening, as we saw in chapter 2, is not under our control. It arises spontaneously, through grace. Moreover, we need enormous grace behind us in the struggle with our own limitations and egocentric delusions. To see through the illusions that trap us, the genetic patterning, the imbalances of intellect and emotion, the warring desires, the fears, the cultural biases, and the sheer weight of our physical senses is impossible without help of the Shakti. Ramakrishna, the nineteenth-century sage whose disciples helped bring Vedanta to the West, was a priest in a Kali temple and adored the Shakti, constantly praying to her for a vision of truth. He felt such longing that he once seized the ritual sword from the Kali statue and threatened to stab himself with it if she didn't reveal herself to him. Perhaps we don't need that level of passionate desperation, but we do need to admit our neediness.

THE GODDESS REVEALED

Back to the story.

At last, the air shimmers with an unmistakable force, sweet and fierce, tender and diamond hard. Durga appears out of the air, glistening and dark, with blue-black skin and flowing, lustrous hair, her form of light clothed in robes whose colors shift and slip, revealing and concealing the beauty of her breasts, the curve of her belly. An erotic perfume surrounds her, and yet her aura of untouchability keeps the gods on their knees. She rides a lion.

"What brings you here, Indra," she says, as if she did not know what havoc the asuras had wreaked in their world.

"O Durga, O Ma," says Indra, "Our world is in ruins and no male god can save us."

"So, only in extremis do you come to me for help?" she asks.

Indra knows enough to let that pass. He knows that she can do no less than save her world. A moment later, she agrees. "Yes," she says, "I will intervene to restore the balance of the world."

Enchantress that she is, the goddess has no sooner spoken than she has taken herself to the scene of the coming battle. (Imagine her as Angelina Jolie in the movie *Tomb Raider:* lithe, exotic, and deceptively innocent.) As she sits carelessly on the back of her lion, her silken skirts brush the grass. Flowers drip from her fingers, and clouds form and dissolve in her hair. Her body emanates rays of sensual bliss, and her eyes—well, no one has ever looked into her eyes without falling in love. She is beauty personified, sexuality clothed in form, enchantment itself. Riveted, enchanted by her beauty, by her graceful poise, by the gentle power of her divine self-confidence, the palace guards send messengers to the inner chambers, and within moments the demon kings have come to their windows to look at her. They are connoisseurs of feminine beauty. They have never seen a woman like this before. Some celestial maiden, they agree. Perhaps one of the devas has sent his wife or daughter as tribute. Of course, they want her. Why wouldn't they?

The palace majordomo saunters out to the garden and salutes Durga with only the slightest hint of menace. "Since you are in the garden of their majesties," he says, "I must assume that you have some interest in my lords. And, fortunate one, they have seen your beauty and are delighted to invite you to join the legions of their wives."

The goddess looks demurely at the ground. "Indeed," she says, "I have longed to know the asura kings. But there is one difficulty. I am the daughter of a warrior race, and must marry an equal. In my girlhood, I took a silly vow that I would only marry a man strong enough to defeat me in battle. You know how girls are—full of fantasy and romantic notions. But a vow is a vow. If your masters really want me, they'll have to fight with me."

"Lady, you are either mad or suicidal," says the majordomo. "No one has ever defeated my masters. It would break my heart to see such a delicate maiden die."

"Nonetheless, that is my condition," says Durga, giving him such a languorous glance that the majordomo feels stirrings of lust in every part of his body.

"And if your masters are afraid to do battle with me themselves, I am happy to take on their army."

"Very well, I will convey your message," he says, and hurries back to the palace.

The demon kings are intrigued. The lady has spirit, they agree, almost equal to her allure. They send messengers of increasingly higher rank and persuasive powers, but she will not back down.

Finally, Shumbha gets impatient. He tells the captain of his guard, "Go out and drag her in here by the hair."

The captain marches forth, accompanied by a small platoon. As he approaches, the goddess says, "Why are you here? I have challenged your masters."

"Madam, they do not fight women. We are here on their behalf."

"So be it," she says. A sword appears in her hand. She points it in their direction and, swifter than light, the captain and his men dissolve on the ground into puddles of disjointed matter.

At this point, wisdom might suggest to the demon kings that there is more going on here than meets the eye. But the ego, especially in its inflated state, is not necessarily wise. The demons send a larger company. The goddess, with the same languorous smile on her face, bids her lion open his mouth. The soldiers are drawn inexorably into the lion's huge jaws.

Now, the demons realize what they are facing. They remember the loophole and realize that they must defeat her or die. Their magical host, under the command of the generals Chanda and Munda, springs forth from every corner of the kingdom, converging on the slender figure in the garden. Fierce demon warriors with bared teeth and buffalo heads; creatures with teeth and fangs; lion-bodied, many-armed creatures of flesh and illusion attack the goddess. At this, the terrifying goddess Kali emerges from Durga's third eye. Emaciated, wearing a garland of skulls, roaring, she falls upon the army. As she cuts off the heads of the generals, she offers them to Durga.

But the battle doesn't stop. Now, comes the army of the demon general Raktabija, whose name means "drop of blood." Every drop of his blood has the power to turn into a clone of this magic warrior. To wound him is to give birth to a host of other Raktabijas—each with the same magical power. Raktabija represents the different faces of the self-seeking mind, which pops up every time you think you've knocked it down, always with a new disguise.

Suddenly, Durga lets out a roar that shakes the heavens. From her body emerges a host of beautiful light-forms: goddesses who each hold the full Shakti of the gods themselves.

They ride celestial vehicles and carry innocent-looking implements that hold deadly powers. Indrani, the Shakti associated with Indra, rides an elephant that tramples the demons underfoot. Saraswati, astride a celestial swan, sprinkles water from a monk's bowl, and as the drops fall on the soldiers, their bodies dissolve. Vaishnavi, the beautiful Shakti of Vishnu, carries a mace that she whirls with deadly accuracy and extraordinary effect. And finally, from out of Durga's body fly more terrible goddesses: Tara, Chinnamasta (the headless one), Bhairavi (the fierce). Along with them, Kali challenges the host of Raktabija, her tongue licking up the blood of the soldiers so that they can no longer be reborn from the spilled blood. Within half an hour, shockingly, the army is vanquished.

Now, Shumbha and Nishumbha have no choice. They have to fight the goddess themselves. By now they know who she is. It is the ego's last stand, and they approach the battle with full pride in their strength. Nishumbha is the first to die. Now roaring and as large as the palace itself, Shumbha advances upon the goddess.

"You challenged my army saying that you would fight single-handed," shouts Shumbha, in a voice so loud that it shakes the nearby hills to powder. "But look, you have helpers. Your challenge is forfeit."

"Not so," roars the goddess, vibrating the sky with rumbles of celestial thunder. "These goddesses are parts of myself. I alone exist in the world; what second, other than me, is there? O wicked one, behold these my powers entering back into me." With that, the other goddesses melt back into her form, leaving just Durga, shining with an almost blinding light.

"When I showed myself here in many forms, it was by means of my extraordinary power. Now I've withdrawn them. I stand utterly alone." And she calls out the warrior's blessing: "May you be resolute in combat."

The goddess's eight-armed form swells until it fills the sky. Twirling with one hand her great sword like a baton—and with axes, maces, spears, and crossbows in the others—she flies through the air, dancing between the demon kings, rising with them into the heavens, sinking below the earth, until finally, they lie on the ground, wounded, bleeding.

"Ma," says Shumbha with his dying breath, and then a smile comes over his face as the ecstasy of the goddess fills his being. In that instant, both the demons are transfigured, dissolving into Durga's body, dying into the mystery. When the ego dissolves, even the most demonic soul comes home, back to the heart of the mother.

TRANSFORMING THE EGO

Why would a battle story be the root myth of the goddess? Is it simply one of those stories, found in every tradition, about how in humanity's darkest hours the divine comes to save us? (Is the fact that, in normal times, the Goddess Durga remains inaccessible intended to reassure the masculine that feminine power, though potentially dangerous, remains under wraps unless summoned by the masculine himself?) Is the Devi Mahatmya, as so many spiritual teachers have pointed out over the centuries, a story about the battle of essence against the forces of ego?[4]

Like all powerful mythic stories, it makes sense on all of these levels. From the point of view of the environment, the goddess is the power of nature overwhelming human hubris. Her roar is the tsunami, the lightning strike, and the earthquake. From another point of view, it's a story about how we are supported and protected when we admit we are powerless over the forces of darkness and take refuge in the higher power. It's a commentary on the danger of underestimating the feminine. And of course, it's a story of rescue, the promise of protection in a world where we are so often victims of warring powers.

At yet another level, the Durga story is about the transformation of the ego. The mighty battle between Durga and the demons is the inner struggle that invariably begins when we undertake real transformative practice. Like the demon kings with their austerities, the ego enters into spiritual practice with its own agenda. Ego seeks control—control over circumstances, control over the body, control over the people around us. Power and mastery are what matter to the ego. So naturally, the ego will resist surrendering to higher powers, letting go of its agendas, or giving up control on any level. But the evolutionary Shakti has a different agenda. She wants to move us away from egocentric consciousness to the recognition of our nondifference from each other and the cosmos. To do this, she must put the ego in its place and ultimately dissolve it. The ego, however, will fight her to the death.

The demons personify the most primitive and intransigent forces of ego. They are the part of us that unabashedly craves power over others. The demonic part of the self sees everything and everyone, including the higher powers of the universe, as tools in its personal agendas. The gods, as we've mentioned, also represent aspects of the self, but they represent the higher self, the unique personal qualities of essence. The devas are our love, our dedication, our good intentions, the forgiveness and compassion we display when we're aligned with spirit. Durga arrives in our inner world to strengthen those higher qualities, whether for the sake of accomplishing good in the world, for progress on the spiritual path, or for the evolution of collective consciousness.

As postmodern practitioners, we may prefer to take a gentler attitude toward our own dark side than the myth describes. Most of us long ago rejected authoritarian religion, with its talk of sin and insistence on eliminating the darker forces in the self. If we practice one of the new thought paths that emphasize our innate goodness, we might prefer to ignore the negative qualities in the self, on the principle that fighting the ego only strengthens it. If we're psychodynamically oriented, we might be interested in bringing our shadow qualities into the light so we can integrate the power tied up in anger or greed or pride. If we aspire to be modern-day Tantrikas, we might practice diving into the feeling within our passionate impulses and discovering the primordial Shakti at the heart of anger and fear and greed.

All these approaches are useful, some on the level of personality, others as practices for enlightenment. Later, we'll look at these approaches more deeply. We'll meet goddess energies that cradle the ego in a gentle, transformative embrace. We'll also learn to invoke the Tantric goddesses who can show us how to enter the heart of passion for the sake of transformation.

Before we can access them, we need to bow to Durga—without reembracing authoritarian ideas of submission. For there are moments when the only way to put our narcissism in its place is with a sword—the sword of wisdom wielded by a warrior who takes no prisoners. This is Durga's role, whether she is operating in the outer world or the inner world.

In my life, the energy of the warrior goddess with her upraised sword shows up to remind me to get my striving, performance-oriented ego out of the way so that the deeper power can unfold my life according to her evolutionary imperative. Durga, in my inner world, is the unstoppable energy of spiritual growth. When I resist that, I often encounter an unexpected setback. She might get in my face as a kind of cosmic "No!" to my egoic illusions—and then manifest as the deeper awakening that follows when I let them go. Over the years, I've been through this cycle often. At times, egoic agendas pile up, balloon out, and take over my world—until, like cataracts, they ripen and become so swollen that they are ready to come apart of their own weight. Then nearly always, I hear the roar of the goddess's lion sounding through my dreams.

Just as often, Durga's battle cry is "Yes!" She manifests as a surge of courage, a "Yes, you can!" that forces me to stop and inspires me to take a new path. Maybe she shows up to guide me through a maze of my own making or speaks through a friend's word of encouragement. Sometimes I'll make some horrific mistake and hear her laugh as she points out that even mistakes can be teachers. More and more, I've learned in those moments to bow to her, to follow her lead, to recognize the Shakti's agenda for my growth.

When you feel caught in one of those moments—when your personal will seems blocked by immovable obstacles or when you want to move in a new direction but don't know how—consider that it might be a signal from the Shakti. Then, consider sitting for a few minutes in meditation and using your imagination to bring yourself into the presence of Durga.

Accessing Durga

For this exercise, you will need a quiet place to sit, a journal, and something to write with.

Become aware of the Durga Shakti as a shimmering presence around you. You can visualize her seated on her lion (though sometimes she rides a tiger— see which animal feels right to you!). Her dark hair streams over her shoulders. She wears a golden crown; a scarlet, silk sari; and golden necklaces, rings, and bracelets.

See Durga's magnificent arms, strong and bristling with weapons: the bow, the sword, the trident, the mace, the discus. See also the lotus she carries.

She is watching you with an intent gaze. Her eyes are large and dark.

Offer your salutations to her.

Ask her: "What is the major inner obstacle I have to face now? What do I need to let go of? What should I be paying more attention to?"

Close your eyes and turn to your heart. Ask the question in your heart.

Begin to write. Let the writing come naturally, without thought. Keep writing until you feel that there is no more to say.

Look over what you have written.

Now take the radical step of turning this over to the universal power of grace. Offer the obstacles to Durga, saying, "I offer all this to the Durga Shakti, asking that your grace dissolve all obstacles, inner and outer."

FIGURE 3: THE GODDESS DURGA

WHO IS DURGA IN YOUR LIFE?

Durga Shakti doesn't cradle you or coddle you. Instead, she lends you strength to do what you have to do. The seventeenth-century freedom fighter Shivaji, whose bands of Maratha warriors drove the Moghuls out of their home territory in Western India, claimed to have received his sword from Durga. Famously partial to warriors and leaders, Durga is especially available when you're struggling to right a wrong.

This is true up and down the chain of being. If Durga the cosmic queen is a world-protectress, the Durga woman is the protectress of her world.

Sasha, a lawyer and mother of two girls, first discovered the Durga Shakti when her daughter Lee began failing in school. It turned out that Sasha's husband, Lee's father, was engaging his daughter sexually. Sasha vowed that, whatever it took, she would protect her daughters. She filed for divorce, insisting that her husband not be allowed unsupervised visits with their girls. He fought hard for joint custody, deploying a high-powered legal team. As a lawyer, Sasha's field is wills and trusts, and she had never litigated. But she decided to be her own lawyer.

In the midst of this, Sasha took a class I was teaching on the goddesses. She felt an immediate affinity for Durga and created a meditation in which she imagined Durga's strength inside her own body. She would visualize each of Durga's eight arms holding a particular power. In one hand, she imagined the power to use words skillfully. In another, the power to read financial statements with care. In another, the skill to face down her husband's lawyers. She imagined all of Durga's weapons as energies empowering her to protect her daughters. She won the case, and soon afterward she realized that an enormous weight had lifted from her daughter. The fact that Sasha had fought on her daughter's behalf seemed to give the teenager her own sense of purpose and a new understanding of her own feminine strength. Lee's grades improved, and she went on to a good college.

THE DURGA PERSONALITY

Sasha's experience was a classic example of a Durga-style intervention. Like Sasha, we can tune into our own Durga energy by invoking the figure of the goddess. When you feel drawn to this goddess, it usually indicates one of two things: either you need an infusion of Durga-like strength, or you carry the Durga archetype as part of your personality. A woman tuned to the Durga archetype has a natural capacity for warrior-style leadership. She will naturally create zones of protection around the people in her life. (She's also an effortless multitasker, like a mother who manages three children while cooking a five-course meal, or like an executive running a team of diverse employees). The Durga woman makes space for people to flourish, fighting their battles when needed—as Sasha did for her daughter—but she is just as likely to push them into fighting for themselves.

My friend Ruth is an environmental activist and seasoned political operative who runs a family, cooks creatively and brilliantly, buys and sells houses, and has an almost limitless ability to make friends. She came into my life when I was just beginning to teach publicly, and she enlisted herself to help me create a teaching world. For two years she ran retreats for me, helped me plan programs, and used her formidable social skills to bring people into my life.

Durga women have a natural generosity, combined with a no-nonsense, "pull up your socks" sensibility that can be abrasive when the Durga shadow is in force. "Pull up your socks" *is* a Durga mantra. She herself gives no quarter to her own weaknesses and has little patience for anyone who stays stuck in theirs. Come to her with a problem, and she will immediately suggest a solution—but may lose patience if you don't act on it. Durga women are formidable. Hillary Rodham Clinton is the quintessential Durga woman—beloved by her friends, worshipped by her staff, regarded with suspicion by people who are uncomfortable with the kind of feminine power that won't disguise itself.

Hillary doesn't ask for sympathy, and as a result, she may not get it. Durga women don't cry easily. In fact, they often don't show emotion, especially not negative emotion. A Durga woman may believe that her job is to hold up the world—one of my more Durgaesque friends calls it her Mighty Mouse syndrome. She believes she can take care of anyone, solve anyone's problems. Helen Mirren's TV show character, Inspector Jane Tennison, epitomizes Durga energy. So did Queen Elizabeth I, who gave her name to the era of Shakespeare and the first British explorers of the New World. Angelina Jolie holds the Durga personal archetype in many of her films, as well as in her activist personal life.

In Indian mythology, Durga is sometimes described as a cosmic queen, and the Durga woman is definitely queenly. In ancient times, royalty felt themselves directly linked both to the land they ruled, to its people, and also to the subtle realms of gods. True royalty acted as a kind of channel between earth and heaven. An evolved Durga woman has that sense of global connection and global responsibility—whether her sphere is a family, an organization, or a project. At the same time, she intuits that the power that moves her is not her own. A true Durga woman will at some point in her life feel the transpersonal source of her own guardian energy.

"I was meditating at a shrine in Mexico," a student of a shamanic activist told me recently. "At one point, I had a vision of myself sitting on a throne. My back was open and energy was rushing into it from a kind of sun behind me. But the front of my body was in a formal, upright pose, very authoritative. I felt that I was seeing my soul. I saw that my authority comes from this stream of energy that was entering me from behind."

This woman had sensed the presence of the Durga archetype in her larger, transpersonal form. She felt that energy as the force that empowered her call to social action. An evolved Durga woman holds a big, often radical vision, and she has both the energy and the strategic skill to actualize it.

Invoking Durga as the Protectress

Find a comfortable seated position in a quiet location, and begin to focus on your breath.

With eyes closed, imagine yourself in a mountain grove. You are high in the wild mountains, in Durga's secret abode. As you look around, you see tall, snow-covered peaks on all sides. In the grove, the grass is soft and the air is sweet.

Know that you have come to ask Durga's protection. You may want to ask for her help in a personal battle or for some action for the benefit of humanity. Perhaps you want to request her help in protecting the environment or in righting some social inequity. Perhaps there is an illness in your body, or a friend is in trouble.

You call Durga in by reciting the following mantra ("I bow to Durga") nine times:

Om dum durayai namaha
ohm doom door-gah-yai nuh-muh-huh

You ask, using the following words or your own, "Goddess Durga, great warrior, protector, and mother of the world, please be with me."

Now you see the goddess forming out of the mountain peaks. She moves toward you, riding on her lion, moving over the mountains until she is only a few feet from you.

You gaze at her raptly, seeing her beautiful face under a golden diadem; her fierce, loving eyes; her long hair and firm mouth. She wears scarlet silk, gathered around her waist by a golden girdle, so that her legs can sit astride the lion.

She says, "Speak to me."

Folding your hands, you tell her your situation and ask for her help. You wait to hear her answer, which may come as words, as an inner feeling, or as a sense of her energy moving through you.

Now, imagine that a red light flows from Durga's heart to yours. As you inhale, you draw that light into your heart. You feel it filling you with strength and certainty, the qualities of Durga's Shakti.

Repeating the mantra "Om dum durgayai namaha," breathe with the feeling that you are drawing the goddess into your body. Let your pores open to receive the powerful, protective energy of Goddess Durga. Realize that you are taking in the power that can fight your battles, speak your truth, and in every sense fight for the preservation of the world.

Let go of the mantra. Rest in meditation. Meditate with the feeling that you are filled with the Durga Shakti.

SHADOW DURGA

As you uncover the Durga Shakti in yourself, it's important to be alert to the ways her shadow manifests when she is invoked in the service of egoic aims. Durga's shadow is harshness and the need for control. In her relationships, she needs to be in charge, and when Durga is manifesting her shadow, her control extends to a level of micromanagement that can disempower anyone who lives in her shade. She needs to shine, even to outshine, and her pride can verge on haughtiness. In the film *The Devil Wears Prada*, Meryl Streep's character embodies the essence of the Durga shadow, using her power to reduce the women around her to menial status. When a woman carries her Durga qualities in shadow, her protectiveness can become a protection racket, and every gesture of help carries an unspoken price tag.

As an employer, she expects perfection, and she can be capricious. Like the Red Queen in *Alice in Wonderland*, negative Durga is likely to command you to paint the roses red, in one breath, and an hour later insist the roses be painted white. (Never mind that the roses don't need painting!) One Durgaesque boss authorized a complex renovation project in her office, then when it was done, announced that it was both ugly and way too expensive; that if the people who requested the renovation had told her exactly what they had intended, she would never have approved it. This is Durga's shadow in action. Her shadow qualities are the negative aspect of her power to protect and transform.

Negative Durga can be self-righteous and critical. In your inner world, the negative Durga voice can show up as a relentless inner critic. She knows every one of your faults and failings, and she is likely to recite them to you at the slightest sign of a mistake. Durga is sure of her rightness, her moral high ground, her political correctness. She has a tendency to stake out ethical territory and allows no deviation from her standards. The 1970s model of the angry feminist, an Andrea Dworkin ("Heterosexual sex is rape") or a Catharine MacKinnon, incarnates the hard-ass side of Durga. Ripping through obstacles, she can also rip apart the fabric of things. Fighting injustice, she visits her sword on anyone or anything that stands in her way. If you earn Durga's disapproval, she is likely to stick you in her box marked "demon" and keep you there for a long time.

THE HEROINE: RIGHTING WRONGS

Durga is heroic in the old-fashioned sense. Like Wonder Woman, Durga is ready to leap into action at a moment's notice—and mobilize armies of helpers, usually female.

In the 1980s, psychotherapist Ruth Berlin noticed that her son's asthma got activated during the times when local crops were being sprayed for pests. She organized a group of mothers to protest aerial spraying in her area; after several years she was able not only to have it banned in Los Angeles, but to have the pesticide removed from circulation entirely. Now, besides her day job as a psychotherapist, she runs an environmental group focused on lobbying against airborne pesticides.

As this anecdote shows, the Durga energy can give a woman an acute social or political consciousness. Many of Durga's fiercer forms, like Bhadrakali and Chamundi, are famously goddesses of the margins, which means that they protect people who live at the edge of society. Durga energy is often behind a woman's instincts to champion the underdog or to organize for change. Dorothy Day was a bohemian rebel, a journalist who flourished in the Greenwich Village counterculture of the 1920s and 1930s. In her thirties, she converted to Catholicism and, in a move that was deeply radical for her time, recognized that it was possible to marry her socialist politics with her Catholic theology and mystical intuitions. Along with another mystical activist, Peter Maurin, she held the Durgaesque vision that Catholicism could become a force for living Jesus's original ministry to the poor. She and Maurin founded the Catholic Worker movement, which ran hospitality houses for homeless workers and served generations of desperately poor people in New York's Lower East Side. Her work helped inspire the liberation theology movement in South America, and it continues to inspire Christian activists.

On a more universal level, Durga's energy is often the fuel for popular uprisings and the will to fight social and political injustice. The early agitators for women's voting rights were filled with the Durga energy. So were the "rebel girls" of the labor and civil rights movements. So were my contemporaries in the second-wave feminist movement of the 1970s. The quiet "Enough!" of Rosa Parks keeping her seat in a segregated bus; the lunch counter sit-ins, Freedom Rides, and voter registration efforts in the 1960s; the wave of democratic feeling that created the Velvet and Orange revolutions in Eastern Europe; and the winds of popular protest that swept through the world in 2011—bringing down dictatorships in Tunisia and Egypt. All are expressions of the Durga Shakti. Durga energy is beyond political partisanship, of course; her energy flowed through Sarah Palin's famous acceptance speech at the 2008 Republican National Convention as much as it flows through Nancy Pelosi or through Leymah Gbowee, the Liberian peace activist.

One way to get a felt sense of the Durga Shakti is to remember a moment when you recognized, from the deepest place inside you, that something was wrong; that it *had* to change. If that recognition comes from the Durga Shakti, it goes beyond mere frustration. It goes beyond cognitive awareness of a social problem. Durga's transformative power carries a conviction that comes from deep inside the body, and with it often comes a sense of "Now!"—meaning *the time is now*. When that knowing is strong enough, it is followed by action. You will willingly put your body and your speech on the line to change the situation— whether it is an internal or an external one.

When the Durga energy is moving in society, it will naturally bring people together, raise up leaders, give impetus to a cause. Before the Durga Shakti is activated, we often feel powerless, confused, unable to act. Our forces are scattered and our will vacillates. If our will is strong, it may be powered by egoic agendas, anxiety, or fear. It's self-aggrandizing and manipulative—and limited in its power, which is why movements for change burn out or devolve into internal power struggles. Once Durga rises within us and descends through us (for the process of being activated by the Goddess involves both the calling from above and the ascent from below) there is purpose, will, direction, and a sense of inevitability. Of course, the ego can distort the pure instinct of the Shakti, and when the Shakti in her radical form has been unleashed, it requires great discernment to keep hold of the thread of the pure evolutionary impulse and not let the ego come in to claim it. Even when human confusion distorts the impulses of the Shakti, once Durga has sounded her battle cry—blown her great conch and clanged the bell of transformation—the movement of evolution cannot be stopped. When Durga's revolutionary energy sweeps through the world, there is no going back to the way things were before.

The phrase "winds of change" actually describes the way Durga energy moves, both in the world and in our bodies. Anyone who has ever been caught up in such a moment will recognize the feeling of heightened pranic energy— the dopamine surge that fills you, impelling purposeful action and seeming to carry you beyond anything that you could have done under ordinary conditions.

DURGA AS THE FORCE OF INNER REVOLUTION

The same quality of purposeful action can be invoked when what we need is the will to change a deep-seated habit or addiction. Anyone who has ever done personal transformative work knows that the desire to change a self-destructive or addictive habit has to mature into an intense will to transform before it galvanizes into action. In my experience, tuning into the Durga Shakti is like tuning into an almost cosmic sense of purpose. W. H. Murray, the Scottish polar explorer, wrote, "When there is a definite commitment, providence moves too."[5] Durga is that providence.

As a force in the transformative process, Durga Shakti gives you the power to face the parts of yourself that are in the way of your evolution, in every sense of the word.

Contemplation: Invoking Durga to Transform Yourself

For this exercise you will need a pen, a journal, and a quiet place to sit in contemplation.

Consider one quality in yourself that you know needs to change. Perhaps it's an aspect of your personality that others have pointed out to you, or that you know causes suffering to yourself and others. Or perhaps you notice a regressive trait in yourself like indecisiveness, deceitfulness, or lack of discipline. Perhaps it is an addictive behavior or a psychological pattern that seems to be keeping you from stepping into your best self.

Write a paragraph about how this trait manifests in you.

Now imagine yourself in a garden. See before you the form of the Goddess Durga. She sits astride a lion, draped in red silk. Her hair is black, lustrous,
and covers her shoulders. She wears bracelets, rings, and other ornaments.
Her dark eyes blaze with kindness.

As you are seated before her, gaze into her eyes. Imagine that with each
exhalation you offer this negative trait into her radiant presence. With each
inhalation, you breathe in her strength and purity, her power to transform.

Finally, sit with the feeling of Durga's presence, allowing her dynamic,
loving, awakening energy to fill you. Imagine that you are filling yourself with
Durga Shakti.

In her most secret and inward manifestation, Durga is the power behind radical
spiritual awakening. She's the Shakti that descends into us and ignites the subtle
body, beginning a process that can eventually change the way we think, feel, and
see ourselves and the world. In the Tantric traditions, this awakening is called *shaktipat*, the descent (*pat*) of Shakti. It's an extraordinary mystical process in which
Shakti from above meets Shakti from below and sets in motion the kundalini—the
so-called coiled inner energy that orchestrates the dance of internal revolution.
The Tantric traditions tell us that kundalini is the inner form of the goddess and
that when the human body forms, it holds both the divine dynamism of the goddess and the transcendent spirit of the divine masculine principle. The awakening
of kundalini is actually the awakening of the Goddess's powers within the human
body, and it may be the most radically transformative event in one's life. It can
set in motion a complete reordering of your priorities, opening up the gates of
the inner body, giving you the capacity to perceive the inner meaning of events,
unlocking creative gifts, kindling love in the heart, setting in motion the process of
self-questioning that can change the way you live every aspect of your life. In the
goddess traditions, what we call the awakening of kundalini is the moment when
the goddess decides to show you her liberating face.[6]

Until that moment, all the energy in the system is outgoing, spent in
powering the senses and the heartbeat, drawn outward to complete immersion in the external. When kundalini awakens, all of that changes. You get
the capacity to turn your attention inward, to see beneath the surface of
things, to sense the deep connections between yourself and others and yourself and the world. The awakening of kundalini is something like a dynamite
blast that cracks a rock—in this case, the rock that cements us into the

feeling of separation and duality. I once watched workers dynamite a huge boulder in the midst of a field where they were building a house. When the dynamite exploded, the boulder rose a foot in the air, then settled back, cracked in a hundred places. The shape of the boulder remained, but it no longer held together. In the same way, the edifice of dualistic understanding is cracked during a kundalini awakening. You may not immediately realize that this has happened. The old structures of your mind and body and heart may stay in place for some time after the initial upheaval, but the cement that holds them together has been dissolved.

Only a mighty force like the Durga energy can crack the embedded rocks of our deep karmic habits. As kundalini, Durga Shakti can dissolve the neuronal patterns that keep us stuck in our woundedness and constrict our responses to the world. More than that, the awakened Durga Shakti has the power to turn around the ship of your consciousness. She can literally reverse the polarities of your awareness so that you can begin to see into the inner world. Kundalini awakening is soul stirring. A subtle kundalini awakening will give you a deeper access to meditative states. A dramatic kundalini awakening can dissolve the forms around you so that for a few moments you experience your body, mind, and external surroundings evanesce into emptiness. It can send light and energy shooting up your spine, waves of bliss coursing through your body. It can pluck out your sense of alienation, your feelings of darkness and low-grade anxiety, and give you an effortless feeling of connection to all that is. It can overwhelm you with feelings of love that come from the depths of the earth and reach up to the sky. It can also draw out your shadows and show you the rage, fear, and grief you've hidden from yourself in your addiction to the light side of your existence. But kundalini will also release them out of your system, layer by layer, so that you are no longer ruled by "demonic" emotions.

When the Goddess Durga awakens in you as the kundalini Shakti, she awakens as all her divine aspects. In the root myth of Durga, there is that moment when different Shaktis emerge from her body in the form of goddesses like Lakshmi and Saraswati. That scene could be a metaphor for the emergence of different energies after a kundalini awakening. Once activated, the inner evolutionary energy acts in the psyche in three distinct ways, each personified by one of the goddesses. These stages often occur simultaneously, but they can feel very different. In the first stage, our system is gradually cleared of obstructions and karmic blocks, the residue of old wounds, genetic predispositions, and traumas—any resentment, grief, and fear that darkens our energy body and prevents the free flow of our natural life-force. This purification stage is associated with Kali, the fierce energy of the Goddess.

The second stage is often experienced as the awakening of your sense of inner abundance. Sensations of bliss might pour through your body, or you might feel spontaneous impulses of kindness and gratitude. You feel joyful for no particular reason. Problems resolve themselves. You may see lovely visions in meditation or experience inner and outer gifts showering on you. Your life begins to feel graced. You get a job offer or an inheritance. You have a breakthrough in a creative project. You become pregnant after years of trying unsuccessfully. Your relationships with people you've been estranged from become friendly again. You feel loved, loving, fortunate. Your inner life seems to unfold almost effortlessly, as if guided.

These inner and outer gifts are manifestations of Lakshmi, the energy of good luck, love, and delight. The expansion of Lakshmi's energy can happen early in the process, but the experience of inner harmony and abundance becomes stronger each time another limiting pattern or negative emotion is released from your system. Dammed energies are freed and begin to flow through channels that you might not have known were there.

When Lakshmi energy is moving in the body, your desires begin to be fulfilled, both the inner ones and the outer ones. As a young woman, I'd always had a secret desire to be irresistible. At one stage of my awakening process it seemed as though this was being fulfilled: I became so magnetic that men were constantly flirting with me—to the point where it became uncomfortable. Both women and men have shared similar experiences with me. When the Lakshmi energy is operating in you, your body becomes particularly radiant.

The danger here is that you might become intoxicated with your own good fortune—attached to the sweets of life. You might find yourself living in your own version of the god realm, the domain of infinite pleasure, where desires are more or less instantly fulfilled and your worst problem is having to make choices between one great experience or another. The problem with the god realm is that it's easy to get stuck there—but of that, more later!

SARASWATI RISING

In the third stage of kundalini awakening, you begin to experience the gifts of Saraswati, the power of knowledge. In the external world, Saraswati Shakti might manifest as a new eloquence, the gift of verbal expression, or the power to make delicious music. In the inner realm, however, the mark of Saraswati's presence is the opening of your capacity for insight. You're able, effortlessly, to recognize divine presence in the world. The enveloping consciousness of the witness arises in you. You understand subtle energy, and you can express it. Your intellect becomes powerful and refined. You can read philosophy or physics or mystical texts, understand them, and make connections between disciplines. Richard Sclove had a spontaneous kundalini awakening as a student at MIT. One result was that he began to know what the professor was going to say before saying it, and he also could discern when the professor was wrong. In one stunning emergence of Saraswati Shakti, Sclove guessed the answers on a calculus exam for an advanced course he hadn't expected to pass. Instead, he received the highest grade in the class.[7]

The difficulty here is that your understanding and eloquence—the expression of Saraswati's gifts—will often outstrip your realization.

In my early years of kundalini awakening, my insights about spiritual life arrived so compellingly that I felt as if I understood all sorts of subtleties I'd never realized before. Texts came alive. When other people would be confused by spiritual paradoxes, I could almost instantly understand the unity behind apparent contradictions. I could speak intelligently about all this, and yet my inner embodiment, my assimilation of the knowledge that flowed through me, was unbaked and superficial. I had grown up in a family of writers, and I already tended to overidentify with my intellectual prowess, such as it was. Whenever Saraswati unfolded a new insight, my ego would identify with it, and I would feel as if I had "succeeded" in my spiritual life. Often, at that point there would be a setback, a moment of humiliation. I'd forget something, or misstate something I should have known, and I'd realize that I wasn't intellectually omnipotent at all. It was as if the Goddess were reminding me that worldly and spiritual gifts are just that—gifts, leant to us for a purpose.

FULLNESS, INFLATION, AND DURGA'S SWORD

The process of assimilating the gifts of the goddess swings naturally through phases of expansion and contraction. The goddess expands in you. You experience the fullness of her gifts. You fall in love with the energy moving in you. Often, you experience profound humility and gratitude. Then the ego seizes the gift, identifies with it, and begins, subtly or less subtly, to overreach itself. At that point, Durga's sword might appear in the form of a smack from the universe or a sudden and precipitate feeling of having fallen from grace. Or the boons and meditation experiences might seem to evaporate, leaving you with the feeling that you've lost touch with love, or that Saraswati's graceful gifts of speech have deserted you. Sometimes, it can seem as if your vision is once again clouded, the world once again opaque and flat.

The path of the goddess is all about learning to ride the expansion and contraction until you can recognize her different faces in the ups and downs of your inner journey. You become familiar with her subtle hints, the signs that a path is opening for you, the warnings to back off, back down, go deeper inside, or turn more attention to a part of your personal self that needs development. Little by little, Shakti partners with your own efforts and practice to subtly reshape your character and nature. The more you understand the process as the natural expression of the goddess's acts of revelation and concealment, the more easily you can partner with her unfolding inside you.

Durga

door-gah—Warrior Goddess of Strength and Protection

Other Names for Durga:
  Ambika (*uhm-bi-kah*)—Little Mother
  Katyayani (*kaht-yah-yuh-nee*)
  Aparajita (*uh-pahr-ah-ji-tah*)—Unconquerable One
  Mahishasuramardini (*muh-hish-ah-soor-uh-mahr-di-nee*)—Slayer of
  the Demon Mahisha
  Mahamaya (*muh-hah-mah-yah*)—Great Illusion, referring to her
  power of creating the worlds
  Vindhyavasini (*vin-dya-vah-si-nee*)—Dweller in the Mountains
  Sheranvali—(*sheyr-uhn-vah-lee*)—Lion Rider
  Bhagavati (*bhuh-guh-vuh-tee*)—Blessed Lady
  Mahadevi (*muh-hah-dey-vee*)—Great Goddess; the Great Goddess is
  often identified with Durga

Recognize Durga in:
  • strong winds
  • crashing waves and high surf
  • the season of autumn, when the leaves turn colors

- bonfires
- all forms of bravery in the service of truth
- the will to battle
- powerful leaders who take groups of people through a crisis or a war
- feelings of triumph and satisfaction after doing something difficult
- strong foundations, whether physical or cultural
- mountains
- upheavals that lead to new forms of culture or government
- courage that comes from the heart
- the impulse to protect
- truth-telling
- measured risk-taking

Invoke Durga for:
- physical, mental, and emotional strength
- personal empowerment
- standing up for yourself in an argument
- starting a project and getting down to work
- completing a project
- willpower to create positive habits, such as eating healthy foods, getting exercise, or sitting for meditation
- help in challenging situations, such as getting your kids to do their homework, chairing a meeting, facing a difficult boss or coworker, litigating, keeping your integrity under challenging circumstances, calling someone out, controlling unruly emotions
- taking care of you in bad neighborhoods or negative situations
- rescuing someone in trouble
- protecting other people
- ending relationships
- political power and savvy
- fighting for justice
- facing up to (and facing down!) the negative side of your own ego

Bija Mantra
Dum (*doom*)
Seed mantra for Shakti as pure strength

Invocational Mantra

Om dum durgayai namaha
ohm doom door-gah-yai nuh-muh-huh

Om, I bow to the one who overcomes all difficulties

Gayatri Mantra
(Called "Mother of the Vedas," the Gayatri mantra is foundational in Hinduism, second only to the mantra "Om" in its importance. The Gayatri mantra is used as praise, as petition, and simply to connect your consciousness to the deity or energy invoked. Most deities have a Gayatri specially dedicated to them.)

Om katyayanyai cha vidmahe
Kanyakumaryai dhimahi
Tanno Durga prachodayat

ohm kaht-yah-yuhn-yai chuh vid-muh-hey
kun-yuh-koom-ahr-yai dee-muh-hee
tun-no door-gah pra-cho-duh-yah-tuh

Om, may we come to know the goddess Katyayani
May we meditate on the maiden goddess
May that goddess Durga, who overcomes all difficulties,
impel us forward on our path

Durga's colors: red, gold, yellow, orange
Durga's festival: Dasara, in the Hindu month of Kartika
(September–October)
Durga's mount: lion, tiger
Durga's consort: Shiva

CHAPTER 4

Lakshmi

Goddess of Abundance and Good Fortune

Bestower of intelligence and success, O goddess,
giver of worldly enjoyment and liberation,
with the mantra always as your form,
Goddess Mahalakshmi, I bow to you.

MAHALAKSHMI ASHTAKAM
Eight Stanzas to Great Lakshmi

[Lakshmi] throws the spell of the intoxicating sweetness of the divine; to be close to her
is a profound happiness and to feel her within the heart is to make existence a rapture
and a marvel; grace and charm and tenderness flow out from her like light from the sun
and wherever she fixes her wonderful gaze or lets fall the loveliness of her smile, the soul
is seized and made captive and plunged into the depths of an unfathomable bliss.

SHRI AUROBINDO
The Mother

There is in all things an inexhaustible sweetness and purity, a silence
that is a fountain of action and joy. It rises up in wordless gentleness
and flows out to me from the unseen roots of all created being.

THOMAS MERTON

Let the beauty of what you love be what you do.
There are many ways to kneel and kiss the ground.

RUMI

I n the old days, Lakshmi was invoked for fame and prosperity. Traditionally, in India *fame* meant something like "good repute," "good name." To possess fame was to be known in your village or district, with Lakshmi's grace, for your good qualities: your generosity, fairness, and skill. Prosperity was more quantifiable. It could be counted in gold, grain, or sons, and when the count was high, it showed in your face, in the contentment that beamed from you, the satisfaction of security. For a man, it brought power and respect. For a woman, prosperity manifested in beauty, children (preferably sons!), and the good luck to be cherished by your family.

The boons Lakshmi bestows reflect her own golden qualities; what the goddess gives you is always, in the end, herself. Shri Lakshmi, says the "Shri Sukta," the earliest known of her praise hymns, incarnates food, universal sovereignty, noble rank, authority, power, spiritual luster, kingdom, fortune, bounteousness, and beauty. A story goes that the other gods envied these qualities so intensely that they plotted to steal them from her. They're still trying to steal them; Lakshmi's worldly gifts are the greatest prizes of life on Earth—wealth and power and beauty—so alluring, so desirable that human beings as well as gods are tempted to extremes for their sake. One of her names, Shri, actually means "auspiciousness."

All the goddesses confer power. Shakti, after all, *is* power. The fierce goddesses offer us the power to fight our battles, the inner ones and the outer ones. The wisdom goddesses give us inspiration and insight and the skill of speech. Lakshmi and her queenly sister goddess, Tripura Sundari (who we will meet in chapter 12), embody the skills of success—worldly and spiritual. They also carry the inner qualities that make life lovely: love, harmony, kindness. When we have Lakshmi, the old mythic texts tell us, we have everything, inner and outer, for a beautiful life. Without her? Well, without her we're impoverished, both inwardly and outwardly. Without her, the world is a desert.

We know this, because it happened once, as the following story reveals.

Indra, king of the gods, is riding his celestial elephant through the glorious kingdom of the gods. Indra has the natural arrogance of an absolute ruler. He's proud of his royal status, proud of his warrior prowess, proud of the rich offerings in the sacrifices he receives from sages. He's having a good day.

As his procession moves in its slow progress, he sees the sage Durvasas standing before him with matted hair and road dust covering his body. He holds a dusty garland. "Indra, Indra!" calls Durvasas. "I bring you a great blessing. This garland appeared before me after meditation, and an inner voice told me to offer it to you. It contains the very essence of auspiciousness (shri) and prosperity. Guard it well!" Indra leans down and takes the garland. He offers a respectful but absentminded salutation to the sage. Then, without waiting until he is out of sight, he drops the garland around his elephant's neck.

Durvasas stands for a moment, shocked at Indra's carelessness with what, after all, was a divine gift. Then he utters a curse. "Just as you dishonored auspiciousness, auspiciousness will abandon you," he says.

The moment Durvasas speaks, every flower in Indra's kingdom wilts. Every tree droops. The garland, you see, was the form of Lakshmi herself, the goddess of abundance, auspiciousness, and all-around goodness. Her flowering form represented the flowering of the natural world, and the sage had offered it freely to Indra. When the king of the gods dropped the garland so carelessly around his elephant's neck, Lakshmi simply disappeared from the three worlds. With her went beauty, fertility, and the luster of every realm and every being. It wasn't just that the crops stopped growing. Every form and expression of goodness dried up like an abandoned lake. Prayers and sacrifices stopped; the sages no longer had the will to perform them. People stopped giving gifts, or offering food in charity, or helping their neighbors. No one cleaned the roads. Parents became indifferent to their children, and couples quarreled bitterly with each other. Rulers forgot to consider their people and raised taxes mercilessly. But because no crops grew, the taxes went unpaid. Even the sun and moon dimmed, and a dull cloud lay over the earth. That's how it goes when the power of auspiciousness leaves the land.

In desperation, the gods approach Lord Vishnu, who is the true ruler of the worlds. Vishnu's cosmic task is to maintain the material universe in balance. He does this from his abode, Vaikuntha, where he maintains a heavenly court. But it is Lakshmi who gives him the power to do this, and when she disappears from the worlds, even Vishnu can't keep things going. He looks deeply into his vast awareness to discover the explanation, and he finds the moment when Indra, in his pride, insulted the goddess. Knowing Lakshmi, he realizes what happened. Lakshmi is not a goddess to roar, or to complain, or to draw a sword. But she does not stay where there is pride or harshness. When she is displeased, she simply leaves, and with her goes everything that makes life sweet. Vishnu, who has presided over many turns of the cosmic wheel, recognizes the symptoms of Lakshmi's departure, even though it had been several eons since such a thing had happened on so large a scale.

Vishnu is the most resourceful of deities, and sitting in meditation he understands what must be done. Lakshmi had enfolded herself into the sea of consciousness, dissolving into the particles of the Milky Ocean, the cosmic sea of love and intelligence that stretches beyond space and time. In Indian myth, the Milky Ocean represents the creative chaos of Shakti, the nourishing fluid out of which life is born. In its natural state, the ocean is simply endless, transcendent, timeless. In order to create life, it must be churned with will and intention, just as milk needs to be agitated in order to produce butter. Vishnu himself, between cycles of time, spends eons floating on the ocean of consciousness. He understands that to bring Lakshmi back, the elemental deities need to make an extraordinary effort. He assembles the gods on one side of the ocean, and the demons, the dark forces, on the other. Don't ask me how they manage to find the shores of the boundless ocean; this is a myth after all, and in myth anything is possible. Vishnu then calls forth, out of his being, two of his cosmic animal forms. Taking the body of a great serpent, Vasuki, he becomes the rope that pulls the vast churning stick. Pouring another part of his being into the form of Kurma, the cosmic tortoise, Vishnu dives to the bottom of the sea and supports the churning stick from underneath.

Then, undiminished in his transcendent perfection, he takes his place with the gods. Together, with prayers and supplications, the gods and demons begin to churn the ocean.

Many amazing and luminous gifts come forth during the churning, but these are for another time and another story. The important thing is that, as the waters swirl into vast waves, the figure of Lakshmi slowly rises up from the center of the whirlpool. She stands gracefully on a lotus, her glorious golden skin gleaming, her lustrous hair flowing to the waist. Her huge almond-shaped eyes and honeyed lips are features so refined and beautiful that gods and demons gasp. She is soft ivory-gold, the color of a lotus, and her breasts, according to the verse that describes her form, are round, high, and close set. She wears a white garland and rosy silk, and her hair is dark and curly over her half-moon-shaped forehead. Her hands are at her sides, palms out in the gesture of bestowing boons. Golden light pours from her. As gods and demons elbow each other for the privilege of courting her, she smiles her tender, lustrous smile and extends her hand to Vishnu, her eternal consort.

As Lakshmi steps from her lotus and takes Vishnu's hand, the earth bursts into flower. The memory of love is reborn, and sages rekindle their sacred fires. The sun regains its fiery splendor, and the moon gleams full in the nighttime sky. Kings call their prime ministers to remind them of the laws of generosity, and rich people invite the beggars at their gates to come inside and feast. With Lakshmi's reappearance, love, generosity, sacred practices, wealth, and fertility return to the world.

When Lakshmi marries Vishnu, the world celebrates the sacred marriage of masculine and feminine, the marriage of wisdom and love. In their union, an age of order and harmony is born. Dharma itself, the principle of righteous action, is Lakshmi's gift. More than that, she awakens love in Vishnu's heart. When Vishnu is out of touch with Lakshmi, he's rather stern—a stickler for the forms of righteous behavior. But when he gets together with Lakshmi, he softens into the masculine deity of nourishing affection.

THE GODDESS OF SUSTAINABILITY

It's easy to see this story as a parable for our own time. Just as carelessly as Indra tossed away Durvasas's garland, our own Indras have used and tossed aside the bounty of the earth, poisoned the atmosphere, and insulted nature in a thousand ways. We see signs of Lakshmi's withdrawal in the desertification of so many parts of the planet, in the pain of starvation and cruelty that afflict so many on the earth, and in the cynicism and violence of so much contemporary art and culture. From a subtle perspective, when we consider what it means to live sustainably in this world, we are actually contemplating what it means to incarnate Lakshmi. Even the word *sustainable* is a reference to her.

Lakshmi is the goddess energy who preserves life. In Tantric nature cosmology, she is the nourishing, cooling power of the *soma*, or moon-nectar, that balances the fiery, lightning-like Shakti of Kali and the blazing solar energy of Durga. Soma was the drink of the gods, and supposedly it contained the power to give immortality. It was one of the substances churned up from the Milky Ocean, along with Lakshmi herself. According to Ayurveda, the traditional medical science of India, soma appears in the body as *ojas*, a vital essence found in the bone marrow. Ojas conveys vitality. Sexuality and meditation both draw their power from ojas. It's connected with rejuvenation (interestingly, the bone marrow is where stem cells are found); it's also the subtle substance that can cool the body when the kundalini Shakti is manifesting in a fiery, Kali-like fashion. Lakshmi's Shakti is life sustaining both in the physical and subtle realms. She is, subtly speaking, the water of life and the subtle nectar that moistens the heart.

Lakshmi is an ancient goddess. The Vedic singers praised her under her most ancient name, Shri, and sang the "Hymn to Shri" ("Shri Sukta") to bring forth whatever is glorious and beautiful in the natural world. Besides being a name of Lakshmi, *shri* is an abstract noun that signifies all the qualities associated with auspiciousness: good fortune, lovingkindness, material prosperity, physical health, beauty, purity of motive, well-being, authority, energy, vitality, and every kind of radiance.

THE POWER OF RULERSHIP

In the old traditions, kings and queens were considered the embodiment of shri and needed the qualities of shri in order to rule. (Western traditions also equated the prosperity of a kingdom with the virtue of the king, though of course they didn't use the same words to describe this royal quality.) Even members of the demon races could have shri. The Vishnu Purana describes how two demon kings, Bali and Prahlad, became filled with the energy of shri through their virtuous character and their devotion to God. As long as Lakshmi favored them, the two kings shone with auspicious qualities. As rulers, they presided over kingdoms where all the fields yielded rich harvests, where all the women gave birth to healthy children, and where love and virtue reigned. But when wily Indra cajoled Lakshmi into leaving Prahlad, this noble king lost not only his prosperity, but his inner strength and joy, and he was soon conquered by his rivals. The right to rule, and the power of rulership itself, was Lakshmi's gift.

Kings "married" shri by rituals that bound them to the fertile fields of their kingdoms, mirroring the sacred marriage of Lakshmi and Vishnu, the union of masculine strength with the blessing-power conferred on him by feminine love. Even today, we recognize shri in the natural authority of a good teacher or leader, one of those people who can draw us to a cause or a project by his or her innate qualities of enthusiasm and by the subtle feeling of *rightness* they project. When Barack Obama was first running for president in 2008, I would watch him as he gave a speech and see shri emanating from him, as though the Shakti of auspiciousness had chosen him to incarnate leadership in a critical moment for his country. (Arguably, her mantle of glamor seemed to slip from his shoulders soon after his 2009 inauguration.) When you have shri, you are not just fortunate, not just successful. You are *right*, trustworthy because your words and actions are inspired by an intrinsic attunement to what is needed in each time and place. To stand in shri is to stand in integrity, like those ancient kings who mediated between the higher world and the earth.

Durga was the goddess invoked by kings for victory in battle. Lakshmi was the one invoked for the blossoming fullness of a land at peace. We follow Durga with the confidence that her strength will protect us. We follow Lakshmi out of love—as the following meditation may reveal.

Invoking Lakshmi on the Island of Flowers

Find a quiet location where you can sit and focus for this exercise.
Once you are settled into your seat, begin the following meditation.

Imagine yourself sitting on a cushioned seat on an emerald green lawn. The grass is dewy and lustrous, and behind you is a spreading tree. The tree is in bloom, covered with fragrant pink and red flowers. As you look down, you realize that the seat you are sitting on is studded with gems, that the cushions are silk, and that everything in the environment is shining with light. In front of you, an aquamarine ocean glimmers, small waves lap on a beach whose pebbles are pearls. The air is fragrant with the scent of blossoms.

Over the ocean, you see the form of the goddess Lakshmi appearing, as if rising from the waves. She is tall and slender with golden skin and long, lustrous hair. Her rosy-pink sari falls over a perfect body. As you watch, she glides over the water and steps onto the pearly beach. As she walks toward you, a jeweled bench appears, and Lakshmi seats herself upon it, facing you, just a few feet away. She is smiling, and her eyes invite you to meet her gaze. Her eyes, which are enormous, dark, fringed with long, curling lashes, are looking into yours with infinite love. Lakshmi has golden skin; a mouth that curves like a bow; and small, white teeth. She wears a crown of gold on her waving dark hair and necklaces of gold, rubies, and diamonds around her neck. Her arms are heavy with golden, jeweled bracelets, and her silken sari is sprinkled with gold dust.

Her smile is infinitely loving. As you gaze into her eyes, you realize that she sees into your soul, that she knows you, that she loves you infinitely. She invites you to ask for a gift of grace.

Now you begin to sense her love flowing toward you as a stream of rose-gold light. You may actually visualize this light-energy, or you may simply feel it as a current of loving sweetness. This light, Lakshmi's blessing, is flowing toward you, and with your inhalation, you draw it into your body. With your exhalation, you feel the energy moving through your heart.

If you feel resistance to the energy of Lakshmi's blessing, breathe it out with your exhalation. Have the feeling that Lakshmi is absorbing your resistance, your feelings of unworthiness or lack, and transmuting them into beauty and light.

Breathing in the Lakshmi energy—the energy of love and blessing, the energy of divine abundance—feel that her blessing is filling you with her own qualities: beauty, love, gratitude, forgiveness, generosity, healing, and the power to bless. Allow yourself to take in the light of Lakshmi with each breath. Allow the light-energy to spread through your being. Breathe out your resistance and your doubts, and allow Lakshmi to absorb and bless them.

BLESSING AND CONFIDENCE

Perhaps this meditation gave you a sense of the subtle effect of Lakshmi's presence within you. Her Shakti manifests inwardly as a subtle trust in the goodness of the universe, as a feeling of contentment and confidence. Lakshmi embodies a kind of heartfelt self-worth, which is why meditating on Lakshmi is a good way for someone with self-esteem issues to uncover their own intrinsic value. "Life is good" is a Lakshmi mantra. If you could see Lakshmi's energy as light, you would see that it is rose-gold—rosy with the color of optimism, good health, and love; gold with the color of abundance, the inner sense of fullness that overflows as joy and sweetness. A hymn from the Tantric tradition implores her:

> O Mother
> Deeply embedded
> Is my fear, my insecurity.
> Have mercy, O Mother, on my wretched state.
> Uproot it
> With the joy that arises from your sweet and compassionate glance . . .
> Plant in us the seed of auspiciousness
> As we make our way in the world.[1]

If Durga is the strength and protective power in nature, Lakshmi is its beauty. As Kali is the darkness of night and the great dissolve into nirvana, Lakshmi is the brightness of day and the expansiveness of teeming life. She can be found in rich soil and flowing waters, in streams and lakes that teem with fish. She is one of those goddesses whose signature energy is most accessible through the senses. You can detect her in the fragrance of flowers or of healthy soil. You can see her in the leafed-out trees of June and hear her voice in morning birdsong. If Durga is military band music and Kali heavy metal, Lakshmi is Mozart. She's chocolate mousse, satiny sheets, the soft feeling of water slipping through your fingers. Lakshmi is growth, renewal, sweetness.

One of her names is Kamala, which means "lotus." The lotus is a symbol of growth, of the life that blossoms in the waters and roots itself in soil. Macrocosmically, the lotus represents the manifest world, which in mythology begins when a cosmic lotus springs forth from Vishnu's navel at the start of each new cycle of creation. This expansive, vigorous moment of blossoming holds the essence of the impulse that brings forth life from the earth. Lakshmi is that blossoming essence, the image of life itself.

FIGURE 4: THE GODDESS LAKSHMI

The lotus also points to Lakshmi's spiritual gifts. In Hindu and Buddhist literature, the lotus symbolizes the absolute purity of consciousness, and that of the spiritual adepts whose personal consciousness has become luminous through practice and realization. Rising out of the mud, yet blossoming in spotless perfection and beauty, the lotus is the "seat" of great sages and saints, buddhas and bodhisattvas, all those who have refined their consciousness to a state where they can root themselves in life's muddy soil and use its fertility as compost to blossom the soul.

Lakshmi has this quality of transcendent purity, which is why the hymns that praise her point out that she is the bestower of intelligence as well as success, of liberation as well as of worldly enjoyment. She is also one of the goddesses most associated with dharma, with virtuous actions and clarity of mind. When you begin to invoke Lakshmi as an inner helper or chosen deity, you often notice that one of her gifts is a certain discernment, a delicacy that is almost finicky. Lakshmi epitomizes refinement. She can give you a rarified eye to discern what is good, true, and beautiful in your daily world.

LAKSHMI IN THE MATERIAL UNIVERSE

Let's not overlook the obvious. In the human world, Lakshmi is the Shakti of success, wealth, romantic attraction, artistic accomplishment, and that indefinable gift that we call "good taste." She's the goddess of the decorative arts, manifest in beautiful furniture and fabrics; in the clothing of designers like Valentino; in the supermodel on the back cover of *Vogue*, wearing a Hermes scarf tied carelessly around her hair. Lakshmi is every beautiful woman in life and art, perhaps most gorgeously captured in Botticelli's *Birth of Venus* (which could be an actual painting of Lakshmi herself, if she had darker hair and a few more clothes).

Lakshmi is also money. Aurobindo, who was one of the first modern spiritual teachers to question the assumption that poverty is more intrinsically spiritual than wealth, wrote, "Money is the visible sign of a universal force, and this force in its manifestation on earth works on the vital and physical planes and is indispensable to the fullness of the outer life. In its origin and true action, it belongs to the divine."[2]

The operative phrase here is "true action." Money reveals its sacred qualities when we use it in the right way. One of the subtle gifts we get when we tune into Lakshmi is that she can help us recognize the sacred quality in money. She can even liberate us from the shadow emotions of fear and greed that seem Velcroed to our modern relationship with wealth. In Mumbai, during the yearly Lakshmi festival, businessmen actually pile their strongboxes and bank statements (and now, their computers) in mounds, to which they offer flowers, sprinkling Lakshmi's material manifestation with water, naming it with Lakshmi mantras.

Even though they may be doing so to increase their bottom line, there's great wisdom in the practice of offering respect to Lakshmi as the physical substance of money. However, to find the depth of the practice (and to raise it beyond magical thinking) we need the discernment to recognize the subtle energy behind wealth's physical manifestations. Money is a physical symbol of two deep principles within Lakshmi's energy: the principle of value and the principle of giving and receiving—the exchange of energy that underlies every process in the physical world.

We estimate the value of something by what we are willing to give for it—whether it is our money, our labor, our commitment, or our care. To respect Lakshmi is to respect the value of everything that matters to us—including our own bodies and the worth of our labor. Someone who has mastered the energy of Lakshmi has an instinctive sense of what can be given and how much to give in exchange for value received. In the subtle economy of the Lakshmi Shakti, what ultimately counts is our ability to recognize the subtle source of physical wealth, to honor it, and to share our bounty in just the right way—not too little, not too much.

SHADOW AND SACREDNESS

When we worship Lakshmi's gifts without recognizing her subtle sacred essence, we open the door to some very shadowy manifestations of the Lakshmi energy. All the goddesses have their binding and their liberating faces. When Lakshmi's energy is in shadow, it binds us through attachment to material goods. The corruption, greed, and unbridled acquisitiveness of contemporary society, the compulsive consumerism, the wildly disproportionate difference in wealth between the people at the top of the income ladder and the rest of society—all these are manifestations of Lakshmi's dark shadow. When we can recognize the subtle essence of Lakshmi, we will honor material wealth as her physical form, but we'll also understand that money is only one type of currency. It can't, as the country song goes, "buy back your youth when you're old, or a friend when you're lonely, or a love that's grown cold."[3] There are other ways of measuring wealth, and these are also in Lakshmi's gift.

THE INNER FEELING OF ABUNDANCE

Several psychological studies have revealed that although material security definitely increases happiness, beyond a certain income level, the correlation between income and happiness drops significantly. One reason for this is that a major ingredient of happiness is a sense of sufficiency. Satisfaction—a primal Lakshmi feeling-state—is the felt sense of having enough. In a society where we are trained to consume voraciously, many of us have lost the ability to recognize the feeling of satisfaction. Just as we get indigestion when we eat past the point of physical satisfaction, so too when we go on acquiring for the sake of having more and more and more, we lose access to the inner feeling of "enough." Being in tune with Lakshmi is not necessarily about having more, or spending more, or looking better. It's about feeling the fullness and satisfaction that comes with the sense of sufficiency.

Here is Lakshmi's first lesson: what we really crave is not more stuff, but the inner experience of abundance and beauty. Lakshmi is famous for giving material boons, but her deeper gift is the subtle ability to experience innate perfection and beauty. Because Lakshmi is an aspect of our life-force; the sense of sufficiency, abundance, and beauty is built into us, and so is the need for it. Love of beauty is an expression of the goddess. It's true that when we pursue it greedily, we end up chasing an ever-receding prize. But when we deny it or are denied it, our hearts wither.

When I was twenty-one, just out of college, I lived in a ground-floor apartment on the Lower East Side of Manhattan. It was a vibrant and exciting neighborhood, but there was nothing beautiful about it. I would wake up some mornings feeling starved for cleanliness and symmetry—starved for beauty. So, once or twice a week, I would take the subway up to Fifty-Ninth Street and walk over to the Plaza Hotel. Dressed in my jeans and T-shirt, I'd assume my haughtiest expression, figuring that if I looked entitled enough I could pass for a bohemian heiress. I'd saunter through the lobbies of the Plaza and the Pierre and literally inhale the fragrance of opulence. (As I remember, it smelled like freesias.) I'd walk over to Madison and admire the bibelots and French furniture in the shop windows. I'd stroll through the east side of Central Park, where huge trees shade the walkways and the lawns are especially blue-green and lush, and I'd stop off at Eighty-First Street to sit for an hour or so in the marbled coffee shop at the Metropolitan Museum. I was getting my Lakshmi injection. These days, I see young people from the ghettos of Harlem and Brooklyn strolling the sidewalks in front of Bloomingdale's and Barney's, doing exactly the same thing. Like me, they're there for their wealth fix, and like me they may not realize that what they are craving is not really the consumer riches on display. What they are craving, at heart, is Lakshmi.

In those days, it never occurred to me that I would ultimately find my connection to this kind of abundance and beauty inside myself. What I did know was that the visible expressions of Lakshmi's Shakti nourished me. I could get that nourishment from a garden, a lushly watered lawn, or a symmetrically arranged living room. I could find it in the sculpted face of my college friend Garland, whose youthful beauty was so dazzling that people stared at her on the street, and the jazz giants in the clubs we frequented would regularly get down from the stage to ask if they could buy her a drink.

I never thought to own the gold jewelry or the couture dresses, any more than I thought I could look like Garland. I simply admired them. Beauty entrances us, in all its forms. I remember, years later, being asked to counsel an unhappy actress. As I listened to her recitation of woe, I was unable to take my eyes off her perfect face. Someone so beautiful, I remember thinking, can say almost anything, and you'll want to listen. Emerson was right: beauty is its own excuse for being.

There are different ways of being beautiful, of course. The fierce goddesses, for example, are often gorgeous (even when they have fangs) and so are their manifestations (even when they are scary). But Lakshmi's expression of beauty has an unmistakable set of qualities. It is sweet, ripe, symmetrical, pleasing. There is no irony about Lakshmi, and nothing that shocks you. Lakshmi can be simple—Armani rather than Versace—but she doesn't wear safety pins in her nose or rips in her stockings. Often, Lakshmi-like beauty has the quality of being cultivated, nourished, polished. Lakshmi's gifts are enhanced through a certain effort and craft.

That said, Lakshmi's manifestation as beauty, like her manifestation as wealth, has its very obvious shadow side. Shadow Lakshmi is on full display in the excesses of the contemporary beauty industry, with its often painful cosmetic enhancements and its pervasive message that a woman's desirability is determined by how closely she matches the ideal of the currently fashionable body—long-legged in size 2 jeans, breasts pouring out of her cami, silky of hair, and creamy of skin. Yet, no matter how much she is perverted, Lakshmi continues to invite us to worship her by making ourselves beautiful—inwardly, outwardly, each of us in our own way. The human instinct to adorn our own bodies and our surroundings is one of Lakshmi's signature expressions.

Contemplation: Lakshmi

Sitting in a quiet, comfortable place, ask yourself the
following questions and write down the answers.

What is my current relationship with the Lakshmi energy, the divine feminine power of abundance, beauty, harmony, and balance?

In what ways do I experience abundance?

What do I experience as beautiful in myself? In the world around me? In others?

Look at what you've written. Is there anything that surprises you? Is there anything you see about your attitude toward Lakshmi Shakti that you'd like to change?

THE LAKSHMI WOMAN

Lakshmi is a consort goddess—a wife. In the villages of India, the good fortune of a family depended on the wife; certain ancient texts state quite specifically that when a man has an auspicious woman in his home, that man's life would be successful and prosperous. The *Ananga Ranga* and other classical Indian texts even list the marks of an auspicious woman—including the shape of her eyes and the marks on her belly. Each has its own significance. The Lakshmi woman, if not beautiful, was attractive and symmetrical. She was gracious, nourishing, skillful, and, well, compliant.

In our society, of course, the Lakshmi woman might appear as the prom queen, the supermodel, the beautifully groomed and dressed trophy wife a successful man "acquires" as the visible sign of accomplishment and a necessary social enhancement. Some Lakshmi women naturally give their power to the male and enjoy being ornamental. Lakshmi, though often brilliantly diplomatic, may look to be honored for her beauty and her sweetness rather than for any worldly accomplishment. The traditional Lakshmi woman is responsive, receptive, not aggressive. She wants to be desired, and she is not unwilling to be possessed. Her defining quality is radiance, the subtle inner light that emanates as Lakshmi's golden glow.

A woman in touch with her Lakshmi essence is palpably radiant. There's a kind of light around her, a shine to her skin, a powerful magnetism that comes off her like a miasma and draws the eye or the heart. Singer Beyoncé Knowles and actresses Halle Berry and the young Michelle Pfeiffer have this quality, as though their bodies are touched with golden light. That Lakshmi glow often appears in young women as they come into the fullness of their beauty. Of course, for centuries, the Lakshmi quality has been the subject of the most ardent male gaze.

Helen of Troy was the great Lakshmi woman of the classical world, which is one reason why her husband had to fight to get her back: by stealing his wife, Paris stole not only her beauty but the very symbol of her husband's royal authority. When the singer-model Carla Bruni married then-president of France, Nicolas Sarkozy, she automatically conferred a mantle of glamor on a short, notably unglamorous figure.

Jacqueline Kennedy Onassis was the Lakshmi icon for the mid-twentieth century—not just beautiful, but possessing the goddess's qualities of charm, graciousness, and great fashion sense. When President Kennedy introduced himself to a French crowd as "the man who accompanied Jacqueline Kennedy to Paris," he was actually acknowledging a profound symbolic truth: her presence by his side sealed his own authority and called forth the ancient mythology of the young king and his auspicious goddess-consort.

In the movie *A Place in the Sun*, Elizabeth Taylor plays a rich girl whose beauty and love so lure the hero that to be with her he kills his lower class girlfriend. In the movie, Taylor incarnates the dual power of beauty and wealth—Lakshmi's twin boons—which promise to adhere to the man she smiles on, and which, of course, are traditionally bestowed on the man who carries the corresponding masculine qualities: authority, courage, and wealth. Lakshmi might flirt with a surfer, but chances are she'll marry the lawyer who can keep her in Christian Louboutin shoes. (Of course, a contemporary Lakshmi woman is equally likely to become the lawyer, like Reese Witherspoon in *Legally Blonde*.)

THE FORTUNE OF KINGS AND THE BELOVED OF GOD

Lakshmi is sometimes said to have two faces. As Vishnupriya Lakshmi (literally, "beloved of Vishnu"), Lakshmi showers her lovers with auspicious qualities and lasting inner wealth. As Raja Lakshmi (literally "the luck of kings"), she gives power to rulers and leaders and bestows sweeping success and good fortune—but not always the kind that lasts. Vishnupriya Lakshmi embodies fidelity, integrity, and virtue. Raja Lakshmi is notoriously fickle; she can be with you today, and hanging out with someone else tomorrow. The lush, brunette actress Catherine Zeta-Jones often plays this sort of role—as in the films *Intolerable Cruelty* and *Chicago*. Michelle Pfeiffer as the singer Susie Diamond in *The Fabulous Baker Boys*—who brings two musicians good luck, then takes it with her when she leaves them—offers an electrifying version of Raja Lakshmi. So does Sharon Stone as the fickle wife of a Mafia-linked casino owner in the film *Casino*.

In the classic old movie, *Gilda*, Rita Hayworth plays a beautiful, mysterious singer who lives with a rich casino owner. In one memorable scene, she hangs over one of her suitors at the roulette table, placing bets for him. In this moment, she incarnates Lady Luck, the sultry, alluring power of fortune itself—infinitely desirable and infinitely elusive—and in this case dangerous, since Gilda works for the casino. Raja Lakshmi is desired intensely, yet she can be destructive to anyone who tries to hold her. A woman who carries this archetype holds so much unearned power that she can come to rely on her beauty and power to charm, and neglect inner qualities. Rita Hayworth, who with all her beauty was unlucky in love, used to say, "My men fall in love with Gilda, and they end up with me."

Without consciousness, a woman who incarnates the power of Raja Lakshmi can lose herself in being the object of desire, becoming what others see in her, eating their sexual projections as well as the anger and jealousy that are often projected onto beautiful women. And she can fall into the opposite trap—giving away her power and radiance to serve men who seem to validate her existence by desiring or needing her.

When the Lakshmi magnetism is joined with empathy and genuine concern for others, such a woman can bless others by her presence. Kate Middleton, the wife of England's future Prince of Wales, stepped into the Lakshmi archetype in 2011, incarnating a radiance that shines through even from the photos in supermarket tabloids. When Kate married William—in a ceremony that millions of people watched on TV and YouTube—it wasn't just a mundane event. Lakshmi walked up the aisle with her—so much so that people all over the world felt personal joy at the sight of Kate in her wedding gown. The ultimate modern-day Lakshmi figure, of course, was William's tragically beautiful mother, Diana. Diana, with her shining blondness, her clothes, her empathy for the suffering, and her air of vulnerability created around her a vortex of goddess energy that was never more in evidence than in the emotion that surrounded her tragic death. Even fifteen years later, watching the clips of Diana's funeral on television, I found myself in tears, like the million mourners who silently lined the procession route to watch her funeral cortege. Perhaps it was the power of collective emotion. I suspect, however, that what made Diana such a luminous and beloved figure was a kind of transfiguration—a descent of Goddess Lakshmi that at critical moments appeared through her beautiful body.

LAKSHMI AS BLESSING

Lakshmi's capacity to nourish and bless is symbolized by the lotuses she holds in two of her four hands, and by the shower of golden coins that drips from the other two hands. She blesses with material wealth, but also with inner abundance. If her aspect as Raja Lakshmi incarnates material good fortune, beauty, and success, her aspect as Vishnupriya Lakshmi offers the most lasting forms of wealth—integrity, empathy, compassion, and the capacity for relational love.

Vishnupriya Lakshmi is a goddess of relationship. She is that aspect of the feminine that nourishes and lubricates relationships of all kinds—friendship, marriage, and family life. The radiance of Vishnupriya Lakshmi is connected to the deep Shakti of balance and universal harmony. It manifests as fertility in nature, emanating from the earth in spring or as the glow of a healthy woman, happy in her pregnancy or satisfied in love. But the real essence of Lakshmi is that inner balance at the heart of the partnership relationships that support the human world. Empathy, the quality that nourishes relationships, is one of the gifts of Lakshmi, whether it manifests in a woman or a man.

In mythology, Vishnupriya Lakshmi is the perfect wife, the beloved consort of the male deity who himself symbolizes balance, harmony, worldly skill, leadership—everything that sustains life in the human realm as well as in the subtle spheres.

Lakshmi is Vishnu's power to nourish life, which means that she is conservative and supportive in the best sense of the word. In paintings of Lakshmi and Vishnu, Lakshmi is often shown clinging to her husband's breast or massaging her husband's feet. When Vishnu takes earthly avatar forms, Lakshmi appears with him. She is described as Vishnu's radiance, the world-mother as he is the world-father, and the source of his unconditional grace.

In the Shri Vaishnava tradition, Lakshmi is the mediator, the one who intercedes like a mother between the children and the father. Her grace, it is said, is unconditional, and comes without being asked. Vishnu must be solicited, but Lakshmi gives always, and she gives to anyone. In fact, there's a story that describes Lakshmi as an agent for social change.

GODDESS OF GENEROSITY

Once, the story goes, Lakshmi and Vishnu were living in the city of Varanasi, manifesting as the deities of a big temple known as Jaganatha. It was a particularly rich, upscale temple where only members of the higher castes were allowed. That didn't stop the poor and low-caste folk from worshipping Lakshmi. One year on the Lakshmi festival known as Diwali, Lakshmi decided to visit all the untouchables in town. She went from house to house, bringing food and money to everyone who had said her mantras or lighted a candle in her honor—and, so the tale goes, even to those who hadn't.

When Vishnu heard that Lakshmi had been hanging out with untouchables, he got very angry and forbade her to visit their houses again. At that, the normally submissive Lakshmi rebelled. She swept out of the Jaganatha temple, and went to live with a community of sweepers.

From the moment she turned up there, the formerly impoverished sweeper community began to prosper. Food mysteriously appeared, crops began to grow around the houses, and people began cleaning and rebuilding their huts. Meanwhile Vishnu's temple became, mysteriously, impoverished. No one brought offerings anymore. Even the trees outside the temple withered. Vishnu finally had to travel to the community of so-called untouchables to beg her pardon. Lakshmi agreed to come home only if he promised never to restrict her grace-giving impulses again.

Wendy, married to a film producer, is a Vishnupriya Lakshmi-style wife. She runs a quietly lavish home, raises two children, gives large parties, and entertains houseguests and family members with informal, gracious good humor. She's the person you go to when you need someone to drive you to the doctor or chair your charity event, and she's the natural anchor of the spiritual center that she attends. When her husband complains about the time and money she spends helping other people, she reminds him that this is their nonnegotiable bargain. She will create a beautiful home, family, and social life for him, and in turn, he will support her drive to help other people and support her in using her time and money to take yoga retreats and travel with her spiritually minded friends. This is their balance of giving and receiving.

LAKSHMI AND THE CYCLE OF GIVING AND RECEIVING

Like the natural flow of breath, the natural action of the Lakshmi Shakti expresses itself in the fine balance of giving and receiving. In Vedic times, this idea was expressed through the fire sacrifice (*yajna*) in which the fruits of the earth were offered into a sacred fire along with mantras and prayers. The fire ritual was both a physical ritual and a metaphor for keeping in right relationship with the earth, the ancestors, and society itself. In the Bhagavad Gita, one of the most potent texts on right living in religious literature, Krishna—Vishnu's avatar—explains the unspoken contract between humanity, the physical world, and the higher powers of the subtle worlds as a mutuality of giving and receiving.

FIGURE 5: VISHNU AND LAKSHMI

The heavens offer gifts to the earth—both the physical gifts of sun and rain that make crops grow, and also the subtler gifts of fertility and growth and happiness that we can feel inwardly when we tune into the soul of the natural world.

In return, human beings conserve the earth and offer back gifts to the Shaktis that play as the world. You give with your body—giving part of your wealth to others, offering service where it is needed. You give with your speech—saying kind words, or sincere praise, or chanting mantras, or giving blessings. And you give with your mind—maybe through prayer, by dedicating whatever you do to the benefit to others, or perhaps by starting your meals remembering all the living organisms who worked or gave up their lives so that you could eat. You express not only gratitude, but also the hope that the food nourishes you so that you can, in turn, nourish life.

It's in the balance that Lakshmi manifests. Without receiving, you feel dry and undernourished. Without giving, you become narcissistic, arrogant, and entitled. When you can allow yourself to receive with the feeling that you deserve the gifts of life, and then give with the feeling that others deserve them also, you find yourself in what one of my teachers called the auspicious state of mind, the state where shri is simply flowing through you. You feel Lakshmi's presence as internal abundance and also as gratitude and as the desire to bless others. It's then that you can begin to feel Lakshmi's energy as your own.

Invoking the Lakshmi Shakti of Giving and Receiving

Set aside half an hour, find a quiet location, and take some
time to write in your journal about giving and receiving.

PART ONE: RECEIVING
Ask yourself, "What would I like to receive more of now?" Consider all the areas of your life, including:

- money and material wealth
- love
- acknowledgment or praise
- spiritual experience
- success in your career

- the ability to have children
- beauty
- fun
- health
- fame

Write down your answers in your journal. If there are specific people from whom you would like to receive these boons, list them as well.

PART TWO: EXPLORING THE GIFTS YOU WOULD LIKE TO RECEIVE
From the preceding list, choose the three most important gifts you would like to receive in your life now. For each of these gifts, answer the following questions.

- Why do I want this?
- How would I benefit from it?
- How would others or the world benefit from it?
- In what ways am I blocking myself from receiving more in this area of my life?

PART THREE: GIVING
Now consider the gifts that you, yourself, have to share. How can you offer a gift or blessing as an exchange for what you want to receive? One way to do this is to literally or symbolically help someone else to receive the very gift you desire. Think of how you might make this kind of offering, and then write about what that might look and feel like.

Close your eyes, and imagine yourself blessing this other person with the gift you want for yourself. What would that look like? Be as extravagant as you can. In case you have a hard time imagining the specifics, imagine yourself offering this person the experience of being totally happy, satisfied, and fulfilled. Then, imagine this person feeling totally happy, satisfied, and fulfilled.

Take a few moments to write about this visualization in your journal.

Once you've finished writing, ask yourself, "What physical or symbolic action could I take to turn this desire to give something into an actual offering?" Then, when you're ready, take the action. It can be something very small— making a little contribution to charity, giving a massage to a friend, or grocery shopping for someone who is very busy or ill.

HONOR LAKSHMI BY *BECOMING* LAKSHMI

The goal of Tantric deity practice is not just to honor the goddess, or even to attract her blessings. The real purpose is to *internalize* the energetic qualities of the deity, to actually *become* the deity in human form. This is not so much a matter of identifying with the archetype as it is downloading her qualities into your being. You do this through meditation and also as a conscious practice of enacting her qualities of generosity, balance, and carefulness.

Much Tantric ritual involves a graduated series of meditations and ritual actions. You begin by contemplating the external face of the goddess. You repeat one of her mantras. You make literal or symbolic offerings to a statue or picture or inner image of the goddess. You meditate with her yantra, a geometric symbol that replicates the internal light-pattern that is the goddess's visual energy signature.

Classically, the ritual would begin with a formal installation of the goddess within your physical body. You touch each part of your body—physically at first, later with your attention. You say or think her mantra—"Om shrim lakshmyai namaha," or simply "Shrim"—while thinking, "Lakshmi is in my foot—my foot is Lakshmi's. Lakshmi is in my ankle, my ankle is Lakshmi's." As you become familiar with the felt sense of Lakshmi's Shakti, your formal practice of installing her in your body begins to feel real.

You might also visualize her physical form, as in our first contemplation, drawing her energy into your body. Eventually, you might practice embodying Lakshmi. Walk with the feeling that you are walking as Lakshmi. Ask yourself, "How would Lakshmi enter this room? How would Lakshmi speak? How would Lakshmi behave in this moment? How does she eat? How does she handle her money?"

Being Lakshmi

Find a comfortable seated position for this exercise. You will be working with Lakshmi's bija mantra, *shrim*, pronounced "shreem." A goddess's bija mantra carries her presence, just as an acorn contains the potential oak tree. The difference between the mantra and the acorn is that the goddess's presence can fully manifest inside the bija. If you recite the mantra with the feeling that the mantra is truly the sound form of the goddess, it will powerfully affect your own energy body, and eventually give you a powerful feeling of the goddess's presence within you.

PART ONE: INSTALLING THE GODDESS

Begin by invoking Lakshmi through the bija mantra, *shrim*. Repeat it silently with each inhalation. As you do, imagine installing the felt sense of Lakshmi in your body.

Now, call to mind the quality of radiance, either visually or as a felt, kinesthetic sensation. How does radiance look? How does it feel in your body? Is it glowing? Pulsing? Magnetic?

As you tune into the quality of radiance, imagine that Lakshmi, in the form of radiance, of golden light, is in your feet. Sense your feet and calves filled with radiance, golden and sweet.

Now sense that radiance, the Lakshmi quality of light, sweetness, and sufficiency, flowing into your thighs. Feel her radiant, abundant energy as a golden presence in your hips and pelvis and in the organs in your lower body.

Sense the presence of Lakshmi's radiant, golden sweetness flowing through your spine. Sense her presence in your stomach and lungs.

Feel Lakshmi as a golden, loving, generous radiance in your heart. Lakshmi's radiance fills your shoulders and arms with sweet sensations of comfort and ease.

Your neck and head fill with radiant light and love. Now, feel the sensations of Lakshmi's radiance in your face, as golden light filling your bones and skin. Feel that your body is filled with radiance—the radiance of health and vitality, the radiance of Lakshmi's abundant energy. Notice the sensations of a radiant body.

Now, imagine your mind glowing with radiance, glowing with light. How does it feel emotionally to be radiant? What does a radiant mind feel like? Perhaps you imagine golden light coursing through your brain. Perhaps you create inner radiance by feeling grateful for your life, or thinking of someone or something you love.

Now, imagine yourself moving through the world as Lakshmi, giving gifts. You bestow radiance and blessings, simply by your presence. As Lakshmi, how do you show up in the world? How does Lakshmi walk? How does she eat? How does she speak to people?

Consider someone who is in need of money or healing. Imagine that you have the power to give them what they need. Stretch out your hands, and imagine that your hands emanate golden light. As the light flows into that person, imagine that it makes them shine with love, good fortune, and abundance.

PART TWO: ACTUALIZING YOUR MEDITATION BY BRINGING LAKSHMI INTO THE PHYSICAL WORLD

First, decide on a physical act you can perform that embodies Lakshmi's quality of blessing. This could be anything from cooking a meal for friends; to making donations of clothes, food, or money to individuals or organizations that benefit the homeless; to "adopting" a family and giving them some needed goods or money.

Second, decide that today you will go through your life with the sense that you carry radiance. Have the sense that your presence bestows boons. Move through the world with the intention to bless the people around you. Do this unselfconsciously, silently, and humbly. You might begin by blessing the chair you sit in, the clothes you are wearing. Offer a blessing to what you see in the room. Bless the doorstep before you walk over it. Bless the car you drive or the bus you ride. When someone comes to mind, bless them. Above all, bless yourself.

In the next days, make a point of offering blessing to everyone you meet. Silently bless them with abundance, with successful love, with health—with whatever you sense they need.

CULTIVATING AN AUSPICIOUS MIND

When you give blessings with the recognition that you, yourself, embody the Lakshmi Shakti, you may get a palpable feeling of her energy coursing through you. But even if you don't "feel" it, you should find that the practice of blessing will subtly change your inner state. When you feel alienated, offering blessings creates subtle connection. When you're having a hard time with another person, offering them a silent blessing seems to activate the subtle intelligence that knows how to fix the apparently unfixable.

This practice of acting as if you were Lakshmi will subtly, over time, show you how to consciously express Lakshmi's attitudes in your daily life.

As an inner guide, Lakshmi teaches the practices for cultivating what is sometimes called an auspicious mind. Anyone who has cultivated Lakshmi over time knows that when you ask her for boons in meditation, your request will often bear fruit. Though Lakshmi answers prayers, her gifts won't stay with you if you don't practice embodying her qualities—generosity, loving-kindness, balance, carefulness, unselfishness, gratitude, and the more mundane qualities like discipline, cleanliness, and order. Aurobindo writes in his book *The Mother* that Lakshmi "does not stay where love and beauty are not willing to be born." He goes on:

> If she finds herself in men's hearts surrounded with selfishness and hatred and jealousy and malignance and envy and strife, if treachery and greed and ingratitude are mixed in the sacred chalice . . . in such hearts the gracious and beautiful Goddess will not linger. A divine disgust seizes upon her and she withdraws . . . or, veiling her face, she waits for this bitter and poisonous . . . stuff to be rejected and disappear before she will found anew her happy influence.[4]

You might find these words sententious—I sometimes do. There's truth in them, however. Mental habits like criticism, judgment, envy, and anger create an atmosphere in the mind that makes it hard to access Lakshmi's subtle quality of light and harmony. Lakshmi's presence can transform the texture of your consciousness, but you may need to cultivate her to do so—both by how you behave and how you think. Because she is so deeply connected to the physical world, Lakshmi practice always seems to demand that we look into our attitudes and imbalances around money, authority, and health.

LAKSHMI AND MONEY

Lakshmi is the Shakti of sustenance, and so one of the crucial attitudes for honoring her is to practice sustaining the abundance you have. The fundamental principle around Lakshmi and wealth is to find the balance between carefulness and generosity, between trusting in abundance and taking care of what you have.

Knowing that the universe is always ready to offer support, you live without fear, and you use money generously. At the same time, when you look at material wealth as Lakshmi's expression, you take care of it. On a day-to-day level, Lakshmi's energy flourishes when we keep budgets, conserve water and energy, and maintain ecological balance in all its forms. So, one of the core practices for honoring Lakshmi is to take care of your money in all the obvious ways: from paying your bills on time and keeping down your credit card debt, to maintaining a savings account and managing your investments, and even to keeping the money in your wallet tidy.

Money, along with sex and power, is one of the main ways in which the goddess's energy can be misused, misunderstood, and cast into shadow. For most of us, learning to honor Lakshmi will involve some clear-sighted awareness of our own imbalances around money.

The following ritual is not, by itself, enough to balance your relationship with money. But if you do it along with some basic, practical strategies for coming into a healthy relationship with physical wealth, it can help you open up to the divine energy within Lakshmi's physical expression.

A Ritual for Worshipping Your Money as Lakshmi

Gather some flowers or flower petals, a cup of water, a candle in a secure holder, a beautiful tray or dish, your wallet, checkbook, credit cards, and a recent bank statement. Then sit somewhere comfortable and complete this exercise.

Take the money out of your wallet, and put it on the tray or dish. Be sure to include some coins, since coins have more "real" value than paper money. Add your checkbook, credit cards, and bank statement.

Light the candle.

Sprinkle a few drops of water (just a few) over the money, the checkbook, and the rest of the items.

Recite the following mantra (which translates to "Om, I honor the auspicious goddess of abundance") nine times:

Om shrim lakshmyai namaha
ohm shreem lucksh-myai nuh-muh-huh

Then, place the flowers one by one on or beside the money and credit cards. As you do, say, "I offer these flowers to Lakshmi, the goddess of abundance."

Sit with your eyes closed for a few minutes, sensing these visible symbols of your wealth as symbols of Lakshmi.

To close, write a check for as much as you feel is appropriate, and send it to a worthy charitable cause.

Notice the inner effect of this ritual. Repeat it whenever you feel drawn to do so—even once or twice a week.

PURE AND SIMPLE

In India, the yearly Lakshmi festival begins with a thorough housecleaning. Everything in the house is scrubbed and polished, and only when the dust and dirt have been removed is the household considered ready to welcome Lakshmi. The tradition says that Lakshmi won't visit a dirty house. In one tale, she plans to visit a couple who have been devoted to her for years, but their house is so dirty that she can't find a place to lay her gift. Finding that the only relatively clean place in their home is the stove, she turns it to gold. Generous as she is, Lakshmi is also something of a stickler, which is why lovers of Lakshmi will also tend to be lovers of physical and mental clarity and order.

Cleaning your house in honor of Lakshmi is also a powerful way to clean your heart, especially if you do it with intention and a sense of ritual. ("The state of your room is the state of your mind" is a good Lakshmi proverb!) Perhaps because I'm a congenitally untidy person, I've found over the years that washing dishes and cleaning floors is one of the quickest ways to dissolve feelings of anger and emotional turmoil. There's human wisdom in this: a study of poor neighborhoods in the Bronx revealed that when residents painted over the graffiti on the walls and cleaned up the trash in the streets, the crime rate went down.[5] It's simply easier to respect yourself and others when your body and environment are clean.

Of course, the equation of external purity and inner purity of heart can be taken to compulsive lengths, which is why some of the most famous Tantric practices are designed to break the obsession with external purity by taking "unclean" substances in a ritual context, or practicing in "unclean" places like cemeteries and cremation grounds.

But in general, an auspicious life is a life that is "clean." When you feel shadowed by bad luck, poverty, or feelings of confusion or unworthiness, one of the very best antidotes is to clean up your physical environment—then give yourself an internal Lakshmi shower.

Lakshmi Cleansing: Bathing in a Shower of Gold

This inner cleansing ritual can be done while you are taking your daily shower. However, you can also do it as a meditative practice while seated in a comfortable position. I like to do inner cleansing at night. I bring to mind anything that hooked or disturbed me during the day and let Lakshmi's golden light wash it away.

Close your eyes and imagine yourself opening a doorway into a lush tropical garden. The walls of the garden, draped in flowering jasmine, enclose it completely, creating a secret private world of sunshine and shade.

The garden is filled with flowering trees and bushes—gardenias, blossoming orange trees, bougainvillea, and fat roses. The temperature in the garden is perfect, warm but not hot. You walk barefoot down a path carpeted in moss and find yourself in front of an outdoor shower, set under the trees.

Your clothes are peeled from your body by invisible hands, and as you step into the shower, you feel its water streaming as gold and silver light, liquid light that flows over your body, washing away the dust of your life.

The memory of your hesitancies, mistaken choices, and karmic impediments melt away in the cleansing stream of sacred light-water. You are being bathed by Lakshmi's radiance, and where her water touches your body, it turns your skin to a golden, radiant glow.

Let yourself open to the stream of Lakshmi light, which cleanses and rejuvenates your mind as it cleanses and rejuvenates your body.

LAKSHMI AS VALUE

My guru often told a story about Vidyaranya Swami, an aristocrat who started out his adult life as minister to a South Indian king. In the middle of his career, he decided to give up politics and just worship Lakshmi. He believed that because Lakshmi is the goddess of wealth, if he meditated on her she would take care of his livelihood. This turned out to be a doomed project; Lakshmi generally doesn't shower material wealth on people who haven't done something to earn it. Eventually Vidyaranya lost everything. But by that time he'd been so marinated in mantras that he only wanted to do spiritual practices, so he took the vows of a monk.

Shortly after completing his vows, he was sitting in meditation one day when Lakshmi appeared to him. "I'm here to give you the boons you've earned from your worship," she told him.

"But now I'm a monk," said Vidyaranya. "I don't even touch money. Why didn't you come before?"

Lakshmi smiled prettily. "You had a lot of impurities that needed to be washed away," she said. "Your monk's initiation took care of the last ones, so here I am."

"But what can you give me now?" he asked.

"I'll give you knowledge," she said. From that moment on, Vidyaranya was a fount of insight on spiritual matters. His name, Vidyaranya, means "forest of knowledge."

My guru used to tell that story to make the point that any practice we do will eventually bear fruit. I like it because it reminds us that Lakshmi appears in our life as whatever we value, which could manifest as external gifts or as inner qualities. You experience the energy of the goddess at whatever level of consciousness you're able to access at any moment, and through whatever it is you value.

At our ordinary level of consciousness, we tend to see Lakshmi's gifts as external to us. As we go deeper into spiritual practice we recognize that Lakshmi's deeper boons are the qualities of character and soul that she can inspire in us.

As practice deepens, we begin to recognize her esoteric gifts of subtle radiance and bliss, aspects of Lakshmi that reveal themselves in meditation, in dreams, and eventually in daily life.

Someone who meditates on Lakshmi will recognize her across an entire spectrum of different flavors of happiness. She is the thrill that rolls through the opening heart, the expansive love that can make the pleasures of meditation so deep that they can seduce a meditator into wanting nothing so much as long sessions of sitting. She gives the feeling of being embraced from the inside, and the simple experience of easeful well-being and peace. A friend of mine, who suffered from a lifelong feeling of insufficiency, describes her own first awakening: "A beautiful light, like a sunrise, appeared in the center of my chest. It was golden, brilliant, and as I looked at it, a voice said, 'This is you. You are this beauty.' I've never forgotten this. I believe it changed me forever."

A woman from one of my classes, about to undergo an operation, sat for meditation before being wheeled into the operating room and saw a wash of golden radiance surrounding her. "I sensed this as the presence of Lakshmi—Lakshmi as this endless abundance of love and protection that lies beneath everything."

Over the years, as I've listened to dozens of stories from meditators whose kundalini is in the process of unfolding, I've heard tales of wishes fulfilled, money coming unexpectedly, strange coincidences that feel as if the universe was giving boons. To call these gifts of Lakshmi may be unscientific, but there is a reason why her devotees swear that to a lover of Lakshmi, good fortune is like a flower in the palm of your hand.

Lakshmi

luhk-shmee—Goddess of Good Fortune, Wealth, Love, Fertility, and Royal Authority

Other Names for Lakshmi:
>   Shri (*shree*)—Auspiciousness
>   Kamala (*kuh-muh-lah*)—Lotus
>   Mahalakshmi (*muh-hah-luhk-shmee*)—Great Good Fortune
>   Vishnupriya (*vish-noo-pree-yah*)—Beloved of Vishnu

Recognize Lakshmi in:
- money
- plump fruits and vegetables
- lush gardens, meadows, and fields
- cloudless summer skies
- calm, tropical oceans and blue lakes
- the Hawaiian island of Maui
- jewels and gold
- precious fabrics like silk and cashmere
- neighborhoods like Manhattan's East Sixties between Fifth Avenue and Park, London's Knightsbridge, Bel Air in Los Angeles, the Tuscan countryside, private Caribbean islands, Capri
- yachts
- designer clothes and lush décor
- beautiful people
- roses in bloom
- the music of Mozart, Vivaldi, Verdi
- symmetrical and harmonious art

Invoke Lakshmi for:
- money
- all forms of abundance
- being content with what you have
- good health
- good luck
- support in worldly life
- developing qualities like gratitude and generosity

- feeling good about yourself
- allowing yourself to receive
- improving your luck
- getting pregnant and delivering a healthy child
- getting a good job or finding a comfortable and beautiful house
- experiencing beauty in your life
- diplomacy and mediation
- gracefully exercising authority
- skill in cooking, decoration, and fine arts
- attracting a desirable and loving mate
- harmonious relationships
- enjoying every form of pleasure
- love in general
- skill in all worldly activities
- giving blessing
- inner radiance
- happiness

Bija Mantra
Shrim (*shreem*)

Invocational Mantras
To invoke Lakshmi, seat yourself in a comfortable upright posture, and bring your attention into your heart center, behind the breastbone.

Feel that Lakshmi is present within your heart.

Imagine her seated on a pink lotus. She has golden skin, lustrous dark hair, large almond-shaped eyes filled with love. She wears golden necklaces and bracelets. Her sari is pink or rose-colored silk. One hand is raised in a gesture dispelling fear. The other drips golden coins, which fall as blessings into your heart.

Begin to repeat one of the following mantras, having the sense that you are dropping them like flowers into your heart. Repeat the following mantra 108 times.

Om shrim maha lakshmyai namaha
ohm shreem muh-hah luhk-shmyai nuh-muh-huh

Om, I offer salutations to the great goddess of good fortune

You can also invoke Lakshmi by chanting the following stanzas, from the Mahalakshmi Ashtakam (Eight Stanzas to Great Lakshmi):

Namaste'stu mahamaye
Shripithe surapujite
Shankha chakra gada haste
Mahalakshmi namo'stute

nuh-muh-stey-stoo muh-hah-mah-yey
shree-pee-tey soo-rah-poo-jeet-ey
shan-khuh chuh-kruh guh-dah huh-stey
muh-hah-luhk-shmee nuh-mo-stoo-tey

Salutations to you, great world enchantress,
Home of fortune, worshipped by gods,
Bearer of conch, discus, and mace,
Great goddess of fortune, homage to you.

Sarvajne sarvavarade
Sarva-dushta-bhayankari
Sarva-duhkha-hare devi
Mahalakshmi namo'stute

suhr-vug-nyey suhr-vah-vuh-ruh-dey
suhr-vuh-dush-tuh-bhuh-yun-kuh-ree
suhr-vuh-doo-khah huh-rey dey-vee
muh-hah-luhk-shmee nuh-mo-stoo-tey

Knower of all, grantor of all boons,
Fearsome to the wicked,
Remover of all suffering
Adored goddess, Mahalakshmi, we bow to you

Siddhi buddhi prade devi
Bhukti mukti pradayini
Mantra murte sada devi
Mahalakshmi namo'stute

si-dhi boo-dhi pruh-dey dey-vee
bhuk-ti muk-ti pruh-dah-yee-nee
muhn-trah moor-tey suh-dah dey-vee
muh-hah-luhk-shmee nuh-mo-stoo-tey

Giver of intelligence and success,
O goddess, giver of worldly enjoyment and liberation,
With the mantra always as your form,
Goddess Mahalakshmi, salutations to you.

Gayatri Mantra
Om mahalakshmyai cha vidmahe
Vishnupriyayai cha dhimahi
Tanno Lakshmih prachodayat

ohm muh-hah-luhk-shmee chuh vid-muh-hey
vish-noo-pree-yah-yai chuh dee-muh-hee
ta-no luhk-shmee pruh-cho-duh-yah-tuh

Om, may we come to know the goddess of Great Good Fortune
May we meditate on the beloved of Vishnu
May that goddess Lakshmi impel us forward on our path.

Lakshmi's colors: red, pink, gold
Lakshmi's flowers: the lotus, the rose
Lakshmi's festival: Diwali (Festival of Lights)
Lakshmi's consort: Vishnu

CHAPTER 5

Kali

Goddess of Revolution

Isaac spent all his time reading in a dark house, refusing to go out into the sunshine.
His next-door neighbor was a hidden spiritual master, who periodically dropped by
to say to Isaac, "Don't spend your whole life hunched over your desk in this dark
room. Get out and look at the sky!" Isaac would nod and keep on reading. Then
one day his house caught fire. Grabbing what possessions he could, he ran outside.
There, he saw the master, pointing upwards. "Look," said the master, "Sky!"

In this story, there are three elements that represent the process of
awakening: the fire, the master, and the sky. Kali is all of them.

• • •

O Kali, my mother full of Bliss! Enchantress of the almighty Shiva!
In your delirious joy you dance, clapping your hands together!
You are the mover of all that moves, and we are your helpless toys!

RAM PRASAD

Wild women don't worry.
Wild women don't have no blues.

IDA COX

Just before I began work on this book, a friend loaned me a painting of
Kali. It's done in the richly detailed style of traditional Nepali religious
art, filled with complex and significant detail. The goddess is shown as a
beautiful young woman, with dark blue skin, naked except for what looks like
a hula skirt made of severed arms. Her round breasts are full and firm enough
to burst off the canvas. Wild black locks flow down her back and over her
shoulders. Her wide, lustrous eyes are set in a dark face so luminously beautiful that it is impossible not to be drawn to it. Her tongue sticks out just a bit,

delicately touching her upper lip. There's the slightest suggestion of fangs, or perhaps that's an illusion. The sword in one of her four hands is not an illusion: it drips with blood. Nor is the severed head she holds in her other hand. Around her neck is a necklace made of skulls. She squats over the pale, prone body of Shiva, holding in her open vagina Shiva's erect phallus, which gleams white and foaming between her red-tinged labia. He lies on a lotus-shaped bed supported by four skulls.

Flames, blown by an invisible wind, flow from Kali's head and shoulders, and from Shiva's feet. One of her hands is raised in the gesture that signals "Fear not." Another points downward, bestowing boons. She is, to say the least, formidable.

People who came into my house when I had the painting would often sneak side glances at it or stand in front of it for a few minutes, staring. There were moments when I understood their reaction. Even though the image was so familiar, even though I could rattle off the esoteric meaning of all those skulls and severed arms, the painting often startled me. Every time I looked at it, I remembered that Kali, the fiercest aspect of the feminine, is not a goddess to take lightly.

THE BLOOD DRINKER

In Indian mythology, Kali first appears as a frenzied, battle-maddened demon slayer, who comes into the world at moments when dark forces—demons— threaten civilization and especially the feminine. In the core myth of Kali's emergence, she appears out of Durga's third eye at one of the key moments in the *Devi Mahatmya,* when the Devi is threatened by two demons called Chanda and Munda. Durga's face darkens, and Kali emerges with a roar, her sword swinging, cutting down demons and crunching them in her teeth. At last, she slashes off the heads of Chanda and Munda, and presents them to Durga. Later in the battle, Kali confronts the demon chief Raktabija. Raktabija has a magical power: when drops of his blood spill, they turn into warriors. Kali, with her long tongue, licks up his blood before it can touch the ground.

Many images of Kali show her with a long tongue, caught in the act of licking the blood of warriors. In these images, she often appears as a hag, emaciated, ugly, with fangs, and with blood dripping from her tongue. But as human consciousness evolved over the centuries, so, it seems, did the image of Kali. Her body became beautiful, as it is in most modern representations. Instead of seeing her as an almost demonic presence, devotees meditating on Kali began to find esoteric resonance in her gestures and implements. Raktabija's blood became a symbol of the uncontrollable desires that agitate our minds, and Kali's tongue became the power of yogic will to eat up desires and thoughts so that the luminosity of our essential awareness can reveal itself.

TWO FACES OF KALI

Kali appears differently depending on the level of consciousness with which you approach her. Anthropologists note that there are two basic versions of Kali in popular Indian religion. There is the village or forest Kali, where she and her alter-ego forms—such as Bhadrakali, Chamunda, and Bhairavi—are often seen as goddesses of the margins: scary, half-demonic forest deities. They are invoked for protection and magical purposes by mostly uneducated rural people, often in nighttime rituals and seasonal dances in which goddess-possessed worshippers enact the myths with lots of shouting and roaring, fueled by home-distilled local liquor. Black magicians worship this same aspect of Kali with mantras, for the sake of acquiring magical powers and killing enemies. In Nepal, as in many parts of Bengal, Kali worship is accompanied by animal sacrifice, and her temples often smell of the blood of goats.

In more modern, urban Hindu religious practice, Kali is Kali Ma—Mother Kali—a benign and loving source of every kind of boon and blessing. This is how Kali appears in American Kali temples and on the website for Kali Mandir in Laguna Beach, California.

At this level, her wildness is interpreted symbolically. The skulls around her neck are not dead victims, but the letters of the Sanskrit alphabet, through which she manifests both liberating mantras and deluding ideas. (Remember the goddess's dual nature as both the force that binds us and the force that sets us free.)

The hands on her apron represent the karmic tendencies she removes from her devotees, as well as her own manifold capabilities. The skull in her hands, which her sword has just lopped off, is the ego that separates us from her. Kali's nakedness shows that she has cast away illusion; in her, the entire truth about life and death is revealed. Even her color is esoteric; Kali's dark colors stand for the ultimate void state, where all differences dissolve into the absolute beyond all form. Her sword is the force that slices through delusion, ignorance, false hope, and lies. Her position on top of Shiva reveals that she is the dynamic force in the universe, the power that churns the stillness of the void, so worlds can be created inside that transcendent nothingness.

In fact, Kali holds both these energies—the spiritually liberating and the fearsome—which is why she always remains wildly, dynamically paradoxical.

She is multifaceted and multilayered, both as an inner force—a spiritual and psychological power—and as a force in the universe. The nineteenth-century Bengali poet Ram Prasad, in his songs to Kali, caught her paradox. He sang of a goddess who embodies love and destruction, who is both the Shakti at the heart of this confusing world and the power who dissolves our pain:

> O Mother! Thou art present in every form.
> Thou art in the entire universe and in its tiniest and most trifling things,
> Wherever I go, and wherever I look
> I see Thee, Mother, present in thy cosmic form.
> The whole world—earth, water, fire, and air—
> All are thy forms, O Mother, the whole world of birth and death.
>
> O mother, who can understand thy Maya?
> Thou art a mad Goddess; Thou hast made all mad with attachment.
> Such is the agony caused by the mad Goddess
> That none can know her aright.
> Rama Prasad says, "All sufferings vanish if she grants her grace."[1]

In the meditation that follows, we invoke her paradox, and the mysterious quality of her love—the love that this devotional poet saw in her.

Meditation: Kali

Sit or lie down comfortably for this exercise.

Close your eyes and focus on your breath for a few minutes, until you feel calm and centered.

Imagine yourself lying on a beach on a beautiful summer night. You're completely comfortable, very close to the earth, and the earth is warm. As you look up into the moonless sky, you sense a sacred feminine presence in the darkness, a presence filled with pulsing energy. As she comes closer, you recognize the form and the energy of the goddess Kali. You may envision her body as luminous blue-black, full-breasted, shining. Or, you may sense her kinesthetically. As she comes closer, you find yourself gazing into her eyes, which are shining with love. You sense within her an absolute love and an invitation to freedom.

FIGURE 6: DANCING KALI

As you tune into the cosmic energy of Kali, let yourself recognize that this sacred feminine presence sees you completely. She sees your beauty, your woundedness, your doubts, your fears, your karmic blocks, the ways you've hurt others. She sees your mistakes, your longings, and your innate goodness. She sees everything that's apparent and everything hidden. . . . She sees you; she adores you; she holds you. She is fierce wisdom incarnate, the liberating force of grace. She is freedom itself.

Let your breath connect you to her glowing sacred heart, to her pulsing, utterly free energetic core, which is also your own heart.

With each inhalation, you draw in the liberating grace of her presence, letting it flow through your body, your being. And with each exhalation, you allow the sense of whatever within you needs to be released, to be let go, in order that she can dissolve it.

Your inhalation and your exhalation are almost like a prayer. "I accept freedom. I allow whatever can be released in this moment to be released."

KALI AS THE MIRROR OF OUR INNER STATE

Ram Prasad, like all great lovers of Kali, was able to hold her light and dark sides together, finding within her a path that transcends duality. She invites us to do the same, which may be why Kali so fascinates modern practitioners. Kali challenges us by daring us to look her in the face and find the love behind the pain of life.

The way we see Kali at any given moment has everything to do with where we are in our own journey. Whether Kali seems terrifying, fascinating, or loving depends on our state of consciousness and our level of both emotional and spiritual development. But she always invites us to a radical form of ego-transcendence.

Swami Vivekananda, one of the most important Hindu teachers to come to the West in the early twentieth century, deeply understood this truth. In one of his songs, he says:

I am not one of those . . .
Who put the garland of skulls round thy neck,
And then look back in terror
And call Thee "The Merciful."
The heart must become a burial ground.

Pride, selfishness, and desire all broken into dust,
Then and then alone will the Mother dance there![2]

I discovered this ego-destroying quality of the Kali Shakti the first time I taught a class on Kali at a retreat center in the 1980s. Preparing for the class, my contemplation of Kali literally intoxicated me. The idea that divine grace can take the form of fierce, destructive blood lust; of wild freedom; of bared teeth and naked breasts seemed both deeply exciting and deeply mysterious. I soon found myself identifying with Kali's strength and wildness, invoking her with poems to the volcano and the hurricane, feeling myself expanding in a kind of participation mystique as I considered the ways in which Kali manifests in nature and in human life. Contemplating her, I felt strong enough to step beyond any rules or conventional forms—I felt like a Kaliesque Tantric hero.

Two days before the course was to take place, during a meeting with the other speakers, the program director began shouting at me. She was normally a volatile person, but this display went beyond mere volatility. As the others in the room sat open-mouthed in shock, she railed for five minutes about how my conception of Kali was nothing like what she had in mind. Her rant was so far out of proportion to the circumstances that it finally struck me: this woman was enacting a manifestation of Kali's wrathful face. As I listened to her, I sensed the goddess saying, "You think you know me? You think you can identify with me? Before imagining that you are ready to embody me, you might want to learn to bow to me!"

Afterward, as I tried to make sense of the event, I suddenly remembered Ramakrishna Paramahamsa, the great nineteenth century devotee of Goddess Kali. Ramakrishna always identified himself not as a tantric hero, but as the goddess's child. He practiced as a devotee, allowing his ego to get out of the way of his adoration of the goddess.

I went to my room and threw myself on the floor in the classic position of spiritual surrender. "I'm not strong," I said to the goddess. "I'm not a heroine. I'm your child! Please show me what to do!"

In the days to come, I was informed that I should not stand at the podium to give the talk on Kali, but to speak from the back of the hall, in the dark, as if I were narrating a slideshow. There was no question that this was a move meant to lop off one of the heads of my ego: specifically my pride in myself as a teacher.

As I sat there in the dark, something powerful and free began to move through me. The words began to speak themselves. Simultaneously, a tidal wave of love poured through the room. The ecstasy that swelled up from inside my chest felt almost unbearable. The man sitting next to me gasped "Wow!"—clearly the same thing was happening to him. Some powerful alchemy had arisen in that moment, and Kali was manifesting not in her fierceness, but in her melting sweetness. I heard from many of the people in the room that afternoon that they had had a similar experience. Kali had, at least temporarily, cleared my egoic persona out of the way and then come through herself.

KALI AND THE EGO

That experience—which I am grateful to have had in the safety of a meditation retreat—showed me something about Kali that I've never forgotten. She is a massive love-force that is literally death to the ego. When she erupts in your life, Kali will cut away whatever is extraneous, whatever is indulgent. She is especially hard on arrogance, including the arrogance that makes us believe prematurely that we are outside the rules, before our earned wisdom has legitimately given us the right to set aside rules in the service of higher values. Though Kali embodies transformative anger, she also, paradoxically, destroys anger—especially the anger that comes from thwarted egoic desires.

KALI'S FIERCE FORMS

In the Tantric tradition, Kali's role in the transformation of consciousness is embodied in ten different flavors, or sacred roles, called the Mahavidyas, or Great Wisdoms. (We'll look deeply at several of these goddesses later in this book.) Her fiercest form, Bhairavi, erupts with the boundary-busting force of a volcano or a massive forest fire. Then there is Bagalamukhi, the Crane-Headed One, who has a beak like a crane and is also known as the Impaler. She is the force that stops you in your tracks—impeding forward movement and forcing you to internalize your energy. Chinnamasta, the most resonant and mysterious of all, holds her own head in her hands, and has two streams of life-force running from her neck into the open mouths of two attendants. Dhumavati is the crone-goddess who compels renunciation of everything worldly. Tara dissolves boundaries and protects. Kali manifests in all these forms, both as an external force and as an internal energy.

In nearly all of them, she compels you to bow down.

One of the myths of Kali's origin has Kali emerge out of the body of Shiva's consort Sati during a critical moment in Sati's marriage to Shiva. If you'll remember, the story of Shiva and Sati turns on the debacle of Daksha's fire ritual. In this version, however, Daksha, who believes Shiva is not an appropriate husband for Sati, invites her to the celebration, but not him. Not wanting to miss the event, Sati asks Shiva for permission to go without him. Shiva refuses. Furious, Sati takes on her fearsome form as Kali. Shiva is terrified of her and tries to flee. But Kali fills all of space with innumerable forms of herself until Shiva finally surrenders, sits down before her, and asks, "Where is my beautiful Sati?" She answers that this is her real form, and that she has taken on the sweet body of Sati to reward Shiva for his austerities. It is in her fearsome form, she tells Shiva, that she carries out the divine functions of creation and destruction.

Violence is part of the creative process. (The big bang, after all, was an explosion.) The energy that pushes a baby out of the womb, in a process that is bloody and full of the threat of death, is full of creative violence. Like anything to do with Kali, once the birth process begins, it is inexorable. Of course, in our time we employ drugs and surgical knives to "civilize" the process, to make it more convenient and often save the lives of mothers and children. But in the essential truth of the body, the process of birthing belongs to Kali, and for many women it offers the first great recognition that here is a place where the human ego has to get out of the way.

Another of Kali's teachings is that in order for something new to be born, old structures must be destroyed—whether in nature or in society or in your personal life. Her name, Kali, is the feminine form of Kala, or Time, the great destroyer of even those things that seem permanent. As I wrote this chapter in the summer of 2011, tornados were sweeping through the American South, and every other day brought news of the huge swathes of wind that flattened every structure in their path. In Santa Cruz, California—a town near my own home—they were rebuilding the port that was smashed by a relatively small swell from the great tsunami that rolled over coastal Japan in 2010, destroying cities and creating a meltdown in the Fukushima nuclear power plant.

It's not hard to see these earth upheavals as Kali's work, as nature's great "No!" to the poisons human beings have dumped into her air and soil and oceans. Ancient people saw earthquakes and hurricanes this way, as the anger of gods like Kali and her male counterpart Rudra-Shiva. Nowadays, we understand their physical causes. Yet for a Tantrika, who looks at the world and the psyche as a play of Shaktis, or divine feminine energies, the physical forces that create upheaval are also Kali's manifestations in the world of tide and wind, no less filled with her mystery for being scientifically explainable.

Aurobindo wrote, "There is in her an overwhelming intensity, a mighty passion of force to achieve, a divine violence rushing to shatter every limit and obstacle. All her divinity leaps out in a splendour of tempestuous action; she is there for swiftness, for the immediately effective process, the rapid and direct stroke, the frontal assault that carries everything before it. . . . But for her, what is done in a day might have taken centuries."[3]

KALI AS THE "NO" OF REVOLUTION

Witness the sudden upheavals of the Arab Spring of 2011, when Kali ripped through the Middle East as the force of popular uprisings in Tunisia, Egypt, Libya, and Syria. Durga gives the strength to begin and support the process of change, but Kali has the force to sweep away old structures. Her energy, moving through a group or a nation, can topple a dictator, bring down the Berlin Wall, and melt down the stock market so quickly that it leaves us dazed. Yet it is only from the open freedom—left after old structures are dissolved—that the inspiration to create anew can arise.

Moreover, when Kali is at work, you can trust her to show you what is truly indestructible, both in you and in your world. She does this by dissolving everything in you except that which cannot be destroyed. That's why we need her. You don't know what love is until you've felt the depth and fierceness of Kali's love, which, in my experience, is the strongest force of love and ecstasy in the universe. That's the secret that her lovers know—and Kali has many lovers, including awakened practitioners like the nineteenth-century *siddha* Ramakrishna and contemporary saints like Ma Amritananda. It's a secret that you only come to when you let her dissolve your defensive boundaries. To know her boons, you must, in some way, surrender to her intensity. The biggest experience of Kali's love always accompanies those moments when we have allowed ourselves to let go of our egoic agendas. As she sweeps away a layer of ego, the depth of her care is revealed.

KALI AND SPIRITUAL LIBERATION

Without her ruthless insistence on melting us to the bone, we'll never get down to our essence, down to the apparent nothingness that alone can reveal our true vastness, and out of which real creativity arises. It isn't enough to pay lip service to the beautiful idea that in our essence we are God living as a human being. To actually realize that, to *be* it, demands that we step forward audaciously into our largeness and love, and that we be willing to look into and surrender our own darkness, our shadowy motives, our built-in contraction, and our tendency to identify with the false self.

For this, Kali is the teacher. Her energy can get behind the classic self-inquiry question, "Who am I?" and give it so much passion that the very inquiry becomes a sword to cut away conditional beliefs, false ideas, and everything that keeps you from recognizing your unconditioned self. If you let her, Kali will clean out your dark pockets, bring your shadows to light, and reduce all your excuses to ashes even as she licks up the ragged edges of your karmas.

If that sounds dramatic, it is. (Kali is nothing if not dramatic!) Craig, a California businessman, discovered Kali when the housing crash of 2008 wiped out his real estate development business, and his debts depleted the seventeen million dollars he had acquired over ten years of work. In the aftermath, he lost his house and his girlfriend and was left to live in his car. During that time, he experienced paralyzing fear, rage, and humiliation.

But the destruction raging through his life turned Craig into a seeker. In the painful, fearful months after the crash, he gradually faced into his own heart. He saw how armored his body had become by his relentless focus on pursuing success and how much he had cut himself off from other people and his own center. Craig decided to look at his crisis as a teacher and see if he could discover a motivation for living that was deeper than worldly success. He embarked on a yoga practice, and on the even deeper practice of learning how to follow the intuitive guidance that began to emerge through his long periods of solitude.

In a less dramatic way, one of my major spiritual breakthroughs arrived in the wake of being "fired" by my fiery guru. I was working on a project for him. In the course of it, I shared something he had said to me with someone else. In Tantric spiritual disciplines, the ability to keep the teacher's instructions secret is considered a crucial quality. When my teacher heard that I had shared his words, he called me to his conference room and shouted that he didn't want me to work for him anymore. I was devastated.

I made my way to my room and sat down on the bed, expecting to burst into tears. Instead, I was thrust into a state of open-eyed meditation. In that moment, "I" woke up to the presence of a self beyond ego. That presence "saw" that who I really was had nothing to do with my ordinary personality, my aims, and my neuroses. Lifted out of ordinary body-identified consciousness into a state of radical freedom and joy, it was obvious—beyond obvious—that who I am is consciousness itself. My teacher's Kaliesque gesture, his fiery words, had temporarily cut the string that tethered me to the personality-self.

For three days, "I" lived in that experience of simple, joyful, absolute freedom. At the end of the third day, my guru summoned me back to my job on his staff. In the press of ordinary life, the expanded awareness was gradually covered by daily worries and ideas, but a part of my consciousness had been permanently liberated from identification with my false self.

Contemplation: The Felt Sense of Kali in Your Life

Find a comfortable position, and have your journal or a notebook
and pen handy. This contemplation involves some writing.

Kali comes into our lives in many different ways, including in those moments
that seem part of the "normal" violence of life. Think back to a time when
someone you loved or admired berated or broke up with you. Consider the
moment when you lost a job, or when something of value was taken from you.
Think of a time when you were unjustly accused.

Now, sense your way into the feelings that came up at such a time. What
would the experience have been like if you had been able to see the divine face
of creative destruction in these events? How did the experience change you?

Now, ask yourself, "Were there unexpected gifts that arose from those
losses or changes? What were they?"

If you like, take a few moments to write about what comes up for you in
this contemplation.

Write an invocation, a poem, or a poetic paragraph about or to Kali beginning with the line, "Kali, the wild dark goddess . . ." Let your writing come forth
as spontaneously as possible, without censorship and without worrying about
literary elegance. See if you can let the Kali Shakti write through you.

Next, read through what you've written. Then sit for a few moments
and meditate.

THE TANTRIC KALI: DEITY OF HEROES

To look Kali in the face and receive her gifts is not easy. To actually court her ego-
destroying boons is the work of a hero. In the Tantric traditions, Kali is the central
deity of the left-handed path, where transgressive activities are practiced in ritual
settings for the sake of discovering the blissful state where dualities like pleasure/
pain, pure/impure and even life/death dissolve. To follow that path—in which
the forbidden becomes sanctified and poison becomes nectar—is possible only
for practitioners at an advanced level of consciousness. It demands discipline, a
mind made strong and still by rigorous practice, and a relentlessly nondual vision.
In *The Count of Monte Cristo*, the hero feeds his daughter small amounts of poison,
which make her immune to any attempt to kill her through poison. Similarly, the

Tantric hero subjects himself to experiences that make him familiar with the dark side, particularly with death, so that he cannot be moved by them.

Practicing in cremation grounds, sitting on corpses, even drinking blood—these were part of certain Tantric rites, which might be undertaken for the sake of radical self-purification through renunciation, or, at a lower level of consciousness, for the sake of acquiring magical powers.

The left-handed path is notoriously tricky—even dangerous for those who are not ready, because more often than not, the "poison" is simply poisonous. However, it's more than possible to practice worshipping Kali like a Tantric hero without engaging in transgressive rituals. It can occur in the context of life itself. Vivekananda wrote thrillingly of seeing Kali in a storm:

> The stars are blotted out,
> Clouds are covering clouds,
> It is darkness, vibrant, sonant
> In the roaring, whirling wind
> Are the souls of a million lunatics,
> Just loose from the prison house, wrenching trees by the roots,
> Sweeping all from the path. . . .
>
> The flash of lurid light
> Reveals on every side
> A thousand, thousand shades
> Of death begrimed and black
> Scattering plagues and sorrows,
> Dancing with joy,
> Come, Mother, Come!
> For Terror is thy name,
> Death is in thy breath,
> And every shaking step
> Destroys a world for e'er,
> Thou "time," the All-Destroyer!
> Come, Mother, Come!
> Who dares misery love,
> And hugs the form of Death
> Dance in destruction's dance,
> To him the mother comes.[4]

A young woman journalist told me of a transfiguring vision—profoundly Kaliesque—that came to her as she witnessed a horrific scene in wartime Bosnia:

"I was standing in a village square. Every building had been burned out, and the stench of burning bodies was everywhere. I can't even describe the horror of the human destruction I saw there. Then, it was as if I went into an open-eyed trance. Suddenly, with my naked eyes, I saw the horrible scene suffused with light. Light streamed through it, dissolving every charred house, every broken body. I could see—so clearly, the way I see you now—that it was all one light, one substance. My heart was breaking with love.

"Who could understand with the mind how light and, yes, love could be present in such a moment?" the young woman said to me. It was only years later, hearing the mythology of Kali, that she was finally able to make sense of her vision.[5]

THE KALI WOMAN: ARCHETYPE OF FEMININE POWER, SEXUALITY, AND RAGE

When a world-transforming energy gets modulated through an individual's unconscious, it becomes a personal archetype. For many contemporary Western women, Kali represents not the inhuman power in nature or culture, but the possibility of an audacious fierceness that has historically been denied both to the divine feminine and to individual women. Almost always, when a woman says "I need to find my Kali side," or "I need some Kali energy," she's looking for a way to stand up for herself, to discover her inner fierceness, or to express the outrageous side of her sexuality.

One of my students, whom I'll call Annie, is a graduate of a Catholic girls' school, and a really nice person. Her yoga and Buddhist practice had centered on developing peaceful qualities: nonviolence, surrender, contentment, and detachment. But as sometimes happens, her spiritual aspirations had gotten somewhat mixed up with the values of her middle-class upbringing. As a "nice girl," the product of twenty-five or so years of acculturation, Annie had disowned her own anger, her jealousy, and her sadness. When she became a yoga student, these qualities began to seem particularly unacceptable.

Then she found herself in the midst of a knotty sibling battle over the care of her bedridden mother and the disposition of the family property. As she attempted to make herself heard by her strong-willed sisters, Annie realized that her carefully cultivated tendency to seek peace at any price was making her impotent. She understood that being nice was not always the most enlightened response. She needed something else, some kind of cut-to-the-chase aggressiveness—some fierceness. Without it, she was in danger of giving in to her siblings' unabashedly self-seeking agendas, which she knew both she and her own children would regret.

For Annie, invoking Kali offered a doorway into her own strength. It sharpened her discernment and woke her up to the recognition that her niceness was actually a mask: it was based on socially conditioned roles and responses, and on old family dynamics. As she inquired deeper, she saw into the fear that lay behind her politeness.

Annie began working with her Kali energy by doing a yoga pose that was half a squat: raised arms, tongue stuck out, vocalizing "Ahhhh" as loud as she could. She would imagine herself shouting "NO!" to her siblings and also to her own passivity. Her passivity, she realized, was based on fear, the core refuge of her egoic false self and the more she questioned and liberated it, the freer she became to speak out. She was able to insist that she and her siblings put her mother's money in a trust, in care of a lawyer who was answering to all three of them. For the first time, Annie's sisters began to listen to her views and treat her as an equal.

Kali Asana

Place your feet wide apart, so that you can comfortably bend your knees. With bent elbows, raise your arms. Begin standing straight, then swiftly bend into a squat, pulling your arms down, elbows first, and sticking out your tongue. As you do, shout "AHHHHH." Try to do this from the belly rather than the throat. Inhale up to standing, and take a deep breath, filling your lower chest, middle chest, and upper chest. Then repeat the movement. Do this five times. Notice what you feel.

THE POSTMODERN KALI

Until recently, it hasn't been easy to find role models for incarnate Kali, since most Kaliesque characters in fiction are depicted as demonic or crazy. (Think of the grungy serial killer played by Charlize Theron in *Monster*, or the murderous lover played by Jessica Walter in the early Clint Eastwood film, *Play Misty for Me*.) Martial arts films sometimes have Kali-style heroines. Uma Thurman in the film *Kill Bill* and Ziyi Zhang in *Crouching Tiger, Hidden Dragon* are

Kali-touched warriors, both deadly and beautiful. Rock singer Patti Smith in her heyday channeled Kali's wildness. So did other punk rock bands like The Clash. (It's no coincidence that soldiers in Iraq in 2003 and 2004 went into battle with earphones blaring heavy metal music—Kali music!)

Despite her problematic aspects, or perhaps because of them, Kali fascinates contemporary women. As feminist-oriented anthropology, goddess-centered spirituality, and yoga have spread through the Western world, the image of Kali has surfaced in Western culture more visibly than any other Indian goddess.

As a postmodern goddess, Kali irradiates popular culture as the incarnation of the fiercely in-your-face side of feminine power. A twenty-year-old friend pointed me to a Lykke Li music video called "The Only," which she told me expressed her own experience of Kali. The singer, wearing a jeweled goddess-girdle dances in and out of flames, grinding her hips against a board full of throwing knives.

Kali is the force many young women call on in those moments when they courageously face and move beyond their own trauma, or when they want to break through sexual shyness, politesse, insecurity, and discomfort. Kali's image offers an entrance into a wild audacity that has historically been denied both to the divine feminine and to individual women. Lady Gaga exemplifies this edgy, Kali-like quality in songs like "Edge of Glory." and "Marry the Night."

Contemplation: Kali's Audacity

Sit in a comfortable position, close your eyes, and contemplate the Kali energy in your life.

How has Kali energy empowered your audacious or unconventional behavior?
How has she inspired you to push the edge—in both positive and negative ways?

SHADOW KALI

If Kali symbolizes feminine audacity and youthful intensity, she also symbolizes more shadowy and problematic forms of power, especially the angry and aggressive energies that are hard for many women to own and for men to handle.

(Even in India, to call a woman "a regular Kali" is not a compliment—instead, it's shorthand for foul-tempered or rageful). Kali, like all divine forces, is much bigger than our human ego. So when she shows up in the feminine psyche, it can feel as if we've been possessed, literally taken over by something that has nothing to do with our normal, "daytime" personality.

Kali's power, suppressed, will often turn in on us, fester in the form of rage, attack our bodies in the form of illness and accidents, and surface in ways that can destroy our love and the love others have for us. (It seems telling that one of Lady Gaga's music videos takes place in a hospital, in the aftermath of what seems to have been a suicide attempt.) It was not until the 1980s that clinicians realized that many women suffering from depression and eating disorders had been the victims of rape or sexual abuse of different kinds. Their rage and pain had been "stuffed inside," and needed to be expressed as well as cleared in order for the women's bodies and psyches to heal.

Women, as we know, have suppressed their power for thousands of years, becoming masters of passive aggression and vicarious backstage manipulation. So the process of finding and harnessing that energy in ourselves is fraught with missteps. We don't always know how to separate the transformative anger that can stand against injustice from the rage of the wounded feminine, which all of us, whether we know it or not, hold in our cells. The boldness and audacity that is as much a part of the divine feminine as her softness can be channeled into powerful and effective protest. It was witnessed by the Mothers of the Disappeared—who demonstrated silently and publically during the days of the Argentinean junta, and helped bring public attention to the regime's atrocities—and it fuels the efforts of former sex workers and others who now toil to end sexual trafficking around the globe. Divine feminine anger can also erupt in ways that destroy the structures of our lives.

KALI AS THE INNER VOICE OF DESTRUCTIVE RAGE

When Kali appears in the dreams and poetry of contemporary Western women, she often serves as a hook for everything in us that feels uncontrollable in our psyches. Witness the invocation of Kali on yOni.com, a neofeminist website:

I am the Bitch from Hell
I think you know me well
I am the dark goddess
Kali, Hecate, Lilith, Morrigan, Ereshigal.

From an article on this same website: "The dark goddess lives in us all. Often suppressed and denied, she will eventually leak out in hostility and sarcasm, with sly cutting digs, nagging gossip, and putdowns . . ."[7] For many women, especially third-wave feminists in their twenties and thirties, owning their Kali side is a metaphor for learning to love their own rage and sexuality. Kali storms through us as the repressed power that women hide as they try to live up to the image of the loving, nurturing feminine archetype that every society idealizes. It's no wonder that "Kali" and "Kaliesque" are more often than not used as shorthand terms for feminine rage. On the other hand, some women use the Kali image to justify shadow behaviors: uncontrolled outbursts, PMS symptoms, and acts of vengeful anger against family members and former partners who have abused or betrayed them.

The following version of the Kali myth carries the scent of this uncontrollable quality as it appears in the personal psyche.

A demon has appeared who can only be killed by a woman. So, at Shiva's request, Parvati enters his body and transforms herself by drinking the poison that Shiva holds in his throat. In this way, she takes in all the negativity of the collective consciousness, which she turns into wrath. She emerges as the naked, bloodthirsty Kali with matted hair and a blazing, red third eye in the middle of her forehead.

Kali quickly dispatches the demon, but afterward she's so intoxicated by battle lust that she refuses to return to her beautiful form as a devoted wife. Instead, she wanders into the forest, where she dances so wildly and with such force that she threatens to bring down the worlds. (Revolution, once started, can tend to get out of control.)

The local sages petition Shiva for help, but even he is unable to get Kali's attention. Finally, he challenges her to a dance contest. He begins his own dance, which is so intense that it creates craters in the earth and shakes the planets from their orbits, causing so much destruction that it arouses Kali's compunction, and she comes to her senses and returns to her "normal" form.

This story comes from the Shiva Purana, a text in which Shiva is the dominant partner and the goddess merely a consort. From one point of view, it expresses both male terror of the uncontrollable side of feminine power and the masculine instinct to show his strength in order to control the feminine. In this instance, Shiva tames Kali by acting so wild that she has to calm down in order to soothe *him*. (In another version the story, Shiva transforms himself into a baby, which arouses Kali's mother instinct.) From a neuropsychological point of view, we could look at Kali in this story as emotion and Shiva as reason; Kali as the amygdala and Shiva as the neocortex; Kali as passion while Shiva is insight.

This story also expresses our collective terror at the rage of the feminine. After several thousand years of patriarchy, we're used to masculine anger and rage, even when we fear it. But the rage of the feminine—the terrible face of the mother—seems to threaten the very ground of existence. It reminds us that the earth itself could turn on us, could refuse to play its supportive role, and could erupt as a volcano or a tornado.

From the point of view of conventional society or of modernist rationalism, the Kali appearing in the personal psyche carries the blood scent of chaos—the all-bets-are-off chaos that arises when the abused and betrayed feminine rises up in vengeance or simply with a cry of "Enough." When women are seized by the rage of shadow Kali, it can wreak massive personal destruction.

The most dramatic story of this shadowy side of Kali comes not from Hindu but from Greek mythology. It's the tale of Medea, the princess of Colchis, who uses her magical powers to help her lover, Jason, shear the golden fleece from two indomitable rams. For the love of him, she abandons her family and her home and goes with him to the city of Athens. Then, several years later, Jason is offered the hand of a younger princess who happens to be the daughter of the ruler of Athens. Medea begs Jason not to abandon her, but when he refuses, she fashions a magical cloak that incinerates his bride—and then she kills her own children.

In modern times, there's a Kaliesque quality in the shocking story of Lorena Bobbitt, who put up with her husband's infidelity until one night her suppressed rage overtook her and she cut off her husband's penis. (Fortunately for him, he made it to the hospital in time to get it reattached.) In the 1980s and 1990s, as women began for the first time to speak about their experiences of sexual abuse in their families and date rape in their peer relationships, I witnessed confrontations between daughters and their fathers, confrontations that sometimes came close to tearing the families apart. Women who get "possessed" by Kali sometimes seem to me to be carrying the pain and rage of millennia, as if they had opened themselves to the accumulated anger of millions of wounded women, layered into the collective unconscious, demanding some form of release.

DISTORTION AND ESSENCE

Like all shadow behaviors, the expressions of negative Kali energy are distortions of the positive qualities of Kali Shakti. They twist and mask a quality that is essential and sublimely transpersonal: the force of liberation through radical change. Kali can manifest sublimely through the intense activism of the women who fight to expose human sexual trafficking, factory farming, and the exploitation of workers in electronics factories. But she also acts through the rages of people like Jane, a gifted and loving therapist, who holds power in her family and tribe through her destructive eruptions of anger, which cause the people around her to walk on eggshells. Most of the people close to her yield ground immediately rather than stand up to Jane's emotional tsunami.

Tellingly, Jane's uncontrolled anger is the shadow side of her most profound gift. She's a master facilitator of transformation who can cut through the masks of politeness that keep a group from coming together authentically. Her positive Kali energy has all the force of the goddess's power to destroy the outworn and make room for the new. This doesn't make Jane any easier to be around when she's in a rage, any more than understanding what Kali is about will necessarily make your experience of a life upheaval more comfortable. But if you pay attention, Kali can teach you how to channel power so that you recognize, integrate, and deeply honor the forces of change, including the change that comes about through your encounter with the dark energies of the world.

Contemplation: The Shadow Kali

You will need a journal and a pen for this exercise. Find a comfortable seated position and contemplate the following questions.

How do you see the shadow forms of Kali in your own life?
Does Kali come out in your tone of voice, in the way you talk to your family members, in inner feelings of rage and resentment?
Is your inner shadow Kali rebellious? Angry? Hurt? How does she manifest?

The beginning of any process of integrating the shadow Kali is to learn how to recognize her, and as I said earlier, this often doesn't happen except under some kind of inner or outer duress. Sometimes it takes a breakdown to get us to look into our shadow Kali.

For me, it happened during a health crisis. At the time I was living a classically yogic lifestyle, actively "working on" my anger and personal ambition through the time-honored practice of total denial. Like many people involved in spiritual self-cultivation, I believed that any form of personal willfulness was selfish (i.e., bad) and took for granted that being spiritual meant witnessing, and hopefully transcending, my shadow qualities. Since I have a lot of rebellious and eccentric qualities, this was not easy or natural for me. As so often happens when we disown our shadow, my creative energies went underground. I was tired all the time. My unadmitted anger tended to pop out in sarcasm or in sudden outbursts that created problems for me with other people. Finally, my digestion started to go south.

One night I had a scary dream. In the dream, an animal was trapped inside my body, eating his way out. I happened to be reading Robert Johnson's book, *Inner Work*, which describes a classical Jungian process of active imagination that is a powerful way to get in touch with your own shadow energies. I decided to start a process of dialogue with what I recognized as suppressed Kali energy. It often happens this way: we seek Kali at the moment we realize that we are living in dissonance with the parts of ourselves we may not fully understand or know.

Sometimes people do this kind of shadow work aloud; I did it as a written dialogue. I began by writing with my right, dominant hand, "I'd like to speak to Kali." Then I took the pen in my left hand. As I did so, I felt a leaping in my heart and saw these words flowing through my pen: "I am anger, I am power, I'm the girl in the corner, I'm the wild dancer, I'm you, I'm you, I'm you!"

"What do you want?" I wrote.

"I want out," wrote my other hand. "To be free! To be wild! To be in control!"

The process went on for several hours, and ended only when I got a cramp in my hand that finally made it too uncomfortable to write. In the process of writing, I had felt myself swinging from wild exhilaration to resentment and back again, but always with a feeling of mounting energy and excitement.

After a few weeks of this process—which I've often come back to over the years, with Kali and other goddesses—I began to notice the near miracle that occurs when we begin to tune into any divine archetype, and especially to allow it to consciously speak through us. I began to find that positive Kali qualities—a natural kind of assertiveness and freedom—were coming back into my life. My health improved, but more to the point, I began to be able to speak my truth in the moment in ways I hadn't in years. Talking to Kali had actually allowed me to integrate these energies.

Dialoguing with Kali

Find a time when you can be alone to complete this exercise.
Light a candle, and keep your journal and pen handy.

Using the illustration on page 121, saturate your vision with the image of Kali.

Close your eyes and imagine her standing before you. Imagine her with three eyes, wild hair, and a beautiful dark blue or black face. See her long tongue and her fangs. Feel the energy emanating from her.

Breathing in, feel Kali's energy flow from her third eye into your heart. Exhaling, allow that energy to flow through your body.

Now, begin to speak to her. Ask Kali to tell you about the ways she manifests or would like to manifest within you. Ask:

"Who are you for me, goddess Kali?"

"What do you have to teach me?"

"How do you express yourself in my life?"

"How are you suppressed?"

"How and when can you help me?"

"How would you like to be recognized by me or expressed through me?"

Ask these questions with complete openness, without anticipating how the answers will come. Write down the answers. Alternatively, you can write your questions with your dominant hand, then immediately write Kali's answers with your nondominant hand. Write without censorship, letting both the questions and the answers come out as they will.

Read over what you have written.

Finish by sitting with the energy of Kali, breathing in and out, sensing her Shakti flowing from her third eye into your heart and enlivening your body.

Afterward, journal about this contemplation. Notice how the energy of your personal Kali feels emotionally and in your body. Is there a difference between the empowering, enlivening form of Kali and the shadowy Kali qualities that you experience?

THE ANIMAL SACRIFICE

Kali and her alter-ego goddesses—Bhadrakali, Tara, and others—are said to like animal sacrifices, and in certain parts of India goats are still offered to her during festivals. On the subtle level, however, the "goat" to be sacrificed is egoic selfishness, and one of Kali's boons is her power to help you clean your heart of negative energies—desire, fear, anger, and jealousy. More than that, she gives a kind of radical freedom from attachment, especially the attachment to the structures of the persona and the personality-identified ego. This is one reason for the tradition of worshipping Kali in cremation grounds, where the presence of death reminds you that all the things you desire and fear will pass away.

KALI AS THE HUMAN TEACHER

In the Tantric traditions where Kali is most deeply understood, the ego-smashing side of the Shakti is often carried externally by the human guru, who in the traditions is held to embody the enlightened power to cut away those aspects of ego that no one seems to be willing to give up on his or her own. This function of the teacher is subtle and problematic, because it can sometimes degenerate into abuse. (For this reason, the *Kularnava Tantra,* one of the key surviving texts of the Kaula Tantra tradition, lists several pages of qualities that a trustworthy guru should possess and that a disciple is supposed to look for in his teacher. These include control of desires; absence of qualities like greed, anger, and pride; freedom from ego; unshakable contentment; constant engagement in deep practice; mastery of both the teachings and the inner pathways of enlightenment; and much more.[8]) For someone who genuinely wants to change, who has the right teacher, and who is able to stand the inevitable heat, practice with a Kaliesque guru can be one of the quickest paths to inner freedom. Susan, a longtime student of an Eastern teacher, described her experience to me in a letter:

"During the years I lived and worked with my teacher, I often saw her unleash Kaliesque verbal blasts, hurled with such precision and force that you sometimes felt that she had taken a sword to your deepest hidden wounds. She had a scorched-earth policy about any manifestations of ego. She pounced on both willfulness and weakness. If you manifested lack of confidence she would shoot down anything you said. But if you were arrogant, willful, or careless, she could be even more merciless. She once shouted at me in front of a roomful of people, and one of her favorite ploys was to accuse you of someone else's mistake. It's said that the quickest way to recognize the ego is to notice the part of you that reacts when you're falsely accused. My teacher had a genius for raising that defensive inner voice, the voice that wants to shout 'I didn't do it!' One of her greatest gifts to me was the mirror she held up to that angry, self-justifying instinct, so that I came to recognize it as the reaction of my contracted self, and learned to be its witness.

"What made this bearable," Susan wrote, "was the undercurrent of deep love that permeated her environment. Often, even while I was reeling from one of my teacher's Kaliesque sword cuts, I'd be aware of an expansive opening through my heart, and a feeling of extraordinary joyfulness, a sort of self-generating bliss. It wasn't masochism as people who don't understand the guru path sometimes believe. It was a glimpse of my own essence, the deep love that arises when a piece of the ego lets go. That love kept me in place for years, despite the acute psychological discomfort I often experienced. Something in me knew that there was a greater prize at stake than simple comfort or short-term enjoyment.

"I've never regretted that decision. Over the years, Kali's sword, manifesting through my teacher's words, caused real attrition in my instinct to identify with my false self. At a certain point there was a shift. It's hard to say what happened, but it had something to do with letting go of my desire to have her like me, and at the same time recognizing that my own inner issues—resentment, fear, arrogance, and of course, childhood wounds—were calling forth her behavior toward me. As I took responsibility for my own shadowy qualities and began to be able to let them go, I not only stopped blaming her for "misunderstanding" me, I stopped being triggered by it. Gradually, the process had burned away enough of my fear and anger that there was less and less defensive ego to pop out. She would send a verbal arrow in my direction, and it would simply fly past me: the inner "hook" was gone. I even began to see the underlying playfulness behind many of her barbs—and as I lightened up, our relationship became much more open and playful."

Sometimes, the way through Kali's fire is utter surrender. Sometimes, as in Susan's case, it is pure endurance. And sometimes, it's quite simply our ability to love her even in her terrible form. One story goes that her consort Shiva adores her so completely that he asks that she dance on his prone body, and that she grants this as a boon to him. As many lovers of the fierce feminine can attest, once the "test" has been passed and the lover has shown his or her willingness to hang steady in the face of the terror, the goddess will reveal that behind all her forms is love itself—love that reveals itself as the very substance of the universe.

Sacrificing Your Negative Tendencies to Kali's Fire

Find a comfortable seated posture in a quiet place to complete this exercise. Before you begin, consider the qualities in yourself that obstruct your happiness, your love, your wisdom, and your freedom. It might be anger or the kind of pride that makes you hold back from life. It might be resistance to practice and to the path. It might be fear—including the fear of letting go of your egoic contractions and opening to your capacity for clear, powerful action.

Once you have several qualities in mind, begin the exercise.

Imagine that Kali stands before you. In front of her is a fire, its flames rising in jeweled colors. Imagine yourself bowing before her. Imagine the negative tendency you chose as a cloak that covers your body. Peel away the cloak, and drop it into the fire. Watch it dissolve in the flames.

Choose another quality of egoic consciousness. Peel it away like a cloak, and drop it into the flames.

Repeat this several times until you feel an inward shift.

Over the next few days, notice any shifts in your emotional state, in the way you are with others, and in your perceptions of situations. You may notice that your inner state becomes more intense for a while. This is the rumble of your tendencies leaving your system. In moments of intensity, imagine them being offered into Kali's fire and dissolving in the flames.

UNLOCKING THE HIDDEN KALI

Kali offers us the freedom that lies beyond death. You can enter her freedom through many doorways—looking into her force in nature, examining the hidden forces behind your shadow rage, or invoking her fire to help you dissolve emotional patterns and negative tendencies. Ultimately—and this is the secret that Kali reveals only to those who seek it—Kali's essence is the vast, empty, ultimately fertile void itself. Kali's blackness is the darkness of the ultimate mystery, the transcendent womb of black light out of which reality is always arising and into which it constantly subsides. She's the cloud of unknowing described by the Christian mystics; the presence behind all things. When you tune deeply into Kali's energy, letting the calm presence behind her eyes open you to the presence in your own, you discover that her death-dealing implements, her take-no-prisoners attitude toward ego, her revolutionary forcefulness and her vast love are simply aspects of her ultimate power to draw the mind within. Kali does indeed dissolve our structures, but it's always in service of the heart. She reverses the process that brings form out of the formless and takes us back to the absolute. The yogi's Kali is that power that can turn the mind inward in deep meditation, dissolving our body sense, dissolving our thoughts, liberating emotions into energy, and drawing all our energies into their source in the inner heart. Her great dissolve carries us into the recognition that all things are one in the Self. In the heart of hearts, Kali lives as the magnetic draw of ultimate oneness, the call of the Self to let go of everything that would separate us from what we always already are.

Meditation: Kali as the Void

Once again take a comfortable seated position somewhere
quiet. Once you feel present, begin the meditation.

Imagine for a moment a vast, endless black sky. Let your entire attention focus
on that blackness. Breathe it in, and breathe it through your body.

Now, with your exhalation, see if you can let go, just for this moment, of
whatever stands in the way of opening to that fertile darkness.

KALI AS THE GREAT VOID

In the modern world, it is hard to come across absolute darkness. But camping in the California mountains on a moonless night, with the stars blotted out by the tent canvas, I meditated on blackness and found myself engulfed in it. For a moment, my body and mind disappeared, dropped away as in the old Zen tales, and there was nothing at all but a pure sense of aliveness. No me, no other, no here, no there. In that absolute darkness, pulsating with energy, Kali's love rose up as a fierce ecstasy, and for that brief time I understood in a pure wordless way what the poets mean when they say that Kali is the Absolute, the reality that remains when everything else dissolves. In that context, I saw that Kali's wild hair, her crazed bloody dance, her flailing limbs, and her hand raised in the gesture of "Fear not" really do represent the absolute freedom of release from karma and time. Absolute freedom is found in the pristine inner space between now and then—the inner sky that opens on its own—in the heart of any moment when thoughts drop away.

Kali

kah-lee—Black One

Other Names for Kali:

Shyama (*shyah-mah*)—Dark One

Chamunda (*chah-mun-dah*)—Destroyer of Ignorance and Duality, as represented by the demons Chanda and Munda

Bhavatarini (*bhuh-vuh-tah-ri-nee*)—She who saves from the ocean of worldly suffering

Bhadrakali (*bhuh-druh-kah-lee*)—Auspicious Black One

Chandika (*chuhn-dee-kah*)—Fierce One

Chandi (*chuhn-dee*)—Fierce One

MahaKali (*muh-hah-kah-lee*)—Great Black One; Kali as the source of all-that-is

Goddess of:

- the dissolution of outworn structures
- radical rebirth
- dynamic power of change
- the process of childbirth
- death
- the fury of battle
- release of constriction and stuckness
- radical purification and detoxification—both physical and internal
- righteous anger
- wildness and radical audacity
- liberation through "dying" to the egoic self
- absolute voidness beyond all forms
- fierce love and ecstasy

Recognize Kali in:

- lightning storms
- volcanic eruptions, tornados, and tsunamis
- battlefields
- wild outbursts of ecstasy
- the act of pushing the child out of the womb
  (literally and figuratively, as in a dramatic creative process)

- radical creative freedom
- purification experiences
- sudden changes in life, especially those that involve disruption
- sudden enlightenment experiences

Invoke Kali for:
- transformative strength
- burning limitations and karmic veils
- purifying the inner body and the chakras
- awakening the kundalini energy and inspiring her to rise
- discovering the truth in a confusing situation
- letting go of outmoded structures or egoic tendencies
- seeing into the mysteries of life and death
- all forms of enlightenment, especially the kind in which we move from the relative to recognition of the absolute reality
- purifying and strengthening the heart
- transcendent ecstasy in meditation, lovemaking, or in the midst of troubles

Bija Mantra

Krim (*kreem*)

or:

Krim hum hreem (*kreem hoom hreem*)

Krim activates energy.

Hum brings strength.

Hreem arouses sweetness.

Invocational Mantras

Om aim hrim klim chamundayai vicche svaha

ohm aim hreem kleem chah-mun-dah-yai vich-ey swah-hah

Om: the primordial sound

Aim: the seed of wisdom

Hrim: creative manifestation

Klim: transformative power

Chamundaye: a name for Kali as the destroyer of the "demons" of ignorance and duality

Vicche: cut (as in cutting the bonds of ignorance and ego)
Svaha: the mantra that signifies offering

Jayanti mangala kali
Bhadrakali kapalini
Durga kshama shiva dhatri
Svaha svadha namo'stute

juh-yuhn-tee muhn-guh-lah kah-lee
bhuh-druh-kah-lee kuh-pah-li-nee
door-gah kshuh-mah shi-vah dah-tree
swah-hah swuh-dah nuh-mo-stoo-tey

Auspicious and victorious Kali
Bhadrakali! Wearer of the skull garland! O mother, hard to know!
Compassionate and benevolent mother
You who embody the sacred syllable offered in all rituals,
I bow to you!

Gayatri Mantra

Om Mahakalyai cha vidmahe
Parameshwaryai dhimahi
Tannah Kali prachodayat

ohm muh-hah-kahl-yai chuh vidmahe
puh-ruh-meysh-wuhr-yai dhee-muh-hee
tan-nuh kah-lee pra-cho-duh-yah-tuh

Om, may we come to know the Great Kali
May we meditate on the Supreme Goddess
May that goddess Kali impel us on our path.

Kali's colors: red, black, midnight blue
Kali's flowers: red hibiscus, blue lotus
Kali's consort: Shiva

CHAPTER 6

Parvati

Goddess of the Sacred Marriage

The moment I heard my first love story, I went looking for you.

RUMI

translated by Coleman Barks

Love, enjoyed by the ignorant
Becomes bondage.
That very same love, tasted by one with understanding,
Brings liberation . . .
Enjoy all the pleasures of love fearlessly,
For the sake of liberation.

CITTAVISUDDIPRAKARANA

I n Indian mythology, there are two archetypal romances. One is the teenage love affair between young Krishna and his lover Radha, the milkmaid who abandoned everything to dance with him in the moonlit forests. (We will meet Radha in chapter 10.) The other is the story of Shiva's long, layered marriages to two different forms of the goddess: his first wife, Sati ("She Who Is"), and his second wife, Parvati ("Mountain Maiden"). The first marriage leads to a tragic act of sacrifice. The second becomes one of the great cosmic partnerships in the mythic history of human culture: the union of Parvati, the supreme yogini, and her yogi husband, Shiva.

I'm thinking about Parvati as I listen to Laura, a student of mine who works as a financial analyst in Manhattan. Laura is an artist of precise analysis, a gifted economist, with a business degree and a serious yoga practice. She's also in trouble in her relationship with her boyfriend, Brian, a man she is sure she loves but doesn't know how to live with. Laura is confronting one of the classic dilemmas of a contemporary woman. Her work life demands focus, sharpness, and quick, penetrating intellect—qualities she associates with the masculine. Her sharpness and strength have a tendency to turn into armor, so she can't open herself to her lover. When she lets go of her carapace, she turns needy and demanding.

"I have two settings: armored and collapsed," she tells me. "The armored me has no clue how to be vulnerable with another person. The collapsed me is like mush—no spine at all, just neediness and insecurity."

Laura needs to create a new image of femininity for herself. Her strength is almost completely masculine; crafted, as it is for many of us, from her banker father's style of dealing with the world. She associates femininity with her neurotic mother, who felt overwhelmed by a powerful husband and who spent many days in dark rooms nursing her migraines.

For someone like Laura, as for so many women struggling to find a balance between strength and softness, Parvati can be a key inner-goddess archetype.

Each individual goddess can be seen as part of the wholeness of the divine feminine, which Tantric texts describe as the ultimate reality itself. At the same time, each goddess has her own unique personality. In the tradition, these individual goddess personalities are called sakala forms. As discussed earlier, *sakala* means "with qualities," as opposed to the "higher" *nishkala* aspect of divinity, which is without limit or qualities. When we do deity practice, we focus on the personality of the goddess with its specific attributes and unique energy. In classical Tantric practice, we do this with the understanding that the goddess is not a separate entity, but an aspect of our own higher self. Invoking her unique personal presence is like tuning into a specific channel for energy and blessing, which exists in the field of the collective consciousness. Eventually, that individual form will dissolve into consciousness itself, revealing the vast spaciousness beyond forms. Along the way, as you open the borders of your psyche to the energy of the goddess, you draw her into yourself. Her qualities begin to infuse your personality, enlarge your psyche, and even create seemingly miraculous changes in your outer life.

As you court intimacy with the divine feminine, you'll also notice that she can be met at any level. Depending on your intention, she might manifest as a felt sense of energy, as a nonphysical presence you see in visions or feel around you, as inner guidance, or as a doorway into the Absolute. She takes on different forms, leading you into subtler and subtler states, then shows you how to bring out those subtle qualities into your life. Invoking Durga, you invoke your own hidden qualities of protective strength, the fierceness of the feminine activist who can run a family or a business or summon the tribe to collective action. Invoking Lakshmi, you summon the shimmering quality of feminine beauty and the energy of abundance and wealth.

Parvati's energy is a mixture of these two feminine poles. Related to Durga and Kali, Parvati is one of the strong goddesses. She's also a goddess of love, with a seductive radiance directed at her beloved, yet at the same time focused inward, on her own essence. She's a mother. She's a yogini, a seeker of truth who inquires deeply into the nature of reality. She's powerful and she's tender, she's willful and she's playful—both at the same time. Moreover, Parvati is a goddess of relatedness. When you tune in to Parvati, you tune in to your own longing for sacred partnership. Parvati incarnates the feminine side of a form of marriage that many modern romantics crave: the union between the fully realized feminine and the fully realized masculine, the dance of intimacy where two powerful beings become one without sacrificing their individuality.

Parvati's image in bronze often shows her dancing, large-breasted, sinuous, and somehow mischievous with coy, lowered eyes. She represents the dynamic feminine in active partnership with her beloved masculine counterpart. Since her beloved is the notoriously untamable outsider-god Shiva, there's an element of danger and illicit delight in their relationship, a quality of mystery that makes even their domesticity seem fraught with potential chaos. Parvati confidently embraces the great void where no forms exist. She fills it with her blissful presence, and voilà—that formless emptiness becomes a cozy plenum, a space in which life can flourish. Parvati can know the unknowable, tame the untamed, and then tango with it. Who wouldn't want to participate in her cosmic romance?

A ROMANTIC FANTASY COUPLE

I first came across the Shiva-Parvati story early in my spiritual journey, and I immediately recognized it as my ultimate romantic fantasy. The story is told on page 152. Shiva is the Heathcliff of Indian spirituality: the cool, brooding outlaw, the bad-boy deity whose secret nature (unlike Heathcliff's) is blessing itself. He is also the one deity who embraces anyone who turns to him, including criminals, thieves, and heretics. My guru used to describe Shiva as "the Lord even of those people who have no Lord." Because, ultimately, he is consciousness itself, the infinite intelligence within which everything takes form, Shiva has no preferences, no favorites. That makes him both quick to give blessings, and impregnable to seduction. He's the freest of free beings, the ultimate detached witness. Left to himself, Shiva never gets entangled in the chaos of ordinary life.

He disdains the idea that there might be some reason to enter the manifest world. Like a hermit in a cave, he needs the feminine to bring him down to earth, even to allow him to act and give blessings.

Parvati, of course, knows that Shiva actually needs the very thing he resists. The divine masculine cannot act in the world without her, his dynamic counterpart. Even though she has to go through all sorts of trials to win him, she never doubts that he belongs to her nor that she has the will and strength to make him see it sooner or later. Any devotee of woman's fiction will recognize the situation: the Mr. Rochesters, the Mr. Darcys, the aloof cowboys of contemporary Harlequin romances are all replicating (albeit in radically reduced form) the Shaivic cool. Actors Marlon Brando and Robert Mitchum had a Shiva-like quality in their youth, as does Daniel Day-Lewis. Parvati herself is a divine prototype of all the plucky, independent, gorgeous heroines of fiction, from Elizabeth Bennet in *Pride and Prejudice* to Marguerite in *The Scarlet Pimpernel* to Julia Roberts in *Erin Brockovich*, or Emma Stone in *The Help*. Teresa of Avila, the sixteenth-century nun and devotee of Jesus, was a romantic mystic in the Parvati mold, who founded convents and wrote spiritual classics while carrying on an inner romance with Jesus.

In any case, Shiva and Parvati's story became my personal story of spiritual/erotic love, though for me it always remained an inner archetype rather than a model for actual relationship. Their story taught me some things about the spiritual path that I had never known. First, that the spiritual journey is not necessarily a hero's quest, like the story of the Buddha. It can also be a romance, a tale of separated lovers—the soul and the supreme soul, the heart and the mind, the body and the spirit—who find the path back to each other. It also tells us that the ultimate task of the inner life is not to separate spirit from its entanglements in the body and the world, as some Eastern and Western mystical traditions teach, but to marry spirit and body, wisdom and love, detachment and adoration so that the spirit and the body can exist in harmonious balance, and infuse divine awareness into the world.

In short, Shiva and Parvati taught me Tantra.

UNPACKING THE MYTH

Of course, like all the great myths, this one needs to be unpacked at different levels. It's a metaphor for the cosmic truth that reality has the quality of duality-in-unity, that it is a dance of polarities. Shiva and Parvati ultimately stand for the union of stillness and power, or wisdom and bliss. It's definitely a myth about the inner journey to wholeness, the yogic merging of energy with spirit, inside you and me.

That doesn't make the love story any less alluring or any less of an archetype we can live out in life. Parvati—the lover as yogini, the chosen disciple of the cosmic guru, the universal feminine in partnership with the cosmic masculine—is a powerful, if often unconscious, role model for contemporary women—especially for women who want to do their spiritual life in partnership. The Shiva-Parvati archetype can be lived out in same-sex couplings as in heterosexual ones, and in relationships where the partners interchange their masculine and feminine roles. Power couples often unconsciously model the relationship between Shiva and Parvati. The woman (or man) who gets romantically engaged with a mentor, and the woman (or man) who falls in love with her yoga teacher or her guru, is enacting the Parvati archetype. The relationship between Michelle and Barack Obama seems like a Parvati/Shiva pairing. Jivamukti Yoga founders Sharon Gannon and David Life or yoga teachers Colleen Saidman and Rodney Yee mirror the Shiva-Parvati relationship. We see its traces in the partnerships of artists like John Curry and Rachel Feinberg or John Lennon and Yoko Ono. One of my male friends has been through three marriages looking for that ultimate partnership. His personal archetype can be seen in the film *Mr. and Mrs. Smith*, where Brad Pitt and Angelina Jolie play married assassins who fight their climactic battle standing back to back, guns blazing at their assailants.[1]

THE COMPLETION OF ENLIGHTENMENT

In the esoteric traditions of left-handed Tantra, the figures of Shiva and Parvati symbolize what Buddhist scholar Miranda Shaw describes as "the completion of enlightenment."[2] This is a state of primal, ecstatic wholeness between the masculine and feminine sides of ourselves, and between the various polarities in consciousness, like unity/duality, spirituality/sexuality, and life/death. In the Buddhist Tantric tradition that flourished in Kashmir, side by side with the Shakta tradition of Hinduism, Shiva and Parvati are transformed into the male and female buddhas Vajrayogini and Vajrasattva, often shown in explicit sexual union.

Though Parvati is inextricably connected to her partner (one image of the two of them, called Ardhanarishvara, "The Half-Woman Lord," has the lovers occupying two halves of one body) she also fully embodies her own powerful yogic will. She is beautiful, sexy, and athletic; she can actively pursue yoga without regard to traditionally feminine delicacy, yet she remains fully feminine. Part of Parvati's mystery is that even as a wife she remains a virgin, in the sense that her independence is always intact. Even when she becomes a mother, it is by a form of parthenogenesis: the son of her body, Ganesha, is produced without benefit of insemination, out of her own sweat and the skin flakes of her body.

Of course, the Shiva-Parvati love story is not just an external relationship. For an individual, the Shiva-Parvati love story ultimately takes place in the psyche, and it symbolizes a powerful stage of embodied enlightenment. When the god and the goddess come together in the individual and collective psyche, we experience what is sometimes called the inner sacred marriage: the full integration of spirit and feminine heart, intellect and feeling, freedom and fullness. For real self-actualization, the masculine qualities of transcendence, freedom, penetration, intellectual principles, and ideas need to come together with the feminine way of earth rhythms, connectivity, paradox, relationship, and change. They can then be enacted in the world, their transcendent values can become immanent, and we can recognize the interconnectedness that flows between our bodies and souls.

In fact, the cosmic masculine and the cosmic feminine are never two. In the process of differentiating, individuating, and embodying, they *seem* to separate—their apparent polarity becoming the world of polarities. The ecstasy and the pain of life in a body is precisely in the illusion of separation in which wisdom and love seem to come apart and have to be brought together again—at which point we recognize that separation was purely illusory.

THE ROMANCE OF THE GODDESS

As the story begins, Brahma, the creator god, looks around the cosmos one day and realizes that Shiva, the third member of the triumvirate of cosmic rulers, is not playing his part in the drama. Shiva is supposed to be functioning as the great destroyer, bringing about endings so that there can be new beginnings. Instead, he's dissolved himself in meditation. He's so immersed in the stillness of the void, reveling in his absolute freedom, that he is utterly unconcerned with the affairs of the cosmos.

This has happened before. As we've already seen, eons earlier, Shiva had married Sati, "She Who Is." He lived with her in exquisite, romantically erotic passion for a few cosmic centuries—until Sati's semidivine father, Daksha, barred them from a ceremony to which every other god, nature spirit, and elemental entity in the universe had been invited. In protest, Sati immolated herself in her yogic fire. After her death, Shiva immersed himself in an unshakable state of *samadhi* (meditative union), tuning out the world.

As the cosmic centuries rolled on and Shiva never opened his eyes, the gods realized that something had to be done to re-engage Shiva in the world-play.

FIGURE 7: PARVATI/SHIVA AS ARDHANARISHWARA—THE ANDROGYNE

For one thing, a new, nearly invincible demon was taking over certain critical zones, and Shiva was needed to engage him. Obviously, Shiva's desire needed to be kindled, since it is desire that is the engine of every form of engagement. For that, also obviously, a woman was necessary. But what woman could tempt the great yogi?

Brahma is the first to understand. He realizes that he must once again enlist the goddess Maya herself—the enchantress, the allurer, the divine feminine force whose erotic power is at the very heart of the game of embodiment. Only the cosmic power of allurement herself could possibly find her way through the barriers of Shiva's unbreakable meditation and draw him back into the game. Brahma betakes himself to a mountaintop, and for thirty thousand years he sings her praises to the four corners of the universe. He invokes her as the one whose being is both world-transcending enlightenment and the world-beguiled, tormented ignorance of every creature: "The Queen who wants no rest yet remains unmoved for all eternity, the Lady whose body is both the tangibility of the world and the supersensuously subtle material of the heavens and hells."[3]

"You are wisdom and increase, stability and compassion," Brahma prays. "Queen of the world, you are alive in every nuance of feeling and perception; feeling and perception are your gestures. Your nature can be sensed only by one who realizes that you are the union of opposites. You produce the round of mortal delusion, yet you open the way to liberation. You are wisdom and ignorance; you illumine what is already self-luminous."[4]

At last, the goddess appears. She's in her dark form, blue-black and shining, seated on her lion, smiling with the full power of cosmic allurement. Her voice is like thunder, and she says, "Make your wish known. The very fact that I am here guarantees its fulfillment."

Brahma explains that Shiva has lost himself in meditation, and that without his involvement the worlds cannot go on.

The goddess smiles. She tells him that she will take form as a human woman. In his gorgeous retelling of the Sati myth, called "The Romance of the Goddess," mythologist Heinrich Zimmer has the goddess saying, "Just as I trap the newborn babe into life, so shall I draw this God of gods. As all the children of earth are allured by the charm of the beautiful feminine, so shall it be with him. For when in his meditation he splits the inmost kernel of his heart, there he shall find me melted into it, for I am his bliss. Bewitched, he will draw me to himself."[5]

This time, the goddess is born as the beautiful daughter of Himavat, the incarnate deity of the Himalayas, and his wife, Menaki. She grows up with eyes like lotus buds, six-inch eyelashes, and Shiva in her heart. By the time she is fourteen, she transports herself daily to the Himalayan grove where he sits in meditation, taking him flowers and often sitting for hours, ecstatic just to stare at him.

Invoking Parvati

Sit in a place where you will not be disturbed for fifteen to thirty minutes. Seat yourself a comfortable meditation posture.

Close your eyes and summon the image of Parvati. You may imagine her in the form of the Meditation on Parvati as the Yogini on page 163, or follow the simple form that follows:

Imagine Parvati as a young matron with skin the color of an apricot sunset or dawn sky.

She has large breasts, long wavy hair, and dark eyes slanted upward. Between her eyebrows is a vermilion dot, and she has three horizontal white stripes of ash across her forehead. Her lips are red, and she wears several golden necklaces. Around her waist is a golden girdle that anchors her red silk lower garment—a pleated length of fabric gathered around her waist and fastened between her legs, so that it leaves her calves free, like the skirt of an Indian dancer.

She is seated on the back of a white bull, Shiva's mount, in half-lotus posture, with the top of her right foot resting on her upper left thigh. She is smiling, and her eyes bless you.

Say to her, inwardly, "I offer my salutations to you, goddess Parvati. Please bless me and fill me with your Shakti."

Recite either the Parvati invocation mantra, or the Parvati Swayamvara mantra (found on page 176) nine times.

Then, ask for a specific blessing, sit for a short meditation, and/or practice the contemplation exercise on page 159 called The Heart's Desire.

THE MAIDEN

Parvati at this stage is the archetypal maiden, just awakened to love and infatuated with an unattainable male. She's young, naïve, and unaware of the consequences of her infatuation or what it takes to enter into partnership with a masculine figure who is himself consumed by his internal passion for truth. Like a student falling in love with her yoga teacher or a young woman falling in love with an artist and loving him from afar, Parvati is enacting a fantasy, and at this stage she is completely immersed in her worshipful, hopeful aspiration toward Shiva's love. Anne Roiphe, in her memoir *Art and Madness*, describes how she and other young women of her generation fell in love with art and literature, and enacted their love by aspiring to become not artists, but muses. In the prefeminist days of the late 1950s and early 1960s, women rarely became writers themselves; women's fiction was considered trivial, and many women who loved art settled for loving artists. Roiphe, after graduating from Sarah Lawrence College, married an impassioned, good-looking, hard-drinking playwright and supported him while he wrote his first play. She continued worshipping writers and being their lovers until she had an awakening and realized that she could write novels herself.[6] Parvati at this stage is just that sort of young girl, not yet self-empowered, even though she is a goddess.

One day, Brahma summons Kama, the god of desire, and Kama's wife Rati, whose name means "delight." He commands Kama to enter the grove where Parvati sits in contemplation of Shiva, and shoot his desire-arrows into Shiva's heart. Kama is terrified, for he knows that in so doing he risks the formidable anger of the lord of yogis.

THE INCITEMENT

But Brahma is his father, and though Kama argues, he has to obey. He, Rati, and their friend Spring tiptoe into the grove. They bring with them a cloud of erotic fragrance. Flowers burst into bloom, sending intoxicating scents through the air. Gentle breezes cool the air. Brightly colored birds appear in the trees, calling to each other with magical love songs. Parvati is enchanted. The spiritual love she has for Shiva suddenly inflames her desire, and her body becomes moist and rosy. Her lips part, her eyes become languorous as she gazes at her beloved, who is still lost in meditation. At that moment, Kama raises his bow and sends three of his five arrows—the ones named Inciter of the Paroxysm of Desire, Inflamer, and Infatuator—into Shiva's heart.

Shiva feels his awareness contract from formless pervading vastness into a specific sense of his surroundings. He senses the breeze on his face. He inhales the perfumed air. As he partially opens his eyes, he sees Parvati, and a familiar stir

FIGURE 8: THE GODDESS PARVATI

arises in his heart. When the stir moves down to his groin, Shiva realizes what has happened. "Who has stirred sexual desire in me?" he thunders. Without a second's hesitation, Shiva opens his third eye, sending out a beam of fire that incinerates Kama.

Rati, Kama's wife, collapses in agony. Parvati, too, begins to cry. "Would you have Desire leave the world?" she begs. "Without him, no creature will mate and the generations will die out!"

Grudgingly, Shiva agrees. He restores Kama—but without a body. Then Shiva goes back into meditation.

Now Parvati is desperate. She is deeper in love with Shiva than ever, and she senses that he too has been touched by her. He has also demonstrated that he is not willing to give in to his feelings. Something else is required. She will have to earn his love through yoga.

Of course, this is one of the universal moments in the arc of romance. It's the moment when Psyche spills the wax on Cupid, and he disappears. It's the moment in *When Harry Met Sally* when Billy Crystal freaks out after his first night with Meg Ryan. At this stage of separation, the plot thickens, and the lover's seriousness is tested.

In our inner life, it's also the moment in a creative project when we catch our first glimpse of possible fulfillment. We recognize that something is ready to emerge, but that we'll have to work for it. In spiritual life, it represents an initial awakening in which we actually experience what it is to meet the Beloved. For a moment, the Beloved seems to be present, to see us, to touch us with an intimate glance. Or we enter a state of fully awake presence and recognize our own essence, realizing that this is what we have always been.

Then the moment passes, and we are left in the sadness of separation—a separation made far more painful by the fact that we had that glimpse.

THE COMMITMENT

If, like Parvati, our desire is strong enough, we make a full commitment. We see that it's not enough just to be inspired, to feel longing, to be in love. We have encountered the beloved, but now we need to make ourselves into the vessel that can hold the emerging vision, the vessel that can be the beloved of the Beloved. Rumi wrote, "God too desires us."[7] But God's desire is for us to *become* God, to realize our identity with the divine. For this, transformative practice is required. Yet this practice will not be powered by egoic will. The will behind it is the will of the universe itself, the pull of the evolutionary imperative, the will of the Shakti.

PARVATI AS DIVINE WILL

Parvati in her moment of decision is both the individual—the girl in love with a god—and the power of will itself. She makes a momentous decision. She decides to practice yoga, *tapas* in Sanskrit, the psycho-physical process of heating the energies in our body and mind through intense concentration for the purpose of internal transformation. In the Native American vision quest ceremony, the young warrior stands inside a circle, unmoving, for a set period of time, until his body and mind are opened through concentration to the appearance of a guiding vision. The practice Parvati undertakes is much more intense. She proposes to go to the forest and stand on one leg in a Himalayan stream while repeating the name of Shiva, until he comes to her.

Her mother forbids her to do so. "Such austerities are for men," she says. "You are a delicate girl, a princess."

"Give up this insane idea," Menaki pleads.

Parvati refuses. "No," she says. "I am the daughter of a mountain, and I am tough."

This is the moment when Parvati the maiden steps into her power. She's moved by love, which combined with her now intensely focused will is powerful enough to shift the order of the cosmos. The story goes that from that moment, she receives the name Uma ("maiden"), which came from the sound of her "No, Ma." The name Uma is often used to describe Parvati as the incarnation of focused will, a will so strong that it could only have arisen in the heart of the creative power itself. Uma's will simply says "No" to objections and obstacles. Shiva has rejected her? No, he will not do that. My family doesn't want me to practice yoga? No, I won't accept their limits.

Contemplation: The Heart's Desire

Gather your journal and something to write with, and find
a comfortable spot to complete this meditation.

Write down a list of your deep desires. Include desires that would nourish you and others emotionally, like the desire to have more love, to be with a certain person, or for your family to be happy. Include material desires, such as the wish to live in a certain place or to have a car or some other physical object. Include desires that have to do with your career or calling. Also include desires that have to do with your inner growth and your spiritual life, such as the desire to cultivate compassion or to experience deep peace. Include desires that have to do with the welfare of the earth or of other people.

As you look over this list of desires, ask yourself, "Of these desires, which feel most in line with my deeper destiny? Which of them will take me closer to my true Self or to God? Which of them are in line with the highest evolution of consciousness—my own and others?"

Now, close your eyes and summon the image of Parvati. Feel the presence of the goddess as you imagined her in your first meditation. Sense her energy in and around you. Inhale, bringing Parvati's energy into your heart. Exhale, allowing it to flow through your body.

Ask yourself now, "What is the deepest desire of my heart?" Then begin to write, and write down whatever arises.

Once you have completed your writing, once again anchor yourself in the Parvati energy. Now, ask yourself:

What will it take for me to realize this desire?

What will I need to let go of?

What qualities in myself will I need to cultivate?

Who is available to help me?

What is a first step I can take?

Now, offer your desire to the goddess, asking for her help in bringing it about. Take some time to write about what you have discovered.

There's a sutra in the *Shiva Sutras,* a great text of yoga, that says that the divine power of will—the generative impulse behind the evolution of consciousness—*is* the maiden Uma. Parvati's focused intention, her will to union with her beloved, is identical with what is sometimes called the evolutionary impulse, the cosmic and individual drive to evolve to higher levels of awareness. Because her intention is nonegoic, it carries a certainty of fulfillment, as well as a sure knowledge of the action to take to accomplish her goals. In creating a world, she created a separation from her other half. Now, the moment has come to reunite—not just in the transcendent formless space where all differences are dissolved, but in bodies, on the earth, *inside* the creation. Parvati's yoga is focused not on personal attainment or self-cultivation. It's all about love.

In that sense, Parvati's story is a demonstration of a fundamental Tantric premise, and it's meant to show us something about our own possibilities. Parvati and Shiva are the poles of consciousness itself, which means that they exist fully within our own consciousness. So Parvati's "No, mother!" moment is meant to reveal, first of all, that truly focused intention carries within it the seed of fulfillment. It is a truth that applies to every human endeavor.

She's also showing us a deeper truth about spiritual life: that if we're willing to make the necessary sacrifices, we can have it all. We can have enlightenment and intimacy together. We can know our transcendent bliss-self, and we can realize that bliss in passionate relationship. The secret Parvati shows us is that the relational form of self-realization requires just as much conscious effort as to realize the transcendent self. Both paths begin with self-cultivation. Parvati has realized that she can't "have" Shiva unless she cultivates in herself the qualities of stillness, stamina, and devotion. To embody love requires absolute commitment, radical courage, and rigorous self-cleansing. The great desire has to be separated from smaller desires and tested in its own fire.

Meditation: Parvati as the Yogini

Once again, find a quiet spot to complete this exercise.

PART ONE: RECEIVING THE ENERGY OF PARVATI

Close your eyes and center your attention on your breath. Notice thoughts flowing like clouds through your mind.

Imagine yourself sitting in a grove on top of a mountain. Your seat is a soft bed of moss beneath a tree whose leaves are living jewels of light, emerald-green in color. On the branches are flowers made of light: sapphires, rubies, and topaz. As you sit beneath the tree, you feel the light from its branches embracing you from above, and flowing around your body, holding you in a radiant, rainbow-like cloak of light.

Standing on the outskirts of the grove is a young maiden, luminously beautiful. Her body is golden, the color of a dawn sky. She has large, bare breasts and long, well-muscled limbs. A red silk cloth is twisted low around her hips. Her belly is well-defined, yet sensuously round.

The maiden's body radiates warmth, and as you look more closely you see that the gold of her skin is illuminated by her inner power, the heat of her yogic fire. Her face is turned toward you, and she is smiling. Her smile radiates playfulness and love. Her eyes look into yours with a penetrating gaze that sees past your fears, your excuses, your confusion, your assumptions of smallness and limitation. In her eyes, you read an uncompromising recognition of your highest possibilities. She is summoning you to recognize yourself as the yogini, the goddess herself.

Still holding your gaze, she balances on one leg, with the other bent so that the sole of her foot touches her inner thigh. Then she unbends her leg until her foot touches the ground, toe first, and she begins to dance. With one hand she gestures toward you, palm down, fingers relaxed. From her fingers flash sparklers of fiery red light. Particles of that light flow toward you and into your heart with each inhalation, filling you with strength and power. She turns her palm upward, and from her fingers flow sparklers of pink and gold light, emanations of the goddess's playful love. As you inhale, you draw these light particles into your heart, filling it with tenderness.

As she continues to dance, holding your gaze with her luminous eyes, the shimmering particles flow more and more thickly from her hands, red and gold, flowing into your heart. As your heart takes in the light, you let it flow through the whole region of your chest. Parvati's strong and tender love-light now illuminates your heart, purifying it of wounds and blocks, dispelling the armor that you've erected around it. As your heart opens and releases its blocks, tears might come. Let them flow. Let the power of Parvati's radiance fill your heart until it expands with passionate strength and tenderness.

As your heart fills with the light, let it expand out from your heart and form sparkling clouds of light around your body so that you are completely immersed in red and golden sparkles of radiance. Your body begins to sway. For a few moments, you enjoy the full expression of Parvati's light in your heart.

When you are ready, inhale the light down from your heart to the belly, feeling it fill your pelvis and sexual organs with sparkling particles of red and gold. Allow the light to expel the wounds, the scars, the grief stored in your pelvis and sacrum. Little by little, you feel the light of Parvati's power and love filling your lower body, loosening and expelling shame, fear, and mechanical lust. With each inhalation and exhalation, the light streams through your legs and feet, filling them with the free and playful love-charged energy of goddess Parvati.

PART TWO: IGNITING YOUR OWN POWER OF DIVINE WILL
When you are ready, let the light stream back up through the center of your body, igniting the area around your navel. Here, allow the light of the goddess

FIGURE 9: PARVATI AS A MAIDEN YOGINI

to energize your own will. The Shakti of Parvati's will is free of ego, free of partiality. It is wholly focused and concentrated, full of absolute one-pointed determination.

How does it feel to tune into the divine will? Notice that it is free of conditions and free of stray thoughts.

Toward what aim will you direct that divine will? What will you focus it on? Realize that the object of Parvati's will should be worthy of its divine origin. Where you place your will determines your life, your direction, your action.

Let the felt sense of divine will, expanding as golden radiance through your belly, show you what it wants for you, what you truly desire for your life.

THE YOGINI PATH

In the spiritual world of India and Tibet, there are other stories of young yoginis who left home to live in the wild. Sometimes they left concupiscent husbands, as did the South Indian yogini Akkamahadevi, who fell in love with God in the form of Shiva and roamed naked in twelfth-century Karnataka, singing songs of longing and meditating on the void. Sometimes, like the Kashmiri poet Lalla, they sang of nonduality, declaring that consciousness itself is one, that Shiva and the soul are never separate. The Buddhist yoginis described in Tibetan Buddhist texts were spiritual descendants of Parvati and came from the same region of the Himalayas. According to recent contemporary research, these yoginis sometimes found their Shiva in a Tantric partner and enacted the drama in a physical body.[8] In Daniel Odier's book *Tantric Quest*, he tells the story of receiving initiation with just such a naked Tantric yogini. She teaches him the Kashmiri Shaivite practices where the seeker learns to take his awareness back through the stages of material manifestation to the state of pure awareness. In the process, she initiates him in a Tantric sexual ritual.[9]

Parvati, the maiden, stands in her frigid stream for uncountable months, perhaps years. (We're talking here about deep time, after all, which is the timing of gods; thousands of years are contained in a moment.) Eventually, the fire of her yoga begins to penetrate the upper worlds. Shiva can feel the heat. In his meditation, he senses the unwavering devotion of this young woman and remembers her beauty and his own response to it. Perhaps he also recollects the bliss he had known with his divine consort and recognizes that though solitary meditation has its own joy, there is something about relationship that can't be beat.

Shiva decides to test her. Taking the form of a Brahmin boy, dressed in white, with his tuft and sacred thread, he appears on the bank of the stream. Parvati stands there unmoving, deep in meditation on the mantra, "Om namaha shivaya." The radiance around her nearly takes his breath away.

Parvati receives him reverently and asks why he has honored her with his presence.

"Princess," he says, "the gods have noticed your efforts and have decided to reward you. But they have asked me to point out to you that you are focusing your attentions on the wrong deity. Shiva is an outcast, a wild-haired madman, an eccentric who hangs around with ghosts and goblins and who worships corpses. He has no lineage, no family, and everyone knows he drove his first wife to suicide. This is no partner for a maiden like you. Instead, I've been empowered to offer you the hand of Vishnu. Now, *there's* a deity any maiden would love. Handsome, a master of the art of love and statecraft, he would give you the life you need and, moreover, he would love you because he is, after all, the divinity of erotic love."

Parvati begins to shake with outrage. Her yogic fire blazes up around her so furiously that even Shiva is a bit awed.

"Shiva is my cosmic husband, my love, and my lord," she roars. "If he has no lineage it is because he himself is the source of all lineage. He gives refuge even to creatures that others consider inauspicious. And since you have come here to insult him, I must ask you to leave my grove."

At this moment, Shiva throws off his disguise, appearing in all his naked, ash-smeared, blue-throated beauty. "Be my wife," he cries out. "You have won me."

Shiva, of course, is the ultimate postconventional deity, and he wants to consummate their marriage then and there. But Parvati, thinking of her mother's feelings, insists on a formal wedding. The wedding procession is a story in itself. Vishnu—resplendent in yellow silks—precedes Shiva, and Parvati's mother assumes that this is the bridegroom. She nearly faints when Shiva himself arrives on his great bull, surrounded by weird creatures with animal heads and mis-shapen bodies and long fangs—his goblin host.

THE DIVINE MARRIAGE

Shiva carries his bride to the mountains, to his favorite haunt, Mt. Kailash. There, they consume eons in erotic play, making love on clouds and mountaintops, and in subtle heaven-worlds, surrounded by clouds of peacocks and acres of mountain flowers. Shiva worships his consort, massaging her feet, kissing her all over her body, and gathering flowers to place in her lap.

Their love-making is so intense and fiery that the cosmos trembles with the force of it, and the gods become terrified. On one particular occasion, the gods sense that the two are about to make a child. Frightened that the child born of such a union will be too powerful, they find a way to interrupt the two of them in the middle of intercourse. Shiva's seed is discharged outside Parvati. It is so fiery and hot that no container can hold it, until it is finally held in the Ganges River, where it is incubated and finally born as the child Skanda, or Karttikeya. Karttikeya eventually reunites with his parents and becomes the general of Shiva's celestial army.

That same fire periodically erupts into marital arguments. Parvati becomes jealous because Karttikeya is being raised by the river goddess Ganga. On another occasion, Parvati wins at dice and insists that Shiva forfeit his loincloth. Annoyed, Shiva turns her into a parrot. Parvati takes refuge in what is now the city of Chennai, and becomes a goddess named Minakshi—always shown holding a parrot. But most of the time, Parvati keeps trying to domesticate Shiva, to bring him into relationship. He's only partially domesticable, of course. When she complains that she doesn't have a real house to live in during the rainy season, Shiva takes her to the high mountain peaks above the clouds, where it doesn't rain. Sometimes, he responds to her pleas for an ordinary home by pointing out that as an ascetic, the whole world is his dwelling place.

In essence, Shiva and Parvati are Tantric partners. They are the prototype: the divine couple whose union models the ideal for every practitioner of sacred intimacy. Despite the fact that they are a family, their unconventional way of living fits the classical Tantric lifestyle: in the tradition, Tantric pairings take place in caves and forests and cremation grounds—places where ordinary people don't have the stamina or daring to approach.[10] More than that, the two of them embody the qualities that will become the standard for Tantric practitioners, whose coupling will be seen as practices for embodying both the state and the union of the divine pair. In the Tantric texts like Chandamahroshana Tantra, a Buddhist scripture that echoes the principles of the Shaiva and Shakta Tantras, the requirements for Tantric partners are described. They must both be equally strong practitioners, motivated toward enlightenment, skilled in meditation, belong to the same spiritual tribe, and filled with erotic passion. Passion is crucial, because without strong erotic desire there is no energy to be transmuted into divine bliss. The Tantrikas understand that sexual energy is also the force behind spiritual evolution. What makes sexual energy spiritual is how you choose to direct it. "Bliss is gathered by passion," says a Tibetan commentary on the Chakrasamvara Tantra, but it's passion tempered by rigorous and careful discipline.[11] The sexual ecstasy of Tantra can only be cultivated by yogis who have perfected a state of thought-free, meditative attentiveness, without lust or ordinary grasping attachment. Parvati, through her long austerities, has attained this state of absolute clarity, which Shiva has perfected through his own practice. So when they come together, their intense, prolonged sexual encounter is a shared meditation on nondual bliss. It's a celebration of wholeness, connection, and exquisite love.

Meditation: Opening to the Divine Yogi-Lover

Find a comfortable place where you will not be disturbed. Have
your journal and pen handy in case you want to record anything
about this meditation. Allow the meditation to unfold naturally,
without forcing any of it. Often, as you practice this meditation, it
will take its own course, and if this happens, let it happen.

Close your eyes, focus on your breath, and let your awareness flow inward. Imagine yourself in Parvati's grove. Invoke her presence as in the first meditation on page 155. As you feel Parvati's presence in your body, let her radiance fill you from head to toe.

Now become aware that before you in the grove is the figure of a godlike male. He has the slim, muscular body of a yogi. He wears a tiger skin around his waist, and his skin is pale blue, the color of awakened consciousness. As you revel in the power and light scintillating within your own body, you become aware of his heart opening to you. Waves of attraction and love flow from his heart to yours. Your heart opens to receive him.

Without moving, your bodies are drawn toward one another. The energy from your hearts merges together. A fiery sparkle of light and desire flows from your womb to his belly and joins your bodies even more deeply. Your head falls back, and you receive showers of white light flowing from his third eye, flowing in through your wisdom eye and mingling with the red and golden sparkles that fill your body.

You allow your light body—free, powerful, filled with love—to merge with the body of the yogi. As you embrace, your power and love merges with his stillness, his spaciousness. Your light bodies dissolve completely.

You rest in space, filled completely with the one light—pulsing with love and awareness—that comes together in your merging.

THE ENLIGHTENED DIALOGUE

As a couple, Shiva and Parvati are in constant conversation. Esoteric teachings are part of their pillow talk. Metaphysical scriptures and yogic texts flow from their intimate conversations and enliven the dialogues with which they entertain themselves during the spaces between their lovemaking. Among these are the meditation aphorisms of the *Vijnana Bhairava,* a compendium of brilliant and effective concentration practices, beloved in both Shaivite and Tibetan Tantric traditions since the eighth century CE.

The conversation begins when Parvati asks Shiva, "My beloved Lord, please tell me, what is your true nature and how can it be known? There are so many practices, so many rituals, that people are confused. Tell me, what is the essence of practice?"

"Goddess, you are my own Self," says Shiva. "Let me explain. No ordinary practices or rituals can touch my deepest essence. I am found in that space of stillness where the contraction of ego dissolves, and where the highest bliss arises." Then he goes on to teach her a series of short exercises, each discrete and independent, each one a doorway into the heart of reality. They include meditation on the space between the breaths; meditation on the void at the crown of the head; meditation on the space inside a cup and the darkness in a well; and also meditation on the bliss that arises when savoring food, during sex, and in the memory of its caress. These practices span every moment that arises in the life of a human being. At the core of the conversation is the profound recognition that we can enter into that ego-free, thought-free, bliss-saturated state at the heart of any moment and any activity.

This endless conversation between the lovers is consciously offered as a gift to human beings who long for the secrets of enlightenment. The power in the conversation is not just in the intensity of Shiva and Parvati's engagement in the truth. It also comes from their enormous sense of shared presence. Because they experience themselves as one heart, the mystical dialogues between them loop in and out of the same inner source, like a verbal infinity sign, in which questioner and questioned are constantly doubling back into themselves, drawing insight out of their own center. Parvati's question draws out Shiva's insight.

FIGURE 10: SHIVA AND PARVATI WITH THEIR SONS, GANESHA AND KARTIKKEYA

Her presence inspires him to turn into himself and find words to express truths that come from the place beyond words.

Because they are together, because there is an "other" who needs to hear words, the wordless can be expressed in language—which then becomes the basis of some of the great texts of yoga and Tantra, the revealed scriptures of the Shaiva and Shakta traditions of Indian philosophy.

It's a tradition in Tantra that the core teachings arise as revelation out of this primal relationship of love. The teachings of hatha yoga, for instance, were supposed to have been demonstrated by Shiva to Parvati one day as they sat on the banks of a sacred lake. In a wonderfully improbable twist, a sage named Matsyendranath happens to be shadowing them. He has taken the form of a fish who swims up to the bank, pokes his head up just enough to hear the discussion, and later passes down the knowledge as the asanas of yoga.

Or, so the story goes. My suspicion is that this particular myth concretizes a process of channeling that goes on in meditation, when we go into a state of stillness and drop a query into the heart. In that state, teachings and revelation and insight arise, which do feel as if they have been downloaded from a much larger field of wisdom.

We replicate Shiva and Parvati's conversation every time we sit together as lovers, as teacher and student, or in a group and seek revelation, transformation, or the insight for change. Shiva and Parvati symbolize the moment when we get spiritually naked together, when our love and trust is great enough to let us be vulnerable and thus make space for revelation to arise. This intellectual merging involves a subtle Tantric embrace of thoughts and energies rather than a physical merging. It is no less an embrace for being subtle.

The image of Shiva and Parvati sitting together in a grove on the crest of a mountain not only carries the archetype of divine lovers, it also stands for the mysterious creative moment when two or more people enter a "we" space together. In the "we" space, our essences connect, and we are then hooked up with superconscious source of insight. Physicist David Bohm called this process "dialogue." Dialogue happens when, like Shiva and Parvati, we recognize our fundamental unity, our interdependence. Instead of being a conversation between separate individuals trying to find solutions with their minds and from their egoic selves, dialogue happens in a shared space of presence. It comes from the inspired, revelatory, transformative energy that shows up when a group of people allows boundaries to come down and real mutual vulnerability to emerge.

Dialogue always starts with a question, an inquiry. In their coupling, Shiva and Parvati epitomize this fundamental creative conversation in which truth always comes out of the silence behind words, rising into expression through verbal exploration.

THE TENSION OF OPPOSITES

Parvati and Shiva hold a creative tension of opposites. He represents the eternal drive for freedom, the yogi's need to disentangle himself from the world; she represents the feminine drive toward expressive fullness—emotion, rhythm, even the creative flow of thoughts.

When Shiva—who stands for everything that is antithetical to society—unites with Parvati and creates a household life, they are making an enormous statement. Their partnership resolves one of the most embedded dualities in culture: the duality between life in the world and life of the spirit. In Indian life as well as in Christian mysticism there has always been an opposition between the ascetic yogi, who withdraws from the world in order to realize his nature as spirit, and the householder, entangled in domesticity. Traditionally, the demands of the world, epitomized by family life, are diametrically opposed to both the spiritual path and also to the path of the artist. The mystic and the artist are both said to need solitude and disengagement for the practice of their discipline. In the film *Bright Star*, which tells the story of the love affair between the poet John Keats and young Fanny Brawne, Keats's friend Brown argues that marriage to Fanny will destroy Keats as a poet, since he will then be tied to domestic concerns. In Indian and Buddhist mythology, yogis are routinely tempted by nymphs and beautiful girls, the understanding being that to give in to the temptation of desire is to fall from yoga.

In the Tantric path, however, this dichotomy is transcended. Worldly life and spiritual life, spirit and flesh, are recognized not as a duality, but as manifestations of the same power, which is Shakti. The *Vijnana Bhairava* describes a practice where you discover the ecstasy of the ultimate reality by going into the throbbing heart of pleasure, inside the joy of sex, of song, of delicious food, then meditating on the "perfect condition of that joy" until the supreme bliss reveals itself.[12] Tantric adepts say that the highest spiritual initiations are given by women. "Without woman, there is no bliss," says the Chandamaharoshana Tantra, a Buddhist text. It goes on to say:

To renounce [the world]—don't do it! . . .
Inhale scents,

Taste delicious flavors,
Feel textures.
Use the objects of the five senses—
You will quickly attain supreme Buddhahood.[13]

Tantra is the Goddess's path, which means that it is for people who know how to use the physical and imaginal world as doorways into the ultimate, as well as for worldly delight. The Goddess is the mistress of these worlds as she is of the physical world, which is why at the heart of Tantric practice there is deep respect for the feminine as spiritual authority. In *Tantric Quest*, Daniel Odier's teacher tells a story about how a group of hermits debated all day about whether the ultimate truth is a self or a non-self. Finally, one of the ascetics says that the argument can only be resolved by a dakini, a woman practitioner. The yogini then goes into meditation on the nondual oneness between self and non-self, and in the space of presence that opens up in the circle, all agree that the discussion has been resolved. They recognize that spirit is not higher than matter, nor is matter devoid of self. Instead, it is the nature of spirit to creatively express itself in form, just as it is the nature of silence to express itself in sound.[14]

This is the recognition that arises out of the union of Shiva and Parvati. Parvati is Shiva's capacity to express himself in action. Without her, he is simply inactive, inert. Parvati, in scholar David Kinsley's words, "not only compliments Shiva, she completes him."[15]

Meditation: Parvati and Shiva as the Two Halves of Your Body

This meditation can surprise you because it allows you to tune in to the presence of the divine masculine and feminine within yourself. As mentioned earlier, the interdependence of spirit and matter, masculine and feminine, intellect and feeling, is epitomized by the figure of Ardhanarishvara, God as Half Man-Half Woman. The right side of this androgynous being wears a tiger skin, has matted locks, and carries a trident. The left side has a bared breast and a delicate skirt; her hands dance in mudras. In the tradition, the left side of the body is considered feminine, while the right side is masculine. (Refer to figure 7 on page 153 for a representation of this figure.)

Find a comfortable seated position for this meditation, and be sure to have your journal and something to write with.

Begin by making a list of the qualities and behaviors in yourself that you consider feminine. Then, list the qualities you consider masculine.

Now list the qualities of the divine that you consider feminine and the qualities you consider masculine.

Now imagine that the left half of your body is filled by the divine feminine as the Goddess Parvati. Sense the qualities of the goddess in that half of your body: beauty, devotion, playfulness, charm, sweetness, nourishing love, erotic tenderness, gracefulness, feminine strength.

Imagine that the right side of your body is occupied by the divine masculine in the form of Shiva. Feel his energy in your body. Sense his qualities: stability, steadiness, penetrating intellect, clarity of vision, peace, vastness, ruthless swiftness, masculine strength.

Let your attention move from the feminine side of your body to the masculine side of your body. Notice the differences. Feel these two sides of the divine nature held within you. Sense them held in balance in your own body.[16]

The Goddess Parvati manifests herself for the sake of inciting spirit—formless, transcendent, uninvolved—to grow down into the messy, fruitful karma-laden world of the body. It has to happen, otherwise there would be no life, no world. Unlike the story of Adam and Eve, where Eve's temptation wrecks everything, the Shiva-Parvati story makes Parvati's allure the very basis of life in this world. It also offers us a model of the feminine as a fully integrated mother/lover/yogini who is playful, willful, independent, yet utterly devoted.

Laura, the young woman I mentioned in the beginning of this chapter, discovered this for herself. When she meditated on the image of herself as Parvati, she began to discover the erotic yogini behind her armor. The internalized image of Parvati's steadfastness helped her maintain her assertiveness and strength. She also began to feel her way into a sinuous, yielding quality that she hadn't found in herself before. In the moments when she could touch Parvati's quality of loving flexibility, she saw a way to open to her lover, without collapsing her will, and a way to maintain her independence without sacrificing closeness.

Not all of us get to live that story as part of a couple, but anyone who deeply wants to can live that story as a process within his or her own psyche.

As an interior process, the Shiva-Sati-Parvati story is all about the integration of spirit with form, of freedom with fullness, of knowledge and love. Robert Johnson, in his famous book *We*, uses the Tristan and Isolde myth to point out that romantic love is often a displaced version of love for spirit, for God. His point is that when the love that belongs to the divine is placed on the shoulders of a human being, it can only lead to disillusionment and tragedy.[17] The Shiva-Parvati story, however, points to another outcome for romantic love. It describes a relationship in which yoga, inner knowing, and self-cultivation are natural to the lovers. Both are complete in themselves, yet they also complete each other. Unlike the duality-based spirituality of the West, where the human and the divine are permanently and inalterably separated, Tantra assumes that the human being—both body and soul—is made of the same stuff as the divine. So the story of Shiva and Parvati becomes a tale of consummation, of learning to live in unity while dancing out the ecstasy of relationship—an ecstasy that is a constant rhythmic dance between unity and separation, passion and detachment, movement and stillness.

Parvati

pahr-vuh-tee—Mountain Girl

Other Names for Parvati:

Gauri (*gow-ree*)—The Fair One

Minakshi (*mee-nak-shee*)—She with Eyes Like Slender Fishes

Shivaa (*shi-vey*)—Feminine form of Shiva

Girija (*gi-ri-jah*)—Daughter of the Mountain

Uma (*oo-mah*)—Maiden

Haimavati (*hai-muh-vah-tee*)—She Who Belongs to the Mountain King Himavat

Goddess of:

- sacred and mundane partnership
- patron deity of yoginis, discipleship, and esoteric study
- marriage and motherhood
- asceticism, commitment to practice, power to practice intensely in yoga, meditation, or athletics
- homemaking known for civilizing the wild aspects of the ascetic masculine

Recognize Parvati in:
- forest groves and mountains
- yoga studios
- partnerships between self-actualized individuals
- unusual domestic situations
- working mothers
- peacemakers and mediators
- sunlight
- fertility
- sensuality
- dance

Invoke Parvati for:
- strength and commitment
- unbreakable willpower
- devotion
- finding a desirable mate, getting married
- success in relationship
- conceiving and bearing a child
- creative activity
- uniting the masculine and feminine polarities within yourself
- breakthroughs in yoga practice
- will and power in athletic training
- power of self-transformation
- balancing of the worldly and spiritual sides of life
- commitment to practice

Invocational Mantras

Sarva-mangala-mangalye
Shive sarvartha-sadhike
Sharanye tryambake gauri
Narayani namo'stu te

suhr-vuh-muhn-guh-luh-mahn-guhl-yay
shi-vey suhr-vahr-thuh sah-dee-key
shuh-ruhn-yay tree-um-buh-kay gow-re
nah-rah-yuh-nee nuh-mo-stoo-tey

175

O auspiciousness of all auspicious things!
O benevolent fulfiller of all our goals!
O fair three-eyed goddess, you are my refuge.
O Narayani! Salutations to you.

Swayamvara Mantra

The Sanskrit word *swayamvara* refers to the ceremony in which young women chose their husband. This mantra is said to be particularly powerful for attracting a mate.

Om hrim yogininam yogini yogeshwari
Yogabhayankari sakala sthavara
Jangamasya mukhya hridayam mama
Vasam akarshayakarshaya svaha

ohm hreem yo-gee-nee-nahm yo-geysh-wuhr-ee
yo-gah-bhuh-yuhn-kuh-ree suh-kuh-luh stah-vuh-ruh
juhn-guh-muh-syuh mu-khyah hri-duh-yum muh-muh
vuh-sum ah-kahr-shuh-yah-kahr-shuh-yuh svah-hah

O yogini of all yoginis, O goddess of yoga,
Who dispels fear through her yoga,
Who is first among all living beings:
Attract, attract the one I seek into the abode of my heart.
I offer the results to you!

Parvati's flowers: red hibiscus, rose, lotus
Parvati's colors: red (but Parvati can also be seen clothed in many bright colors)
Parvati's consort: Shiva

CHAPTER 7

Saraswati

Goddess Who Flows as Language, Insight, and Sound

> You are intelligence, intelligence, intelligence. Your names are memory, resolution, mind, and hymn of praise.
>
> **ABHINAVAGUPTA SARASWATISTOTRA**

> May Saraswati—goddess of knowledge, who is praised by the wise, who is the wife of the creator—reside on my tongue.
>
> **HYMN TO SARASWATI**

The story goes that once there was a famous Brahmin scholar who had a good-hearted but very stupid son. In the old Vedic world, the ability to memorize and recite sacred texts was a crucial skill and the mark of a man's worth. The son couldn't even pronounce the Sanskrit correctly. So, instead of being educated like other Brahmin sons, he was put to menial tasks—woman's work, like cleaning the house and carrying jugs of water from the river.

Then one day, when the son went to the river, he came across a beautiful woman in distress. Perhaps robbers had stolen her purse; perhaps she had been abandoned by her family. It doesn't matter; the point is that the son rescued her, gave her water to drink, and took her home for a good meal. She was profuse in her thanks. As she said goodbye, she did a strange thing: she touched her finger to the boy's tongue. Suddenly, the boy burst out with a verse of Sanskrit poetry so subtle, so sinuous in meter and rhyme, that everyone present could only gasp in amazement. From that moment on, the boy displayed powers of speech, memory, and rhetoric so far beyond his father's that in only a few years he became the most famous orator in his district.

That mysterious woman was the goddess Saraswati, demonstrating the power of her grace. A verse says, "When Saraswati gives her blessing, a dumb person becomes a poet." Swami Vivekananda, the great Hindu teacher whose eloquence captured the American imagination at the Chicago Parliament of World Religions in 1893, related that as he stepped on stage to deliver his paradigm-shifting address, he did so without notes or even a plan. Instead, he asked for Saraswati's grace and winged it, utterly confident that she would give him the words. She did, and in that one address, Vivekananda changed the way educated a pivotal group of Western religious people understood Hinduism. To be blessed by Saraswati is to be able to transform the world through words.

In Tantric understanding, the grace of the goddess is the catalytic force that arouses the powers hidden in the self. Goddess energies connect you to your highest capacities for understanding as well as action. Saraswati Shakti will often show up as moments of sudden understanding. When words flow easily, when ideas come up out of nowhere, when you say something so powerful and profound that it surprises even you, you are experiencing Saraswati. The gift for languages is a manifestation of Saraswati, as is every expression of intelligence or capacity for innovation. As a spiritual energy, Saraswati can help you penetrate through the thickets of thought—which are also, paradoxically, an expression of her energy—to recognize your own awareness as the field of enlightenment.

Above all, Saraswati is wisdom. This has been her function ever since the beginning, when Brahma, the creator god, asked for help in order to make a world.

ORDER OUT OF CHAOS

In the beginning, surveying the formless chaos of inchoate matter and energy, Brahma felt confused and at sea. He had no idea how to fashion something out of that disorganized swirl. In desperation, he turned into himself and asked, "How can I create an ordered cosmos in the midst of this chaos?"

From within him, the Goddess spoke. "Through knowledge," she said. "And from knowledge will come creative action."

With that, she emerged from Brahma's mouth as the power of the creative word. She rode a snow-white swan—the *hamsa*—and carried a *veena*, a kind of lute. Fair-skinned, glowing with moonlike radiance, throbbing with power, her being vibrated with the mantra "Om." That sound, carried on Brahma's breath, would eventually manifest as all the worlds.

Saraswati's grace, her Shakti, kindled Brahma's creative wisdom—as well as his passion to make universes.

From Saraswati's stringed instrument, sacred mantras took form in cosmic space. Saraswati showed Brahma how to shape these sounds into energies that could become space, fiery suns and planets, the earth with its landmasses and seas, and the heavenly and earthly creatures who dwell in all the spheres of the cosmos. Ecstatic, he called her Vagdevi, the goddess of speech and sound.

GODDESS OF CREATIVE SPEECH

All the Indian goddesses are connected to creativity, because Shakti is inherently creative. But Saraswati is the one whose cosmic function it is to embody the creative flow through language, speech, and sound—both cosmically and personally. If you are a writer or musician, you might recognize how the energy of Saraswati functions in you as the unmistakable drive that moves you when your work is flowing. The impulse of the Saraswati energy is passionate, but in an impersonal way. It's exciting, yet there's a subtle clarity about it. When Saraswati is in charge, you're operating from a deeper center than usual. The ego is out of the way, and even thought is harnessed to her agenda.

THE SARASWATI WOMAN

A Saraswati woman gets her deepest satisfaction from being in touch with that source of inspiration and creativity. She loves solving intellectual and artistic problems, discovering connections and new paradigms. She can pore over a text for hours, and what interests her in relationships is not so much communion as discovery. Caroline Myss, the medical intuitive who writes books in which she looks for connections between the Hindu Tantric structures in the subtle body, the Kabbalistic Tree of Life, and the Christian sacraments, is a classic Saraswati woman. So is Naomi Klein, the left-wing political science writer, a vibrant personality whose brain seems to spark new connections hourly. So is the spiritual teacher Gangaji. In an era when there are notoriously few meaty roles for actresses, actress and director Julie Delpy has created quirky, postconventional characters who incarnate Saraswati's quality of flowing speech, creative chutzpah, and romantic independence.

Saraswati women are often unconventional, not so much because they are trying to break the rules as because they don't notice that the rules are there. And though they can be beautiful and popular, their hearts will tend to be not so much in their relationships as in the intuitive realm where the connections are being downloaded. Saraswati women wrote the first novels, and have gone on writing novels to this day. In traditional societies like Greece, they were often the *hetaerae*, courtesans who escaped the prison of marriage to write poetry and advise statesmen like Pericles (whose mistress, Aspasia, Socrates claimed as one of his teachers). Margaret Fuller, the transcendentalist philosopher, was a Saraswati woman. Victoria Woodhull, the controversial early feminist and practiced con woman, was endowed with Saraswati's gifts. There's a sparky, surprising quality about Saraswati women. They have a profound ability to think on their feet, no doubt the result of their connection with the intuitive realms.

But Saraswati is also my sixth-grade science teacher, Mrs. Ballard, who first taught me the uses of rigor. And she's all the teachers who know how to ask the right question—the question that elicits a new way of thinking or a different way to look at a problem.

THE GODDESS OF FLOW

Saraswati's name means "the flowing one," and in one of her oldest forms, she is the goddess of a sacred river. It seems that once, Shiva opened his third eye to destroy the world by fire. Every deity panicked—except Saraswati. She took the form of a river and carried the fire to the bottom of the sea, where it remains until this day.

The Saraswati River flows from the highest causal heavens to the earth. It is hidden underground, invisible to human eyes. In the same way, the creative force flows invisibly through the universes, connecting the dense world of forms to the world of subtle intelligence and light. In paintings, Saraswati is often seen sitting next to a flowing stream, accompanied by her vehicle, the swan. The first part of her name, *saras*, means "flowing." The last part of her name, *vati*, means "one who is associated with."

Saraswati is associated with flow in all its aspects: with flow as water—the nourishing water of life, the water from which life first emerged, the water without which there can be no life, the water of the womb, the water of essential creativity. She's associated with the moon, which governs the flow of tides and which in Hindu iconography is said to radiate cooling beams of purity and grace; with intellect and inspiration, which flow from the subtlest level of mind; with eloquent speech, which at its best flows directly from that primal grace source; and with music. Classical Indian music characteristically flows in a way that Western classical music never quite replicates. Notes stream like water from the *sitar* of Ravi Shankar, or the *sarod* of Ali Akbar Khan. Their improvisation arises within a pattern, but it is never forced. Instead, it flows so easily and effortlessly that it can seem to come from the air itself. Indian musicians keep pictures of Saraswati on their altars, for musical inspiration is impossible without her.

THE CREATIVE MOMENT

In you and me, Saraswati flows through that moment when we choose a creative path or make an intention. She lives in the ever-new creative instant when inspiration arises within the field of your consciousness. When an idea takes form, you can find her as the inner impulse that comes from somewhere deeper than your ordinary mind, ready to dance on your tongue. She undulates in the stillness before the notes come forth and ripples forth as your power to make connections between apparently disparate things, as the power to understand language, as intelligence in all its forms, as insight and rhetoric, and as the intuitive knowing that lets you recognize your own awareness as the field of enlightenment.

In the old Vedic tradition, as in the Tantras, speech and mantra are regarded as creative powers. The Rg Veda speaks of how the world came into existence using a phrase uncannily like that in the Gospel of John: "In the beginning was the Word, and the Word was with the Creator, and the Word was the absolute."[1] That word, *pranava*, flows on the breath of the divine as Om. It evolves into fifty-two sound-energies that take form as the *matrikas*, or phonemes of the Sanskrit alphabet. The word *matrika* has the same root as the Latin *matrix* and *mater*. The fifty-two letters of the alphabet—the matrikas—are the "little mothers" of all that exists, while the overarching power of the matrika Shakti, the energy behind language, is the creative source or mother of worlds. At her subtlest, Saraswati lives in that pulsing space at the root of sound, where silence gives birth to creative possibility. A hymn to Saraswati by the Tantric sage Abhinavagupta praises this subtlest form of Saraswati like this: "No one knows your nature, nor is your inner reality known. You are the whole universe and you exist within it."[2]

SARASWATI TO THE RESCUE

In the realm of human action, Saraswati is the deity you invoke when you just need some help with your communication. You don't need to be seeking ultimate knowledge to invoke Saraswati. Like all the goddesses, she has both an exalted, otherworldly form, and a homey, intimate presence. You can call on Saraswati when you need help with your term paper or your overdue report. When your computer is frozen and tech support has run out of suggestions, Saraswati can help you bring it back to life.

She's the original energy behind the Internet, and she dances in the virtual world as the very force that facilitates connection. Computer wizards are children of Saraswati, heirs of the Vedic sages who deployed mantras in the service of their practical aims. If you ask people who played with computers in the early 1970s, you'll often hear them say that their ideas came out of nowhere. They arose in the ether, perhaps during a conversation or a late night's noodling over the mainframe in the Stanford computer lab with an open bag of Fritos and a bottle of wine. Saraswati is the cosmic downloader, the mother of innovation, who lives as the source code behind your computer's programs as well as in your inspirations and your capacity to follow them to a real-world manifestation.

SHADOW SARASWATI

The following is a useful thing to know, along with its corollary: when there are glitches in your communication—whether in receiving communication or expressing yourself—you are experiencing blocks in the Saraswati energy. Like all goddesses, Saraswati can operate in the sphere of maya, in shadow forms, to increase density and confusion. (Think of propaganda, lies, disinformation, Internet chatter, false rumors, formulaic fiction, and all varieties of spin.) In fact, since language *is* creative power, Saraswati's maya is perhaps the most persuasive and compelling of all. We shape reality through narrative. Every story we spin will literally change some piece of our world, for better or worse. Words can destroy reputations, dissolve family ties, bring down governments, start wars. A casual put-down, a big or small lie, an accusation made in error, and our own negative self-talk all linger in the heart, subtly and dramatically affecting the way we hold ourselves and others. Since the brain is wired to remember the negative much more easily than the positive, the shadow side of Saraswati can program you for a lifetime, as the skew of negative interpretations takes root in your memory and forms the lens through which you look at yourself and others.[3] Eloquence in the service of falsehood will make a lie seem true, until we lose all faith in words. It's said that in our age, the good stands on only one leg, the leg of truth. To fall into the shadow of Saraswati is to lose sight of the difference between truth and falsehood, and to be willing to use your gift for speech to spin tales that obscure truth for the sake of gain.

WORDS THAT BIND US

The sages point out that discursive thought itself is Saraswati's shadow. Anyone who sits for meditation will recognize the mayaic flow of the endless mentalogue that runs through his or her mind. And if you doubt the power of the goddess, an hour of trying to stop the mind will convince you that Saraswati's creative flow is indeed a river, or perhaps a fountain—endlessly running. You can't control her, you can only flow with her, using a mantra or your own awareness as a boat you can steer along those channels that lead to expansion and joy rather than suffering and constriction.

Abhinavagupta wrote of thought's binding tendency in a marvelous phrase: "The fettered soul is like a dancing girl who, wishing to leave the stage of maya, is collared by the doorkeeper in the form of thoughts and dragged back onto the stage."[4] Just as the shadow of Lakshmi's energy manifests as greediness and mindless accumulation, the shadow of Saraswati's Shakti can trap us through words unconnected to meaning, and through communication that doesn't consider the consequences of one's words. Just as Lakshmi's quality of giving and receiving needs to be understood and held in balance, Saraswati's flow of language and information also needs to be balanced—too little, and there's no communication; too much, and there's overload.

One reason it's so important to honor Saraswati in her liberating form is so that she can show us how to see through the mayaic masks of language, cut through the power that language has to turn the world opaque and dense. We need her grace to discriminate when the energy in words is thick or imbalanced, when we are hiding behind language, when communication is stuck. Then, the Saraswati Shakti will give us the words that open hearts, loosen stuck energies, help us partner with the flow of reality, enliven mantras, and show us the pathways into the fertile depths of creative stillness.

Contemplation: Your Relationship to the Goddess in the Form of Speech

With pen and paper nearby, take a few moments
to consider your own patterns of speech.

Look back over the last few days and notice some of the positive or inspired ways you have used the gift of speech. Remember the moments when your words felt true, authentic, wise, connected to your heart. Can you become aware of the feeling that this produced in you and in the people you were with?

What gifts did you give others through words? These might include offering clarity or insight in a way that it could be received, giving genuine praise, explaining something accurately, saying something witty or funny, speaking kindly, or being truthful.

Also, without judgment, notice some of the habitual speaking patterns you fell into—whatever they were: things like speaking to fill a silence, being unnecessarily sarcastic, gossiping negatively, complaining habitually, saying things you didn't mean because you felt they were more "acceptable." Notice when you felt inhibited about speaking, or when you chattered.

Is there a speech habit you'd like to change or break? Is there a gift of intellect or eloquence you'd love to receive? Are you longing for some spiritual, creative, or philosophical insight?

Now invoke the Goddess Saraswati. Imagine yourself sitting on the bank of a stream. Notice your surroundings. There are overhanging trees, soft grass on the bank, flowering vines and shrubs.

You see before you the luminous form of the Goddess Saraswati. Her skin is fair and her eyes are lustrous, with a deep peace radiating from them. She is dressed in a white sari, and around her neck are pearls. She carries a book in her hand.

She is gazing at you, a half-smile on her face. As you gaze at her, a stream of pearly light begins to flow from her third eye into yours. As you inhale, you feel this light entering your own third eye and suffusing your body with glowing, soft luminosity.

The goddess invites you to speak to her. What lack do you feel in your own creative life? How would you like your mind and speech to flower, to become more refined? What spiritual boon, what inner opening do you long for?

Tell the Goddess Saraswati your wishes. Ask her what you need to understand about your relationship with language, speech, and creativity.

Wait to receive an answer, and see if you can discern her response without overthinking it. The response may come as an image, a feeling, or an insight. Or it may arise later, perhaps through something you read or the words of another person.

THE POWER OF REFINEMENT

When you are attuned to the ways of Saraswati, her subtle energy can refine your speech and hone your perception. In particular, she'll help you discern the ways language can be used to liberate you—and how speech becomes compulsive or harmful.

FIGURE 11: THE GODDESS SARASWATI

As we know, the social media explosion is communication on steroids, and Internet speech can work with equal facility to liberate or harm. An inspiring message from a friend, shared over Twitter, inspires a group of students to volunteer to build houses for the homeless. An Internet prank played on a high school girl triggers her suicide.

Saraswati energy embodies the power of discernment, *viveka*. Viveka is our ability to separate our lower-self impulses from the ones that come from the higher self. It's no accident that Saraswati's bird is the swan, the hamsa. In mythology, viveka is represented by the Paramahamsa, the Great Swan—Saraswati's vehicle—who lives in a lake in the Himalayas. It is said that if you pour milk into the lake, the Paramahamsa's beak will act as a filter, separating the milk from the water, so he only drinks the milk. One of Saraswati's gifts is the discrimination to separate truthful, liberating knowledge—and words—from the kind of information that creates confusion and fear. She is, for this reason, the prime deity of wisdom and knowledge—especially the knowledge transmitted heart to heart, by the speech of the teacher.

THE ORAL TRADITION

In ancient times, knowledge was passed down orally. Nothing was written down. You couldn't just get knowledge out of a book. Teaching was transmitted through the voice, which meant that every phrase or teaching would be infused with the state of the teacher, as only spoken words can be. It was transmitted through mantras, the words of power that connect the mundane mind to the higher mind and will, and ultimately to the Shakti herself. Because speech actually carried the transmission of the entire culture, speech was worshipped as a deity in Vedic civilization. The gift of speaking truthful teachings and reciting mantras was considered one of the manifestations of Saraswati, and it carried great power.

As the power of Lakshmi is associated with rulers, the power of Saraswati is associated with priests and scholars. Because learning was such a respected and even sacred activity, you had to be chosen to learn not just sacred knowledge, but any knowledge, and you had to demonstrate again and again your capacity to hold it.

The student sat near the master, became very receptive, and listened without judgment, taking in what the master said totally. The master spoke from the heart of his or her own knowledge, with the intention of infusing it into the student's heart. You listened attentively, like a vessel open to receive. Then you held the knowledge in your heart. Again, you fully held it. You submitted to it, you let it work in you by contemplating the words, not trying to interpret or argue with them. At this stage, the teaching had to be received fully, just as it was being transmitted. Only after you had held it and let it permeate your heart and mind, did you begin to question it and offer interpretation. At that point, the original truth would have become part of you, and it would begin to inspire you. You would start to have inspired thoughts, to bring up trains of associations. At that point, you might express the truth in your own words or consider it in a unique way. Then you would have the capacity to give it back—to other students, or in writing.

The whole process would have taken place through the very subtle medium of speech being spoken and heard—Saraswati as speech meeting Saraswati as mind. You always surrounded learning with mantras that would purify and open you to knowledge. You would offer your voice to the goddess before you chanted. So the process of receiving knowledge became very sacred. The teacher and the books were treated with enormous respect—anyone who's studied in India will remember being told never to put books on the floor out of respect for the truth they contain. In one of the prayers that teachers and student chant together, there is a line that says, "May our knowledge turn into light." Saraswati is the Shakti that can turn knowledge into light.

THE SARASWATI STORY

There is more than one story of Saraswati's origin. As we've seen, the root story describes her arising from the mouth of the creative father-god, Brahma. There's an obvious parallel with the origin myth of Athena, the Greek goddess of wisdom, who arose out of Zeus's head. Yet Saraswati is not Brahma's creation, nor is she his daughter. Saraswati embodies Brahma's creative power.

To continue the tale, Brahma takes one look at her and falls wildly in love—as so many of us, ever since, have fallen in love with our own creative power. He grows a fifth face in order to look at her. In one version of the story, she curses him for this act of primordial sexual harassment, saying that in the future, no temples will be built to him. In the more accepted version, he joins his essence with hers, and together they produce Manu, who does the actual supervision of the evolutionary process and its accompanying protocols.

SARASWATI AND KRISHNA

That's what we might call the official (because most often told) version. But Indian spiritual culture has many schools and sects, and several of them claim Saraswati. One version of the story has Krishna dividing himself into male and female, Purusha (pure spirit) and Prakriti (the energy that will become matter). His feminine half takes on five forms, one of which is Saraswati.[5] Her lovely function is to fill the world of material reality with insight, knowledge, and learning.

In another version of this story, Saraswati arises as the tongue not of Brahma, but of Vishnu, of whom Krishna is an avatar. As such, she is the co-wife of Lakshmi. Since Lakshmi embodies wealth, power, and fertility, while Saraswati stands for spiritual and aesthetic values, scholar David Kinsley points out that their rivalry might represent the age-old tension between the sensual and the spiritual, or *bhukti* (enjoyment) and *mukti* (spiritual liberation). My guru, who often talked about goddesses as if he knew them personally, used to say that though they are both jealous of each other, Saraswati is more jealous than Lakshmi, so it is politic to offer worship to Saraswati first.

It's true that the children of Saraswati—scholars, musicians, writers, research scientists, and certainly spiritual teachers—often exhibit fierce envy and malice toward anyone who seems to receive more praise than they. Composer Antonio Salieri's rivalry with Mozart, the subject of the film *Amadeus*, is a classic case of Saraswati-style jealousy. A true Saraswati person doesn't much care about money, but she cares deeply about fame and reputation. She wants to be recognized as the most accomplished, and it pains Saraswati people when a rival is elevated.

Saraswati's jealousy eventually makes Vishnu decide to divorce her in favor of the sweeter tempered Lakshmi. In fact, in all the stories, Saraswati ends up alone.

SARASWATI'S DIVORCE

In the more popular version of Saraswati's story, it's Brahma who divorces her. Brahma becomes increasingly disaffected with Saraswati's refusal to carry out the traditional wifely role. She wants to spend all her time in study and meditation, tending her inspirations. She doesn't cook; in fact, she won't even come to meals, and when she does, she's either totally aloof or chatting all the time about esoteric matters that don't interest Brahma. Brahma—who is after all, the original patriarch—wants a more pliable wife. He gets more and more annoyed.

Matters come to a head when Brahma and Saraswati are supposed to preside together at a religious ritual. She promises to be there but gets so immersed in her study that she doesn't show up until the ritual is almost finished. "That's it," Brahma says. "We're finished." He divorces her and takes another wife.

Ever since then, Saraswati has been alone. Unlike Lakshmi, who's the archetypal consort-wife, and Kali, who has a relationship (albeit a wildly unconventional one) with her Tantric husband Shiva, Saraswati has no partner.

As an archetype of the feminine, Saraswati is the solitary woman, the scholar at her desk, the yogini or the nun who gives up conventional life for something subtler, more pure. She's Jane Austen, writing her novels in the drawing room. She's the lonely woman scientist married to her lab, the dedicated violinist, the artist in her studio, Dian Fossey choosing her Rwandan gorillas over her Australian lover.

In the West we have the image of the virgin as the untouched soul, the soul who is so drawn to the light of wisdom that she doesn't get involved in the world. She's apart, aloof, but she also stands for the profound blissfulness of solitude, meditation, inner contemplation, and hours of practicing our instrument or our craft. She's the offering we make to perfection. Saraswati has this virginal, above-the-world quality, which teaches us that we need dedication and immersion in order to extract the subtle truths of life and art. It's also telling that in the original myth she has no interest in traditional religious ritual. She is, essentially, beyond conventional forms, tuned into the vibrational reality of direct insight and intuition.

But of course, there's another side to Saraswati's marital debacle. In traditional societies, and even in contemporary ones, a woman who dedicates her life to interior pursuits will often have to give up partnership, either for her own reasons or because few men will put up with a partner who is so absorbed in her own creations.

I'm a Saraswati woman, and I can tell you this from personal experience. In my early thirties, after having been in various partner relationships, I began to feel that I would have to choose between being partnered and being a serious practitioner as a writer and meditator. It wasn't a choice that every literary or scholarly or spiritually oriented woman would have to make, but for me it seemed necessary. I had a pattern of making my partner relationships primary, letting them take over my life to such an extent that I would let everything else go. It was only when I was unpartnered that my practice seemed to flourish. In the make-it-or-break-it moment of considering what I wanted my life to be about, I chose practice.

It was a momentous, life-changing decision, and it was probably the decision that made possible any spiritual and writerly progress I've managed to make in the years since. There have been moments of loneliness, though not so many as you might suspect. I believe I would make the same decision again. It is almost as if the archetype inside my soul made the choice, because nothing else would have allowed my life to unfold for my inner growth.

I've seen this solitary tendency in many Saraswati women, though we often tend to fight it. Janey is a case in point. She runs two yoga studios, teaches yoga, counsels scholars, makes films, and spends her life promoting the good, the true, and the beautiful. In the twenty years I've known her, she's had only one boyfriend, and the relationship didn't last. Janey is strikingly pretty and has immense social gifts; her friends are always on her case about why she isn't with a guy, and she claims she'd like a partner. Yet it never happens, as if something in her field, in her inner DNA, has decided that fulfilling her destiny as a teacher and yogini demands a kind of intense focus that partnership would preclude.

Another Saraswati woman, Ariella, has become a contemporary voice for spiritual awareness—an archetypal Saraswati quality. She writes with style and immense rigor, like the swan separating the milk of truth from the muddy water of today's spiritual marketplace. Though she longs for a family and a life partner, her romantic relationships tend not to last, or at least not in the form that her Lakshmi side would prefer. It is as if the Saraswati energy in her simply demands to be expressed as a kind of spiritual solitude, continually asking her to rise to the mandate that goes with the gifts.

In fact, many men with an abundance of Saraswati energy have a hard time with partnership. When you're a channel for Saraswati's flow of inspiration, and especially when you've committed yourself to the rigor that she often demands, you may not have the space for ordinary relationships. The wives and children of male artists, scientists, and philosophers often have to put up with absent, glazed-over eyes at dinner while their Saraswati-ridden father attends to his inner voice. Alexandra Styron, in her memoir about her father, the novelist William Styron (author of *Sophie's Choice*), writes about the fatherly rages and episodes of inattentiveness that punctuated her childhood. In one passage, she wonders whether such an artist would be kinder to abstain from conventional partnership. Saraswati's world is supramaterial, and she has little patience with the mess down here. She plays in the intellect and in the realm of inspiration. The physical world seems to her to be more of an arena where inspiration can be contained or expressed than a place to be engaged for its own sake.

SARASWATI AS MUSE

Of course, Saraswati women are not always artists or thinkers. Often they are muses. A woman with an affinity for Saraswati may long to be the muse of a great artist or writer, or run a salon for intellectuals and artists. My friend Kathy had a successful career as an art dealer (another Saraswati vocation), but she also had muse-like relationships with several gifted thinkers, including Joseph Campbell. She possesses the gift of being able to ask the right question, the question that ignites Saraswati's flow in another person; she also has Saraswati's gift of purposeful gab, the ability to keep a conversation sparky and deep. Barbara Epstein, the late editor of the *New York Review of Books,* incarnated the Saraswati muse energy, not only in her loving way of helping writers bring their work to its best level, but also in her friendships with several generations of writers, including W. H. Auden, Gore Vidal, and scores of others. When her marriage to another distinguished editor ended, she had a long relationship with a writer who worked the long hours that she did, and whom she declined, in the end, to marry. She also recognized the Saraswati need for radical independence.

Saraswati is dispassionate, which is why Saraswati people make good mediators. Saraswati can help you stand outside your emotions and observe them. She is also critical; her swan's beak has an unerring nose for the half-hearted offering or the sloppy sentence. Taylor Mali, a poet and Saraswati-inspired teacher, declared his eighth grade classroom a "like"-free zone, forbidding kids to lard their sentences with the modern teenager's favorite filler word, as in, "I, like, wore blue yesterday."

Each of the goddesses is rigorous in her own way. Saraswati's rigor has to do with keeping the mind and heart pure, one-pointed, and careful. She's a proofreader, a timekeeper, a perfectionist. Think of the young violinist, practicing for hours every day, or the mathematician checking and rechecking his proofs. Inspiration tends to come to the person who courts Saraswati with effort and rigor—and therefore one of her gifts is that aspect of genius that Thomas Carlyle called "the infinite capacity for taking pains."

COURTING INSIGHT

The word *insight* means the vision that sees into something, often something that has been opaque. Insights arise all the time, yet for many of us, they are invisible, and we have to listen hard to discern that voice of intuition.

Because Saraswati is so subtle, her voice is often hidden. When Saraswati takes form as intuition, she can show up as a small voice, often hard to hear behind the chatter of the mind. So when you want to receive an answer or an inspiration, you often have to prime it.

You can prime intuition by asking yourself a question and then holding still until the answer comes. This process works best if it's a question you really care about; inspiration doesn't arise so easily when you're only casually interested in the answers. It's also important that you be able to wait for the answer to arise. Often when you're courting inspiration, you'll ask the question, then try to figure out the answer mentally. There's nothing wrong with thinking something through—in fact, it's a crucial part of the process. To receive insight, you also have to go past the thinking mind, especially the inner, critical voices in the mind. You have to get quiet enough, focused enough, and patient enough to discern the voice of the inspiration or intuition.

There are two ways to practice downloading intuition. One way is through some form of automatic writing. You ask a question and then start to write, without censoring. The second is more subtle and involves a very deep, interior listening.

I learned how to do the first process when I was trying to cure a writer's block. Being a perfectionist, I used to spend so much time agonizing over perfect sentences that writing was torturous, and I was never satisfied with what I did. At one point, someone suggested a tactic that Julia Cameron and other writing teachers later made famous. The idea was to decide on your topic and then write without censorship. So I would ask myself a question or give myself a topic—mundane questions at that point, like, "What does it mean to be friends with someone?" and later, spiritual topics like "Why do we meditate?" or "What does it mean to be truthful?" Then, I would just start typing and continue till there was nothing more to come out.

It worked. Somewhere in the mess on the paper there would be the insights I needed, the truths I was looking for. So whenever I had to write something, I'd begin with this process of regurgitating it onto paper, resisting the urge to edit as I went along. Later, I'd sculpt the mess of words into an article or a chapter or a talk.

I still didn't know how to harvest, or even hear or trust, the real flashes of inner intuition, the sudden insights about direction that we sense are being given by the Shakti, but which can be indistinguishable from all the other thoughts in the mind.

LISTENING TO INTUITION

Then, in the 1980s, I had a life-shifting experience. I was scheduled to give a talk at an intensive workshop for about two thousand people. I was to speak right after the lunch break. The subject had been set in advance, the event carefully planned, and I'd been perfecting the talk for several days. As an introvert, to feel comfortable speaking in front of such a large audience, I needed to be well prepared.

Right before lunch, to my horror, another speaker unexpectedly began to speak on my topic. As I listened to her covering one after another of my points,

I panicked. I had a talk to give in just two hours, and my planned presentation was rapidly becoming redundant.

I had no choice: I turned inside and asked for help. I waited intently, listening for a cue, a hint, a word. After a while, from a deep reservoir of inner spaciousness, I heard a sentence arise, word by word. If I hadn't been desperately listening for an answer, I would have ignored it as just another stray thought. But because my need was great, I clung to each thought. I wrote them down. And for the next hour, I listened inside, writing down the ideas as they came more or less randomly into my mind. I gave the talk, and it was fine. Most important, I'd received a crash course in listening to inspiration. What I discovered in that afternoon is that inspiration is always there, always available—what we need is the motivation to seek it and the container to hold onto it.

BREATHING IN INSPIRATION

The English word *inspiration* comes from the Latin *inspire*, which means to breathe. In the Greek and Kabbalistic traditions, inspiration was sometimes described as breathing in God, who is breathing life into us. Just as in the Bible, God is said to have breathed life into the original man, so the Vedic *Devi Sukta* (Hymn to the Goddess) has the goddess saying, "My breathing forth gives birth to all the worlds and yet extends beyond them."[6] Deity meditation practices nearly always include a moment when we breathe in the energy or the light of the deity, literally taking her energy into our own being. We can breathe that energy in her Kali form, as power itself, fast and strong like a rapidly flowing river or vast wave of light. We can breathe her in as the gentle power of abundance and beauty: Lakshmi, who offers us nourishing sweetness. And we can gently inhale her as Saraswati, the subtle clarity that connects the mind to the subtle world and infuses our thoughts and speech with wisdom. The gift of Saraswati is said to be the power to speak truth—such that even your casual words turn out to be true. When you are in tune with this goddess, speech comes from the place of truth inside you. In Saraswati's realm, words are a direct expression of cosmic realities, not superficial and meaningless.

Asking Questions of the Goddess

In this exercise, we'll contact Saraswati as the power of inspiration. Find a quiet place where you can be alone to complete it, and make sure to have your journal and pen nearby.

Find a question that concerns something important in your life at this time. It doesn't have to be something deep and profound, but it's best if it's a question that is important to you.

Write your question down. Read through it a few times.

Then, close your eyes and recite nine times this Saraswati mantra:

Om aim saraswatyai namaha
ohm eye-m suh-ruh-swuh-tyai nuh-muh-huh

I bow to the Goddess of Speech

Ask inwardly for an answer to your question, stating the question clearly. Imagine the form of Saraswati before you, recalling the image of the goddess as a luminous beauty with almond eyes and lustrous black hair, milky skin with a hint of rose, delicate features, and a stringed instrument in her hand. Or feel her as a presence, an energy like a luminous white cloud.

Breathe with the sense that you are breathing with her. With each exhalation, allow your question to flow toward her as an offering. As you inhale, allow a subtle current of knowing to flow from her into your mind, entering through your forehead.

Now begin to write, not censoring, letting the words or the image flow onto the paper.

Read over what you have written. Ask, "Is there more?" and take down whatever arises.

INSIGHT ARISING

Saraswati's inspiration arises in two ways. In both Indian and Kabbalistic traditions, it's said to come in the form of arousal from above—from the invisible realms—and also as arousal from below. Arousal from above is the download from the Shakti that seems to arrive full-blown in the mind—as in the musical downloads that Mozart received or the inner voice that dictated "Kubla Khan" to the English poet Coleridge. When you're courted by inspiration, it can feel like taking dictation and can show up at random times. Songwriter Randy Newman, who seems to have an active dialogue with his muse, once scolded her for downloading a song lyric while he was negotiating traffic on a

Los Angeles freeway. "Don't give me a line when I can't write it down!" he is reported to have shouted at her. "If you're going to show up while people are driving, go bother Leonard Cohen."[7]

Arousal from below is the inspiration that comes up as a result of your own effort, your rigorous practice, your research, and the hours you sit in the chair. Musician Brian Eno, in an interview on the creative process, says that it "requires a practice of some kind. It frequently happens that you're treading water for quite a long time. Nothing really dramatic seems to be happening . . . And then suddenly everything seems to lock together in a different way. It's like a crystallization point where you can't detect any single element having changed.[8] One writer calls it "ass-piration"—meaning that it comes from keeping your ass in front of the computer for a certain amount of time until the gift starts to flow.

In studies of creative artists and scientists, there's evidence that the great inspirations come to people who've put in endless hours of practice or contemplation. You tussle over a problem in science: How is the genetic code constructed? What happens to objects when they are freed from the pull of gravity? Then, at some point, when you've worked it over as much as you can, there will be a moment of relaxation, when the mind shuts off. In that moment, the inspiration—the "Aha"—arrives.

Of course, it's because of your effort that you have a container for the insight. It's the same with spiritual experience. "The reason to keep working is almost to build a certain mental tone, like people talk about body tone," says Eno. "You have to [be able to] move quickly when the time comes, and the time might come very infrequently . . ."[9] When I'm teaching, I get many questions from people who've had a big moment of recognition or insight—or an inner opening to the energy of the higher self—and felt unsettled by it or just sorry because it didn't last. But after practicing for some time, after cooking their mind in meditation for a few months or even a few years, not only does the initial experience make sense, not only is that big opening no longer scary, but they actually start to integrate it at the level of subtle experience so that it becomes a natural part of their being. It's only after we've practiced and created a strong container that the states we experience in meditation become integrated into our bodies and minds, and the flashes of insight actually become deep wisdom that can be translated into daily life.

So whether it manifests as inspired ideas, art, or scientific or spiritual insight, the Saraswati Shakti is the inspiration that arises through personal effort and also from the subtle noosphere, the collective higher consciousness. Her Shakti expresses itself through the inner work we do to hone the mind, to study, to practice—the careful, rigorous effort that allows us to become a container for wisdom and inspiration.

Courting Saraswati for Creativity

For this exercise, set aside half an hour when you can
be alone. Use pen and paper, rather than a computer, so
that you can feel the tactile sensation of having a writing
implement in your hand and moving it over the page.

Begin by closing your eyes, and repeating the mantra "Om aim saraswatee namaha om" nine times, out loud or silently. Sit for a few minutes breathing with the sense that you are breathing in clear, luminous energy from the air. Turn your attention toward your heart, and ask that your inner power of inspiration, the sacred feminine in the form of insight, flow through your pen.

Start with the phrase: "The sacred feminine asks to express herself within me as . . ." and write without stopping for at least five minutes—allowing whatever comes out to emerge. Then write: "I will know that the sacred feminine energy is expressing herself through me by the following signs . . ." Again, write without censorship until nothing more comes out.

ALTERNATIVE PRACTICE OPTION

You may also do this exercise as a song. Simply open your mouth, and without censoring begin to sing: "The divine feminine wants to express herself through me as . . ." Let the words and notes come spontaneously.

Then sing: "I will know that the sacred feminine energy is expressing herself through me by the following signs . . ."

You might want to do the singing version of this exercise while walking or while in the car—sometimes moving your body makes the practice freer.

You may also draw, paint, or dance your intuition—whatever would allow you to express the inspiration of the sacred feminine at this moment.

Saraswati

suh-ruh-swuh-tee—Flowing One

Other Names for Saraswati:
Bharati (*bhah-ruh-tee*)—Eloquence
Mahavidya (*muh-hah-vid-yah)*—Great Knowledge
Vach (*vahch*)—Speech
Brahmi (*brah-mee*)—Vastness
Sharada (*shah-ruh-dah*)—Autumnal
Vani (*vah-nee*)—Speech or Sound

Goddess of:
- speech
- learning
- music
- creative intuition
- insight
- spiritual discrimination

Recognize Saraswati in:
- the swan (her mount)
- crystal
- clear-running water
- mantras
- flowing speech
- refined singers and musicians
- inspired writing, oratory, and scholarship
- computer programs
- computers
- libraries
- classrooms
- Google searches
- language
- intellectual acuity
- literary conferences, writers' workshops, bookstores, and mathematical formulations

- musical instruments, especially stringed instruments
- the first quarter of the moon

Invoke Saraswati for:
- study
- learning
- enhanced memory
- musical skill
- skill and eloquence in speaking or writing
- deeper meditation
- insight
- answers to questions—both intellectual and practical
- mathematical insight
- help with computer glitches
- communication problems
- taking tests
- learning languages
- intuition
- auspicious speech

Bija Mantra
Aim (*ai-eem*)
Seed of creative speech and inspiration

Invocational Mantra
Om aim hrim saraswatyai namaha

ohm ai-eem hreem suh-rah-swah-tyai nuh-muh-huh

Om, I bow to the flowing one whose essence is wisdom

Gayatri Mantra
Om saraswatyai cha vidmahe
Brahmapatnyai cha dhimahi
Tannah devi prachodayat.

ohm suh-ruh-swuh-tyai chuh vid-muh-hey
bruh-muh puht-nyai chuh dhee-muh-hee
tun-nuh day-vee pruh-cho-duh-yah-tuh

Om, may we come to know Saraswati
May we meditate on the consort of Brahma
May that Goddess impel us on our path.
Under Meditation Verse:

Meditation Verse
Ya kundendu-tushara-hara dhavala
Ya shubra-vastravrta
Ya vina-vara-danda-mandita-kara
Ya shveta-padmasana
Ya brahmacyuta-shankara-prabhrutibhir
Devaih sada vandita
Sa mam patu saraswati bhagavati
Nihshesha-jadyapaha

yah kun-dayn-doo-too-shah-ruh hah-ruh duh-vuh-lah
yah shuh-bruh-vuhs-trah-vri-tah
yah vee-nah-vuh-ruh-duhn-duh-muhn-dee-tuh-kuh-rah
yah shwey-tuh puhd-mah-suh-nah
yah bruh-mah-chyu-tuh-shuhn-kuh-ruh pruh-broo-tee-beer
day-vai suh-dah vun-dee-tah
sah mahm pah-tu suh-ruh-swuh-tee bhug-guh-vuh-tee
nih-shay-shuh-jah-dyah-pah-hah

May Saraswati, goddess of learning, protect me by removing my
intellectual dullness. She is white as the kunda flower, the moon, or snow.
She is dressed in white and seated on a white lotus flower. She plays the
lute and is adored by all the gods, led by Brahma, Vishnu, and Shiva.

Saraswati's colors: white, yellow
Saraswati's flowers: white lotus, jasmine
Saraswati's mount: swan
Saraswati's consort: Brahma (for a time)

CHAPTER 8

Sita

Goddess of Devotion and Mystical Submission

The tears we shed for the Beloved are pearls . . .
Grief for the Beloved is the polishing of the heart and soul.

RUMI

Can you imagine the eyes of Sita when she refused another test?
When she looked at Rama, a man she loved enough to die for, a man who was a god, and
knew it was over? Can you imagine her eyes in that moment, as she asked her mother to take
her back, to swallow her back into the earth? I think my eyes are like that now, leaving you.

JASON SCHNEIDERMAN

amakrishna, the great nineteenth-century lover of the Goddess, used to weep whenever he thought of Sita. For years, so did I. Sita floats on an ocean of tears. Sita—beautiful, pure, the maiden bride, the stolen and then abandoned wife—stands as the radical interface of love and suffering much as Mary stands for the loving, suffering feminine in Christian culture. Sita exists only for love. She personifies loyalty. She incarnates devotion. On an archetypal level, she stands for the feminine principle of loving submission—submission to the masculine, submission to the divine, submission to life itself. We can see Sita, the daughter of the earth, in the natural world and mourn the suffering of this earth goddess as we watch the life of our forests destroyed by clear-cutting, our waterways polluted by chemicals, entire species dying out.

As a human archetype, Sita lives as the virgin bride, the traditional wife who accepts her husband's opinion as the final authority. She's also the integrity of a woman who keeps her vows and protects her own intact quality, her purity of soul.

Sita is an avatar of Lakshmi, whose habit it is to accompany her divine consort Vishnu whenever he incarnates. When Rama, the king-hero avatar of

Vishnu, appears on Earth, Lakshmi comes as Sita, just as she is said to have come later as Krishna's erotic paramour, Radha. In paintings and statues, you nearly always see Rama and Sita sitting together on a single throne, and if you practice *kirtan,* devotional chanting, you hear their names chanted as one—Sita-ram. There is no question that Sita is Rama's Shakti; indeed, she has almost no existence without him. The heroine of the *Ramayana,* the national epic of India and a core mythological text of Hinduism, Sita is *the* icon of traditional Indian womanhood. Even today, unmarried girls in India are taught to be like Sita—sweet, obedient, faithful, and above all chaste. In the 1980s, when the *Ramayana* was performed as a fifty-part maxi-series on Doordarshan TV, the whole country watched it; TV screens were set up in villages and in city streets and parks, and people would often perform worship in front of the screens. There was a huge national furor when the actress playing Sita appeared in public smoking a cigarette—how could Sita, the very incarnation of purity, smoke?

DAUGHTER OF EARTH

Sita's name means "furrow." She was literally found in a furrow, discovered as a glowing, golden child by her famous father, King Janaka, and accepted as a gift of the Earth. Janaka is celebrated in several Upanishadic texts as the quintessential enlightened king. He is a profound seeker of wisdom, a disciple to several of the forest sages whose teachings form the heart of nondual Vedantic philosophy. Janaka represents Eastern masculine spirituality at its best: detached, wise, rational, authoritative, ruling over the physical realm yet always slightly above it. Janaka had learned to identify his real Self with the nondual consciousness beyond forms—not with the body, with his thoughts, or with his emotional human self, and certainly not with his role as a king. In one famous story, Janaka is approached by a proud young renunciant, Shuka, who believes that he has nothing to learn from such a worldly king. He finds Janaka sitting on his throne with one leg thrust into a fire, while the other is being massaged by a beautiful woman: Janaka's awareness is so poised in the absolute that pleasure and pain are equal for him. From one point of view, we could say that Janaka is the first real Tantrika in the world of Indian philosophy. He lives the life of a king, sports with his consorts and courtesans, and carries out the duties of a ruler, yet maintains yogic equanimity in the midst of it all.

Sita arrives in the life of this profoundly detached being as an emissary and a reminder of the values of earthiness. To those familiar with the old rituals of early agricultural societies, it would seem likely that she is born as the result of a ritual act of Janaka's—perhaps even a ritual coupling with a woman who represented the land. We could say that she incarnates the land, the feminine Earth principle: passive, fertile, beautiful, ultimately supportive—in need of the dynamic masculine to "awaken, arouse, and inseminate her."[1]

At the same time, the fact that she is Janaka's daughter argues that she shares his capacity for enlightened renunciation and devotion—which she will enact through her own yogic path of absolute submission to her husband and her fate. All we know of her early life is that she is beautiful and good, famous for her beauty and virtue, and sought after by the princes of every city-state in the land.

Among the princes who come to seek Sita's hand is Rama, prince of Ayodhya, a hero as well as a man of transcendent virtue: Janaka's ideal son-in-law. Rama comes to the contest for Sita's hand (which he wins handily by bending an outsized bow) as the hope of his generation, heir to his father's kingdom, and the eldest of four brothers who are all devoted to each other. Like Janaka, Rama is a Vedantic adept; when Rama meets Sita he has just completed an intensive spiritual training with his guru, the sage Vasistha. Vasistha taught that the world as we know it is unreal, that everything is a dream within consciousness itself, brought into being by the illusions of the mind. In short, by the time Rama sees Sita he is beyond passion and attachment, committed entirely to dharma, the cosmic law that unfolds through right action and submission to the laws of life. So even though she is beautiful and alluring, Rama's marriage to Sita is more about dharma than passion. It is dynastic, but beyond that, it is archetypal: the righteous prince, schooled in the quintessential masculine principle of spirit-as-transcendental-reality, joins the quintessential feminine principle of embodied form. The soon-to-be king marries the land and literally plows her, thus insuring fertility and prosperity for the kingdom. The masculine joins with the feminine, heaven marries the earth, purusha ("the soul") marries prakriti ("matter"). It is a cosmic mating, like a key entering a lock, the hero claiming his foundational power, incarnate in his mate.

THE EXILE

Back home in Ayodhya, a drama of betrayal is about to unfold. Rama's stepmother, his father's youngest queen Kaikeyi, has had her mind poisoned by an evil maidservant who has been telling her that it is in the queen's best interest to have Rama step aside in favor of Kaikeyi's own son, Bharata.

Kaikeyi had once saved her husband's life, for which he had promised her one unconditional boon, a boon he was bound to honor no matter what the cost.

Kaikeyi asks that Rama be banished from the kingdom for fourteen years. As a matter of honor, the king complies—though the grief will eventually kill him—and Rama obeys his father's command. Sita begs to accompany him, along with one of his brothers, Laksmana. The now-favored son Bharata swears that he will hold the throne in trust until Rama returns.

When Rama tries to persuade Sita not to come with him to the forest, she says, "Deprived of her consort, a woman cannot live; you cannot doubt this truth as far as I'm concerned . . . O thou of pure soul, I shall remain sinless by following piously in the steps of my consort, for a husband is a god."[2] Because of her devotion, Sita is what the *Manava Dharma Shastra* describes as the ideal Hindu wife, who is always faithful to her husband: "Though destitute of virtue, or seeking pleasure elsewhere, or devoid of good qualities, a husband must be constantly worshipped as a god by a faithful wife."[3] Such a woman is called a *pativrata* ("husband-vowed"), one who is committed to unconditional selfless loyalty to her husband, who is essentially her deity. Her vow has all the power of yoga; through her intense selflessness, a pativrata generates yogic fire, and this gives her immense *siddhis*, or yogic powers. Of course, modern feminist scholars see her as receptive to the point of passivity. Jungian psychologist Gareth Hill would describe her as an archetype of what he calls the "static feminine"—completely yin, unconditionally supportive, and utterly faithful.

The forest becomes the stage for the drama at the heart of the *Ramayana*. Trouble starts when a demoness falls in love with Rama. When Rama rejects her by pointing out that he is already married to Sita, the demoness invites her own brother, the powerful demon-king Ravana, to steal Sita. Ravana is delighted. Not only is Sita beautiful, but she is the prized possession of an enemy king. Ravana arranges for a magician named Maricha to take the form of a magical golden deer, who so entrances Sita that she begs Rama to catch him so she can make him her pet. In a sense, Sita brings on her own fate, for Ravana seizes her while Rama and his brother Laksmana are chasing the deer, and he bears her away to his island kingdom of Lanka.

Ravana expects that Sita will realize her powerlessness and give into him. He hasn't reckoned on Sita's radical fidelity to Rama. Frustrated in his attempts to woo her, he ends by confining her to a barren prison, where she stays for years until Rama rescues her, aided by the monkey-god Hanuman and an army of simian warriors. During her long captivity, Sita is taunted by demons and visited daily by Ravana in his demonic splendor, demanding her surrender and threatening to kill her if she refuses him. Sita despairs completely, but she

FIGURE 12: RAMA AND SITA

never stops her one-pointed contemplation of Rama. At one point, Ravana tells her that if she will not become his wife he will cut her up into pieces and eat her. Sita replies that if she wanted to she could incinerate him with her yogic fire, the accumulated power of her fidelity and chastity. "I do not do this only because Rama has not given me permission!" she says. When Ravana tries to convince her that Rama is dead by showing her a magically produced head of Rama, Sita's main thought is that Rama's death must have been the result of some flaw in her devotion.

Having followed her through this ordeal, we can hardly believe it when the rescued Sita is brought before Rama, and he refuses to take her back. We feel her shock that he cannot recognize the power of her purity and love. Rama stands in the dharma of patriarchy, which holds that a woman who has lived with a man is considered, de facto, impure. He declares that he fought Ravana only for the sake of family honor, not because he is attached to Sita. He says it would be improper for him to let her return to his bed after she has been with Ravana, who must have had sex with her while she was living in his palace. He makes her what he considers a generous offer of protection: "You can marry one of my brothers," he says, "or one of the demon warriors. But I won't have you."

Sita swears that she was taken against her will and that she has remained faithful to Rama throughout her captivity. If he rejects her, she says, there is nothing left for her but death. She tells Rama's brother Laksmana to make a fire. She walks around Rama three times with folded hands, and then prays to Agni, the god of fire: "Since my heart has always been true to Rama, give me your protection." She steps into the fire. The fire blazes up around her, leaving her untouched. Agni himself emerges from the flames, leading Sita out of them. Even her flower garland is still dewy, unsinged by the flames. As Agni presents her to Rama, he declares that her purity is unmatched in all the worlds.

At this, Rama melts. He takes her back, and together they return in triumph to Ayodya.

It seems that everything will turn out well. Then Rama begins hearing rumors. The citizens of his kingdom are whispering that Ravana had his way with the queen, and that Rama is nothing but a cuckold. To stop the gossip and to save face (though he calls it setting a good example for his subjects), Rama decides to banish Sita, even though he has just learned that she is pregnant with twins. He has Laksmana take her to a deserted place and abandon her in the forest.

Experiencing the Passion of Sita

This is a practice that comes from the Christian tradition, and it's
a powerful way to tune in to the mystical quality of sorrow and
sacrifice. We normally don't think of sorrow as a spiritual feeling, and
especially we don't think of it as a spiritual process. So this practice
can open you to a new and radical relationship with grief that will
let you bring out stored grief as well as fresh grief and express it
not in broken sobs, but in cleansing, healing tears. Find a quiet
place to contemplate Sita's passion in this three-part exercise.

PART ONE: IMAGINE YOURSELF IN THE BODY OF SITA
You are young, no more than eighteen years old, and your soft, golden-skinned
body is emaciated. You wear tattered clothes, and your hair is loose around
your shoulders. You are alone on an island surrounded by ocean, sitting in
front of a small hut.

Imagine that you have lived with the love of your life, a being you have
been joined with heart and soul, body and mind, in a profound soul union. Now,
he is absent. You don't know if you will ever see him again. Your heart is turning over with sharp, intense grief. Let yourself feel that grief, the stored grief
of lifetimes of separation from loved ones. Feel its sharp edges. Feel where it
is in your body. If tears want to come, let them. Fully feel your grief. Now go
into the grief. Enter into it completely. How does grief feel in your heart? Can
you feel the release in it, the joy hidden in grief?

PART TWO: FEEL THE POWER OF FEMININE ENDURANCE
Imagine that your captor stands in front of you. He is dark-skinned, handsome, and muscular, wearing red silk clothes studded with gold and pearls. He
exudes sexuality and deep power. You know that if you give into him, he will
give you riches and pleasure, and that if you don't, he will eventually kill you.
Feel the war within you, the power of attraction to the dark masculine, fighting
with your deep love and grieving for your lost soul mate. Feel the temptation
to give in. Feel it fully.

Then summon from within the power of your unbroken vow of fidelity,
and feel the strength of it filling your body. Let yourself feel sacred pride and
sacred anger at your captor. Recognize the power you hold within you: the
power of the feminine spirit that has nothing left to lose.

PART THREE: FEEL THE ACHE OF INJUSTICE AND THE JOY OF VINDICATION

Imagine yourself walking toward your beloved soul mate. You have been brought to him. Your heart is alight with happiness as you see his face. Then you notice how stern he looks, how dark and closed is his face. You walk closer. He makes no move to embrace you. You feel a sharp pain in your heart, the pain of complete rejection. Now he is speaking. He is telling you that you haven't loved him enough, that the mere fact that you have lived with another man makes you unworthy of his love. You want to scream and cry. What do you do? What do you say?

Filled with the desire to prove your loyalty, you offer to die if you have been untrue. You ask the universe to bear witness. If you have been loving and loyal to your mate, you will step into a fire and emerge unscathed.

Feel what it is to step into a fire, knowing your purity of motive, knowing that your life is at the mercy of the universe.

Feel your amazement at the miracle.

When your love opens his arms to you, are you able to go to him joyfully, without resentment? With total love? Can you forgive him for doubting you, because your love is so total that it has no room for anything but love?

_____

Invoking Sita Seated in a Fire

Find a quiet place and set aside fifteen minutes to a
half hour for this contemplation. Have a journal and pen
handy in case you want to write anything down.

Sitting comfortably, spend a few minutes following your breath. Then, bring your attention into your heart. Repeat the invocation mantra for Sita three times (see page 219).

With your awareness in your heart, begin to bring to mind the image of Sita.

Imagine Sita as a young woman with pale skin and long dark hair. She wears a white sari, a necklace with small black beads, a flower garland, and bangles—brightly colored glass as well as gold—around her wrists. Her long-lashed eyes are closed. In the middle of her forehead is a vermilion dot. She wears gold earrings. On her lips is a gentle smile. She gazes at you calmly.

FIGURE 13: SITA SITTING IN THE FIRE

> Sita sits in the midst of a blazing fire. The flames are golden, and they leap around her without touching her body. As you breathe in, inhale her love, faith, and compassion. As you exhale, imagine that love filling your body and flowing out into the world.

SITA'S VOW OF TRUTH

Back to the *Ramayana*. Years go by. Then one day, while hunting in the forest, Rama meets his twin sons, Lava and Kusha, who have grown into mighty archers. Intrigued, he decides to take Sita back, but demands that she undergo another public ordeal to prove her fidelity. Sita seems to agree. She comes to Rama's palace. There, standing before Rama's throne, Sita petitions her mother, the Earth, in what was known in ancient India as an "act of truth."

"If I have always been pure and faithful to Rama in thought, word, and deed, may the sweet Earth receive me," she says.

At her words, a throne rises from the Earth. Sita sits on the throne, which then sinks into the ground. The goddess has returned to her origins.

Rama, it is said, mourns her forever. He never remarries; he always keeps a golden figure of Sita at his side.

Why does Sita disappear? Is she showing Rama that even unconditional love, at the end of the day, can be lost when asked to prove itself beyond a certain limit? That even the earth's patience wears thin? Does she realize, like the wife of an abusive spouse, that Rama will never change, that he cares more about his dignity than about her? Is the moment of Sita's disappearance a watershed moment in the development of culture? The ascendancy of Rama, righteous warrior-king, may have symbolized the triumph of a warrior culture, where legality and reputation, masculine honor and dharmic rigidity would trump more feminine values of personal love and relatedness. Rama's descendants would go on to dominate the Earth, and in the millennia of human history that followed, the feminine would be dominated as well, her values denied. Perhaps Sita's disappearance back into her origins represents her values disappearing from the world.

You'll have noticed how the motif of disappearance runs through several of the goddess stories, especially those of the consort-goddesses. You'll recall that in the most famous of all these stories, Sati, the first wife of Shiva, immolates herself in her own yogic fire. In the patriarchal versions of the story, she does this because her father has insulted Shiva by not inviting him to a ceremony. In the Shakta version, in the *Kalika Purana,* and the *Devi Bhagavat Purana,* the Goddess vows before incarnating in her form as Sati that if she is not respected she will instantly leave her body. Her self-immolation is the fulfillment of that vow: she kills herself not because her father didn't invite Shiva, but because her father disrespected *her.* The implicit threat here is that if the life-force isn't honored, it simply disappears. The yin aspect of the feminine, like the fertile Earth, doesn't fight to protect herself. Fierce goddesses—like Durga and Kali—fight to protect the world, to protect the gods, to protect life. They "punish" pride and disrespect with weapons. The gentle goddesses simply withdraw.

The wifely goddesses, the traditionally "feminine" goddesses, can only fight injustice by passive resistance, of which allowing yourself to die is the ultimate expression. Committed to the path of submission, it is only through passive resistance, especially self-immolation, that they can force the masculine to look at his own cruelty or impel him to turn back to the values of love and justice. In the world based on traditional Hindu values—which are essentially heart values—a loved one's self-sacrifice implicitly commands obedience. In a fair universe, the sacrifice cannot go unrewarded—even if the only reward for the selfless person is an accumulation of inner power. In human politics, the only power of the truly powerless is to appeal to the moral sense of the powerful. Sita's tactic would become the underpinning of Gandhi's *satyagraha* movement and, through his example, of the American civil rights movement and, later, of the Argentinian Mothers of the Disappeared, whose silent protests did so much to call world attention to the atrocities of a dictatorship. All these revolutions employed the essentially feminine tactic of passive resistance to arouse the higher values of an unconsciously cruel dominating power. It's a tactic that doesn't work against conscious cruelty, as Winston Churchill pointed out when Gandhi suggested that Britain try nonviolent resistance against Hitler. The demonic powers are not convinced by righteous displays of nonviolence. And as a personal tactic, passive resistance easily turns into passive aggression.

SITA: THE ARCHETYPE OF THE FEMININE AS VICTIM

As an archetype of the ideal feminine, Sita can appear as outdated as foot-binding. Mythologist Jean Houston writes about an evening when she watched the TV version of the *Ramayana* on a village square in rural India. As Ravana was flying away with the captive Sita, an old woman whispered to Houston, "Women in India need a different story."[4] I've heard the same complaint from several young Indian women. One girl told me, "I don't care if I never hear another word about Sita. My mother was always telling me to be like her, and that's the last thing I would ever want for myself!" If contemporary art is any indication, educated modern Indian women prefer the Durga archetype to Sita; in galleries in Mumbai and Delhi, I have seen contemporary paintings of Durga on her tiger, sometimes with the artist's face. Sita is not, for sure, a favorite goddess of feminists.

In a world where women can still be bought and sold, where brides are set on fire because they haven't brought enough dowry, and where women and girls are oppressed by rigid religious laws—as in Saudi Arabia and other Arab countries—or raped in acts of war as in so many places in Africa, the loving, receptive, suffering image of Sita has enormous relevance. Ravana is still kidnapping Sita, and Rama is still punishing her for having been kidnapped. Unlike Kali, who storms forth from the earth as a volcano or an earthquake or a tornado, Sita is herself the sacrifice. She represents the sacred Earth which continues to bring forth crops and support life even as her pastures are paved with concrete and her life-sustaining rainforests are cut down. She is a symbol of every woman still deprived of voice by clueless patriarchy, yet who manages in her suffering to keep love and forbearance alive.

Sita embodies the feminine insistence on the primacy of relationship. In these stories, Rama incarnates patriarchal ethics, which honor principles above persons. The Harvard psychologist Laurence Kohlberg famously taught ethics classes by giving students case studies in which the "right" answer was based on principles of law and justice. In the 1980s, another Harvard psychologist, Carol Gilligan, conducted a series of studies that revealed a different but equally significant feminine ethic based on relationship. In feminine ethics, the need to take care of another person trumps the rule of law, and ethical development is judged not by how closely you adhere to the laws of abstract justice but by your felt sense of responsibility for those you care about.[5]

THE SELFLESSNESS OF THE SITA WOMAN

Both the power and the tragic potential in the Sita archetype lie in the fact that she is entirely defined by her relationships. The Sita woman is utterly selfless in her celebration of the good of others, transcendent in her devotional offering, enduring whatever comes her way. As the selfless wife, the good daughter, she carries an eternity of feminine hopes and feminine tears. In the West, we've transformed the Sita archetype into Cinderella, where the passive, beautiful woman is carried away by the handsome prince—or into the story of the Goose

Girl, where a princess is banished from the palace by a jealous stepsister and made to live as a goose girl until rescued by the prince. She is that part of the feminine spirit that knows how to conceal itself in the inner room of the soul, waiting quietly with folded hands for the masculine to rescue her, inseminate her, inspire her, or show her who she is.

Sita is the exact opposite of Kali and the other fierce goddesses. She is that in the feminine that most needs protection, because it is most open to violence and betrayal. She is the submissive daughter-in-law of Hindu and Islamic tradition, the fifty-year-old wife divorced by her husband for the sake of a younger woman. She is the generations of women who believed that by being good wives, good daughters, and good mothers they would be protected, that their connections to others defined them. Contemplating Sita's story can bring up all the grief of the collective feminine and a deep rage at the masculine, with its rigid notions of honor and its assumption that women are property. But to see Sita as either a victim or as the embodiment of wifely virtue is to miss who she is at her core.

Ultimately, Sita is the holding quality in love. She is the essentially feminine power of unconditional embrace, embodied in the energy that holds a child in the womb. Kali's dynamic force pushes the child out of the womb. Sita is the womb itself. Her Shakti flows as the mother's vital fluids as they nurture the embryo. It appears as the maternal bliss that, for many women, makes the act of caring for a child so ecstatic. That aspect of the feminine appears self-sacrificing to a masculine consciousness (even though it also appears in fathers), but to the woman filled with Sita's particular flavor of love, it is as nourishing to the self as it is nourishing to the other.

SITA'S LOVE

The Sita energy is both the divine, transcendent component of human love, and the most intimate aspect of divine love. We find Sita in that mysterious feminine capacity to create "home" around the people they love and to be grateful for life's goodness even in the midst of terrible pain. Sita is that quality in the feminine whose unconditional love draws out the innate goodness in someone whom the patriarchal mind considers irredeemable. Sita is that quality in the divine feminine that can hold us in all our confusion and that has the power to transmute our darkness in its holding light. Sita's love is profoundly redemptive.

The psychologist Milton Erickson tells the story of Joe, a young man who'd been in prison for robbery, and who'd been in trouble since his earliest youth.

Joe came to a small midwestern town and found a job in a gas station. Since everyone knew his priors, he was shunned by all the good people of the town.

One day a girl came into the station. She was the daughter of a prosperous farmer—way above Joe's social station. They got to talking, and a couple of weeks later, he asked her to come with him to a dance at the grange hall. We have to assume that Joe had some kind of bad-boy charm—we know how much girls like bad boys. In any case, she accepted, but on one condition. "I'll come with you if you'll act like a gentleman," she said.

That night, Joe put on a sports coat, bought a corsage, and behaved like a perfect gentleman—which he continued to do for the next fifty years or so because he married her, went to work on her father's farm, and eventually inherited it.[6]

That girl held the power of the loving divine feminine, the redemptive gaze that Sita emanates from every pore of her golden body. Sita's love appears in the spaces between people, as the energy within relationship, and as the love that life has for every animal and plant and insect that she brings forth.

Contemplation: Finding Sita's Love within Yourself

Find a quiet spot and a comfortable position for this contemplation exercise.

Consider a time when you felt deep, melting love for another person. It might have been for a lover or a child. Feel the all-embracing instinct to love and protect that person. Find it in your body. What are the sensations of love? Feel its softness, its expansive quality, its bliss. Feel its strength. That feeling is the Shakti of Sita. This love asks nothing, expects nothing. It simply gives. Let yourself experience the pure feeling of giving love. Notice what comes up to obstruct it—holding back, bargaining, fear, resentment. Let those feelings go. Rest in the purity of that original, core feeling of unconditional love.

MYSTICAL TEARS

On a mystical level, the tears that Ramakrishna shed when he thought of Sita were not tears at her victimization. They were the cleansing mystical tears that well up in the heart at the sheer beauty of love's enduring sweetness. Sita's endurance is passive, but it's never weak. Her devotion to Rama is a profound act of yoga, a joining with the divine through the path of selfless love, loyalty, and service. One way to join with the divine is to identify with its vastness. But that's not the only way. We also join with the divine when we throw ourselves on the ground in complete loving surrender and say "Thy will be done" or "I am yours" or "Let me serve you." That impulse to surrender is as deep within the human heart as the impulse to transcend, the impulse to love, or the impulse to help another person, and it comes from the same intuition of fundamental oneness with the whole. The Sita archetype carries a profound mystical truth: selfless, devoted service is a doorway to inner power, love, and, yes, ecstasy.

Of course, this mystical style can feel incongruent with the modern Western values of individuality and personal power. Moreover, there's no question that, in its distorted form, the celebration of the Sita archetype and the sacrificial gesture it stands for has been used to oppress not only women, but powerless people and religious devotees in every culture. But if you cut to the internal core of who Sita is, you'll find that she can show you what it means to offer yourself entirely to love—even when love seems to have deserted you.

MYSTICAL SUBMISSION

The gesture of submissive service has been a mystical doorway in many traditions; certainly in Christianity and the Sufi sects of Islam as well as in the Hindu devotional tradition. In fact, the attitude of service is probably the quickest route to spiritual progress we have, at least for those who have the capacity to serve with love. The great insight at the spiritual heart of the Rama-Sita relationship is that it's possible to serve the divine by serving the human beings in your life—serving the teacher, serving the parents (who have, after all, served you), and serving the spouse.

In this sense, the Indian teaching that commands a woman to look upon her husband as God actually pointed out a yogic path that allowed a woman to transcend the irritability and resentment that is normally a part of any marriage. The teaching dignifies the hardships of her married life as yogic austerities and expressions of mystical devotion. There was a reason besides cultural habit that Anandamayi Ma, one of the greatest woman gurus of the twentieth century, remained in some respects submissive to her husband— even after he became her disciple!

Many of us, men as well as women, have enacted the Sita archetype in ourselves when we've been in love.

One of my most memorable experiences of the Sita-style ecstasy happened during a period when I had a crush on someone I worked with. One evening, during meditation, I was seized with a powerful longing to serve this person, to give my life to help him. Suddenly, a river of love began to pour into me. It seemed to come through my crown, as if a faucet had been opened above my head. No question that this was a transpersonal love, coming from a source that had nothing to do with my human beloved. A moment later, the feeling shifted; I began to feel the love pouring up from inside my own heart.

The message seemed clear: the source of my love was not the person, but something beyond him, something that shone through him. At the same time, I feel sure that my spiritual attitude, the intense desire to surrender and serve, had triggered the opening.

That deep, self-offering impulse is the Shakti of Sita. Though it can be misplaced and misapplied, twisted and manifested in innumerable shadow-ways, it is nonetheless one of the greatest of all mystical instincts.

Invoking Sita as the Power of Loving Surrender

Again, find a comfortable position in a quiet location for this exercise.

Remember a time when you loved deeply, when you desired to surrender yourself to love. Can you access in that love the desire to surrender yourself totally, even to collapse your individuality into love?

See if you can fully access that feeling of surrendered love. Feel your way into it. With that feeling, bow. Bow with the sense that you are opening yourself fully to the divine, in loving service.

SITA AS THE COMPASSIONATE FEMININE

What else was it in Sita that made Ramakrishna cry for her? Was it the depth of her suffering and her ability to love right through it? Perhaps. But in weeping with Sita, he was also weeping for the world, for the Earth, and for the very pain of loving itself. When you identify with Sita, you are attuning to the heart of the compassionate feminine, much as Kuan Yin incarnates feminine compassion for Chinese and Japanese Buddhists. Sita's suffering, loving heart has made her a compassionate intercessor for people in pain—especially for women who are misunderstood or mistreated or unloved. The tears we cry for Sita are for all beings held captive in painful life circumstances. They are for animals as well as humans, for anyone whose only power lies in the strength of their fidelity and love. They are also for the beauty of divine love. They are for the unbearable pain of separation from God, and the longing to be reunited with your deepest self.

Sita can help anyone resist feeling bitter in the face of harsh treatment and stay in touch with her love in the face of abandonment. When you want to learn how to face and endure a painful situation, you ask Sita for help. When your lover leaves you, Sita will be there to support you. When you are lonely and in grief, you can invoke Sita to stand with you. And when you feel the pain of the earth itself, let yourself feel Sita's tears and recognize that grief itself can be a healing and deeply mystical pathway.

To tune in to the love and strength of Sita, try the following meditation. Sometimes, passionate grief for others can be a doorway into love.

Meditation: Taking in the Sorrow of the Earth

Once again, this meditation requires a quiet,
uninterrupted space and a comfortable posture.

Sitting quietly, breathe in and out through your heart, as if there were a nose in your chest wall. Let the breath touch your heart center and soften any hardness or armor around your heart.

Imagine yourself in a forest. You are sitting on a bed of moss, breathing in the scents of the trees and flowers. Breathing in, take in the feeling of Sita's love. Feel that you absorb her sweet, encompassing love through your heart.

Now, imagine that around you are creatures of the forests and streams, creatures whose survival as a species is threatened, species that are disappearing or have disappeared from the earth.

Consider the gray wolf, the leopard, the ocelot, the brown bear, the tiger, the chimpanzee, the Indian elephant, the many species of birds and animals that have already disappeared.

Consider the oil on the seafloor of the Gulf of Mexico, the melting polar ice caps, the drying up of lakes, the droughts across the American West, the trees and plants no longer living.

What emotions come up when you consider these things? Rather than trying to name the emotion as anger, or fear, or grief, notice where you feel it in your body.

What is the emotion saying to you?

Now, feel the presence of Sita in those feelings. Ask her to speak to you through the feelings in your body. How can you hold the pain that unfolds daily in this world, with love, without despair? How can Sita reveal to you the mystery of loving acceptance of what is, the "full catastrophe" of life, and your response to it? Stay with the feelings and the question as long as you need to.

Imagine all this being embraced by the vast, compassionate, sorrowing heart of the goddess Sita. Feel the vast spaciousness of her love and her understanding encompass your grief and feeling of having been abandoned. Feel the grace that comes to you through this.[7]

Sita

see-tah—Furrow

Other Names for Sita:
>Janaki (*juh-nuh-kee*)—Daughter of Janaka
>Rama (*ruh-mah*)—Splendor
>Narayani (*nah-rah-yuh-nee*)—Feminine form of Narayan, or Vishnu

Goddess of:
- fidelity, loyalty, and self-sacrifice
- surrender and service
- wifely love
- maternal ecstasy
- the womb and its fertility
- forests and desolate places
- sorrow leading to transcendence and love
- comfort for those who are abandoned
- nonviolent resistance

- strength to endure suffering
- unconditional nurturing love

Invoke Sita for:
- support in conceiving, carrying, and nourishing a child
- unconditional love
- enduring harsh and difficult circumstances with patience
- tuning in to the earth and the natural world
- compassion
- receiving the love of nature
- fidelity and loyalty in marriage and friendship
- devotion
- empathy with suffering

Invocational Mantra

Udbhava-sthita-samhara
Karinim klesha harinim
Sarva-shreyaskarim sitam
Nato'ham rama-vallabham

ood-buh-vuh stee-tuh suhm-hah-ruh
kah-ri-neem kley-shuh hah-ri-neem
sahr-vuh-shrey-yuhs-kahr-eem see-tahm
nuh-toe-hum rah-muh-vall-luh-bahm

I offer salutations to Rama's beloved Sita, the source of creation, maintenance and destruction, the remover of all inner obstacles and the bringer of all things bright and beautiful.

Gayatri Mantra

Om janaka-nandinyai vidmahe
Bhumijayai cha dhimahi
Tannah Sita prachodayat

ohm juh-nuh-kuh-nuhn-din-yai vid-muh-hey
bhoo-mee-jah-yai chuh dee-muh-hee
tun-nuh see-tah pruh-cho-duh-yah-tuh

Om, may we come to know the daughter of Janaka
May we meditate on she who was born from the Earth
May that Sita impel us on our path.

Sita's colors: white, gold
Sita's flowers: wildflowers
Sita's consort: Rama

CHAPTER 9

Dhumavati

Crone Goddess of Disappointment and Letting Go

One who knows the Absolute as both knowledge and ignorance, by ignorance
crosses beyond death, and by knowledge enjoys immortality.

ISHA UPANISHAD

Perceived as the Void, as the dissolved form of consciousness, when all beings are dissolved
in sleep in the supreme Brahman, having swallowed the entire universe, the seer-poets call
her the most glorious and the eldest, Dhumavati. She exists in the form of sleep, lack of
memory, illusion, and dullness in the creatures immersed in the illusion of the world, but among
yogis she becomes the power that destroys all thoughts, indeed [she is] Samadhi itself.

GANAPATI MUNI
Uma Sahasram 38, 13–14

Do not be afraid to suffer, give
the heaviness back to the weight of the earth.

RAINER MARIA RILKE
Sonnets to Orpheus IV (translated by Robert Bly)

Disappointment is a multilayered teacher. Not many of us would choose to
apprentice with her, yet sooner or later, most of us do. People disappoint
us. Luck runs out. Status declines. Strength fails us. Then, the goddess
Dhumavati flies into our awareness, accompanied by her crow, a harbinger of
worldly misfortune who ironically also bestows the inner gifts of detachment,
emptiness, and freedom.

Dhumavati—her name means "the smoky one"—is also called "the widow."
In traditional India, especially in the higher castes, there was no more inauspicious form of the feminine. In a culture where status for women is given by the
husband, widowhood is the worst thing that can happen to a woman. The film

Water depicts life in a house of widows, where young and old women live together in poverty, begging for food. Shaven-headed and wearing white, women in these widow houses received one meal a day and were supposed to spend their time in prayer and meditation. A widow in such a culture is at the bottom of the social order, often thrown out of her children's houses, wandering homeless, living in the outskirts of temples or in wild places.

From a worldly point of view, Dhumavati stands for despair, sadness, and failure. Yet she has significant and subtle boons to give, especially for someone on the path of awakening. Without passing through Dhumavati's winnowing basket, we remain trapped by our dreams of success and our fear of loss, especially the losses that come with age and sickness. With her grace, we can mine the exquisite wisdom hidden in the heart of life's most difficult moments.

Dhumavati is one of the group of ten goddesses known as the Mahavidyas, or Great Wisdoms. They are goddesses who incarnate different stages on the path of self-realization, or states of unfolding consciousness. In the Tantric tradition of the Mahavidyas, Dhumavati represents the void stage which we all must go through on the path of higher awareness.

A TRADITIONAL VIEW OF THE CRONE

Dhumavati is described in a verse in the *Bhairava Evam Dhumavati Tantra Shastra* as "tall, ugly, unsteady, and angry."[1] She wears dirty clothes. She rides in a chariot decorated with a crow banner. She has four hands in which she carries a winnowing basket as well as a broom, a torch, a sword, a spear, a skull bowl, or a club (depending on which text you read). Another verse says, "Her complexion is like the black clouds that form at the time of cosmic dissolution. Her face is very wrinkled, and her nose, eyes, and throat resemble a crow's . . . Her face has a venomous expression. She is very old . . . she has disheveled hair, and her breasts are dry and withered. She is without mercy."[2] These lines capture the paradoxical, even ambiguous quality of Dhumavati, who represents everything that a "normal" person rejects.

In short, Dhumavati is that familiar figure from both Eastern and Western mythology: the crone, the eternal bag lady, the witch. Dried-up, inauspicious, and forbidding to anyone who craves the comforts of life, Dhumavati is one of the rare goddesses who is not conventionally beautiful—perhaps because we view disappointment as ugly. If we allow ourselves to look her clear in the eye, we see that she is pure beingness in its raw form. She has the power to teach us that outer beauty fades, but our divine Self always remains intact. If we can see ourselves this way regardless of what falls away, we've tapped into Dhumavati's strength.

There are two myths about Dhumavati's origin. In one, she rises from the smoke of Sati's funeral pyre after Sati immolated herself at her father's sacrifice. Her face blackened by the flames, Dhumavati comes into the world filled with the outrage and despair of the insulted Goddess Sati and also with the evanescent, nearly transparent quality of smoke. Smoke dissolves, it wanders, it has no abode—thus the social invisibility of the Goddess Dhumavati.

The second story tells us that Dhumavati is born when Shiva curses Sati for an act of unwifely aggression. Sati is living with Shiva in their Himalayan abode. One day she asks him for something to eat; Shiva, ascetic that he is, refuses. "Then I'll have to eat you," retorts Sati, whereupon she swallows Shiva. He doesn't die, of course. Instead, he talks her into disgorging him. The moment he's freed, he lays a curse on her, saying that henceforth she will be a widow. So in one reality, Shiva and Sati remain consorts. In a parallel reality, Sati manifests as the form of the goddess who is rejected by the masculine; punished for her moment of assertive anger by being condemned to live outside masculine protection and thus outside mainstream society. Dhumavati is the feminine unsupported by male authority. In many paintings, she sits in a chariot with nothing to pull it, a position that, as author and Hindu scholar David Kinsley points out, underlies the fact that in the conventional sense she is a woman going nowhere.[3]

THE STILLNESS AT THE HEART OF LIFE

That stalled chariot has deeper esoteric meaning as well. It can also represent the stillness of the eternal present, the action that arises from nonaction, the void state where forms dissolve in deep meditation. In Indian cosmology, Dhumavati represents the Shakti present during Mahapralaya, the cosmic dissolution in which the physical world melts back into the void, and all beings, ready or not, are freed of their bodies, desires, and karmas. In other words, she stands for the cosmic moment of complete renunciation. As an energy in the physical world, she represents the absence of fertility and life-giving moisture. She lives in whatever is desolate, abandoned, unfortunate, and unpleasant. Think of Dhumavati energy as a dry lake bed, as the barren rice fields in a drought-ridden landscape, or in places where clear-cutting has turned rainforest into desert. She is dead coral reefs and foreclosed houses with broken windows. She is refugee camps and displaced peoples moving without passports over desolate ground. In all these ways, she denies the ordinary sweetness of life. She is everything that we want to turn away from and refuse to admit to our lives. But she is also the dignity of the outcast and the power that turns bad luck into enlightenment.

The trick with Dhumavati is to find her enlightened core, the transformative power within hopelessness and failure. This requires inhabiting your worst fears and facing into your losses. Gloria Steinem once said that many of her friends—skilled and successful professional women—had at one time or another confessed to their terror of ending up as bag ladies.[4] When women on their own, women without a man, wake up at three o'clock in the morning to confront their inner demons, it's often with a vision of being homeless in an alleyway or forgotten in some urine-scented corner of a nursing home. For some of us—men as well as women—that is a genuine possibility.

DHUMAVATI AS THE BAG LADY

In a class on the Tantric goddesses, I once asked the participants, as an exercise, to give five dollars to a bag lady while looking into her eyes. People had many different experiences, from confronting their own aversion and fear, to facing the anger of a ranting paranoid schizophrenic, to getting into conversations and hearing genuine wisdom. Afterward, I got a letter from Tina, a forty-year-old beauty who had found that the exercise confronted her for the first time with the realization that not only would she grow old and lose the privilege that comes with youth and beauty, but that all her life she had been terrified of anything ugly or unpopular—of finding out that underneath her skin she was akin to Dhumavati. Dhumavati reminds us that any one of us could lose everything, that when safety nets break down, no one is immune from losing their health or their money or their mind. War or famine or the breakdown of a nuclear power plant could take away everything you relied on.

Dhumavati asks the questions: Can your inner equilibrium survive that level of collapse? Can you find your yogic groove when everything falls away?

These are two of the great questions that yogic practice is meant to answer. Tantric practitioners contemplate the dissolution of the body as a way of transcending fear of death and also as a way of acquiring various yogic powers. Investigating Dhumavati can give you empathy for the unlucky (and for your own unlucky self) and can show you how freedom really does come when there's nothing left to lose.

DHUMAVATI'S BOONS

Even for a person walking a worldly path, it pays to look closely at the old woman with the crow on her banner. Behind her scowl could be a boon. We know from

FIGURE 14: THE GODDESS DHUMAVATI

myths and movies that bag ladies and homeless men sometimes turn out to be sages, loving beings who have chosen to be ignored or overlooked because it gives them freedom, and who have wisdom to impart to someone who knows how to give them honor. In European mythology there is the story of Dame Ragnell, who gives King Arthur the secret of the riddle that will save his kingdom. Fairy tales are full of crones who, when treated kindly, will whisper the magic word that lets the courteous young man find a treasure or helps a goose girl wed a prince. Dhumavati is one of those Shaktis who looks fierce but is actually tenderhearted. She's supposed to give her devotees whatever they desire—when you look lovingly into the face of disappointment, you tap into her love and power.

Contemplation: Confronting Failure

This contemplation may allow you to open to parts of yourself
that you have disowned. Find a comfortable posture and spend
a few minutes focusing on the breath before beginning.

First, think about your own life. When you've failed or been let down, how do you see yourself? Can you look at yourself with the same love that you do when you've had a great success? Or do you subtly reject yourself?

Now, note the feelings that arise when you think of people who have been disappointed, or who have failed. Do you feel empathetic toward them? Do you want to avoid them? What is your usual reaction—inward and outward—to a homeless person? To a very sick person? Do you distance yourself? Do you feel pity? Do you identify with them?

Now, bring to mind a human embodiment of the Dhumavati energy. It could be a sick friend, a homeless man, your grandmother, or a person with Alzheimer's. Imagine yourself taking that person in your arms. Feel your own feelings in that embrace, and sense the feelings of the other person.

GUIDANCE THROUGH SPIRITUAL DISAPPOINTMENT

In any creative or growth process, there is a difficult but necessary stage of void. All your efforts have been fruitless. You know there is further to go but you don't know how to get there. At such a moment, the only way through is to let go of expectation, hope, and your desire for comfort, money, recognition, or even spiritual experience. These are the times in life when you come face to face with your inability to control outcomes, when your skills seem to have deserted you. You find yourself in a state of emptiness and vulnerability, broken open by disappointment or loss or by your own failure to live up to your expectations of yourself.

In failure, Dhumavati is our guide. She takes us down into the cave of the soul, and when we follow her, she shows us the spring that bubbles up out of the empty places in the heart. In a line made famous by Robert F. Kennedy, Aeschylus says, "Even in our sleep, pain that cannot forget falls drop by drop upon the heart, and in our own despite, against our will, comes wisdom to us by the awful grace of God."[5] That wisdom, and the grace that brings it forward, is the work of Dhumavati.

At the age of forty-six, a clergyman I know was subjected to false complaints of wrongdoing. Within a few days, he lost his congregation, access to his children, his profession, and his reputation. He went to live in a different city, and one evening he was invited to dinner at the house of a local family. When he was introduced to the other guests, one of them whispered to the host that she wouldn't sit at the same table with someone who might be a criminal. The host, with some embarrassment, asked the clergyman to leave. It was a moment of soul-grinding humiliation for this man, who was used to being the beloved center of such gatherings and was actually innocent of the complaints.

That night, he sat on the side of his bed, weeping and praying for hours. Early in the morning, out of nowhere, waves of ecstatic energy began to run through his body. He felt completely alive with the recognition of the divine in the universe, living as his human self. At that moment, he remembered a statement of St. Francis that a friend had quoted to him. Asked what he considered perfect joy, Francis said that to be kicked out of a house where he was begging for food and left in the gutter with the dogs would be perfect joy. My friend had found that statement incomprehensible, but that morning, he understood for the first time the gift of being an outcast.

Intuiting Dhumavati's Gifts

In this exercise you will work with the bija mantra of Dhumavati. The seed syllable *dhum* literally means "smoke"; the whole mantra means "Smoke,

smoke, the one who is made of smoke—I salute her." Find a quiet,
comfortable place for this practice, and have your journal and a pen nearby.

First, repeat the Dhumavati mantra nine times out loud:

Dhum dhum dhumavati swaha
dhoom dhoom dhoom-ah-vuh-tee swah-hah

Now, consider times in your life when your hopes and expectations were
disappointed, when you experienced feelings of emptiness and failure. How
did these times contribute to your growth? What gifts did you find in failure?
Write down any insights that arise.

Not everyone can go into the cave of disappointment and find the secret well-
spring. Most of us do our best to avoid failure, as indeed we should—which
is why Dhumavati is not a popular goddess. In fact, orthodox Hindu priests
will often say that married people and people with families should avoid her
because she has a reputation for dissolving family ties. But for someone with a
renunciant's bent, or someone who genuinely wants to dismantle the barriers to
communion with her deep soul, failure and disappointment can be real doorways into self-realization.

Because Dhumavati reveals the transience of pleasure and the unsatisfying
quality of worldly satisfaction, she is very much a goddess of the later part of life.
Most young people have too much bubbly energy and urgent desiring to fully surrender to a path of giving up and letting go. As a life guide, Dhumavati has most
to teach those who've worn out the path of pleasure and effort, and those who are
willing to sit in nondoing, letting come what may.

When your goal is to move deeply into meditative consciousness, she is an
essential guru, even a way station on the spiritual path. Leonard Cohen is one of
the great poets of this stage of life, singing of disillusionment and the love that
remains when all hope fails. In his sixties, he left a Zen monastery where he had
lived for years. Shortly afterward, his manager ran off with all his money, and
Cohen was forced to go on a series of concert tours. To see him in the concert
video, *Live in London*, is to look into the open heart of disappointment. He
comes across as humble, devoted, and profoundly reverent of the audience and

the musicians on stage with him. His face—lined, creased, just plain *old*—is a map of the gifts that can come from moving consciously into loss and despair.

Dhumavati can also open the doorway to the state of thought-free meditation and a very powerful and lasting form of awakening. The contemporary teacher Eckhart Tolle describes in *The Power of Now* a sudden awakening that he experienced during a period of great internal darkness. He had spiraled into depression, a misery so intense that one night he realized he no longer wanted to go on living. With that, the strange thought came to him, "If I cannot live with myself, there must be two of me: the 'I' and the 'self' that 'I' cannot live with. Maybe . . . only one of them is real." With that, his mind stopped, and he seemed to spiral into a void state from which he awoke to an experience of peace and bliss that lasted for months.[6]

Another teacher of nonduality, Byron Katie, had her own awakening in a treatment center for alcoholism. She awoke one morning face to face with a cockroach and, in the midst of recognizing how far "down" she'd come, had a profound realization that reality is exactly right just as it is. That realization was for her the beginning of an apparently permanent opening into bliss and peace. Her journey through loss opened her to the underlying presence behind everything.[7]

THE TEACHING IN SPIRITUAL FAILURE

Anyone who's ever grasped after enlightenment or spiritual experience will recognize that moment when you realize that spiritual striving is never going to work, that all efforts have been in vain. This is a critical turning point in inner practice, and it's one that any serious practitioner will face sooner or later. In Christian contemplative practice it's called a "dark night of the soul." The juice goes out of your practice. You feel dry, disconnected, even disinterested in your path. None of your usual strategies seem to reconnect you. Often this stage goes along with a loss of faith, a disbelief in old certainties. It also accompanies a feeling of being disillusioned with your church or your teacher. As a teacher, I've spent hours listening to people talk about their loss of faith in a guru or a path. James Fowler, in his book *Stages of Faith*, points out that this is a normal and important developmental stage, because it's the passage out of conventional faith into the key developmental stage of skepticism.[8] You may feel that all your props are dissolving, but this feeling has the potential to make room in your psyche for a profound sense of not-knowing, which can eventually morph into a genuinely mystic faith based on inner experience.

In contemporary spiritual circles, of course, many of us "get" this conceptually, without having actually gone through the stage of striving. In fact, if we have been influenced by a "nondual" teacher like Tony Parsons, we may have been taught that effort is basically useless on the spiritual path because what you are looking for is always already present and cannot be discovered through effort. The problem is that it isn't enough to know this intellectually. For most people, tremendous effort has to be made before that recognition can be earned. The grace in failure doesn't come from lack of trying or from premature surrender. Just as you have to have developed an ego before you can experience letting go of ego, you have to have given yourself wholeheartedly to your quest, your work, your practice before you've earned the right to realize that effort won't take you there. You can't give up before you start or because the work seems too hard. That kind of failure does not engage transformative power.

All my moments of Dhumavati-inspired grace have happened in the aftermath of intense effort, often from the kind of driven effort that brought on some form of burnout. In other words, they came from pushing myself to the limit and finding myself stopped by a brick wall in the form of circumstances, or more often, of my own physical weakness or illness. A few years ago, after seven years of intense travel and teaching, often pushing myself past exhaustion, I had a physical breakdown and was forced to take deep rest. For months, I could barely stay upright for more than a couple of hours a day. I kept losing weight, getting weaker, feeling progressively more disassociated from my profession, my life, and my friends. I even looked like Dhumavati—skinny, hollow-cheeked, with dry skin and thinning hair. It was hard to sit up to meditate. I would lie on my back, breathing long full breaths and descending deeper and deeper into my body. As the weeks went on, I became aware of a profound feeling of rightness and comfort. It was as if the isolation and uncertainty of my illness allowed me to touch into a cellular, visceral feeling of undying presence. That presence felt passionless and neutral, yet loving and—above all—unbreakable. I sensed that it would uphold me through death and beyond. There was nothing dramatic about this knowledge. It was simply a recognition of what is; the undying tensile strength of life, present even in the void.

The fierce goddesses all bestow this experience in their own way. Kali and her alter ego, Bhairavi, do it through sudden, fiery, explosive change. Dhumavati does it by relentlessly forcing the recognition of your marginality, your inability to know anything for certain, the dryness and emptiness of the void states of experience, when action becomes impossible.

This will happen to all of us when we face death or lingering illness. In the path of awakening, there will be many times when you're called to die to some deeply held desire. At those moments, Dhumavati holds out the hidden hand that guides you through disappointment to peace and freedom. The phrase in the Bhagavad Gita, "Peace follows renunciation," is a simple statement of truth. Normally, though, the renunciation is, in a sense, forced on us by having things we counted on fall away. A relationship ends, a child leaves, a job dissolves, you lose your health. But sometimes in a moment when the worst happens, you discover an enormous dignity and peace in simply standing in what you are. In such a state, it doesn't matter how things look from the outside or even what you think your life should be. The teachings of the Taoists are filled with this insight. The Chinese wise man Chuang Tzu compares the Taoist sage to a withered, useless tree that is able to survive because no one wants it for firewood or building.[9]

In a classic Zen retreat, practitioners have the opportunity to incubate this state of all-things-falling-away. Sitting for up to eighteen hours a day, staring at a wall, you feel every possible flavor of resistance: boredom, panic, distraction, physical pain. Then, at some point, thoughts fall away. Everything you think you are seems to dissolve. You recognize the bare awareness behind thoughts. Japanese Zen masters call this "body-mind dropping away." It's a state that can catapult you into what in Zen is called *kensho*, a sudden awakening into who you are behind your ordinary identity, or *satori*, the experience of an endlessly unfolding present moment.

Contemplation: Opening into Emptiness

For this contemplation, take a comfortable seated posture and prepare to invoke the energy of Dhumavati by using your imagination.

Begin by repeating the Dhumavati mantra twenty-one times: "Dhum dhum dhumavati swaha." Bring to mind the image of Dhumavati, the goddess who manifests through disappointment and frustration, whose gifts can show us the path to higher awareness that comes in times of disappointment and loss.

Imagine that you are seated in a desert or in a canyon, surrounded by rocks and sky.

The goddess is seated before you, on the ground.

She is dark skinned, skinny, dressed in rags. She has a long nose and pendulous cheeks and breasts. Her face scowls, but her eyes are sharp and powerful. She is looking at you with a clear, neutral gaze, as if asking you, "Can you gaze into the face of hopelessness? Can you find the gifts in failure? Can you see who you really are when everything you relied on is gone?" Looking closer, you recognize that behind her eyes is an infinite, clear space, the space of the peaceful void beyond desires. She is showing you acceptance, the power to enter the void.

As you gaze at Dhumavati, let your attention sink back into yourself. Allow her form to transmit to you her clarity, her absence of any pretension, her stripped-down authenticity. See if you can feel the enormous relief there is in letting go of any expectation or desire. Notice any fear or resistance that arises, and keep allowing the calm, accepting gaze of Dhumavati to dissolve your attachment to anything you think you are.

Ask Dhumavati for a gift of wisdom.

Now, open your eyes, and look around you. Let your gaze focus on the space around objects rather than on the objects themselves. See if you can sense the background spaciousness in which everything is contained. This is the vision that lets you see the formless emptiness that holds and permeates all forms.

THE POWER IN SOLITUDE

Dhumavati, it is said, makes you crave aloneness, the kind of solitude that is happy to stand outside the game. In my life, some of the deepest moments of peace have come when I lost something I valued intensely—a position or a relationship—and let it go. I can remember a time when the decision of an authority put my reputation in serious jeopardy. I fought the decision every step of the way, and lost. After the initial period of regret and bitterness, there came a moment when I just gave up the fight. I gave into reality and walked off the psychic battlefield. The peace that arose in me was as deep as anything I've ever experienced. It shocked me to realize how much tension and anxiety there is in fighting reality, and what a state of relaxation arises when you let go of winning or when you stop clinging to an opinion or to a relationship—even one you thought you couldn't live without.

When a wave crashes over your head, your survival depends on diving into the wave rather than fighting it. As an inner archetype, Dhumavati is your capacity for letting go of the things you thought you needed. It's a skill that can carry you through repeated experiences of radical disappointment; personally, I'm convinced that it is a skill that arises through a particular form of grace. Many of us are crushed by disappointment, like the man who loses his job and then has a heart attack. Grief can wreck your respiratory system—Frieda, a woman who lost her son in an auto accident, developed tuberculosis six months later. My own mother never recovered emotionally from the death of my oldest brother. Those who are poor and marginalized often internalize rage and disappointment, which can turn into hypertension, domestic violence, or depression. To be able to receive the gift in disappointment is a rare skill. It takes a unique type of practice in surrender, and here is where Dhumavati is your infallible guide. "Let go" is Dhumavati's deepest mantra. It arises as the subtle whisper in the heart when you meet her irresistible force and realize that, in crushing you, it expands your borders until borders have no more meaning. Then you flow through reality like smoke and stare out at the world with a vision that understands that you are in everything.

Letting Everything Go

Sitting quietly, meditate on Dhumavati's mantra: "Let go."

Consider the things in your life that feel unfinished or unsatisfying. With an exhalation, have the thought "Let go" and release them.

Consider the things in your life that you feel attached to, that you love. With an exhalation, have the thought, "Let go," and release them, one by one. Know that you can always take them back. This releasing is just for now.

Consider the ways you define yourself. First the obvious: man/woman, daughter/son of _____, mother/father of _____, financial planner, teacher, kind person, shy person, angry person, accomplished, neurotic, intelligent, fat, tired, happy—whatever personal qualities or physical qualities you consider part of "you." As each quality comes to mind, sigh it out with the thought, "Let go."

Now, with the next few exhalations, let go of everything that you think is you. Let it all go with the thought, "Let go."

What is left when everything has been let go?

When you open your eyes, gaze into the space around the objects in your vision, focusing not on the forms but on what holds them. In the same way, notice the space that surrounds any thoughts or images that arise in your mind. Thoughts, impressions, opinions may be there, but they are all held in the emptiness of the mind-space, whose essence is pure awareness.

Dhumavati

dhoom-ah-vuh-tee—Smoky One

Other Names for Dhumavati:
Jyeshtha (*jyey-shthah*)—The Elder
Alakshmi (*uh-luhk-shmee*)—The Inauspicious One

Goddess of:
- disappointment
- old age
- widowhood
- emptiness that can open up into blessing
- the end of life
- navigating the dark night of the soul
- loss of livelihood or status
- thought-free meditation
- void states
- inauspiciousness as the seed of transformation

Recognize Dhumavati in:
- deep sleep
- dark, moonless nights
- homeless people
- old-age homes
- dried-up lakes and deserts
- states of depression and hopefulness
- deep mourning
- the pure experience of the now
- periods of assimilation, when nothing outward seems to be happening

Invoke Dhumavati for:
- the experience of egolessness as a stage in practice
- living with marginalization
- accepting old age
- navigating disappointment
- finding unexpected blessing in loss
- discovering the freedom in letting go
- transcending feelings of being unworthy
- compassion for the elderly, the sick, the homeless
- the humor and wisdom of the crone
- the thought-free state of meditation

Bija Mantra
Dhum (*dhoom*)

Invocational Mantra
Dhum dhum dhumavati swaha
dhoom dhoom dhoom-ah-vuh-tee swah-hah

Smoke, smoke, the one who is made of smoke—I salute her.

Dhumavati's colors: smoky grey, black
Dhumavati's mount: crow
Dhumavati's consort: none

CHAPTER 10

Radha

Goddess of Romantic Longing

Who could cease to tell of that
quintessence of erotic mood
Save one speechless utterly
with ecstasy.

RUPA
Vidagdhamadhava

The sport of love, its glow and luxuries
Are indescribable, O friend,
And when I yield myself,
His joy is endless.

VIDYAPATI
Love Songs of Vidyapati

Have you ever been so wildly in love that you could think of nothing but your lover? Has your heart ever ached with longing for another person, or even for an unknown beloved? Has separation from your lover felt like being torn apart from your own soul? Have you felt ecstatic with your lover's arms around you, in despair when she doesn't call for a day? Has your lover sometimes appeared so numinously beautiful—even when he leaves his towel on the bathroom floor—that you felt an almost worshipful adoration for him? Have you ever had passionate feelings for the divine or for the unknown beloved who can, perhaps, only meet you in your soul?

Then you know what it is to love like Radha.

Radha is the goddess of lovers and desperate romantics. The beloved mistress of the youthful god Krishna, Radha's passionate, erotic drama is one of the world's great myths of love and separation.

The Radha energy is present wherever there is passionate love and the wish to merge with the beloved. She can manifest (and often does) through a teenager's romantic fantasies or in the delicious experience of being immersed in a beloved other. She might also show up as a reckless compulsion to follow your erotic impulses despite all reason and practicality. As a divine archetype, however, Radha's Shakti goes far deeper than the human impulse toward romantic passion. Tuning into the Radha Shakti can uncover the burning heart of universal Eros—the radically impersonal life-force energy that creates life's sweetness—within your desire for a human lover. At the spiritual level, when Radha's energy awakens within you, she can transform a mild interest in inner practice into a wildly personal love affair with the inner beloved. She is one of the secret Shaktis who transmutes ordinary desire into longing and passion into fuel for the spiritual journey.

Teresa of Avila, who carried on a life-long inner love affair with Jesus, was infused with Radha energy. So were John of the Cross, Thérèse of Lisieux, Mirabai, and generations of Hindu and Sufi mystics. Radha's energy is imprinted so indelibly in the collective psyche that to this day she remains one of our great mythic models for passionate devotion.

RADHA AND THE PATH OF DEVOTION

In the original stories of Krishna's early life, Radha appears only as a nameless cowherd girl, one of the group of the young god's teenage companions and lovers, known as the *gopis* (literally, "cowgirls"). She emerged as a full-fledged goddess through the work of a few poets during the medieval flowering of the *bhakti* movement in India. Bhakti—the path of devotional yoga—was from the beginning a movement for spiritual democracy. The more formal Hindu paths of study and ritual were elitist, open only to high-caste men. The bhakti movement welcomed women, illiterates, workers, and outcasts—anyone drawn to God by love. Bhaktas believed that love and adoration were a legitimate path to union with the divine, but they also taught that the path of love is superior to every other spiritual method. In devotion, you lose yourself in the divine, naturally submerging your alienated ego in the relational sweetness of love. The God of the bhaktas was a god of blissful relationship. The great claim of the movement—which survives to this day in India and elsewhere—is that it begins and ends by immersing you in bliss. Fueled by chanting and storytelling, the bhakti movement began spreading over India in the thirteenth century and reached its flowering in the 1600s. By then, every villager knew the stories of Radha and Krishna, chanted their names, and often kept their images in their houses. Along with Sita and Rama, they became beloved deities not only for simple people but for queens, rulers, and scholars. Even today, Krishna's life story is the subject of popular religious comic books and of a six-volume religious page-turner called *Krishnavatara*, a novel that traces his life from infancy through his years of kingship and statecraft.

A key insight of the bhakti path is that any human emotion can be turned toward God. Rama and Krishna, the avatars of Vishnu, were God as human beings. They had real (though definitely idealized) human relationships. For those who understood the deepest lessons of their embodiment, Rama and Krishna's lives implied an even more radical possibility: that any human being can be approached as a form of the divine and can be loved devotionally.

Chandidas, a poet who practiced the most radical form of bhakti, wrote exquisite devotional verses to a teenage prostitute whom he worshipped as the Goddess. He described his Tantric approach to communing with the divine through human love as "the natural (*sahaja*) path." Ramakrishna taught a more conventional version of this principle of natural devotion. He once asked a woman devotee who complained that she couldn't feel love for God, "Who do you love?" When she told him that she adored her baby nephew, Ramakrishna said, "Love him as Krishna."[1]

Like this woman, practitioners of the devotional path were encouraged to love Krishna in whatever way came naturally—as a child, a youth, a friend, or a teacher. Any form of love could trigger the flow of bliss, which would eventually, if properly cultivated, melt into the highest form of bliss. But one particular form of devotion was considered higher than the rest. That was the path of the erotic-romantic lover—the path called *parakriya bhakti*. Like the troubadours of medieval Europe, the bhakti writers believed that the obsession a woman feels for her paramour can transform the heart in a way that no ordinary, respectable love can ever do. It's the greatest form of love, they argued, both because it's dangerous and because it can never be taken for granted. Love outside of marriage, especially in those premodern days, could ruin your life. Your love could be discovered and you could be ostracized for it—or, in a traditional society, killed. At the very least, you risked heartbreak at the hands of a lover who had no legal obligation to go on loving you. To direct such love toward the divine was to court ego dissolution and risk your life (as happened to the poet-queen Mirabai). It also opened you to the highest form of sweetness. *Real* love risks everything.

Radha embodies parakriya bhakti.

Radha is a young woman, growing up in the cowherd village of Vraja. Her lover, Krishna, had been sent there as a baby to escape death at the hands of his uncle, who has sworn to kill him. So Krishna was raised among the village children. He and Radha are childhood playmates, but as they grow, Radha falls helplessly in love with Krishna. According to Indian myth, Krishna is the masculine incarnation of God's irresistible beauty, allure, and love. Krishna, in fact, embodies the power of divine attraction, the radical bliss that turns a lover's heart toward mystical union. Krishna is distracting to the point of addiction. Like a cosmic intoxicant, he draws your attention away from your work, your duties, your very survival. In later life, Krishna would become a king, a statesman, and a world teacher. But at this stage, when he is just past childhood, he is simply, cosmically adorable.

Everyone in the town of Vraja adores Krishna, and everyone has a unique relationship with him. His mother and the older women of the village love him as a son and dote on his baby mischief. The cowherd boys love him as a friend and ringleader. Their sisters, the cowherd girls, are erotically and intensely in love with him.

In another situation, this would be scandalous. But because everyone in the village of Vraja is part of a mythic conspiracy to adore this incarnate deity, the conventional rules don't apply. One of Krishna's incarnational tasks, in fact, is to exemplify the secret truth that true devotion to God allows you to bypass normal social and religious boundaries.

So, in the magical world of Vraja, Krishna's lovers spend their days in ecstasy. Their god is no invisible figure to be reached in prayer, but a living, breathing person. He is audacious, sweet, mischievous—and he also happens to be invincible. (All through his childhood, Krishna keeps casually disposing of the demons sent by his wicked uncle to assassinate him.) In paintings of Krishna, you see him playing his flute for the long-horned cows, surrounded by boys. You see him dancing with the cowherd girls. And you see him with one particular girl, the two of them entwined, embracing, gazing into each other's eyes.

That is Radha. Radha stands out among this village of Krishna lovers because she is his feminine counterpart—his Shakti—and because she loves Krishna to the point of losing all self-consciousness. When it comes to loving God, the devotional traditions tell us, conventional affection isn't enough—or at least not enough to become a radical pathway into the deep heart of reality. The devotion of orthodox religious people—accepting Jesus as your savior, repeating your sixteen-syllable Krishna mantra, praying daily—are fine as practices, but the real

FIGURE 15: RADHA AND KRISHNA ENTWINED

fast track into oneness with God is the kind of supreme love that mirrors the love that is God's nature.

Many charismatic teachers—Ramakrishna, Anandamayi Ma, Ma Amrita-nanda (popularly known as Amma), and my guru, Swami Muktananda—have had Krishna's heart-melting attraction. Anyone who has spent time with such a teacher may have had this experience of ecstatic, expansive, yet utterly personal devotional love. My relationship with my teacher was not at all erotic, yet there were moments in my years with him when an almost unbearable love would explode inside me. Sometimes, in those moments, my heart felt as if it were expanding to take in everyone and everything around me. Radha's story points to the mystery of how a human heart can join with the divine if love is big enough. If you can love God like a lover, Radha's story tells us, the fire of your erotic pas-sion can transform your heart into a melting stream of divine awareness.

So, we have Radha—besotted by Krishna, ready to give up her husband and her position—in a kind of love madness. In one of his songs, the poet Chandidas has her saying:

And now I know
That love adheres wholly
To its own laws.[2]

And:

I took no thought for what would be said of me,
I abandoned everything.[3]

There is nothing practical or calculating in Radha. She wants nothing from Krishna but love. Her passion makes her so immersed in God-consciousness that she lives in a state of natural samadhi, totally free of any ordinary concerns. Not only is she immersed in divine consciousness, she can't escape it:

The yogi yearns for a tiny flash of Krishna in his heart;
Look—this foolish girl strives to banish him from hers![4]

Part of the allure of the Radha story is its intense humanness. She is, above all, *relatable*. In contemporary terms, the Radha-Krishna love affair could be a divine version of a high school romance between the cool girl and the class rebel—who also happens to be a football star and student-council president. It is as if (stretching a few points for the sake of illustration) Emma Stone or Rachel McAdams got together with the young Robert Downey, Jr., or a teenage Brad Pitt or Justin Timberlake. As teenagers do, Radha has her own posse. Radha's girlfriends are in love with Krishna themselves, but they are also devoted to Radha, so they are happy to sublimate their love to support her. In the paintings, you see them clustered around her, helping her bathe, fix her hair, and arrange her sari as she prepares to meet her lover—all the while endlessly discussing the erotic possibilities of the next meeting. "Perhaps he will come tonight!" they tell her. If he doesn't come, she is desolate, and when she sees him next, she tosses her head and refuses to speak to him. The Bengali poets write of their love-play in language that borders on the steamier passages in Harlequin romances:

> He takes my clothes away.
> I lose my body
> At his touch.[5]

But Radha's passionate attachment to Krishna contains its own wound, which is as much a part of her love as the ecstasy. She cannot ever hold Krishna, who will never be tied down to one lover. He loves Radha, but his nature is poly-amorous. Krishna incarnates the personal face of God. He is connected inside and out to every heart, and his task in the world is to share his love—never to confine it to just one person. With Krishna, opportunities for heartbreak and jealousy are endless. When he's with her, Radha is lost in bliss. When he's away, she wants to throw herself in the river. Radha lives in the midst of an emotional earthquake. Her state is the very reverse of yogic equanimity, but it affects everyone who meets her with a similar ecstasy.

KRISHNA AND THE GOPIS

The most famous of the erotic Krishna stories begins when the cowherd girls beg Krishna to dance with them in the forest at night. Smiling his mischievous smile, Krishna tells them, "Yes, we'll dance when the moon is right. But when you hear the sound of my flute, you have to drop everything and come. Whatever you're doing—feeding your child, cooking, serving dinner to your husband—you must come!" He's voicing the ultimate demand that the divine makes of a devotional lover. Call yourself a lover? Then prove it. Don't make love something that you save for your leisure time. Go for it. Throw yourself away for the sake of love!

One August night, as the moon rises over the river, the gopis hear the notes of Krishna's flute lilting through the trees around the village. True to their promise, they put down their babies. They leave their cooking untended on the fire. Half-dressed, they run to the woods where he waits in a clearing by the river.

There, they begin to dance together. The dance is known in Indian myth as the *raslila*, or flavorful game, the sport of delight. One of the most famous images in Indian art shows Krishna dancing in the midst of this circle of young women. He plays his flute. The women sway and bend, so lost in their ecstasy that their clothes are falling off their bodies. In another image, Krishna has multiplied himself so that each of the girls has Krishna in her arms. God belongs to everyone who loves him, and as long as you don't hold back, he won't hold back himself.

Yet, Krishna cannot resist Radha. At one point in the evening, he disappears from the circle. When the gopis look for him, they find him embracing Radha, the two of them lying on a bed of flowers by the river. Radha's love for Krishna kindles his love for her, and it gives her as much power over him as he has over her. And Radha knows it. Sometimes, disgusted by his infidelity, she will refuse to speak to him. Then Krishna follows her, begging her to relent and embrace him. He demands her full attention. She weeps because she can never have his.

As discussed earlier, Robert Johnson, in *We*, says that passionate love for a human being is actually displaced love for the divine. No human being, he argues, can sustain romantic passion forever.[6] Their human foibles—not to mention the issues that arise when we live with another person— make it impossible to sustain the romantic ideal. Of course, Radha and Krishna are not human beings, but forms of the primal divine man and woman. Yet, it's highly significant that Radha and Krishna can never marry or even stay together for long. Their time together is heightened by its brevity; all tumbled hair, languorous limbs entwined, long kisses, passionate arguments, and passionate reconciliations. In the end, Krishna leaves Radha.

He is, after all, the son of a king, and of course he is called back to the city to assume his rightful place. Radha, a peasant girl married to another man, must stay behind. As the chariot carries him away, Krishna looks back longingly at Radha. Radha, for her part, goes mad with grief. Krishna, too, is devastated. The bhakti poets describe how—at least for a while—he sees her everywhere he goes. "How is it," he asks, "that for me the three worlds have become Radha?"[7]

Radha never forgets. For the rest of her life, she spends her days meditating on Krishna. But in her obsession and grief at being separated from her beloved, something amazing happens. She begins to see Krishna everywhere. The whole world becomes her beloved. Every leaf in the forest, the cows, the household butter churn—everything becomes for her the form of Krishna. In the Indian devotional tradition, her state is called "the bliss of the pain of separation" and it is considered one of the highest of all spiritual experiences. When Radha weeps for Krishna, her tears wash away all veils from the heart and everything becomes the form of her beloved.

One day, Krishna, who never stops thinking about the people who love him, calls his friend Uddhava and asks him to go to Vraja and see how everyone is doing. "Especially," he asks Uddhava, "find out how Radha is. She above all others holds my heart."

When Uddhava gets to the village, he is shocked to find Radha and her friends walking around like crazy women. They are beautifully adorned, it is true. They are taking care of themselves physically. But it turns out that they are doing all this because they live in a fantasy. They walk around caressing the trees, embracing the cows, saying, "Krishna! Krishna!" When they walk from house to house to sell their milk and butter, they call out "Buy Krishna! Buy Gopala!"

Uddhava is a great yogi, a master of asana and meditation. He cannot believe his eyes. "These women have gone insane," he reasons. "I have to do something for them."

So he calls the cowgirl maidens together and gives them a lecture on yoga. "Krishna loves you all," he says, in the tone that reasonable people use when talking to children. "He sent me to comfort you. Now, you should take that great love you have and turn it inside. Sit for meditation. Close your eyes and imagine Krishna in the heart. Do some breath control. Try to still those wandering minds!"

The girls look at him indulgently. "Oh, Uddhava," says Radha, "you just don't get it! Why should we close our eyes when Krishna is all we see? You might have to close your eyes and meditate in order to find God in your dry heart. But we see him with our eyes wide open. Everywhere we look, we see Krishna."

Radha's radical love has given her the vision of unity that spiritual practitioners regard as the gold standard of inner practice. She and her friends see the world as alive with their divine lover. Their "madness" is the madness of enlightened ecstasy.

Meditation: The World as Your Divine Lover

Radha's ultimate gift is the experience of your love filling the universe, so that the earth itself feels like your divine beloved.

Every spiritual path is its own doorway into unity consciousness.
This meditation is a practice for touching into the experience of
unification through love. It is a meditation you can do more or less
anywhere, eyes open or closed. Just don't try it while driving!

Begin by placing your attention in your heart.

If there is a person or an image of the divine that naturally kindles feelings of love in you, bring that image into your heart. Or, imagine a soft flame in your heart. Then, with each breath, offer to the flame the thought, "Beloved."

Feel how the thought "Beloved" gently kindles warmth and affection in your heart.

Imagine that the feeling in your heart spreads through your body. Let it gather in your hands and fingers. Then use your hands to enact love in the physical world. Wash dishes with the feeling that your hands are sending love into the plates and that the water runs with love. Touch your friend's arm with the feeling of love running from your heart through your hands.

As you look around you, mentally name everything you see as divine. Look at the trees and name them "God" or "Love." Look at the ground and name it "God." Look around you at the city, and name the stone and wood and metal around you with the thought, "This is God, this is love, this is made of divine consciousness." Look at your food, at the people you meet, and especially at yourself with the thought "This is all God, this is all love."

As you do this, keep your awareness in your heart. This is the meditation of Radha, the highest emanation of devotional love.

THE SECRET PATH

For centuries, Radha has been a model for spiritual seekers called to the secret, difficult path of erotic devotion. It's secret partly because in many cultures eroticism is suspect in itself, but even more so because it goes against our idea that spirituality is supposed to take us not just beyond sexuality, but beyond emotional attachment. Even people who consider themselves to be on a devotional path can be bemused by the intense emotionality of Radha-style devotion. It's hard to see, for instance, how attachment to a divine lover can foster detachment or why obsessive contemplation of your beloved can be a form of meditation.

That's because this kind of devotional love is not something you can fake or manufacture. It arises in the heart as a result of the intense grace of the awakened Shakti. Abhinavagupta, the great master of northern Indian Tantra, says that the experience of radical devotion is one of the great signs of shaktipat, the inner awakening that leads to God-consciousness. In its cosmic form, he says, this power is called "Shakti." In an individual that same power is called "bhakti." Followers of the Vaishnavite devotional paths understand this as well, and some believe that it is necessary to receive Radha's blessing in order to fully enter the mystery of radical devotion.

In short, to fully understand what Radha is about, you need to have had at least a glimpse of erotically charged devotion. In your ordinary state of mind, there is something wildly irrational about giving yourself up completely to a painful and basically unrequited love. The heart of the Radha Shakti is a feeling of longing, an ache in the heart that nothing human can assuage. When the heart wakes up or the kundalini Shakti rises to the heart, one of the first signs is this powerful yearning. It can feel like a yearning to come home, like a longing for some kind of subtle touch, or like a profound feeling that you are missing your beloved. John of the Cross described it in his great mystical poem:

O living flame of love
That tenderly wounds my soul
In its deepest center!

O delightful wound
O gentle hand
O delicate touch
That tastes of eternal life
And pays every debt!
In killing, you changed death to life.[8]

THE LOVE PORTAL

Radha's kind of love is not the quiet, detached compassion that some people associate with spirituality. It's not self-sacrificing, either. Passionate love is demanding. It doesn't take "No" for an answer, and it is as likely to shout in passionate rage as to sigh with passionate affection. Great devotional poets don't only cajole the beloved. They scold God, as Radha does Krishna, accusing him of being unfaithful, of repaying devotion with cruelty. The great Sufi poets like Nazar addressed passionately angry poetry to the eyes of the "cruel beloved." Rumi writes, "As your sword comes down on my neck, I will not take my eyes from your face."[9]

It's not that Radha is masochistic. Far from it: she stands up for her love and her right to be in love. She is willing to dive fully into the passionate bliss not only of her moments of union with Krishna, but also of her moments of separation. This is one of the secrets that Radha imparts, and the reason that Radha-identification has been such a powerful path for single people as well as for those fortunate enough to have a consort who can play the erotic games that are also so much a part of the Radha path.

Erotic devotion, as the stories of Radha and the cowgirl maidens show, is very different than the classical yogic approach to enlightenment. Traditional yogis aim to withdraw their mind from the senses. They privilege a type of meditation that seeks the ultimate spaciousness, the emptiness behind forms. The *Yoga Sutras* define the goal of practice as *chitta vritti nirodha*—the sensation of all movement in the mind.

Devotional yoga—bhakti—chooses to fully engage the senses. The tactic in devotional yoga is to replicate Radha's obsession with her beloved. To do that, you fill your rooms with statues and pictures that remind you of the beloved. You make yourself beautiful for him or for her. You decorate your house and wear brightly colored clothing. You cook food and offer it to the divine beloved. You chant, listen to devotional songs, and repeat the names of God. Like the Sufis with their whirling, you engage your body in trance-inducing movement and dance. You tell stories about God. You hang out with other devotees. Above all, you bring emotion—*bhava* in Sanskrit—into your yoga. Everything in your practice is directed toward kindling and savoring the different flavors (*rasas*) of love and blissfulness in the personal form of the deity.

Even though devotional yoga is a path of practice, true ecstatic devotion is far beyond practice. Just as the awakened state celebrated by the sages is an immediate experience, not a technique or an intellectual understanding, devotion can't be fully understood unless you have it. People who have never felt the passionate sweetness of being immersed in personal love for God mutter dismissively about psychological dependency, spiritual bypassing, and fanaticism. To the rational mind, this kind of devotion looks self-indulgent and crazy. The original Sufi mystics describe themselves as drinkers at a celestial tavern, reeling in drunken ecstasy, sipping the strong wine of divine love, and addressing the beloved as "heart ravisher." The original Hasidim, who sang and danced in wild, all-night devotional frenzies, were called madmen by the conventional rabbis of

Eastern Europe. To the lovers, it makes perfect sense. Why wouldn't you dance if your blood is simmering with adoration?

In later years, just as Hasidism became a rule-bound sect of Orthodox Judaism, the Krishna cult became an orthodox Hindu sect, with strict rules and customs. Most of the devotees merely imitated (or at best, tried to replicate) the original passion. Bhakti movements have a tendency to turn fundamentalist. But originally, Radha and the other cowherd maidens were the models for devotees who lost themselves as they danced crazily in the streets, chanted loudly to the rhythm of cymbals and drums, and welcomed all comers. Chaitanya Mahaprabhu, the sixteenth-century founder of what is known today as the International Society for Krishna Consciousness (ISKCON), led wild chanting parties where he danced through the towns of northern India, transmitting radical love from his heart by embracing everyone he came across. He famously identified himself with Radha. Ramakrishna spent a period of his life dressing in women's clothing and meditating as Radha, in erotic surrender to Krishna. The poet Mirabai fell in love with Krishna as a child and considered herself married to him, even while living as a Rajasthani queen in the town of Udaipur. What all these mystics were enacting was a radical identification with Radha's passion. Even for men, it was ultimately a feminine path—a path of emotion, feeding on beauty and tears.

RADHA IN YOUR LIFE

Some women (and men) have a natural affinity for Radha. A Radha woman often needs intense bliss and pain in her relationships. She makes relationship the center of her life. A Radha woman is likely to be emotional, sensitive, and obsessed with love.

But anyone, male or female, can become Radha when they are in love. The Radha Shakti is the passionate heart energy that brings a love affair alive. She is the Eros of the heart, taking pleasure in longing and anticipation, as much as in fulfillment. The blissful anticipation you feel when you're preparing to meet your lover is an experience of Radha's Shakti. So is the pang of sadness when you have to part. Of course, Radha was a teenager, so she is in a sense the patron goddess of teen romance. The years between the ages of twelve and twenty are the times when many young women play out the fullness of their Radha nature. In those years, your very life seems to depend on being loved by the one you love, and a breakup can feel like a reason for suicide.

You can access one aspect of Radha's energy when you sit with your girl-friends, delighting in conversations about your next meeting with your beloved, plotting how to run into him at the mall. You are being Radha when you bathe and dress and put on your makeup with every thought directed on how you can please your beloved. I first met Radha in myself when I was twelve and in love with an unattainable eighth-grade boy. I had no idea that my obsessive fantasizing, or the lift in my heart when he swung his lanky body onto the school bus, were symptoms of devotion. But at age thirty, when I met my guru and felt that same heart-melting attraction, I actually recognized that the romantic quality in my devotion to my teacher had the same flavor as my romantic devotion to Joey Jay. The difference was that when directed toward my teacher, these same feelings could guide my spiritual path.

You don't have to be young to have Radha explode in your heart. In one of her later novels, *Love, Again*, the English writer Doris Lessing describes a Radha-infused, adoring, unrequited love between a sixty-four-year-old playwright and a young theater director thirty years her junior. The love enlivens every pore of her body, yet causes intense pain because it will never be fulfilled.[10]

Inviting Radha into Your Meditation

First, take some time to prepare your body to meet Radha. You might begin by showering or washing your face. Then, make yourself as beautiful as possible. Put on clean clothes and jewelry, or wrap yourself in a soft shawl. When you are ready, light a candle, and seat yourself in meditation. Make sure you have a journal and pen nearby.

Consider why you have invoked Radha. Do you want help with a problem of love? Do you want to invoke more or deeper love? Do you want to understand divine love?

Gather your intention, and write down your needs, desires, and requests. Place your journal before you.

Repeat the traditional meditation verse for Radha, either in Sanskrit or in English:

Tapta-kanchana-gaurangi
Radhe vrindavaneshwari
Vrishabhanu-sute devi
Pranamami hari-priye

tuhp-tuh-kahn-chuh-nuh-gow-ruhn-gee
rah-dey vrin-dah-vuh-nesh-wahr-ee
vrish-uh-bhah-nu-soo-tey dey-vee
pruh-nuh-mah-mee huh-ree-pree-yay

O Gaurangi, whose complexion is like molten gold
O Radha, Queen of the forest of Vrindavan
O goddess, daughter of Vrisabhanu
O beloved of Krishna, I bow to you.

With your eyes closed, imagine yourself standing in a garden on a warm, scented night. A sweet breeze blows, which you feel caressing your skin.

Ask for Radha, beloved of Krishna, to be present with you.

Now, imagine that she walks into the garden. She is golden skinned, with the face of a fourteen-year-old girl. She has long, wavy hair bound with fragrant white flowers, and she wears a short blouse that bares her midriff and a long skirt. Her breasts are lush. Her rosy toes, with silver toe rings, peek out from beneath her skirt. She is smiling playfully—half girl, half woman.

She seats herself on the grass and invites you to sit beside her.

You sit, and looking into her eyes you see them overflowing with love and mischief. She looks at you questioningly, inviting you to speak to her.

Now, begin to pour out your heart to Radha. Ask her for help in finding love, in finding joy. Ask her to untie a knot in your relationship. Ask her for what you seek in love.

As you speak to her, feel that your requests are received.

Now, if it feels right, ask her that your human relationships be touched with her divine love. Ask that you find the divine through your human loves.

RADHA'S SHADOW

Like all the goddesses, when the Radha Shakti comes alive in human life, she may show a shadow face. Just as the shadow of Radha-style religious devotion is fanaticism, her shadow face in a human love relationship is romantic obsession. We experience Radha's shadow when we just can't let go of a broken relationship, when we pine for an unrequited love, or when we turn a romantic relationship into an emotional roller coaster. Shadow Radha is clingy and jealous. She is also reckless. A woman I know used to read her lover's emails obsessively, convinced that he was cheating on her. When they broke up, she hid in her room, weeping for nearly a month, hardly eating. She even hacked into his email account. She would call her best friend every day to analyze his emails and Facebook postings.

At the extreme end of shadow Radha, you might find someone like Glenn Close's character in the movie *Fatal Attraction* or the anti-hero of Ian McEwan's novel *Enduring Love*.

TURNING HUMAN LOVE INTO DIVINE ROMANCE

When the kundalini Shakti is awake and revealing the liberating face of the goddess as Radha, her ecstatic devotional flow can turn your body and mind into a river of loving energy. Radha's Shakti softens your eyes and brings a playful, gentle smile to your lips. The Radha Shakti intuitively knows how to make your "ordinary" human relationships playful, flirtatious, and loving. She can turn a love affair into an erotic experience of the divine.

If you are doing an internal practice, the Radha energy might infuse your spiritual practice with intense feeling, so that you direct all your normal human emotions—affection and annoyance, anger and infatuation—toward God. On the other hand, if you have enough subtlety and intention, Radha's Shakti can express itself through loving your human lover or your child or your friend as divine beings. You might be drawn to spontaneously worship a lover as the form of the divine. You can treat a child like a sacred being. My friend Nick bows to his wife every morning and evening. She bows to him. They do this even when they aren't getting along with each other. They do it in every mood, at every change of the marital weather. This doesn't mean they don't quarrel, speak sharply to each other, or stand up for their own points of view. Because the Radha Shakti is alive in them, they have learned to hold even the mundane aspects of their relationship in a context of sacred affection.

PRACTICING RADHA

There are two requirements for practicing with Radha energy. The first is that you keep looking fiercely for the divine in your lover or child. The second is that you be willing to keep opening to your feelings, meeting your emotions with the recognition that even the most painful can be doorways into the divine.

At one time in my life I had a lover with whom I could never be together in a conventional partnership. We met every couple of weeks, and our lovemaking had the quality of merging into each other's bodies. The physicality was there, but we were always aware of a deeper and more subtle energy that connected through our skins, through our bones, down to the very soul-essence between us. For days after we had been together, I would feel as if his subtle energy was part of my body. My heart would get soft, sometimes feel as if it were cracking open. At times, I was able to recognize that the very impossibility of conventional couplehood was what made this sweetness possible. At times, it simply felt tragic that we couldn't be together all the time. Over time, the image we held of each other became like an internalized form of the deity, a luminous crystallization of radical emotional presence. Our love for each other was like a wound in the heart, but a wound that carried its own sweetness. We could soothe it with the sound of each other's voice, deepen it by dwelling on the pain of being separated.

In the end, we weren't able to keep it. The passionate longing evolved into a sweet feeling of affection but lost its power to kindle an ecstatic, transformative energy.

There were nights when I would sit with the thought of him and feel erotic energy gather in my genitals, stream through my torso, rising to my heart, flowing in waves up my spine, cresting like light that poured through my body. If I let myself be angry or crave his presence too insistently, the subtle experience wouldn't come to me. But if I could hold his image in my body, let the love-wound be there without trying to resist it or make it go away, I would sometimes dissolve into it, until there was only the sensation of complete oneness. Unlike Radha, I was never able to transfer the erotic devotion I had for my lover to the external world itself. But I was able to recognize again and again how the human form really does hold the divine, and human love the ecstasy of the deity.

Invoking the Love of Radha and Krishna

In this exercise, you will return to Radha's garden, which you first visited in the exercise on page 250.

Imagine yourself back in Radha's garden. This time, you see before you a young couple lying on a bed of flowers. They are entwined in one another's arms. You can hear the sound of their laughter. They are Radha and her beloved Krishna.

As you sit, you see them move from their embrace and beckon you to come to them.

You seat yourself on the ground in front of the couple, and you bow to both of them. Slowly, the figures shift. Now, Krishna and Radha each take one of your hands. They are holding you in the circle of their love, while Radha, seated directly in front of you, gazes into your eyes. She says to you, "Feel the depth of my love."

As if your heart were a portal, feel it open to receive the soft, tender, loving energy that Radha pours into you. Feel what it is like to be completely embraced by their love.

THE WOUNDS OF LOVE

As everyone who has ever experienced it knows, opening the heart can feel like opening a wound. Part of the power of Radha's passion is in its quality of rawness. The other aspect of the secret is in the fact that she accepts every part of it, including the pain. Radha's core state, the previously discussed "bliss of the pain of separation," is a practice that is well worth exploring, even though it might feel counterintuitive. It's especially powerful for people who have a deep longing, whether for a lost lover, for God, or for something unnamed and unknown. If you can recognize your longing as a form of Shakti, you might experience the truth that Kabir celebrated when he wrote, "God is in your longing" and "It is the intensity of the longing for the Friend that does the work."[11] The work is the radical opening toward the inner divine core of yourself. Longing is what fuels that opening.

While I was writing this book, I met a young woman yoga practitioner who was very dedicated to her practice. She had fallen in love with a touring rock musician, whose lifestyle in no way matched her need for regularity and steady discipline. He loved her, but he had a classic rock musician's tendency to play the field. They eventually broke up after she went into a bar in their neighborhood and saw him passionately kissing another woman.

That had happened a year previously, she told me. She had stopped seeing him, but she couldn't get him out of her heart. She knew he was wrong for her, yet being with him had opened her up in a way that had changed her life. "I can't stop loving him," she kept saying. "I don't want to close my heart."

As I listened to her, I actually felt my own heart open. Her state was contagious. I could feel the ache and the sweetness behind it, the crazy ecstatic pain of devotional love. This young woman was experiencing the Shakti of Radha.

I suggested that she try using those feelings in her meditation practice.
"What do you mean?" she asked.

"Feel the pain, let your heart break, and sit with the inner sensation of it," I told her. "Let it be there and make it your starting point for practice. Don't try to get him out of your heart. But let go of thinking that the relationship will work out. Instead, think of the love as a gift of spirit, and meditate on the feeling of love." Radha teaches us to stay open in the midst of heartbreak.

Meditation: The Sensation of Heartbreak

Not for the faint of heart, this exercise involves turning into,
rather than away from, the energetic sensation of heartbreak.
Find a quiet spot and sit comfortably, then begin.

First, draw in the feeling of having your heart broken by a lover. Let yourself feel the emotion. Lean into the feeling, the pain in your heart, as you miss your lover.

Now, let go of the content of the pain, and just feel the wound as an ever-deepening opening in your heart, a softening of the inner armor. Sit with the feelings; breathe into them, sensing all the ways they play in your body and mind. At the same time, breathe out the story, the thoughts *about* the feeling. Don't breathe them out as if you were trying to get rid of them; just breathe them out—until all you are aware of is the pure energy within the feeling of heartbreaking love.

Root yourself in the softness of the heart. Let the ache of separation root itself in the love at its core.

Now, take a radical step. Name the pain as divine Shakti. Name the pain as God. Can you recognize that longing as longing for God?

INVOKING RADHA

As the Goddess of lovers, Radha is the go-to Shakti for all matters of the heart. You might invoke her for finding the juice in your romantic relationship, for attracting romance, and also for supporting you in the midst of a breakup. Radha's Shakti will also kindle in you a generosity about others' romances, because even a vicarious identification with Radha can open your heart.

Radha is also a mediating goddess. Meditating on her or calling on her can help you open your own heart. She can give you the courage to risk vulnerability, and can even initiate you into the path of the vulnerable heart.

Radha

rahd-hah—Golden Girl

Other Names for Radha:
Radhika (*rahd-ee-kah*)—little Radha

Goddess of:
- romance
- longing
- passionate love for the divine

Recognize Radha in:
- passion and romantic love
- intense longing
- romantic settings (like a moonlit forest, lake, or beach)
- romantic intimate sexuality
- devotion to a person or to god
- overflowing love for nature as the beloved

Invoke Radha for:
- blessings on a romance
- winning your lover's heart
- support during a breakup
- relaxing into the pleasure of your romantic relationship
- rekindling a dying love affair
- experiencing your own sensuality
- deepening your love for your pets or for the natural world
- bringing passion into your work, your family, your studies, your friendships
- kindling the flame of devotional love in meditation or chant
- falling in love with the divine
- seeing the divine in the world and in other people

- internalizing a personal relationship with a deity
- bringing passion into your practice by inciting longing and commitment in yourself
- enjoying your life as an offering to the divine

Invocational Mantra

Tapta-kanchana-gaurahngi
Rahdhe vrndahvaneshwari
Vrshabhahnu-sute devi
Pranamahmi hari-priye

tuhp-tah-kuhn-chah-nuh-gau-rahn-gee
rah-dey vrin-dah-vuh-nesh-wahr-ee
vrish-uh-bhah-nu-soo-tey dey-vee
prah-nah-mah-mi hah-ri-pree-yey

O fair-skinned Radha
Goddess of the forest of Vrindavan
Daughter of Vrishabhanu
Beloved of Krishna, I bow to you.

Gayatri Mantra

Om Vrishabhanujayai vidmahe
Krishnapriyai dhimahi
Tanno Radha prachodayat

ohm vri-shuh-bhah-noo-juhy-ai vid-muh-hey
krish-nah-pree-yai dee-muh-hi
tuh-no rahd-hah prah-cho-dah-yaht

Om, may I receive the wisdom of the daughter of Vrishabhanu
May Krishna's beloved illumine my intellect.
May I meditate on Radha

Radha's colors: rosy red and gold
Radha's flowers: night-blooming jasmine and other exotic flowers
Radha's consort: Krishna

CHAPTER 11

Chinnamasta

Goddess of Radical Self-Transcendence

I meditate upon the Goddess Chinnamasta, who is seated in the centre of the
Sun's disk and holds in her left hand her own severed head with gaping mouth;
her hair is dishevelled and she is drinking the stream of blood gushing out from
her own neck. She is seated on Rati and Kamadeva [the god of desire and
his consort] . . . and she is rejoicing with her friends Dakini and Varnini.

MAHIDHARA
Mantra Mahodadhi

That simple but crucial insight—"the sacrifice of self discloses the Eternal"—was the esoteric
insight empowering the mythology of self-sacrifice to the Great Goddess, sacrifice carried
out in prayer, in contemplation, in meditative ritual and ceremony, in symbolic Mass.

KEN WILBER
Up from Eden

On the way to God the difficulties
feel like being ground by a millstone,
like night coming at noon, like
lightening through the clouds.

But don't worry!
What must come, comes.
face everything with love,
as your mind dissolves in God.

LALLA
Translated by Coleman Barks

I n approaching Chinnamasta, we enter again the Goddess's dark realm of
transformative terror and mystery. Chinnamasta is shiveringly awe-inspiring.
Headless, she holds a cleaver in one hand and her own head, crowned with

flowing hair, in the other. Three streams of blood spurt from her neck. Her two naked attendants, each holding cleavers (did they decapitate her, or did she do it herself?) are drinking her blood, which streams into their mouths. Chinnamasta—her name means "head" (*chinna*) "cut off"—is naked, though her breasts and hips are covered with elaborate ornaments. Her yoni is bared. Her feet, adorned with anklets, dance on a couple locked in an embrace.

Even more than Kali and the other fierce goddesses, Chinnamasta demands that we look for the sacred in the forbidden and the terrifying. She was an icon for two controversial Tantric teachers I know of, both of whom loved to talk about the spiritual hero as a practitioner willing to offer his head. The image of headlessness is not unusual in mystical lore. "On this path, the lover is not slow in offering his head at the Beloved's feet," writes the poet Kabir.[1] Other Hindu and Sufi poets—Mirabai, for example, or Rumi—have written fervently of heroes sacrificing their heads to the Lord. To offer the head to God symbolizes total surrender, the complete abandonment of the discursive mind. Symbolically, to be headless is to be free of thoughts, free of self-consciousness, and free of ego. Fine, we say—and more about that in a moment. But we can't ignore the fact that Chinnamasta's image has disturbing resonances. More than any image in the Tantras, her form shows life feeding on itself, the crucial link between love and terror that is such a fascinating and, to many people, horrifying aspect of the Tantric view of life. Who would want to drink their own blood? Someone recently said to me that her first thought upon seeing the image of Chinnamasta was that she symbolized someone in great suffering. Someone psychotic. Someone locked in a dreadful prison, out of sight, and beyond hope of rescue. ("I'd rather be dead than here," a prisoner in a Latin American jail is reported to have said to the *New York Times* in March 2012.)[2] The young "martyr" who straps a bomb to himself, the Burmese monk who sets himself on fire, the member of a religious cult who commits ritual suicide: these are sufferers in any one of the horrific situations human beings experience as much in our hyper-civilized twenty-first century as in less developed periods of history.

But Chinnamasta is neither a figure of suffering, nor of martyrdom. She's a goddess of transcendence and ecstatic empowerment. Christ on the cross symbolizes transcendence of the suffering inflicted on us by the world. Chinnamasta takes us further: she *does it to herself*. For someone in the midst of crisis, physical suffering, or psychological pain, the naked, dancing goddess drinking her own blood could symbolize the intense transformation that can come when we accept the unacceptable, when we "drink" the pain of life. However, if you're a

FIGURE 16: THE GODDESS CHINNAMASTA

meditator working internally with your own kundalini energy, you would see her form differently—perhaps as expressing the mysterious connection between sexual energy and spiritual power. If you're a practitioner on the path of jnana yoga, the path of knowledge, her headlessness might symbolize the capacity to perceive without separating yourself from what is seen. If you're more psychologically oriented, it could be a myth about how mothers, spiritual teachers, (and codependents!) offer their life fluids to the people they love—sometimes with full awareness or consciousness, but at other times in a driven, unconscious way. For anyone on the path of greater awareness, Chinnamasta represents radical transformation of the ego. When you see Chinnamasta in dreams or feel drawn to meditate on her image, you are probably on the threshold of some big shift in consciousness.

THE MYTH OF THE HEADLESS GODDESS

There is more than one version of Chinnamasta's origin. One story goes that Parvati and Shiva have been making love in what the Tantras call "reverse position"—with the goddess on top. As he climaxes, she morphs into her fierce self, PrachandaKali (literally "fierce black one"). From her body emerge two Shaktis, Dakini and Varnini—spiritual daughters who become her attendants.

One day, the three devis go for a bath in the Mandakini River, a celestial stream that flows near Parvati's home on Mt. Kailash. After bathing, her attendants tell her that they are hungry. "Mother, please give us food!" they ask. Smiling, the goddess cuts off her own head. With the three streams of blood that shoot forth, she feeds her two attendants and then herself. Once they have all drunk their fill, she puts her head back on, and once more becomes the lovely Parvati.

Why does Parvati turn fierce at the moment of Shiva's climax? Is she overwhelmed by the sudden infusion of his fiery energy? Is she overcome by passion? Or, does her fierceness symbolize the intensity that comes when kundalini is aroused in the chakra at the base of the spine? The esoteric Tantric tradition points to the last interpretation. The fierceness of the goddess is the intense energy of bliss, rising to unite the couple in the transcendent realm—and then spilling out to nourish the world.

"Dakini" is the name given in Himalayan Tantra to the mysterious female yoginis who serve as Tantric consorts to male practitioners. Dakinis appear and disappear with total freedom, initiating favored yogis, showing up at crucial moments in the spiritual journey. They are elusive, fierce, sexy, and they take no prisoners. In Tibetan culture, spiritually gifted women are often described as dakinis, and given special license to be outrageous, to bend the rules of conventional society, and to realize emptiness as the heart of reality. The dakini is a radically active form of the feminine. In this context, she symbolizes the goddess's power of action.

The root of the name Varnini is *varna*, which translates as "kind" or "category," and is also the word given to the Hindu caste system, which differentiates human beings according to their functions in society. Varnini here indicates the differentiating knowledge that divides life into categories, and makes us see differences. Through these natural powers—knowing and doing—the goddess manifests life and nourishes it. So, you could look at the icon as an allegory that shows the Devi's Shakti eternally nourishing the powers of knowledge and action that manifest through all living beings. Or, Dakini and Varnini could represent the goddess's human "agents," the teachers and adepts who receive, hold, and spread the Shakti through their teachings and examples, and who must be continuously fed from the source.

Another version of the story has Chinnamasta fighting demons in one of the endless wars between the gods and their archenemies, the asuras. When the battle is over, her battle lust is not satisfied, so she cuts off her own head and drinks her own blood. In a third version of her origin, she is said to have appeared after the gods and demons had churned the ocean. Chinnamasta seizes the demons' share of the nectar of immortality, drinks it herself, and then cuts off her own head so the demons can't receive the nectar.

These last two stories, you'll notice, describe the goddess as a fierce nurturer. She sacrifices herself for others, and in this act of reckless self-abandonment, her fierceness and her nurturing qualities are inseparable. The goddess's blood represents her Shakti, the creative energy with which she constantly replenishes life. She offers her life-force, without holding anything back. How free she is, to be able to so exuberantly sever her own head, hold it, feed herself as well as others, then replace it and go home as if nothing has happened!

CHINNAMASTA AS KUNDALINI

Because Chinnamasta is fundamentally a goddess of the inner yogic process, we'll discuss her esoteric qualities before we look at her psychologically. Most Tantric practitioners would tell you that the image of Chinnamasta is a symbolic picture of the rising kundalini. The goddess, in her form as kundalini, takes hold of the sexual energy generated by a Tantric couple (or by an individual who arouses sexual energy internally for spiritual purposes).

Sexual activity normally dissipates the energy needed for yogic power, which is why classical yoga, like classical Western mysticism, wants you to discipline sexual energy through some form of celibacy or, at the very least, moderation. When kundalini awakens and rises, and when the drive toward orgasm has been disciplined through awareness and yogic control, sexual energy becomes spiritual power. Then, the energy that we normally associate with genital sexuality—in a man, the seminal fluid—rises through the subtle channel at the core of the inner spine and melts our bones with the subtle touch of bliss. Tantric writers, because they did not see that any obvious substance was emitted by women at orgasm, considered menstrual blood to be the feminine form of sexual energy. Modern yoginis, of course, know differently. Nonetheless, I know many spiritual women practitioners with awake kundalinis whose menstrual periods either stop or come only every few months—perhaps indicating that some part of their biological energy is "rising" and being transmuted into a more subtle form.

Chinnamasta's image also points to the power of sexual energy as a kind of subtle inner touch. The Tantric master Abhinavagupta writes about touch as the only one of the senses that remains active in advanced states of meditation. In the very highest states of samadhi, you hear nothing, see nothing, taste nothing, and smell nothing. These states are so far beyond either the physical or the subtle senses, but the inner sensation of touch remains active in the highest states of awareness. "Touch resides at the highest level of Shakti as an indescribable, subtle sensation ceaselessly yearned for by the yogin," he writes, "for this contact leads to a consciousness identical with the self-luminous, pure sky of consciousness."[3]

As kundalini, Chinnamasta seizes the raw energy generated by passion and distills it into an exquisitely subtle electrical thrill, which can take a visual form as light, or a kinesthetic form as a sensation of subtle touch. If this occurs as part of a deliberate practice, the yogi will have controlled his or her own energy by a process of focused breathing, and held it inside through *bandhas,* or bodily "locks" of the throat, abdomen, and anus. Then, he draws the collected energy into the central channel—a hair-thin "wire" inside the subtle spinal column. The kundalini slowly ascends to the crown chakra until, with practice, it becomes a fountain of light. Spilling out through the crown, this fountain of Shakti connects the individual's consciousness to the vastness of consciousness itself. Yogic texts like the *Hatha Yoga Pradipika* describe the complex combination of postures and breathing processes that awakens kundalini. Once kundalini is active—however this may have been activated—the rising can become more or less spontaneous. Kundalini rises on its own as the practitioner sits in meditation or engages it through a process of breathing energy up the spine, or meditates by turning her attention into the central channel. Kundalini's active force is an expression of Chinnamasta's graceful energy.

In the hatha yoga texts, this upward flowing current, where the normally outflowing sexual energy is drawn up into the head, is called *vajroli mudra*. Vajroli mudra occurs spontaneously as an inner event when passionate sexuality is disciplined, conserved, then mingles with the upward flowing vital force called *udana* ("rising") *prana*. In its most dramatic form, the energy rises up through the subtle channel in the spinal column, piercing the spiritual centers, then bursts through the head like subtle fireworks, dissolving the mind into a state of sky-like luminosity. When such a Tantric adept engages in sexual tantra, it is for the purpose of providing a driving current to fuel this intense experience of rising kundalini. As all that blissful, transmuted lust reaches the crown, it is said to melt the discursive mind, symbolized by the head. It takes off the "head" of the separative ego, dissolves it into light, and then becomes a fountain-like stream of energy and bliss that nourishes the practitioner and her disciples.

So Chinnamasta, like Kali, carries yoga's enlightening fire. She is the goddess of a yogic process that leads to radical self-realization. Her life-blood represents the energy and wisdom drawn from the stored and transmuted passion of her sexuality. And her realization is the selfless offering of teaching and power that arises when the "head" of the personal ego, the false sense of self, is severed.

Meditation: Chinnamasta

For this exercise, close your eyes and seat yourself
in a comfortable, upright posture.

Center yourself by taking five deep, full breaths.

Focus your attention in the third-eye region, between your eyebrows in the center of your head.

Out loud, repeat Chinnamasta's seed mantra "Hum" (*hoom*) twenty-seven times.

Imagine Chinnamasta standing in the air before you. Her body is radiant with white light. One hand raises a sword, and the other holds her own head, which is smiling. Feel that from her neck flows a powerful white radiance. This is the light of lightning-like wisdom, the power of awakening.

Feel that this light enters your crown and flows through your brain, turning your thoughts to light. The light flows down through your body, filling your body with bright white light. Feel that Chinnamasta's radical blessing is enlightening your very cells, the material of your body.

CHINNAMASTA'S RADICAL SELF-INQUIRY

Another way to look at Chinnamasta's image is as embodied spiritual inquiry: If you were to sever the "head" of your normal, body-boundaried sense of self, who would you be? Without your normal roles, without the "head" of your thoughts, memories, ideas, and self-identity, who are you really? What is left when you surrender all your ideas about yourself? What is left when you actually follow the advice so often given to a meditator and actually let go of your mind?

If you practice this inquiry deeply, giving yourself every possible answer until you run out of verbal answers, you'll eventually realize that what you are looking for is actually the looker, the wordless seer behind all ideas about yourself and your relationship to the world you inhabit. The inquiry opens you to awareness itself, consciousness undiluted by objects. If you've ever tried to meditate on consciousness itself, you know how difficult it is to hold attention steady without an object of attention. One of Chinnamasta's gifts is the power to rest in totally unconditioned awareness, awareness free of thought. The fierceness of her image signals the intensity of her energy, which is a subtle light-saber, the only sword capable of silencing the discursive mind.

THE HEADLESS ONE

One of the more engaging twentieth-century memoirs of a Westerner's experience of enlightened consciousness is by the English writer Douglas Harding. In his book, *On Having No Head*, Harding describes a realization he had while trekking in the Himalayas. One day, quite spontaneously, he lost the sense of having a head on top of his neck. As far as he knew, he had no head. Instead of feeling his "self" to be contained inside the small round circle of his skull, he was pure seeing, pure perceiving. His awareness was open to whatever arose, and everything felt as if it were arising inside him. Mountains, sky, and his own body existed seamlessly inside a single awareness that included his physical self but totally transcended it. With the disappearance of his head, he had also lost his personal ego. He was self-less: thought free, fully open, one with the universe around him.[4]

In the nondual Tantras, this experience of awareness pervading and containing the world is known as the state of Shiva: the recognition that everything exists within your own conscious awareness.

Imagining That Your Head Is the Sky

The meditation of headlessness is described in several Tantric texts. My favorite is from the *Vijnana Bhairava;* what follows here is an adaptation. Find a comfortable sitting position in a quiet location, and begin.

Sitting quietly, close your eyes. Imagine that instead of a head, there is only sky above your neck. Let yourself experience your head as sky.

Open your eyes and gaze out into the world as if you were headless, as if your head were the sky.

What is your experience of the world you see when your head is sky?

A friend who read this chapter just after it was written reported that the preceding meditation felt far too peaceful to be emblematic of such a wild goddess as Chinnamasta. But one of the fundamental paradoxes of Tantric deities is that so-called wrathful deities—the ones who look especially scary on the outside—bring interior peace to those who allow themselves to look beyond the apparent. When you face up to Chinnamasta and let her initiate you into her own freedom, she will show you what that freedom really means: she will open your mind to the universe itself.

THE HEADLESS MEDITATOR

We can think of Chinnamasta's headless state as the absolute purity and courage of someone who has discarded all separate self-sense. Cutting off your own head is cutting off the false-self ego, with its need to preserve your separate personal life at all costs. Having cut off her head, the goddess is able to offer everything to those who need it. Because Chinnamasta cares nothing for personal survival, because she is so unimaginably selfless, she becomes the source of life-force for others. In short, she is a bodhisattva, one whose entire *raison d'etre* is enlightening the suffering of the world. Chinnamasta is often identified with the Buddhist

267

goddess Vajrayogini, who also represents the qualities of radical enlightened wisdom. Chinnamasta's energy shines through the Buddhist prayer that asks, "Nurture me so that I may nurture life."

Casually exuberant, the goddess offers herself to us as the force that awakens in meditation. Fearlessly rigorous, she roots herself in passion and transmutes it into wisdom. Terrifyingly detached even from her own head, she challenges us to follow her example by letting go of all attachment to personal agendas. "I have come so that you may have life, and have it more abundantly," Jesus said, in the most famous statement of enlightened self-sacrifice in Western spiritual literature.[5] When we've sacrificed the "head" of the ego, we can actually work for others without inhibition, without holding back.

THE GODDESS AS THE TEACHER

In the human world, this uninhibited self-offering of Shakti is called shakti-pat—the descent of revelatory energy from the divine into the human realm. Though it can happen without any apparent human intervention, shaktipat is often the gift of the enlightened Tantric spiritual master. In India, devotees of charismatic female teachers like Anandamayi Ma, Mother Meera, or Ammachi often describe their gurus as incarnations of the Goddess. Whether or not this is literally the case, what *is* true is that so-called charismatic teachers, both male and female, are capable of transmitting a powerful spontaneous blessing that acts as an awakening force in others.

One of my favorite stories about Anandamayi Ma is the story of how she initiated her husband. At the time, she was a teenage bride, completely uneducated, living in an orthodox family of Bengali Brahmins. At night, when everyone was asleep, she would be drawn to sit in meditation. Driven by a profound force, an irresistible energy, her body moved, twisted, performed yogic postures, and went into spontaneous samadhi states. As her consciousness expanded, she experienced total unity with all things. For some time, she continued to live as a submissive Hindu wife, serving her husband and her in-laws—even while being guided to behave in extraordinary ways.

One day she said to her husband, "I will initiate you today." Her husband, appalled at the idea of a man receiving initiation from his wife, refused. She said (and you must remember, that this was an uneducated, orthodox Hindu child-wife speaking, not a modern college-educated Indian woman), "If you don't come home at the appointed time, I'll come to your office and initiate you there in front of everyone." He came, received the transmission of her Shakti, and became her disciple.

Describing the process of transmission epitomized by the Chinnamasta Shakti, Anandamayi Ma said, "As the flower gives its fragrance naturally, so the Guru gives *diksha*—by sight or hearing or touch or teaching or mantra or even without any of these, just because he is the Guru. The flower does not make an effort to give its fragrance, it does not say: 'Come and smell me.' It is there. Whoever comes near it will enjoy the scent."[6]

Every teaching lineage carries a particular, unique storehouse of wisdom, love, and energy. Each has its own quality. One lineage may transmit an extremely subtle experience of insight and an expanded awareness. Another may bubble with active energy and passionate spiritual intensity. Some lineage transmissions melt the heart; others convey yogic rigor and intense yogic will. But in a Tantric lineage transmission, there is an offering, by the guru, of heart's blood in the form of energy. That offering can be channeled without intention—or deliberately—through a thought, a mantra, a glance, or touch. My own guru passed on spiritual energy and transformative spiritual awakening on a massive and dramatic scale, even giving public programs in which he awakened kundalini in attendees by a touch—including the occasional light kick to the base of the spine. Though every real spiritual teacher imparts some form of wisdom to students, the true work of a guru, especially in Tantric lineages, is to transmit her own state in the form of accumulated Shakti to anyone who is capable of containing it.

The Tantric texts describe several types of formal shaktipat initiation. In the left-handed Tantric paths, a master will sometimes initiate disciples through a sexual transmission, in which the disciple's sexual energy is made to rise through the central channel and unite life-force with pure awareness in the crown. This is one of the esoteric gestures that Chinnamasta's form suggests. In more conventional spiritual transmission, the disciple sits at the guru's feet (literally or figuratively), hearing wise words, being blessed by the guru's calm gaze and upraised hand. Tantric texts also describe highly formal initiations for qualified disciples, including one that entitles the disciple to become a guru himself.[7] But in practice, especially in the secret Tantric paths, initiation can take place through most unconventional means, including a slap, ritual intercourse, and through other practices not mentioned in any text. In some Tantric traditions, the highest initiation is said to be the initiation by the yogini, the naked female guru whose realization has taken her beyond convention, and gives her the skill to transmit her own spiritual force into another.

THE CHINNAMASTA WOMAN: THE
POSTCONVENTIONAL YOGINI AND HER SHADOW

As the images of yoga goddesses are transmitted across cultures, they take on psychological freight that may have little to do with their original meaning. Released from their original context and from the secretive, esoteric processes that are supposed to bring inner experience of their role in consciousness, the fierce Tantric goddesses often become symbols of worldly freedom. They allow women to envision their own audacity, flaunt their wounds, and speak of what ordinarily would be unspeakable. In fact, it is the shocking quality of Chinnamasta's image that gives it resonance for contemporary women—both as an archetype of freedom and an archetype of woundedness.

As a psychological image, Chinnamasta can represent the exuberant recklessness of the modern yogini—ideally, a beautiful young woman intoxicated by her own life-force, courageous or driven enough to break social boundaries. Her headlessness is a metaphor for her reckless embrace of the anti-conventional. To a woman imbued with the myth of the heroic yogini, Chinnamasta symbolizes the kind of risk taking that is implied in Bob Dylan's famous line, "To live outside the law you must be honest." Hiding nothing, offering her own version of truth through word and gesture, the Chinnamasta woman stands between carnality and the transcendent (in her own mind, at least). She does her best to throw away anything that holds her back from questioning reality. Naked to herself, she is strong enough to withstand the insecurity that comes from radical truthfulness, compassionate enough to use her strength in service, and experimental enough to push the boundaries of what is safe and simple. In an article called "Dating a Yoga Goddess" in the online magazine *Elephant Journal*, the yoga teacher Alex Smith describes yoginis as:

> [those] flexible dare-devils on a spiritual mission who seem to float
> around the world so freely. . . . Most of us don't like societal rules
> and conventions. And most of us don't adhere to them and have
> dedicated our lives to living outside boxes in some way or another. . . .
> A Yoga Goddess can appear to many like an untouchable, statuesque,
> ephemeral . . . theatrical mess on wheels. . . . A Yoga Goddess can
> see souls. . . . Know that [she] is not out to emasculate you but that
> it is her wish and it is within her power to . . . open your heart.[8]

A true Chinnamasta woman may have stepped outside the bounds of the conventional couple, yet hasn't given up coupling. She is a radical thinker, an adventurer.

That means she's often lonely, sometimes confused, but willing to brave the darkness in order to know what is true. The truth she discovers will often come from a remorseless confrontation with the demons in her soul and a willingness to look at both sides of oppositions like life and death, freedom and commitment, success and failure.

CHINNAMASTA'S SHADOW

That brings us to Chinnamasta's complex shadow, and the redemption it offers. At a mundane, first-tier psychological level, Chinnamasta can stand for disassociation. Disassociating or disembodying is one of the remedies we take when we are traumatized or in some other way seized by the shadow of the dark goddess. I can remember, at the age of ten, learning how to move my consciousness so that I stood aside from my body when my mother shouted at me. Like many others, I used that talent for disembodiment to escape feeling painful emotions or to endure attacks from other children, shame, physical punishment and, later, unwanted sex. Children learn to stand outside their bodies when they are spanked, raged at, physically abused or violated, or simply when they are being bullied or humiliated by their peers. In so doing, we cut off our heads—we choose unconsciousness over painful feeling.

Chinnamasta's shadow also manifests in sadomasochistic yearnings and practices. The film *Quills* graphically and dramatically uses the image of headlessness to evoke the violent mood described in the Marquis de Sade's eighteenth-century French S&M novel, *Justine*. The movie begins with a young woman having her head struck off by a guillotine. In 2012, a novel called *Fifty Shades of Grey* topped the bestseller lists with the love story of a dominating lover named Christian Grey and his beautiful younger girlfriend, Anastasia.[9] Commentators noted that many women—including women with good marriages and professional careers—seem to be turned on by masochistic fantasies, if not actual masochistic sex. Perhaps it is their lives of unremitting demands for independent competence that makes women long to be dominated, some writers speculated. Or perhaps it is the Chinnamasta archetype raising her headless head.

THE URGE TO SELF-MUTILATE

For a woman battling disassociation or guilt, unworthiness or confusion, Chinnamasta's act of self-mutilation can seem literal—a mirror of the self-destructive urge that sometimes drives girls and women overwhelmed by their psychological pain. Sandra, who is twenty years old, just "graduated" from a halfway house for girls with eating disorders. She showed me the cuts on her arm, cuts she makes when her feeling of psychological numbness becomes so difficult that she is willing to hurt herself in order to feel something. She wears long-sleeved blouses and confides in one or two girlfriends who also self-cut. She cuts herself slowly, lovingly, and only until she experiences the relief of actually feeling physical pain.

Sandra cut herself for years, partly to penetrate her own numbness, but also because she felt that by hurting herself she symbolically protected her younger sisters from hurt. This girl felt that, like the goddess in the image, she nourished her sisters with her own life-force. Many of the dark goddesses speak to young women battling issues of self-esteem or inner questions about keeping rules versus kicking over traces. A headless goddess in a dream can point out our fear of seeing, as well as our fear of being out of control. We could even, from a certain point of view, identify Chinnamasta with the self-sacrificing gesture of the young woman who "feeds" her friends and family with emotional support, regardless of her own needs, assuming that by nurturing them she will somehow get nurtured in return.

In her book *Dancing in the Flames*, Jungian psychologist Marion Woodman theorizes that the bulimic who eats (nourishes herself) uncontrollably, then vomits compulsively to get rid of the food she's taken in, is someone who has been seized by the shadow of the dark goddess.[10] If so, Chinnamasta—with her luscious body and her triumphant conquest of desire—is a fiercely appropriate icon. She can symbolize the secret life of a woman who, while maintaining her successful façade, cuts off her own needs, desires, and instincts for the sake of an impossible image of perfection, or simply to repress a wound. The young ballerina, Nina, played by Natalie Portman in the film *Black Swan* is driven by a dark mother who pushes her daughter to relive her own dream of success as a dancer. Insecure, perfectionistic, and promoted to a role that demands too much of her, she falls into unconsciousness and loses out to a rival. Her nemesis, Lily, played by Mila Kunis, is a wild girl who is not afraid to embody her own dark energies. The story ends tragically, after Lily gets Nina drunk, seduces her, then leaves her sleeping off the after-effects while Lily dashes off to steal Nina's role. The film, with its undertones of sexual abuse, power dynamics, and exploitation, carries a clear message that unowned dark energies will destroy us if we don't bring them to consciousness.

Contemporary experts say that young women with eating disorders or cutting disorders often have a buried history of sexual abuse.[11] Such a woman's life may have been shadowed by hidden experiences of sexual wounding—a situation that is common in all societies, including (as the film *Monsoon Wedding* points out) traditional India, where patriarchs in joint families might sexually engage their nieces and daughters, and where young girls are often married to much older men. A girl who has been unknowingly sexualized, or whose own sexuality is hidden from her, is "headless" in the sense that she no longer remembers a piece of her past, or even because she has lost a piece of herself as a result of the original wounding. In her disassociation from memory and feeling, she figuratively cuts off her own head, her own ability to be conscious. She then feeds her own false personalities with her energy.

THE SACRIFICE OF CREATIVITY

Another less extreme form of the Chinnamasta shadow is the energy that can imbue a fierce woman with a neurotic fear of keeping her own creative energy for her own purposes. Despite the gains of feminism, many women, especially while raising families, act out the belief that as women, it is their deepest obligation to sacrifice their own creativity, energy, and life-force to feed their partners, their spouses, their bosses, their children, or their students and friends. This is a particularly tricky aspect of the negative side of the Chinnamasta archetype: the brave, strong mother who offers all her power to the ones who "depend" on her can be unconsciously acting out a sacrificial feminine archetype. (Such a woman, as any psychotherapist knows, may also disempower her children or truncate a partner's inner growth through her overgenerosity or lack of boundaries.) For a contemporary woman, to dream of the headless one can be a signal that she is giving away too much of her individuality.

CHINNAMASTA AS DEMOCRATIC
PROCESS AND ITS GROUP SHADOW

Another aspect of shadow Chinnamasta shows up in groups where hierarchy and authority are considered suspect. During my days in the New York Radical Feminists, there were always people in the group who got outraged when one member (usually someone especially articulate, successful, or telegenic) was singled out as spokesperson by the media, or when someone assumed a dominant or leadership role.

On the positive side, in democratic, culturally revolutionary groups like the Women's Movement, the Occupy Movement, and others, Chinnamasta's image can represent a genuinely leaderless group. In a talking circle, leadership passes naturally from person to person as a talking stick passes from hand to hand. In that paradigm, the stream of blood that gushes into the mouths of Chinnamasta's attendants symbolizes the shared stream of leadership and authority. Chinnamasta is a radically experimental goddess, and there is no more radical social experiment than freely sharing governance among members of a group. Such a group might "cut off the head" by rotating facilitation, insisting on decisions being made by the whole, and critiquing any attempt to truncate the democratic process for the sake of efficiency.

As always with strong manifestations of the goddess, the line between light and shadow needs to be walked carefully. In a democratic group, shadow Chinnamasta can become destructive when the group insists that all personal gifts must be subordinated to the collective. The fear that an individual might use his or her charisma to dominate, control, or achieve personal success becomes anger and judgment, and in time the group "drinks" so much of the creative energy out of strong or talented individuals, that the creative ones are driven out of the group.[12]

Which Side of Chinnamasta Are You Expressing?

Find some quiet time to look deeply at the archetype you are most often embodying by asking yourself the following questions. Sit comfortably and keep your journal and a pen nearby.

"In what way am I "mutilating" myself to share power, love, or care with others?"

"In what ways do I hold back from sharing my gifts and power?"

"How am I hoarding or failing to express my natural gifts, my love, and my power?"

Now consider your gifts. Imagine them flowing selflessly into the world. What would that look like? Notice the emotions that arise as you imagine your gifts pouring out of you and nurturing other people. Feel the joy in this. Feel the negative emotions as well. Do you feel drained? Angry? Used?

Now ask yourself, "What appropriate boundaries should I place on my offering of myself? How do I regulate my time? How do I put boundaries on my feelings of 'owing' help to others? How do I nurture my gifts so that they benefit me, so that I reap the harvest of my offering?"

Write down whatever you come up with.

As human beings committed to the process of becoming fully conscious, we're asked to become aware of all aspects of the self. The path of consciousness demands that we look at both our light and our shadow gifts, to know what needs to be contained and harvested inwardly, and what we can appropriately give to others. In this process, there's often a sense of dying to old ways of being with ourselves and others. The image of Chinnamasta so often shows up for us when we are experiencing a form of inner death and rebirth. In a deep transformative process, we willingly become naked, offering up our excuses, our outworn defensive strategies, and our masks for the sake of healing. Anyone willing to look into and heal their own unconscious wounding is actually giving a gift to the culture at large: because they do it, others can share the wisdom of their journey. A stream of wisdom rises up when you have severed the head of your unconscious acquiescence to shadow dynamics. Because you have done it, others can also do it.

To internalize Chinnamasta's image is to agree to a sacrifice. Specifically, to sacrifice an old persona, an old way of defining yourself. The violence of the self-beheading indicates how strong that commitment needs to be for the sake of transformation—a process that always asks some part of us to die. All the fierce goddesses demand this, because they epitomize creative destruction, life emerging from death. When you embrace the fierce goddess, you die to your old ways of thinking about yourself. You die to your illusions. You die to your ego's agenda. This level of sacrifice is always a double-edged, bittersweet, profoundly ambiguous process.

The ambiguity in the figure of Chinnamasta is the ambiguity inherent in the journey of greater consciousness. As a Tantric goddess, Chinnamasta epitomizes *knowing* self-sacrifice, enlightened self-sacrifice. In this sense, she is different than Sita, whose graceful form loves and serves without asking any hard questions or demanding return. Sita never acts for herself. She always places herself subordinate to others: first to her husband and later to her mother, the earth. Chinnamasta, on the other hand, is the radical audacity of consciousness ascending from its embeddedness in life's natural cycle. She dances away from the comfort zone of ordinary life. When a couple "dies" in orgasm, out of their coupling comes new life. When the Tantric practitioner "dies" to ego, she moves beyond the physical level of pleasure to ascend to the greater, subtler pleasure of increased consciousness. She rides her sexuality beyond the physical to the realm of enlightenment, and then offers her enlightenment to enliven the life of others.

The power that Chinnamasta pours into her disciples could be seen as the wisdom of the female sage. Feminine sage energy arises out of the body itself, out of the "darkness" of the space inside the pelvic region, out of the gut. Moreover, it arises from an inner union of the inner masculine and feminine, of intellect and sensuality, of awareness and bliss. Tellingly, the wise woman who rises from this particular bed of passion is single. That may be the reason why Parvati manifests in her fierce form after Shiva's orgasm. Fierceness is what it takes to insist on your singularity when every instinct tells you to collapse into the comfort and restfulness of the postcoital state. Fierceness is what it takes to contain your own energy and turn it into wisdom. Thus, the stream of wisdom that flows from Chinnamasta's transmuted passion is the power that in the West is called *sophia* and that is often associated with the wise old woman, the female elder. Chinnamasta is that same energy poured into transformative activity. We see her wisdom when we look at her severed head drinking the blood that rushes from her body, blood that nourishes herself as well as others on her ecstatic, hard-earned wisdom.

If you are drawn to Chinnamasta, ask yourself at what level you are receiving her message. Is she showing you a place where you are broken; is she asking you to enter a new level of self-transcendence?

Chinnamasta

chin-nuh-muh-stah—Headless One

Other Names for Chinnamasta:
> Vajrayogini (*vuj-ruh-yo-gee-nee*)—Thunderbolt Yogini
> Vairochani (*vai-ro-cha-nee*)—Radiantly Brilliant One
> Vajra-Vairochani (*vuj-ruh vai-ro-cha-nee*)—She Who Illumines Like a Sudden Flash of Lightning

Goddess of:
> • subtle Tantric processes for converting passion into spiritual energy

Recognize Chinnamasta in:
> • a sky full of lightning, a sudden thunderstorm
> • radical acts of self-sacrifice

- sudden spiritual awakening into transcendental awareness
- the "headless" state of thought-free meditation
- egoless states
- the experience of having everything taken away—as though your normal identity is being removed
- kundalini rising
- women's circles in which there is naked sharing of experience
- giving up social roles
- renunciation of your comfort zone, your egoic agendas, and your clinging to personal boundaries
- naked truthfulness no matter what the cost

Invoke Chinnamasta for:
- raising kundalini to the topmost spiritual center, and thus carrying the practitioner to the state of "no mind"
- intense, sudden spiritual awakening
- sacrificing ego in the service of enlightened consciousness—i.e., "dying before you die."
- fearless self-inquiry ("Who am I, really?") with willingness to step beyond all comfort zones
- the bodhisattva or spiritual teacher's willing "feeding" of her disciples
- courage to face your personal demons
- transforming unconscious sacrifice into willing self-surrender
- letting go in deep meditation
- transforming your sexual energy into an awakening and healing force
- becoming psychologically naked

Bija Mantra
Hum (*hoom*)

Invocational Mantra
Om aim hrim shrim Vajra-vairochanyai hum hum phat svaha
Ohm eye-m hreem shreem vuj-ruh-vai-ro-chan-yai hoom hoom putt svah-hah

"Shrim" stands for beauty; "hrim" for transformation and creativity. Vajra-vairochani is the name of Chinnamasta that means "thunderbolt lightning of spiritual awakening."

"Hum" is a mantra for cutting through all illusions.
"Phat" focuses the power in the mantra.
"Svaha" means "offering to the fire of consciousness."

Gayatri Mantra

Om vairochanyai cha vidmahe
Chinnamastayai dhimahi
Tanno devi prachodayat

ohm vai-ro-chuhn-yai chuh vid-muh-hey
chin-nuh-muh-stah-yai dee-muh-hee
tun-no day-vee pruh-cho-duh-yah-tuh

Om, may we come to know the Luminous Goddess
May we meditate on She whose head is severed
May that Goddess inspire/impel us on our path.

Chinnamasta's color: black
Chinnamasta's consort: Shiva

CHAPTER 12

Lalita Tripura Sundari

Goddess of Erotic Spirituality

You are consciousness, ether, air, fire, water, and earth.
You are the universe, O Mother.
But in order to perform your play as the universe,
You take form as the wife of Shiva
And appear before us as exquisite happiness.

SHANKARACHARYA
"Ananda Lahari" ("Wave of Bliss")

With disheveled hair, their upper cloths slipping from their breasts,
their golden belts unfastened because of their haste,
with saris slipping from their shoulders,
hundreds of young women
run after even an old, ugly, and impotent man
who has received just one of your sidelong glances.

SHANKARACHARYA
"Ananda Lahari" ("Wave of Bliss")

I n the Indian city of Varanasi there is a temple dedicated to Rajarajeshwari, a
form of the lovely Goddess Tripura Sundari. People say that when you enter
the temple you can feel the goddess's radical power of attraction. Supposedly,
no one has ever been strong enough to spend the night there. Even her priests
sometimes go crazy with love for her—and as a result there's a lot of turnover
among the temple personnel! Perhaps this story is just a parable about the power
of desire, but if you have experienced the full unfolding of the goddess in this
form, you understand how it could be true. The name Rajarajeshwari means "the
goddess who rules over rulers." It's just one of the thousand names of the goddess Lalita ("Charming One"), whose essence is divine beauty and whose gift is

the bliss that arises when you are able, through her grace, to recognize that every pore of your body, every eyelash, every movement of thought or breath is an expression of her divine play.

Lalita Tripura Sundari ("the charming beauty of the three worlds") is the form of the goddess who most successfully holds together the apparent opposites of executive power and sexuality, and of sexual and spiritual love. Queenly and playful, she represents a most delicious form of the integrated feminine. She is connected to Parvati, who is herself a beautiful form of Kali. In a sense, Lalita integrates the qualities of Parvati—the faithful yogini wife—with those of Kali, the untamable wild woman.[1] Lalita is primarily a Tantric goddess—a mediatrix of the inner realms, a guide through the portals of high stages of samadhi. She is the divine beauty (*sundari*) who permeates the waking, dream, and deep-sleep states—the *tripura*, or "three worlds"—as well as the physical, subtle, and causal bodies in which we experience those worlds.

Lalita reveals herself as the inner rapture that rolls through the body when kundalini colonizes the topmost chakras, and also in the rapturous union of intimate partnership. The name Lalita refers to her capacity for erotic play—one manifestation of which is the natural universe itself, which to an awakened eye appears as a dance of sensual love play, fueled by desire.

GODDESS OF LOVE

In her cosmic form, Lalita embodies desire as the universal creative force. In the Indian view of creation, Desire—Kama—is always the first seed of life. The Greek concept of Eros comes closest in Western language to describing what the force of desire means in the Indian spiritual tradition. Though in our time we have relegated Eros to the sexual, in fact it is something much wider and vaster. Eros is the driving force of life itself, and the erotic is that quality in reality that makes it lively, juicy, and alluring. Cosmic desire brings the universe into being, and the world is, in one sense, an outflowing of the cosmic erotic impulse.

Lalita personifies desire in all its forms—starting with the cosmic desire that impels the formless unborn to explode into forms. In the holographic universe that the Tantras celebrate, that wave of desire is expressed through the entire visible and invisible world. Lalita is the cosmic force that Brian Swimme calls "allurement." The same force that draws atoms together into molecules also manifests as the attractive scent that flowers send forth to attract bees, and as the inner heat and moistness of human sexuality. As a spiritual principle, Lalita's Shakti channels mundane desires into active spiritual aspiration.

FIGURE 17: LALITA SUPPORTED BY FOUR MALE GODS

So when we meditate on Lalita Tripura Sundari, we can access two of the most alluring aspects of the goddess: her creative, life-enhancing generative energy, and her power of spiritual bliss, the inner pull by which she draws the outgoing mind into the spiritual heart.

LALITA'S IMAGE

Lalita sits on a lotus, which emerges out of a bed supported by the reclining form of Sadashiva, Shiva's form as her consort, also known as Kameshwara ("Lord of Desire"). The legs of the bed are four male gods: Brahma the creator, Vishnu the sustainer, Rudra the destroyer, and Shiva in his form as the summation of the previous three deities. Her commanding position symbolizes her status as supreme Power, worshipped even by those who govern the cosmos itself.

Delicately featured, she has a luminous, rosy body. Her rosy color signifies that she is flush with both sexual fulfillment and spiritual delight, and her body is moist with nectar and bliss. She has heavy breasts and a narrow waist. The crescent moon adorns her forehead, and her smile, it is said, overwhelms Shiva.

LALITA'S POWERS

Lalita has four hands in which she holds a noose, a goad, a sugar-cane bow, and five arrows made of flowers. The noose represents that force of attractive love that draws the particles of matter together to form atoms, molecules, and cells and that draws living beings together to form pairs. The noose can operate in two ways: it can bind you to the wheel of life through endless cravings—sexual and otherwise—or it can become longing for the divine and draw you inward, toward the primal union of life-energy with pure spirit.

Lalita's goad represents the suffering caused by craving and anger, which drives living beings and eventually inspires us to wake up to a higher reality. Her bow is the power that incites the mind through attraction and craving, but which can also infuse you with spiritual bliss. The five arrows are the five senses as well as the inner senses that reveal their delight in meditation.

This image shows Lalita as the driving power of life, the Shakti of allurement who makes the world keep revolving in the round of samsara, the endless cycles of life.

However—and this is always the heart of the mystery of the goddess—she also represents the goddess's power to carry us beyond the mundane. Whether she manifests through sexual merging or inner mystical union, Lalita is primarily a goddess of the extra-ordinary, the supramundane. She is unabashedly sexy: in the Lalitasahasranama, the Thousand Names of the Goddess Lalita, she is called the Desirable One, She Who Is Filled with Erotic Sentiments, She Whose Form Is the Desire of Women, and She Who Enchants. But she also represents the subtlest form of bliss—the God-saturated bliss that only comes to one who can sublimate egoic desire to higher longings. In fact, Lalita is a higher octave of Parvati. As Parvati, this goddess functions to bring the divine masculine into embodiment, domesticating Shiva through her yogic powers. As Lalita, she carries him back into the sublime reaches of the upper worlds and merges with him there.

Shankara described Lalita as the one "who dwells in a forest of bliss, whose ornaments glisten with gold, who wears a great pearl necklace, whose mouth rolls with wine, who is the giver of great compassion, who has wide eyes and wanders free . . ."[2]

It's that last phrase, "wanders free," that hints at the radical quality of Lalita's femininity. On one level, of course, her freedom is the absolute freedom of the primordial Shakti, which can create anything or dissolve it at will. But as an archetype of the feminine, Lalita's freedom offers a concrete example of queenly sovereignty. Lalita appears to me to personify the fully alive, balanced, unashamedly enlightened feminine who is never subordinate and is supremely confident that her love can easily join the erotic with the holy. More than any of the forms of the great goddess, Lalita is "allowed" to embody the feminine as the primordial source of everything, without sacrificing the softer qualities of erotic delight and partnership with the masculine.

Like Kali, of whom she is the complementary opposite, she embodies the paradoxical mix of love and power. But while Kali's wildness is scary, and certainly off-putting to the masculine, Lalita is upheld in her power and beauty by not just one, but a host of love-smitten masculine deities. (The jewels she wears are said to have dropped from the crowns of Brahma and Vishnu when they prostrated themselves before her, recognizing her as the supreme mother of the universe.) Lalita is a queen to be unqualifiedly adored and worshipped with rigorous protocols, whereas Kali—even when she occupies the central place in the great temples of Bengal and Orissa—always carries a flavor of the fearsome, blood-maddened dancer.

Unlike Kali, who dances on Shiva like a dominatrix and whose wildness has to be explained away by her mainstream devotees, Lalita sits beside her consort as a respectful, yet equal, wife. (One of her names, Sumangali, literally means "auspicious wife.") Metaphysically, she gives her power to Shiva; she is the Shakti who playfully creates worlds for her formless husband to enjoy in his role as the eternal witness. However, she is never that simple, because Lalita manages to be both a respectable deity who upholds the male-dominated status quo and the main deity in certain left-handed Tantric rituals where the feminine is, at least metaphorically, in charge. Scholar Douglas Brooks points out, "She seeks to uphold the status quo but will not be bound to it; she gives life and fortune, but reserves the right to take it away; she embodies enjoyment, sensuality, and playfulness as well as restraint in her role as chaste wife devoted to her husband."[3]

LALITA THE DEMON SLAYER

Lalita would not be a power goddess if she didn't slay the occasional demon. If she were only sweet, she would have no power to protect us, and she would be only a partial role model for the enlightened feminine. The story that follows is a kind of alternative version of the Shiva-Parvati story, which reveals a slightly different dimension of the goddess as Shiva's consort.

Shiva, you'll remember, has incinerated Kama, the god of pleasure, because Kama was unwise enough to disturb his meditation. In this version of the story, one of Shiva's *ganas*—his weird, semi-demonic companions—starts playing around with Kama's ashes and ends up creating the image of a man. The image comes alive and petitions Shiva for a mantra which, when repeated, will give him one half of any adversary's energy. Shiva praises the man by saying *"bhand, bhand"*—good, good—and for some reason also grants him rulership of the world for sixty thousand years.

The demon, however, is anything but good, even though he takes the name Bhanda. Because he arose from Shiva's anger, Bhanda is especially violent and dangerous, and of course he does what demons generally do: he first builds a huge, architectural mishmash of a megamansion and then attacks Indra, the king of gods and upholder of the righteous.

Bhanda personifies what happens when erotic energy is violently repressed, especially through ascetic denial, as Shiva is doing at this point in his cosmic biography. Natural desire creates new life; it is regenerative. More than that, the energy it generates is the fuel for higher consciousness and creativity. When it is channeled, as in Tantric and Taoist practice, desire fuels spiritual unfoldment: the Tantric yogic traditions pride themselves on their technologies for transmuting sexual energy into spiritual energy. In spiritual life, repressed desire may create a powerful inner cauldron for high-octane meditation breakthroughs. As any long-term meditator knows, it can also morph into irritability and even rage. Western and Eastern mythologies are filled with tales of celibate monks and ascetic yogis so tetchy that they are always ready to hurl powerful, yoga-fueled curses at anyone who crosses them.

To contain and channel desire—which is one of the core projects of the Tantras—requires a resolution of opposites. A practitioner of the left-handed Tantric sexual ritual builds an appropriate relationship between asceticism and unbridled desire, so that desire can work its powerful creative magic as love rather than as lust or greed. Shiva's marriage to Lalita/Parvati provides the necessary balance that lets his ascetic potency take a creative form.

Lalita/Parvati, after her eons-long honeymoon, goes off with her attendant goddess-host to battle the demon. During the battle, both Bhanda and the goddess bring forth various helpers from their bodies. Bhanda produces a number of famous demons, while Tripura Sundari brings forth the avatars of the gods who, in various myths, defeated those demons.

After Lalita has polished off Bhanda, the love god's wife Delight (Rati) begs Lalita to restore Kama, the god of desire, whom Shiva has destroyed. Of course, Lalita does, thus restoring the true balance in the universe. Desire is alive again, but now under Lalita's control. In fact, Lalita Tripura Sundari is often said to infuse the universe with desire and to be the true form of desire.[4] She goes on dancing as the space between atoms, holding the worlds together, entrancing the universe.

THE LALITA WOMAN

As an archetype of the feminine, Lalita incarnates a power that has rarely been realized in the human world. She is the queen who rules through love, standing in her independence but never sacrificing pleasure; she is soft and delicate, yet invincible. On a personal, psychological level, the questions she asks us are: "Can you step into a radical state of empowerment? Can you allow yourself to be that abundant, that loving, that strong? Can you take that much pleasure in yourself and your life?"

To understand Lalita as a feminine archetype, imagine British prime minister Margaret Thatcher (who was famously flirtatious) possessing the beauty and allure of Catherine Zeta-Jones and the intensity of Salma Hayek. Women who carry the goddess Lalita are sexy matriarchs, which means that in the human world they often get a certain amount of bad press. One of the most famous Lalita women was the medieval queen Eleanor of Aquitaine, the renowned beauty who presided over the cult of courtly love that swept through the elite of Europe in the twelfth century. The greatest heiress of Europe, consort of two kings, and mother to two more, she had a well-deserved reputation for intrigue that caused a serious rupture with her husband, Henry II, yet allowed her to accomplish more than any woman of her time. Winston Churchill's mother, Lady Randolph Churchill, was a Lalita woman: beautiful, fascinating to men, and ambitious. She founded a literary magazine, the *Anglo-Saxon Review;* outfitted a hospital ship and took it to Africa during the Boer War; and had several lovers and two much younger husbands. Cleopatra was definitely a Lalita woman, though the conditions of her time brought her to grief in the end. Arianna Huffington, media and political powerhouse, has attributes of the Lalita woman, as does TV personality Diane Sawyer, who from the beginning of her career has been both independent yet supported by powerful men. Sharon Sandberg, the COO of Facebook, carries Lalita's queenly quality. Warm, brilliant, with great business sense, she specializes in empowering women in business and, tellingly, is sometimes criticized for failing to realize that not all women have her natural advantages or her gift for attracting masculine support. Actresses Scarlett Johansson and Penélope Cruz embody some of the ripe confidence of Lalita, as does Queen Latifah.

In her worldly aspects, Lalita Tripura Sundari can seem like a divine queen bee: the goddess who has it all, a diamond-bedecked aristocrat, a queen surrounded by male worshippers, the beauty whose erotic allure so seduces the patriarchy that the male gods bow down to her. When I tune into her on the level of personal archetype, I remember teenage fantasies of having every man in the world at my feet. At sixteen, newly awake to the loveliness of my youthful body, I felt that there was some ultimate power in being desired. The truth was that, in actual practice, my awakening sexuality didn't empower me that much. Quite the opposite, in fact: when I was turned on sexually, I tended to collapse into a kind of swoon, giving up boundaries, losing the protective armor that any intelligent American girl knew was crucial for dealing with teenage boys in the early 1960s. When I wasn't attracted to the boy, the peremptory, clumsy, and often coercive ways that boys expressed their wanting was confusing and disturbing to me, especially because I was shy, more than a little insecure, and always fearful of hurting some boy's feelings. Most of the time, I was either too smitten or too afraid of being rude to stand in the goddess's divine pride and claim her supremacy. Besides, even in my prime, I wasn't *that* beautiful.

So I, like many women I know, had a hard time identifying with Lalita Tripura Sundari. She challenged me to embrace a kind of triumphant femininity that seemed almost hubristic.

LALITA TRIPURA SUNDARI

FINDING PERSONAL EMPOWERMENT
THROUGH MEDITATION

So, entering into meditation on Sundari can be both confronting and healing. For a woman who follows the Tantric imperative to bring the goddess into herself, the goddess's image can make her examine the ways in which she has sold out her own femininity, her desire nature, her natural feminine power. For a man, the goddess may force him to confront the aspects of feminine beauty and sexual power that frighten him and make him feel inadequate.

At the same time, Lalita promises an avenue for opening to a mature erotic feminine—to the aspect of the feminine that can, with full knowledge and power, celebrate the creative source of her life. On one level, meditation on Lalita can help a woman bring out her inner capacity for naked intimacy, and for a man, his capacity for tuning in to the erotic feminine. Lalita's Shakti activates the subtle heart of the erotic impulse, which can be just as intense when it expresses itself in an intellectual partnership or an inner spiritual merging as in a sexual mating.

Futurist Barbara Marx Hubbard has coined a term, "suprasex," that points to the erotic quality that can be present when two minds come together to innovate creatively. This is a good description of how the Lalita Shakti works. Attunement to the Lalita Shakti unleashes creative passion, bringing a quality of unbridled presence to all relationships. In other words, the erotic glow of Lalita's worldly manifestation doesn't only appear in the young, the beautiful, or the sexually uninhibited. She shows up wherever there is creative spark, and spontaneous give and take. Because our society associates Eros almost exclusively with sex, it's hard for us to divorce our erotic energies from the social taboos and fantasies we hold about the erotic impulse. Yet, as Marc Gafni writes, sex "*models* the erotic, it doesn't *exhaust* the erotic."[5] Lalita can help us disengage the inner erotic from culturally received ideas about sexuality. For a woman who longs to embody her innate erotic power, yet is afraid of losing her power in relationship, meditation on *receiving* Lalita's energy can be a powerful key to awakening Eros as your own creative force. And for men, Lalita can be a powerful muse.

For me, the key to connecting with Lalita was to recognize her as the electrical energy that pulses through my body, which I can draw on for creative action as well as in relationship. To realize the empowered erotic in relationship demands first that it be realized inwardly as an autonomous power of self-love. Bringing Lalita alive as an inner archetype, through meditation, is a first step

287

toward incarnating her in your relationship with your own body and in relationship with another.

Meditation: Lalita

Find a comfortable posture in a quiet place to
contemplate the goddess Lalita.

As always with the goddesses, begin by invoking her unique presence.

Imagine her form: slender, delicate, with large breasts. Her skin is luminous and rosy. She wears a red-silk sari without a blouse. Her eyes are large, round, fringed by long lashes. She's smiling. She wears a necklace set with rubies, pearls, and diamonds as well as a golden crown on her long, waving hair. She sits in the air in front of you, and you feel her power infusing your body.

As you draw her Shakti in with your breath, you draw into yourself the power of radiance, fascination, and wisdom. You feel the rosy light of Tripura Sundari flowing from her yoni into your own sexual organ. As it does, you experience her Shakti infusing your yoni and moving up into your womb (or, for a man, flowing into the testicles). As it does, she clears all forms of sexual wounding and the traumas that freeze your sexuality or create different forms of sexual addiction, that create shame, fear or avoidance.

As you exhale, the energy of Tripura Sundari flows as empowered sexual energy from your sacrum up the center of your body, filling you with rose-colored light.

Inhaling, you breathe in the Shakti of Tripura Sundari through your heart. Her rosy light fills your heart, dispelling the wounds of being misunderstood, washing away your timidity and fear of standing in your own feminine heart. As Tripura Sundari's energy expands, you feel compassion and love flowing through your heart. With the exhalation, you recognize that everything within the field of your experience is connected. As your heart expands, the sense of "we" expands. In whatever way is possible, and to whatever degree that you can, you let go of the skin boundaries and feel yourself expanding out to encompass the world around you.

Now you inhale the light flowing from the goddess's third eye into your third eye, drawing in her power of discernment, of discrimination. As her radiance spreads through your brain, you realize that your body is made of her light and that everything you can see or know is irradiated with her light.

Now draw the image of the goddess into your own body. Feel yourself filled with her radiant erotic energy, dancing through you in every atom and molecule of your body. Feel yourself suffused with divine pride, as she empowers you with her dignity and joy. Feel your innate freedom as her freedom dances through you, loosening every block and area of tightness that constricts the energy in your body. Feel yourself filled with her joy and with her tears as you recognize that her radiant body connects you to everybody in the world.

THE INNER FORM: LALITA AS KUNDALINI

Lalita has several esoteric forms, including the famous Shri Yantra. But the most internally dynamic expression of her power is as kundalini Shakti, the evolutionary power that sleeps at the base of the spine until it is awakened by the force of the Goddess. In the Shri Vidya Tantric tradition of South India, kundalini is said to awaken as Bhairavi, the fiercest aspect of Kali. That force blasts kundalini out of her matter-embedded, "sleeping" form. When she rises into the topmost chakra, she moves through a stage of voidness as Dhumavati, then into a mind-free, egoless state as Chinnamasta. At one point, she enters the stage of inner erotic union with the divine masculine, her inner Beloved. This is her expression as Lalita. The Lalita aspect of kundalini is the subtle radiance that transforms our inner sense of duality and alienation into the most radical form of inner wholeness, integrating the sensual and the spiritual in explosions of whole-body ecstasy even as the Kali and Chinnamasta aspects of kundalini are exploding your preconceptions and cleaning out your dangling karmic detritus.

As kundalini, Lalita Tripura Sundari literally cleanses the doors of your perception so you can see the world as it truly is: shimmering with beauty. When you have the grace of Tripura Sundari, you don't need to sit in meditation to revel in the ecstasy of divine presence. You find it in your own mind, just as it is, as well as in whatever flows through your senses.

One of my most surprising shifts of perception happened one afternoon in New York in the 1970s. In those days, the Upper West Side was a run-down neighborhood, inhabited by winos and junkies. (The patch of green at Broadway and Seventy-Second, now an upscale piece of real estate, had been named "Needle Park" because there were so many heroin sales going on there.) On this late-winter afternoon, a few months after my kundalini awakening, I was walking down Broadway in the upper Eighties when the street suddenly turned into what I can only describe as a celestial boulevard. The garbage was still floating in the gutters. The winos were still staggering down the street. But they were all irradiated, shimmering with light and bliss. It was as if a wash of love had spread over everything.

As an inner presence, Lalita Tripura Sundari is the beauty of the world seen through the eye of unity. In ordinary perception, our brain and nervous system carves up reality into disparate chunks, identifies them as separate from each other and separate from ourselves. Our sense of self is confined to the area inside the body, and we are conditioned to identify with our personality and self-image. But when Sundari dances inside you as awakened kundalini, the nervous system begins to give you a palpable experience of unity instead of the normal perception of difference. The self-sense expands so that you can begin to see, eyes open, the world inside yourself.

Another way Lalita Tripura Sundari reveals herself is as the emergence of pure Presence, the dynamic alive awareness that experiences life through your body and senses, and yet stands apart from it. In this very subtle form, Lalita manifests as the enlightened "fourth state" (*turiya* in Sanskrit) of consciousness, the state beyond waking, dream, and deep sleep. Her name, Beauty of the Three Worlds, points to her ultimate nature as the sublime clarity of the witnessing awareness that Tantric tradition says permeates the three ordinary states of consciousness as your capacity to be aware of experience.

The spiritual teacher Adyashanti often speaks about an early experience of Presence that epitomizes this recognition. He was a kid, on the school playground, when his "me" shifted into the background and a vast, loving Presence took over. In an intuitive, unstated way, he realized that this Presence was not only bigger than him, but that it was the force behind the whole of life. He also realized that no one else on the playground could see her or even recognize her existence.[6]

Subtle Erotic Merging

This is an exercise to do with another person. If you are alone, you can imagine that someone you love or feel close to is with you.

Sit with your friend, eyes open. Gaze into your friend's left eye. The left eye is the receptive eye, which connects to the right brain. Let your gaze be soft, and if you notice yourself staring or trying to see into that person, pull your attention back.

Very gently, have the feeling that your energy moves out from your body and embraces them, as their energy embraces you. Let your energies merge. If it feels too intimate to keep your eyes open, close them.

Notice the felt sense of energy in your body. Without trying to direct the energy, allow it to expand.

After a few minutes, bring your attention to the base of your spine and begin to breath slowly up and down your spine, breathing in with the feeling that energy is rising into the center of your forehead, and then exhaling with the feeling that energy flows back down to the base of your spine. Keep the sense of the expansive energy connecting the two of you as you breathe the energy up and down your spine.

THE TOUCH OF BLISS

The Lalita Shakti is also the inner form of the Shakti as lover. As she is a goddess of sexual desire in the external world, in the inner world she is the energy that empowers your longing for spiritual fulfillment. In the deep states of enlightenment celebrated in the Tantras, she expresses herself as the subtle touch of bliss. As mentioned in the last chapter, the Tantric philosopher Abhinavagupta taught that touch is the one sense that does not dissolve in the highest states of awareness. Instead, it morphs into a blissful presence that caresses the inner body, even when all sense of ego and even individuality has disappeared in meditative union. It is the Goddess who brings this level of bliss into meditation.

My friend Michael used to experience the movements of his awakened kundalini as an inner girlfriend dancing inside him, sometimes playful, sometimes stern, always drawing his attention inward toward her palpable presence in his energy body. He discovered as he tuned in to her that she insistently "taught" him which aspects of his mind were helpful and which tended to destroy his bliss. Before the inner erotic explosion, Michael had been characteristically pessimistic, cynical, and dark—a devotee of David Lynch movies and heavy-metal rock. When the subtle feminine energy began unfurling herself within him, he discovered that certain images and thoughts distanced him from her felt presence. Judgmental thoughts, for instance, which normally formed much of his inner dialogue, could cut him off completely from the inner dancer. He found himself walking out of movies he would normally have been drawn to and recoiling from certain kinds of conversations—the kind where aggression, masked as humor, cut swordlike through another person's pretensions or lack of cool. He told me that he felt as if the goddess were guiding him to transform his way of living by granting or withholding her bliss according to whether he followed her inner guidance.

One way to understand what happens when the Goddess, as awakened kundalini, rises through the body and unites with Shiva in the crown is to realize that she is uniting awareness with bliss. Historically, classical nondual practice has been mostly a path for male renunciants. It privileges withdrawal from the world into the detached witness state, where the practitioner stands aside from thoughts and emotions and recognizes his true nature as awareness. When the felt sense of the Goddess's energy is not actively present in your meditation, that witness experience can bring about a kind of desolation, a feeling of detachment from life, and a sense that nothing really matters.

Tantric sadhana takes us beyond that void state. It has as its intention to coax the goddess, who is the bliss and dynamism within consciousness, to infuse the emptiness of the void state with her thrilling presence. It is the goddess who brings blissfulness to meditation and yogic practice.

Invoking Lalita Tripura Sundari in the Sahasrara

The *sahasrara* ("thousand-petaled") chakra is located approximately eight finger-widths above the fontanel (the place at the crown of the head where a baby's soft spot is located). Though it appears to be outside the body, as you meditate there, you will become aware that it is within your subtle body. The sahasrara is considered the seat of the Goddess Lalita Tripura Sundari and the point where the divine feminine in the form of kundalini Shakti merges with the divine masculine in the form of pure awareness—Shiva.

Sit in an upright, comfortable posture. Your spinal column should be erect, and the base of your posture firmly grounded.

Focus on the flow of your breath; sense its coolness as it flows in through your nostrils, and its warmth as it flows out.

FIGURE 18: LALITA AND SHIVA IN UNION

Bring your awareness to the center of your head. Breathe into the center of your head for several breaths.

Allow your awareness to rise through your crown to a spot approximately eight finger-widths above your head.

Imagine the goddess in the form of a golden sun in this spot.

As your breath flows in and out, feel that each breath brings in subtle blissfulness and flows out, allowing that blissful feeling to spread outward through the universe. Allow the seed syllable "hreem" to flow with the breath.

Now, begin to sense the presence of the divine couple within this spot. If you like, you can visualize the goddess, rosy-skinned, with the face and body of a sixteen-year-old girl, reclining with Shiva, who is pale blue in color. Their eyes are closed. Bliss streams from their joined bodies in the form of silvery white nectar and flows down into your head, purifying your brain. It flows downward, filling your body. Let your body open to accept the flow of nectar from the embrace of Kameshwari and Kameshwara, Lalita and her divine consort.

Kameshwari and Kameshwara—Shakti and Shiva as the god and goddess of love—personify the ecstasy that opens in this rare and secret meditation. This ecstasy then spills over into the visionary recognition that the whole realm of experience, both inner and outer, pulsates with light and joy.

When this process starts to take place in meditation, the practitioner might experience explicitly sexual energy flowing in her body. Katherine, a practitioner I counseled, had begun having spontaneous dreams and meditation visions in which her female teacher appeared as the Goddess. Her teacher—who in the waking state was almost straitlaced in her yogic dignity—would appear in Katherine's meditation, embracing her and sending sexual thrills through Katherine's body. In meditation after meditation, Katherine would feel inner sensations of liquid ecstasy dripping down from her crown to her root chakra, igniting powerful sexual desire, then rising up again to her crown. She came to me because she was afraid that her experience was a sign that something was going wrong in her practice, because erotic inner transmission from the teacher was not described in any literature of her extremely conservative tradition. I told her that her experience was indeed a true, and deeply esoteric, expression of awakened kundalini. Tantric teachers have said that such experiences are a sign that the sexual fluid is being transformed into a subtle energy—called *soma,* or nectar—that rejuvenates the entire body.

MEDITATIONS ON DESIRE

Many of the specific practices that work with desire in meditation attempt to replicate that spontaneous inner movement. The practice might start with ritual, which would include a traditional *puja*, or offering of flowers and other articles to the goddess. In the couple's ritual, which is described in *Tantrasara* from the male's point of view, the man would make offerings to his partner as the goddess, then enter her; at the culmination of the ritual, he would ejaculate into the woman while reciting a prayer: "The fire of Atman has been made blazing by the offering of clarified butter in the form of semen; with my mind I am always offering my sensory experience through the central channel, the *sushumna*."[7]

The Tantric sexual practice can also be done alone. A male practitioner might excite his penis and then draw the energy he's aroused up the spinal column with the breath, bringing it finally to the crown to court the ecstasy of that union. For a woman, there are explicit meditations that are designed to bring the goddess energy alive in the yoni and the womb. In some Tantric traditions, it's said that women have a unique ability to realize enlightened states, because they carry within them the generative power of the yoni and the womb. In Merilyn Tunneshende's account of her practice in a Mesoamerican Toltec tradition, her female teacher explains to her that a woman's sexual energy is the fuel of her vitality, both in life and in spiritual self-transformation. When a man ejaculates into a woman, that tradition says, he creates a cord to her feminine energy, which he can continue to draw on for many years, and which is renewed with each intercourse.[8] The teacher goes on to give her practices for removing those cords. In the Taoist sexual ritual, when two adepts are doing the practice, there is said to be a kind of competition to see which partner can excite the other into orgasm. The one who orgasms is considered to have sacrificed his or her sexual energy to the other, who "wins" it. So a clever woman practitioner would withhold her own orgasm, then draw the concentrated energy of her partner's semen into her womb, where it could be used as additional fuel to draw the kundalini energy upward.

What follows is a woman's practice that can be done alone or with a partner. It's a powerful way both to ignite the kundalini energy and to experience the depths of feminine desire in a woman's body.

Meditation: The Goddess as Yoni, Uterus, and Heart

This meditation is for women only. It centers on the yoni, which
is the Sanskrit word for vulva. Lie down in *shavasana,* or
corpse pose, with a pillow under your knees, and begin.

Bring your awareness to the lips of the yoni. You may touch your yoni to center your awareness there. Imagine the yoni as soft, rosy, and moist. Feel the presence of a loving, erotic energy gathering in the lips of your yoni.

Let your attention come to the clitoris, and imagine it as the bud of a rose. Feel the rose unfurling as you now allow your awareness to touch your G-spot, on the inside anterior wall of the yoni. Feel the G-spot as the mouth of an underground spring, oozing sweet water as it bubbles to the surface. Experience the ache of desire within the lips of the yoni, the rosebud clitoris, and the sweet spring of the G-spot.

Now, gathering the energy, allow it to rise with your awareness through the cervix and into the glowing interior cave of the uterus. Feel how the sexual energy can be held and expanded in the uterine cave. Feel that you are growing the embryo of your deep femininity, invoking the presence of the goddess as the form of kundalini in the womb.

Now allow that energy to rise to your heart, and with the inhalation and exhalation, feel the erotic charge of the deep feminine blossoming in your heart like an opened lotus, or deep-pink rose. Rest in the heart as long as you like, then find the energy rising up through your neck, filling your head with soft, luminous, rosy light.

The energy comes to the center of your head, to the third eye. It becomes a glistening full moon, luminous and white, dripping nectar down through your body.

Let your energy rise now to your crown, and see the form of the beloved present on a bed of golden light. He may have a form, a figure. He may simply manifest as a sense of light and presence. Now allow the energy you have collected and drawn upward to merge into the light of the inner beloved. Take rest in the golden light at your crown. Then allow the energy to begin to flow back down your body. That light drips down through your head, infusing your brain; flowing down your neck and into your heart, suffusing your heart and lungs, your entire chest and back; flowing down your torso and into your viscera, your womb, your yoni. The light fills your pelvis and flows down the thighs through the calves and into the feet.

LALITA AS INNER PLEASURE

In our inner world, Lalita is the capacity for radical pleasure. When she is alive in our body, food tastes delicious—even a dry rice cake melts in the mouth. Our relationships delight us; conversation becomes communion, and the silences between us are pregnant with presence. Lalita can manifest as the delight we take in our tasks and as the pleasure of using our bodies and minds or stretching our capacities to the limit. She is the bliss that arises in deep meditation and the pleasure of fully expressing our purpose in the world when we become the best that we know we can be.

We can't find that level of satisfaction only through our own effort. And it doesn't come by sacrificing ourselves for others—that's the role of the Sita archetype. Lalita's Shakti comes to us as the self-empowerment that arises when we are both fully alive to the truth of consciousness and fully present in the body. It is a uniquely feminine kind of self-realization, in which our vulnerability morphs into a complete openness of the heart and our nurturing power is turned back toward ourselves. In internalizing Lalita, women become their own mothers. We learn to protect ourselves not by armoring against the demons of the dark masculine, as Durga does, but by loving that darkness into light, raising it to its heights, and then allowing it to permeate our entire experience, inward and outward. This, I believe is the true Devi Mahatmya: the goddess's victory, her ultimate gift.

Embodying the Qualities of Lalita Tripura Sundari

This exercise is meant to be practiced in active life. Contemplate it here, and then actually take the action you choose.

What qualities of embodied Tripura Sundari do you feel within yourself? How have you expressed the empowered erotic feminine in your life? How have you denied her?

Find one action you can do in the next twenty-four hours that will embody the radiant Eros of the goddess. It could mean dancing to soft or wild music, or lying naked in the moonlight. It could mean creating an erotic ritual with your partner, perhaps lighting candles around your bed; decorating your bed as an alter with fresh sheets and flowers; bathing together; then entering into long, slow lovemaking.

It could mean sitting in silence with your lover or a friend and allowing your heart energy to meet his or hers in a subtle, nonphysical embrace.

Lalita Tripura Sundari

luh-lee-tah tree-pur-uh suhn-duh-ree—Goddess of Emperors

Other Names for Lalita:
Rajarajeshwari (*rah-juh-rah-jey-shwah-ree*)—Queen of Kings
Shodashi (*sho-duh-shee*)—Sixteen-Year-Old Girl
Kameshwari (*kah-mey-shwuh-ree*)—Goddess of Desire
Shri Vidya (*shree vid-yah*)—Auspicious Wisdom
The thousand names described in the hymn "Thousand Names of Lalita"

Goddess of:
- divine desire that leads to skillful action
- sacred sexuality and inner union of body, soul, and spirit
- kundalini when it merges in the highest spiritual center
- queenly embodiment of feminine authority, beauty, and creativity
- power of creation, maintenance, and dissolution
- erotic merging
- grace in every aspect of life

Recognize Lalita Tripura Sundari in:
- beautiful royal architecture like the Taj Mahal, the Lake Palace in Udaipur, or the chateaux of France
- jewels
- the Tuscan Hill Country
- California's Napa Valley
- the ocean in summer
- fragrant flowers
- warm, moist, fertile places
- the moisture of love
- the light of the waxing moon

- queenly women
- young women at the height of their youthful bloom
- visions of light and feelings of bliss
- the experience of inner perfection and fullness
- joyful pleasure—as in good food, wine, company

Invoke Lalita Tripura Sundari for:
- sexual merging and delight
- feminine self-empowerment
- opening the upper chakras, particularly the crown
- feelings of sweetness and fulfillment
- embodied spiritual bliss
- self-realization
- combining worldly enjoyments with yogic liberation
- merging with the inner beloved
- merging with an intellectual partner in inspired conversation

Bija Mantra
Hrim (*hreem*)

Invocational Mantra
Ka e i la hrim
Ha sa ka ha la hrim
Sa ka la hrim

kuh ey ee luh hreem
huh suh kuh huh luh hreem
suh kuh luh hreem

Though there are various explanations of this mantra, here is one way to understand the meaning of the syllables, courtesy of Christopher Wallis.[9]

The first five syllables are said to express the Power of Insight *(jnana-shakti)*, are associated with Vagisvari, and bring about liberation; the second set of syllables express the Power of Action *(kriya-shakti)*, are associated with Kamesvari, and bring about the attainment of one's romantic and sexual desires; and the third group of syllables express the Power of the Will or Creative Urge *(iccha-shakti)*, associated with Para-devi, and removes obstacles.

Gayatri Mantra

Om tripuradevyai vidmahe
Kameshwaryai cha dhimahi
Tannah klinna prachodayat

ohm tree-pur-ah-deyv-yai vid-muh-hey
kah-meysh-wuhr-yai chuh dee-muh-hee
tun-nuh klin-nah pruh-cho-duh-yah-tuh

Om, may we come to know the Goddess of the Three Realms
May we meditate on that Goddess of Desire
May her softness impel me on my path.

Lalita's flowers: red lotus, golden lotus
Lalita's color: rosy red, like the dawn
Lalita's consort: Shiva as Kameshwari

CHAPTER 13

Bhuvaneshwari

Goddess of Infinite Space, She Whose Body Is the World

All the parts of the world, like the limbs of a living being, are dependent
upon the one love, and are bound to one another by natural affinity.

MARSILIO FICINO

Because of the command implied by a single lift of your eyebrows,
Brahma creates this world,
Vishnu maintains it,
Shiva destroys it,
And Sadashiva blesses it.

SHANKARACHARYA
"Ananda Lahari" ("Wave of Bliss")

And in that moment we all thought of the space . . . it would take for the Sun to arrive with
its rays, to ripen the wheat; of the space for the Sun to condense from the clouds of stellar
gases and burn; of the quantities of stars and galaxies and galactic masses in flight through
space which would be needed to hold suspended every galaxy, every nebula, every sun . . .
and at the same time we thought of it, this space was inevitably being formed . . . The point
that contained her and all of us was expanding in a halo of distance in light-years and light-
centuries and billions of light-millennia, and we were being hurled to the four corners of the
universe . . . and she, dissolved into I don't know what kind of energy-light-heat . . ."

ITALO CALVINO
Cosmicomics

O my Beloved
What will you become
When you are through becoming me?

LAWRENCE EDWARDS
Kali's Bazaar

Imagine the biggest space you can—space pulsing with creative fullness and possibility. Try to feel and sense your way into its clarity, its luminosity. Use all your inner senses: sight, hearing, but especially your inner sense of touch. Notice that it pulses subtly. Notice that, within it, little squiblets of thought or ripples of images arise. As you feel your way into this space, recognize that it is hyperconscious. It is aware. It is knowing.

Now see if you can imagine this space as an infinite sky, stretching out forever, borderless and without boundaries. Imagine that everything that could be conceived, as well as the unimaginable—every planet, star, black hole, ocean, planet form, creature, idea, and space-time itself—are contained in this infinite spaciousness. Imagine its sheer freedom. It can become anything. It can dissolve anything into itself. It is filled with possibility, with wisdom, with infinite love. It creates within itself a body—and that body is the cosmos.

You've just tuned into the felt sense of Bhuvaneshwari. Bhuvaneshwari is the Goddess whose body is the space of infinite possibility. She is *ananda*—infinite, creative wisdom/love. She's the matrix, the eternal mother energy who spins the universe out of her own body the way a spider spins a web—and then lives in it. As an energy you touch in meditation, Bhuvaneshwari is akin to the Buddhist goddess Prajna Paramita, the perfection of wisdom, the vast awareness who spirals out and draws you into herself, fully alive to the paradox that form and emptiness are one, that all forms are essentially empty, and that emptiness contains infinite forms. You can't fully realize this without the goddess's permission. Since she herself *is* that paradox, she holds the key to your recognition of it.

Bhuvaneshwari is a wonderful goddess to access in meditation, guaranteeing you that even in the most formless state of awareness, you'll feel a subtle, motherly embrace. When you invoke her presence in meditation, she can gather you into a space that feels like a vast, spacious, cosmic womb. Bhuvaneshwari's subtle meditation presence is formless, detached, an oceanic awareness that you can float in. It will hold you, support you, and renew you. When I want to practice letting go of anxiety or fear, it's often Bhuvaneshwari whom I invoke. Her spaciousness seems to swallow whole whatever needs to be cleared. You can offer her whatever you're holding onto: guilt, loss, emotional upheaval, or just an excess of thoughts. She will take it in, dissolve it, and offer it back transformed. She is the cosmic womb, the great expanse within which all things are held, and out of which they are born.

However, you can't confine or define her simply as space, because Bhuvaneshwari is also layered into the physical world. The world is inside her body, and yet she is at the heart of everything as the space inside every atom. She's

FIGURE 19: BHUVANESHWARI WITH THE COSMOS IN HER BODY

the nothingness behind the big bang, as well as the space that allows your body to exist among other bodies. She is the atmosphere that circles the planet, and she is also deep space, where time bends or dissolves, where distances are only measurable in mathematical formulae, and where matter can expand outward or collapse inward infinitely. Nothing would be if it weren't for her.

Bhuvaneshwari's name means "lady or mistress" (*ishwari*) "of worlds" (*bhuvana*). She's the goddess whose essence becomes the phenomenal universe. She's totally mixed with everything in existence, as space is layered into every atom of even the densest matter. Not just the physical universe, but the whole of reality—all those worlds we can't see with our physical eyes, the universes where there is neither time nor space, the heaven realms and the places no one would want to be. She controls reality, because reality is her own body.

In the *Shrimad Devi Bhagavatam,* the mythological compendium devoted to exalting the divine feminine in her various forms, Brahma the creator tells her story to the celestial bard, Narada.

"Picture the time before creation, if you can," Brahma begins. "I lurch up out of some unconscious realm, to find myself in the midst of a vast, shoreless sea. That's all there is—this endless sea of consciousness. On this sea, I find Vishnu asleep in the coils of the earth serpent, Ashesha. Then I realize that two demons are holding this unformed world captive, ready to swallow it up, and swallow Vishnu too! So I pray frantically to the only one who can help us. I pray to Mother Bhuvaneshwari. To my shock, she appears *out of Vishnu's body,* where she has been holding him asleep. The goddess has been keeping Vishnu unconscious, just as, in her form as Maya, she will keep human beings unconscious of their true origin until she chooses to withdraw her power to delude!

"Do you get this, Narada?" Brahma intones dramatically. "She can even send Vishnu, lord of the worlds, into a state of unconsciousness!"

The moment Bhuvaneshwari withdraws—ta da!—Vishnu sits up, drags the demons across his thigh, and kills them.

But there is still no world!

"Let me show you something," Bhuvaneshwari Devi says. She is in a good mood, now, having created for herself an audience. "Fetch Shiva," she tells Brahma and Vishnu. "This is for all of you." Brahma then relates how the goddess invites them all to sit in a celestial car, a jeweled basket that rises like a hydrogen balloon up through the sky and beyond. They pass through countless subtle worlds and finally reach the subtlest, highest, most infinite plane of all: Devi Loka, the plane of the Goddess. There, Brahma, Shiva, and Vishnu discover that they now have female bodies. They have become celestial maidens, attendant on the goddess Bhuvaneshwari. Brahma doesn't seem to have a problem with this; realizing that he is in the hands of the Mistress, he is able to surrender his need for control, at least for the moment. It occurs to him that she's making some kind of point here, maybe giving a subtle hint that in order to understand the true process of creation, the gods have to feel what it's like to be female?

Breathless, Brahma continues his tale. "Listen, Narada," he says. "This part was fantastic. We saw the *whole universe,* moving and nonmoving, within the nails of the lotus feet of the Devi!" Brahma can't stop talking about the wonder of it. The universe! In her toenails! This is no random Devi. This is a goddess truly worthy of being adored! Here is a form of the feminine they can worship! Which they immediately do, bowing with their heads on her jeweled feet, so that precious gems tumble from their crowns, which have fallen off in the excitement.

"Here is how she looks," Brahma tells us. "Bhuvaneshwari sits on a jeweled bed, wearing red robes, a red garland. Her eyes are dark red. Her face is delicate, with thin lips, and she is overwhelmingly beautiful. Her full breasts are smeared with sandalwood. One hand holds a goad, symbolizing her control of the physical world. Another holds a bowl overflowing with jewels. Her other hands are making gestures of bestowing boons and dispelling fear. Golden earrings in the form of the Shri Yantra hang from her ears, and the mantra 'hrim' sounds from every particle of the air. Even the birds," Brahma says, "are singing 'hrim.'"

Vishnu, always the most quick-witted of the Trinity, realizes immediately who she is. "This is the Bhagavati," he cries, "the one who is the embodiment of *bhaga*—majesty, fame, auspiciousness, detachment, and every other divine quality you can think of! This is the Mahavidya, great knowledge; Mahamaya, the great enchantress. This is the primal creatrix of the world, and it is she into whom the world dissolves in the end!" And the three great gods—overwhelmed, the story says, with devotion—bow again and again to her, saying, "Oh Bhuvaneshwari, mother of the world, this whole universe arises in you and melts away in you. It is only through your will that we create, preserve, and destroy!"

In Bhuvaneshwari, we meet an Indian goddess who closely resembles the Great Mother of Western mythology. Though Durga and Lakshmi and even Kali are called "Ma" by their devotees, and though Parvati is an actual mother, none of them are natural world-mothers in the sense that writers like Erich Neumann and Joseph Campbell use the word. The Great Mother is the form of the feminine in whom the world is embodied; she is the great nurturer who spills out earthly life and gathers it back into herself. Only by a wild stretch of the imagination can you ascribe these qualities to the warrior goddesses, and certainly Lakshmi is popularly invoked for gifts and blessings rather than universal creativity. Of course, Saraswati is a form of the creatrix—in fact, she is worshipped in Trika as Paradevi, the supreme goddess. Lalita is also a world-mother—in fact, Shankara's verses quoted in the epigraph of this chapter were addressed to her. Nonetheless, it is Bhuvaneshwari who is given the name Jagad-dhatri ("she who nurses the world"[1]). She is that beautiful young mother with whom any child can fall in love.

One cozy metaphor from Indian folklore describes the Mother as being something like a farm wife who hoards the seeds in a cachepot. When it is time, she brings them out, plants them, and universes are born. After a while, she gathers them back. Italo Calvino, in his novel *Cosmicomics*, has a Bhuvaneshwari-like character called Mrs. Pavacini, who, at the moment of creation, begins to make a vast, endless pasta—rolling out the dough to make a world. In Sanskrit, this cosmically fertile feminine energy is called *prakriti*. *Kriti* means "making" or "creating." *Pra* means "before." So, prakriti is the matrix of Shakti that is prior to creation. She's the divine space, in short, within which all that is will pour forth and into which it will all dissolve. Bhuvaneshwari is prakriti. But she is also way beyond prakriti, as Brahma points out to Narada. That's what makes her so mysterious. She both contains the cosmos and transcends it.

Invoking Bhuvaneshwari

Sit quietly in a comfortable place. Spend a few minutes attending
to the breath. Then, imagine yourself on top of a mountain, or
in front of the ocean, as vast space surrounds you.

Imagine the figure of the goddess Bhuvaneshwari seated in the air in front of you.
Her complexion is bright red. She has large, lustrous eyes, with a vertical third eye in the middle of her forehead, signifying her all-seeing nature.
On her head is a full moon. She smiles lovingly. She wears a green sari with gold necklaces and bracelets. She has firm, high breasts. In one hand, she holds a red lotus. In the other, a golden bowl filled with jewels.
Love emanates from every pore of her body. You begin to sense the luscious sweetness of her love as you chant nine times the mantra for invoking Bhuvaneshwari:

Om shrim hrim shrim bhuvaneshwarayai namaha
ohm shreem hreem shreem bu-vuhn-eysh-wuhr-yai nuh-muh-huh

Om I bow to the Goddess of Worlds, who embodies creative power and auspiciousness!

Allow yourself to feel the love that flows from her form. Let yourself feel that love as a tender mist of energy that surrounds you. Let her love fill you.

Now imagine that you are making offerings to the goddess. This is a meditation practice called mental worship. Because this is happening in your imagination, you can be totally extravagant. Imagine beautiful flowers—lotuses, roses, fragrant jasmine. Offer them to her. Offer her piles of gold coins and silks, delicious food and drink on golden plates. Imagine offering her jewels and placing them around her neck.

She holds out the bowl of jewels, indicating that you are to take it. You receive the jewels. As you do, sense that you have received the boons and blessings of the goddess.

Finally, feel that you breathe the goddess into your own body. Can you take Bhuvaneshwari into yourself? Can you feel the fullness of her loving presence inside your own body?

THE SPACE BETWEEN

One way to tune into Bhuvaneshwari is to focus on the space around things. Look at this book, and then widen your vision so that you're primarily aware of the space surrounding it. Look at your hand, and see it held in space. When your hand touches the book, the two become one—held in the same space.

When you meditate on Bhuvaneshwari as physical space, the space before your eyes, you might feel first bemusement, then a kind of dawning peace. Your attention will float backward, interiorize. You might even become aware that your own awareness is holding whatever you are seeing or feeling or touching or smelling, and even holding your thoughts. Thus, Bhuvaneshwari will have awakened you to a truth: that the physical world is within your awareness and hence within yourself.

Bhuvaneshwari might also reveal herself inside the density itself. She can throw an internal switch in your brain and show you the world as a shimmering mass of pure light. She can even get you to recognize that a host of sparkly Shaktis are manifesting themselves through every conscious and unconscious activity in your body and mind. If you love reality, love the physical universe, you are worshipping Bhuvaneshwari, who might eventually reward your worship by letting you see how all things in the world are interconnected, arising in space and filled with space. Or, you can invoke her as the space within the lotus of the heart, as the Upanishads suggest.

EARTH AND SKY

Bhuvaneshwari is both earth mother and sky mother. She is not just one-half of the mythological dualism that equates spirit with masculine and matter with feminine. She is all of it; nondual. She is the source of whatever emerges from the earth. She is not only the space that extends outward and up, she's also the space within, the space that extends downward into the depths of the earth and the depths of the heart.

"Vast as the universe is the tiny space within the heart. The heavens and earth are there, and the sun and moon and stars. Fire and lightening and wind are there, and all that now exists, and all that is not."[2]

Bhuvaneshwari is *shunya*—the void. But she is also—and here is another of those paradoxes that the Devi loves so much—described as *purna*, or fullness. A mantra describes reality as follows:

> Om purnam adah purnam idam
> purnat purnam udachyate
> purnasya purnam adaya
> purnam evavashishyate

> *ohm poor-num uh-dah poor-num i-dum*
> *poor-naht poor-nuh-moo-duh-chyuh-tey*
> *poor-nuh-syuh poor-nuh-mah-dah-yuh*
> *poor-nuh-mey-vah-vuh-shi-shyuh-tey*

> Om, it is full here, it is full there.
> From fullness fullness comes.
> If fullness be taken from fullness,
> Only fullness remains.

Just as all numbers are potentially present in zero, all that could possibly exist is potential in the void. Shunya is empty yet full. *Akasha* is space that has no beginning or end, which contains all potentiality. Everything begins and ends in it.

Though Bhuvaneshwari *is* the source of matter, though she *is* the matrix, though she *is* the goddess as Maya—the cosmic measurer who deludes and traps us into seeing matter as separate from spirit—she is *also* a portal back into nonduality. In the *Vijnana Bhairava,* a meditation manual that is beloved by Tantrikas from both the Hindu and Buddhist traditions, there are a number of meditations on the void. Each one of them invites the energy of Bhuvaneshwari to expand inside a deceptively empty space. In the *Vijnana Bhairava,* Shiva calls this space the *madhya,* the "center." The madhya is the gap between one activity and another. Like the still point where a pendulum stops before gathering energy to swing again, the madhya is an empty place pregnant with power.

You find the madhya in the tiny pause between one breath and another. You find it in a mind that pauses between thoughts. You find it above all in the central channel of the body, the subtle pole of energy that runs from the perineum to the crown.

The traditional way to find the inner space of the madhya is to "mind the gap" at the end of each inhalation and at the end of each exhalation. Hold your breath for a fraction of a second at the end of the inhalation and at the end of the exhalation. Keep focusing on the space that you notice there (even if it's so tiny you can hardly find it), as the breath continues to flow back and forth, back and forth. After a while, you'll begin to notice that you can remain aware of the space even as the breath is flowing.

In time, that nearly invisible, hidden space between the breaths can open, imploding inward, expanding into a spaciousness that is infinite—as large as you are able to conceive, and even larger. You find Bhuvaneshwari here, more intimate than your breath. She is "the breath inside the breath," to use the words of the poet Kabir who also pointed to her as "inside the tiniest house of time."[3]

Other goddesses can seem personal and very human. Bhuvaneshwari, however, is far too wide to be anything but impersonal. Yet she is the quintessence of love. Her all-encompassing love is the source of her comfort and power, and when you open up to the Bhuvaneshwari Shakti, you find that she is so accessible and present that you can wrap her around yourself like a blanket.

THE BHUVANESHWARI WOMAN

I first discovered the Bhuvaneshwari energy when I began teaching teleconference meditation classes. Teleconference classes are all about energy; when participants are spread around the world, they are held by whatever energy is generated between the group and the teacher. Though I speak and people ask questions, the most striking aspect of the classes is the soft, spacious Presence that arises between us all. It is like being inside a vast meditative vortex. Over time, I've realized that the spoken words are simply the vehicle for something else: the growing presence of the energy field. Open and spacious, the field holds students as they find their own connection to meditation.

There are Durgaesque teachers, like yogini Seane Corn, whose own powerful activism and gift for words motivates students to make sense of their lives. There are Kaliesque teachers, like Caroline Myss, who can take apart preconceptions with a few choice words. And there are Bhuvaneshwariesque teachers, like Pema Chödrön, who—rather than push students to transcend their limitations—creates an atmosphere of acceptance that allows insight and transformation to occur.

Bhuvaneshwari energy is not passionate like Kali's, not luscious in the same way as Lakshmi's or Lalita Tripura Sundari's, not actively protective like Durga's. Someone in touch with Bhuvaneshwari has the gift of holding space for others. Heidi is a Bhuvaneshwari-style psychotherapist who also runs a treatment center for addiction counseling. Her style of leadership is strikingly nondirective. She leads not by telling people what to do but by surrounding her staff with an atmosphere of support, which encourages them to discover creative ways to solve problems. She is a master of what psychologist Carl Ransom Rogers called "unconditional positive regard." When she disagrees, she does it by asking a question like "Is that what you really want to do?" or "Is that what you think is the best thing to do?" Yet there is nothing passive about her—under her guidance her addiction-counseling center is now among the leaders in its field.

Like Heidi, healers and psychotherapists often function by a kind of nondoing. They extend their psyches to hold another person and in that way provide a trustable sense of presence. There's empathy in it. There's deep listening. Above all, there's a feeling that you're being held. Somehow, that holding presence heals. We don't know how it happens, because it's not done by us. The Shakti does the healing. Bhuvaneshwari—the supreme spaciousness—seeps in among the atoms and subtly knits the broken places.

Bhuvaneshwari people create communal spaces and salons. They are incubators of creative activity. Since her twenties, Alice has been a high-level political operative, managing successful political campaigns for others. In her forties, she began to feel that it was time for her to step out from behind the scenes and run for office herself. As she prepared to run for the state legislature, contacting the powerful people she knew and asking for their support, she noticed that she felt insecure and self-conscious promoting herself. In a series of dreams, she saw herself surrounded by animals and working in gardens, while all around her plants seemed to spring up from the earth. Alice realized that in order to function at her best, she needed to feel that she was nurturing others, planting seeds, and tending them, not acting to promote personal agendas.

At about that time, she was asked to head an NGO that promoted women's education in the developing world. When she took the job, she discovered that she could exercise her gift for promoting the welfare of others while creating a powerful organization of which she is the center.

The Bhuvaneshwari person operates as a still center around which others orbit. She herself may not seem to be doing much of anything. But in her presence, others are inspired to act and create, just as Brahma, Vishnu, and Shiva are inspired by her Shakti to perform their cosmic functions. My hypercreative friend Marilyn couldn't write unless another friend, Kathy, was in the room with her. Kathy served as a sounding board for Marilyn's flow of ideas. Moreover, she possessed calm, centered, approving energy that allowed Marilyn to function without dissipating her energies in endless rewriting. Kathy rarely contributed an idea. She just contributed her presence.

In Taoist philosophy, the best ruler is said to be the one who is most distant from the people, who functions as a benevolent force without directly intervening in their affairs. In just that way, Bhuvaneshwari people extend invisible blankets of loving spaciousness like gifted hostesses. Clair Huxtable, Phylicia Rashad's character on the old *Cosby Show*, had a Bhuvaneshwari-like quality. She carried a strong holding presence—never passive, always grounded, strong without being sharp. Queen Elizabeth II has this same quiet presence and stability. In working groups, there is often one person who, consciously or unconsciously, holds the space for the group. When people in the group argue, or when the atmosphere in the group becomes fractured or spiky, this person will—usually wordlessly—extend his energy over the room and in so doing create an atmosphere that lets everyone resolve their disagreements. Often no one knows that she is performing this function, but most long-running groups have such a person holding space for them. In a working group I was part of for years, people used to give harsh critiques to each other. One of our members, a man named Lee, rarely spoke. But when things got dicey, he would begin to hum very softly, and an energy would flow over the group that, usually within minutes, would calm the ruffled energies.

THE BHUVANESHWARI SHADOW

Bhuvaneshwari also has her shadow side. Someone with a strong shadow aspect of this goddess might hold space like a giant slug or be a space case, given to rambling, unfocused thinking, who never quite tunes in to what is going on around her. "That's fine, dear" is a mantra of one type of shadow Bhuvaneshwari. But Bhuvaneshwari can also manifest as the kind of woman who empowers only those who remain within her orbit, discarding anyone who shows independence or challenges her control. A woman who carries shadow Bhuvaneshwari energy might exercise control from behind the scenes, giving and withholding approval arbitrarily, or creating so much dependence in her circle that everyone unthinkingly does her will. I know a wealthy woman who patronizes artists and writers. She will buy their work and subsidize them while they write or paint. In return, she expects them to drop everything to spend time with her when she feels bored or wants a companion. "I'll send the plane for you," she will tell a protégé, adding that she expects him to show up without his wife or girlfriend. Shadow Bhuvaneshwari can also be the kind of healer who imposes her own agendas on her clients, fostering psychological or even psychic dependence. She can be a form of what Western thinkers like poet Robert Graves and psychologist Erich Neumann called "the devouring mother," whose supportive passivity can act like glue for someone who lets himself become caught in her comfortable ooze.

PRACTICING BHUVANESHWARI ENERGY

Shadow aspects aside, Bhuvaneshwari's capacity for holding space carries a uniquely subtle kind of generosity. So how do you hold that kind of space? You do it by enfolding a situation in the embrace of your own awareness. Perhaps you imagine yourself wrapping a psychic blanket around a person or a situation. Perhaps you mentally step backward, becoming a nonjudgmental, loving witness. Perhaps you station yourself in your heart, become present to the space within, and then extend your heart to hold the other. A few years ago, a colleague of mine was on a car trip with a mother and her teenage son. At one point, they erupted into a shouting match. My colleague had no choice but to stay in the car. At the same time, it would have been inappropriate to actively intervene. So my colleague invoked spaciousness. She imagined her heart as a valley enclosing the mother and son, and imagined spacious energy holding the fiery energy that sparked between them. Little by little, their energy relaxed into calm.

Contemplation: Holding Space

For this exercise, think of someone you know who is engaged in
a difficult task. Maybe he's sick and needs to heal. Maybe she's
trying to sort out her business life. Maybe she's a young person
trying to build a bridge into the future, confused, uncertain, or
simply in need of support. Once you have the person in mind,
take a comfortable position and prepare to contemplate.

Take a moment to create a positive intention or wish for this person. Give it
words, and imagine that you plant that intention inside the field of your heart.

Ask Bhuvaneshwari to be present. You can do this by simply asking her,
by name, to be with you: "Goddess Bhuvaneshwari, please be present here."

Repeat the syllable "hrim" (*hreem*) twenty-seven times, either silently or
out loud, with your attention in your heart. Feel that you offer the syllable into
your heart.

Recognize that whether you are consciously aware of it or not, the syllable
"hrim" *is* the goddess Bhuvaneshwari.

Now, imagine a subtle energy field extending around your body. Feel that
the person you are thinking of is held in this field. No need to "do" anything.
You simply hold this person inside your field, trusting that the power of the field
and the power of your intention will create the space for whatever support the
person needs.

Notice any insights or intuitions that arise as you're holding space.

Do this for five minutes, then consciously bring your energy back into your
body. Feel your energy filling your body from your toes to your head. Imagine
that you are surrounded by a circle of space that holds and protects *you*.

EMBODYING THE GODDESS

Holding space—being Bhuvaneshwari—is a practice that asks you to have
embodied the energy of the goddess. There's a huge difference between holding space as an individual—identifying yourself as the egoic "owner" of the
atmosphere you invoke or as the one who is offering care. As individuals, our
energy is partial, affected by our emotional state. As egoic beings—which all
of us are when we identify with our personal selves—we tend to get inflated,

to take credit for the gifts that manifest around us, and to become attached to our own capacity as helpers or transmitters of power. Moreover, when you try to hold space for another person using your own emotional or physical energy, you will often wind up drastically depleted. The secret of holding space is to get your personal self out of the way and to do it with the feeling that it is the goddess's energy that holds the circle. Your job is to invoke the goddess, to ask her presence to infuse the situation. The mantra "hrim," Bhuvaneshwari's sound form, is a crucial part of this practice.

THE MANTRA "HRIM"

Bhuvaneshwari's mantra is the main Tantric mantra of manifestation, just as Om is the manifestation mantra in the Vedic system. According to the language mysticism of tantra, each of the four components of the mantra—*ha, ra, i,* and *m*—is equated with a particular phase of the process by which cosmoses come into being. Particular vibratory forms, specific deities, and certain aspects of the physical cosmos come out of each of the letters of the mantra, which is the source of the entire cosmic creation.

So it makes sense that hrim would be associated with a goddess whom tantra considers the source of creation itself. However, to say that the mantra "hrim" is associated with Bhuvaneshwari would be misleading, because in Tantric thought, the mantra *is* the goddess. Her anthropomorphic form—her "physical" (*sthula*) shape—is considered a partial form of her. The mantra is her essence. So hrim *is* the Goddess in her absolute form. In fact, there are texts that say that as the goddess in sound form, hrim contains the entire cosmos. When we really take in the mantra, repeating it until it becomes embedded in our being, we literally ingest the goddess, take her into ourselves. If you repeat the mantra with the understanding that it is you as well as the goddess, you will in time come to feel her presence powerfully infusing your body. At that point, your consciousness becomes truly creative, since the mantra "hrim" is creativity itself.

BECOMING THE BODY OF THE WORLD

As you tune into the Shakti of Bhuvaneshwari, you might begin to recognize your own identity with the land and creatures of the earth. Bhuvaneshwari's body is the world, and you are a part of it. Genuinely world-centric consciousness arises from a felt sense; an almost tangible, palpable sense of belonging to the earth.

Author and eco-philosopher Joanna Macy makes a distinction between environmentalism, in which we see ourselves as stewards of the planet, and the movement called "deep ecology," in which we experience the planet *as* ourselves. "I don't work to save the rainforest," she quotes one activist as saying. "The rainforest works to save itself through me."[4] This attitude is an aspect of Bhuvaneshwari consciousness. You begin to tune in to this level of consciousness when you practice expanding the space of your awareness to include the room you are in, the land you dwell on, the city, the country, the earth itself. If you begin such a practice by asking Bhuvaneshwari to be present and by breathing the mantra "hrim" into your heart, you might find that her energy will itself expand your awareness.

Bhuvaneshwari practice also generates natural compassion. The experience of real compassion is not something we manufacture. It flows from an actual felt experience of oneness, and it starts when we are able to take in the perspective of another.

The Tibetan practice of *tonglen*, taking and sending, is a powerful and effective way of helping you tune in to the experience of compassion. In traditional tonglen, you breathe others' pain into your heart and breathe out your own happiness to them. The overriding purpose of this is to experience the truth that others' happiness and suffering is not separate from your own. But to imagine yourself breathing in another's pain can be a daunting practice, especially for someone who isn't sure they have a strong enough experience of their own happiness and strength to withstand feeling another's suffering. The secret of tonglen is to feel that your heart is the heart of a deity and that the deity both receives the pain and offers the blessing. In our ordinary egoic state we do not have the capacity to offer the real healing that tonglen practice can achieve. But when you are open to the presence of deity energy in your heart, the practice of taking in negativities and sending out joy becomes much more effective and powerful.

Meditation: Taking and Sending with the Shakti of Bhuvaneshwari

Years ago, in meditation, I found that by opening up the back of my heart, I could easily expand into the energy of what we could call the "great heart"—the loving spaciousness that supports and contains our individual body, mind, and heart. For some reason, I have always found this practice more effective than tuning in to the space within the heart center. One reason, I believe, is that when we become present to the great heart, we are invoking the goddess as the mother of space, Bhuvaneshwari.

When you are ready, find a quiet, comfortable seated posture
for this exercise and have a timer handy. Then, prepare to open
the back of your heart to Bhuvaneshwari's energy and begin.

With the breath, bring your attention into your heart, the center behind the breastbone.

Feel that in the very center of your heart is a space, and within this space is a small, warm, glowing sun. Bhuvaneshwari is often associated with the sun, the life-giving energy of the cosmos.

Let the breath enter and leave the body through the sun in the center of your heart.

Inhaling, let the mantra "hrim" drift into your heart. Exhaling, allow it to drift out through your heart.

After a time, sense that there is a softening or opening in the back of your heart.

With the inhalation, allow your attention to flow through the back of your heart. Sense that behind you is the great *akasha,* the golden, blissful spaciousness that is Bhuvaneshwari, source of the cosmos. The breath flows into the spaciousness at your back with the sound *hrim*. Flowing back through your heart with the sound of the mantra, it infuses your body with particles of spacious Shakti, pulsing with awareness, freedom, and love.

Now, imagine yourself breathing in your own thoughts—breathing them into your heart and through the back of your heart into the spaciousness of the goddess at your back.

As you exhale with the sound *hrim,* feel that the blessing-energy of the goddess flows into your thoughts, creating auspicious energy in the space of your mind.

When you are ready, inhale any feelings of lack, physical or emotional pain, anger or grief through your heart, into the goddess space behind you.

Exhale with *hrim,* breathing her blessing, light, and spaciousness into your emotional discomfort.

If it helps to have a concrete image to work with, imagine yourself breathing in hot, dark energy and allowing it to dissolve in the goddess at your back. Then breathe light back into your own mind.

Now, imagine another person who is suffering from the particular pain or emotional difficulty that you are experiencing. Feel that you breathe in her or his pain, and offer it through your heart to be dissolved into Bhuvaneshwari's energy at your back.

With the exhalation, breathe *hrim*, filled with spaciousness and blessing, into that person.

After a while, begin to consider all the people in the world who might be experiencing that particular pain. Breathe their pain or emotional discomfort into your heart, offer it to the vast spaciousness of Bhuvaneshwari at your back, and breathe out the mantra "hrim," allowing it to flow into the bodies of all these beings.

Do this for fifteen minutes, until you begin to feel the natural connection between yourself and these other beings.[5]

The taking and sending practice is all about connection. At the least, it can show you that the emotions, and even the physical pain you experience, do not belong exclusively to "you." Everyone has them. The anger isn't *your* anger, even if the reasons for it and the tale you tell yourself about it are unique and personal. The anger is *the* anger, a universal flavor of feeling that sweeps through everyone from time to time. As we recognize its universal, global quality, our own personal anger story becomes less compelling, less *ours*. Anger, held in the open embrace of Bhuvaneshwari, dissolves into a particularly active and assertive form of energy. Breathed back into others, it becomes the motive for active engagement in life. Grief, dissolved into the spaciousness of the goddess, becomes soft-heartedness and compassion. The sense of loss becomes compassion for all the losses that life brings. They are the emotions and pain of all beings. Just as Bhuvaneshwari is the Shakti who manifests all life from within herself, she is also the Shakti who can contain and transform the inevitable suffering of being alive. As the energy of spaciousness itself, she can draw apart the pockets of density and contraction inside your consciousness. She can expand as your awareness and reveal that you are, indeed, capable of holding the world in love.

Bhuvaneshwari

bhoo-vuh-neysh-war-ee—Goddess of the Worlds

Other Names for Bhuvaneshwari:
Mahamaya (*muh-hah-mah-yah*)—Great Enchantress
Sarveshi (*sahr-veysh-ee*)—Mistress of All

Sarvarupa (*sahr-vuh-roo-puh*)—She Whose Form Is Everything
Vishvarupa (*vish-wuh-roo-puh*)—She Whose Form Is the Universe
Prapancheshwari (*pruh-puhn-chey-shwuh-ree*)—Mistress of the Five-Fold
World (all that is made of the five elements: earth, air, fire, water, and
space), and Goddess of the Expansion and Manifestation of All Things

Goddess of:
- sacred space
- the creatrix, mother of worlds
- the divine mother as mistress of all realities, empowering the
  activities that create, maintain, and dissolve the world
- the giver of grace to all beings
- cosmic nature: the subtle matrix from which everything arises
- meditative space

Recognize Bhuvaneshwari in:
- the inner experience of expanding awareness
- mountains, oceans, and landmasses
- landscapes with long views of earth and sky
- the space between one breath and another
- a star-spangled night sky
- the physical world in its beauty
- your own body—especially in states of relaxation—and the energy
  that keeps it alive
- galaxies and nebulae and the space between
- any moment that you recognize the oneness between your body and
  the earth, or that you sense the entire cosmos: earth, air, fire, water,
  all plants, landmasses, and animals

Invoke Bhuvaneshwari for:
- the peace that arises when your consciousness expands infinitely
- the compassion you feel when you recognize that all beings are part
  of one cosmic body
- the capacity to hold space for yourself and others to dissolve
  their differences, create at the highest level, and accept their own
  humanness as part of their divinity
- identifying yourself with the earth and all living things

• the experience of full embodiment: the felt sense of your own body as sacred

Bija Mantra

Hrim (*hreem*)

Invocational Mantra

Om hrim shrim klim bhuvaneshwarayai namaha
ohm hreem shreem kleem bhoo-vuh-neysh-war-yai nuh-muh-huh

Om, I offer salutations to the auspicious Lady of Worlds, manifestor of worlds.

Bhuvaneshwari's colors: red, blue, gold
Bhuvaneshwari's flower: red lotus
Bhuvaneshwari's consort: Shiva

Dialoguing with the Goddesses

Only the images we live can bring transformation.

HELEN LUKE

Awakening Shakti arose out of my own inner dialogue with the Goddess. As I hope you have seen through these pages, this book is an open invitation to deepen your internal conversation with the divine feminine. Shakti is playing in us, as us, and through us, and she is also talking to us. She guides, she plays, and she continually surprises. All we have to do, really, is notice. There is no moment in life when the Shakti is not opening a doorway for us to recognize her and delight in her presence. We spoke in the first chapter about her different "tastes." We described four basic ways in which we experience her—as energies that reveal themselves in the natural elements and in human culture, as distinct divine personalities, as aspects of our own unique personality and essence, and as the awakened Kundalini Shakti, the subtle power that evolves our awareness from within. As you've read and practiced with these goddesses, you may have sensed all these different facets of the Goddess. You may have become more alert to the ways in which these Shaktis interweave with your body, your mind, and your personality. You might have realized the Goddess as an inner force—as a pulsation of energy in your body, as the quality of aliveness in your breath, as the inner river that flows through the thoughts and images in your mind, or as the subtle seeing behind all your experience. You may have enjoyed recognizing her in the natural world—in weather patterns, or the play of light on water, or in the moods of the ocean.

Perhaps you also have a sense of these goddesses as distinct and personal beings. Maybe you've even seen a goddess in a dream vision, or felt her hovering, as it were, in your field—a unique helper or guide you can invoke, pray to, and meditate upon. Or, you might find it illuminating to contemplate these goddess energies as archetypes of personality and to recognize aspects of the goddesses in your own self-expression, or in the people close to you—men as well as women.

WHICH GODDESS ARE YOU?

One of the questions that everyone asks while reading a book like this is "Which goddess am I?" (That's why I've included a quiz in appendix II.) Many of us do seem distinctly related to one of the goddess "types." But recognizing a goddess in yourself is not like, say, Myers-Briggs typing. Most current typologies are related exclusively to the personal self. They are styles of ego expression. The goddesses, however, are transpersonal even when acting through your ego or personality. They always offer you a way to connect your personal self to your transpersonal essence. Moreover, most of us embody more than one goddess. Maybe in your public life you're a Durga-style warrior who burns her way through obstacles at work, or whom others can rely on to confront a bully or a recalcitrant teenager. But you might also have a receptive Sita inside you who comes out in your intimate moments and who sometimes feels at odds with your Durga side. When you discuss ideas, you may have the clarity and precision and intuitive delicacy of Saraswati, but when your emotions are engaged, you fall into the wild, disruptive energy of Kali. Certain Shaktis are part of what we might call the "daytime" energy of your personality. These energies have a familiar and comfortable feel. Others are less developed, more hidden—though they may sometimes come out through dreams or sudden emotional upheavals. These hidden goddesses will come to life for you as you contemplate their myths and consider how they appear as your unique self.

Because the goddesses are *energies*, they tend to energize you when you think about them. Contemplating one of the goddesses, or using one of her mantras, literally awakens some portion of her Shakti inside you.

This could work in several ways.

First, even when a particular goddess energy is already familiar in your life, you may be experiencing her in a mundane, routinized way. She may be connected to a part of yourself you take for granted—your strong will, your nurturing empathy, your talent for making money—but that you may not have identified with anything larger than your personal self. As you begin to recognize the presence of the goddess in certain aspects of your personal self, you will also realize the transpersonal quality that expresses itself through you. Your unique essence—what spiritual teacher Marc Gafni calls your "unique self"[1]—contains both personal and transpersonal elements. Once you consciously connect to a goddess, you'll realize that certain of your traits, skills, and talents are her manifestations or even her gifts. This can radically shift your attitude toward your own life. As you identify yourself with the numinous qualities of a goddess, you may gain a new appreciation of your unique self, your own unique qualities as embodied spirit. Meditating on the goddesses can help free you of the egoic hooks that most of us attach to our own energies. Instead, you can realize that you are, in many ways, a channel for unique gifts or wisdoms of the goddess.

Second, as you get to know the goddesses within you, you will find that they help activate hidden energies in your life. Important threads of your essential self are often operating underground, unrevealed or unknown to your conscious personality. When the Shakti of a particular goddess is dormant, that power is largely unavailable to you. So, an important reason to contemplate goddesses who feel unfamiliar is so they can reveal these closeted powers of your unique self. The process may begin with a dream or meditation experience, as a feeling of being guided from within, or as a sense of connection to energies in nature that connect to these hidden goddess powers. The goddesses can give you access to parts of the self that are unfamiliar and helpful.

Third, you might also discover that certain of your daily activities connect you to particular goddesses. Some of the things you naturally do—painting, singing, gardening, cleaning house, running a meeting, dancing, making love—might be natural doorways through which goddess energies unfold in your life. Long ago, I attended a lecture on the goddess Saraswati in which we chanted Saraswati mantras. The chanting ignited an energetic current inside me. This in itself was not so unusual—I was used to reacting energetically to chanting. What was unusual was the familiarity of the particular energy that I felt in the "presence" of the Saraswati Shakti. It exactly matched a feeling I had first experienced at age twelve, when I began to write stories and essays and discovered that the act of writing made me feel energized and alive. The energy that fueled my impulse to write was, I realized, the energy of Saraswati. That experience made me understand why the act of writing has so often felt blissful to me. Another example is that of my friend Karen, who read an early version of the Radha chapter with her book group. In the conversation afterward, she recalled periods in her life when she, like Radha, had longed for a particular lover. She saw how that same longing had also fueled her entrance into spiritual life and sustained her at crucial moments. Tuning in to her own Radha energy made her realize that the energy of romantic spiritual longing is part of what makes her feel alive in the world.

Finally, your less positive emotions can also be doorways, as any good Tantrika knows. One of the great Tantric practices involves finding the root energy within an emotion, especially strong emotions like anger, joy, fear, and lust. The practice is to let go of the "story" about the emotion, to refrain from acting on it, and to simply feel the pure passion within it. As you enter your anger, you can feel the root dynamism that is Kali's signature energy, which you can use to move through obstructions or even revolutionize your life situation. Your grief can awaken Sita's compassion. The energy within erotic arousal, when you let yourself completely experience it without moving it toward an object, can open into the freedom of Lalita Tripura Sundari, which will then fill your body with blissful feelings.

That, I believe, is part of the gift of getting to know these Shaktis. The more you practice with them, the more you recognize how certain apparently personal qualities or emotions are actually bridges into your unique transpersonal self. This self is not simply an impersonal field. It is alive with particular energies—energies that together create a kind of rainbow of flavors and tastes that are uniquely calibrated in you. Tuning into the goddess Shaktis makes your encounters with both the inner and outer world richly relational, even incandescent. You discover this as you become more familiar with the goddess energies and how they live in you or enhance your personal energies.

As you practice with the goddess energies, you'll notice that there are times when a particular goddess feels particularly alive and resonant for you. This could mean that her energy wants to be more deeply embodied in you. It could also mean that you are actually being "visited" by this unique form of the divine feminine—and are being invited to enjoy her or receive her help!

SHADOW GODDESS

The more we bring a Goddess Shakti into consciousness, the more we can enjoy her unique strengths, as well as the unique flavor of her bliss. (All the goddesses are blissful—but each in her own way.) On the other hand, when you are unconscious of the operation of a goddess archetype, she may operate within you in a shadowy—or, as we've already discussed, in a "binding" fashion. If you won't engage the liberating aspects of the goddesses, you will often get slapped on the side of the head by their shadow. This is, of course, especially obvious when it comes to the fierce goddesses: unacknowledged Kali is notorious for manifesting sudden disruptions or erupting in the form of a fiery tantrum or an impulsive outburst. Durga can be a bossy control freak. It can be equally true of the gentle Shaktis. In her book *Devi*, Indian journalist Mrinal Pande writes about a rich girl who parties like Paris Hilton and who condescends to everyone who comes to her parties—unless they happen to be richer than she. It's a vibrant portrait of Lakshmi's shadow.[2]

Tuning into the kinesthetic sensation of the goddess's energy in your body is one of the best ways I know to bring a shadowed goddess into the light. As you do, her energy will become more integrated into your personality, and she'll actually become a helper. Once brought to consciousness, Kali and Durga can more gently orchestrate your inner revolutions. Lakshmi can expand your sense of abundance without tempting you toward overindulgence or grandiosity. Saraswati can enhance your intuitions without allowing your ego to claim your brilliance or turning you into a nitpicker.

ENGAGE THE DIALOGUE

You may be someone who most naturally relates to the goddesses as personality archetypes. In fact, as aspects of your personality, the goddesses within you are in a continual dialogue. It can be psychologically transformative to bring this subtle conversation to consciousness. Jean Shinoda Bolen, in her book about the Greek deity archetypes, *Goddesses in Everywoman*, suggests treating the goddesses as a kind of committee.[3] This is true of the Indian goddesses as well: each has her own gifts to bring to the project of your life. Once you've gotten a feel for the energy of the different goddesses, you can begin to identify their voices inside you and give them space to advocate different perspectives.

This is especially useful when you're trying to think through how to solve a problem. Lucia, a film producer, was upset when the executives at her studio neglected to include her in a conference with the writer of a film she was producing. Though it seemed like a small oversight, she knew enough about the power dynamics of the film world to recognize that this was a sign of disrespect. But she wasn't sure what to do about it. Ordinarily, she might have taken a conciliatory, Sita-like role or tried to rationalize it with her Saraswati insight. She considered the different voices within her—Sita, counseling patience; Saraswati, strategizing about the dynamics of the situation; Dhumavati, counseling her to let it all go, that maybe this was time to retire from infighting. Kali wanted to kill the deal and take the project elsewhere. Lucia's Durga voice also wanted to show strength. In fact, Lucia's inner Durga insisted that if Lucia didn't stand up strongly, the people she was working with would discount her and her career would be virtually over. As Lucia listened to the inner voices, Durga's voice began to dominate. She realized that this was a situation in which she had to stand up and protest.

With a friend, she strategized a Durga approach to the problem. The next day, she went into the office of the studio executive in charge and crisply told the executive that what he had done was unacceptable. Departing from her usual conciliatory style was difficult, but because she summoned the energy of the goddess, she was able to act with a kind of transpersonal power that she normally didn't experience. The executive agreed that Lucia should have been kept in the loop; the next day, he asked her to produce another movie in addition to the one she was working on.

In Lucia's case, the "intervention" of her somewhat shadowed and hidden Durga energy allowed her to act in a new way. For Miriam, who was trying to overcome her feelings of rejection when her lover couldn't see her one weekend, the solution was to begin by recognizing her suffering Sita energy. Convening a few goddesses, Miriam heard from her inner Sita (who counseled, "Just let him be the way he is"), Kali (who wanted to break up with him immediately), and finally the voice of Lalita Tripura Sundari. This energy felt so confidant, so playful, and so free that Miriam was immediately drawn to her. Lalita advised that Miriam take a trip to the city and go to the opera, something her boyfriend didn't like to do. Miriam was able to see her free weekend as a gift rather than a source of suffering—and when she came back, she was so enlivened that her lover kept asking her, "What did you do to get so happy all of a sudden?" In the weeks that followed, he showed more and more desire to be with her. Lalita's freedom was radically attractive.

Dialoguing with the different goddess personalities can also help you distinguish between what we have already called the "liberating" and "binding" aspects of their Shaktis. When the Durga inside you wants to leap up and fix a situation by fighting or struggling, you might ask your inner Saraswati, with her exquisite sense of timing, to analyze the pros and cons of impulsive action. When your inner Sita feels blindly loyal to a partner, or when you feel passive or reluctant to act without help from another, try tuning into Lakshmi and her capacity for acting diplomatically yet forcefully. You will also notice, as you contemplate each of the goddesses, that there are aspects of the feminine energy that you've never let yourself access. Maybe it's your warrior strength, if your conscious personality is more of a caregiver or a mediator. Maybe it's your deep sensuality. Maybe it's your capacity to shine, to be radiant. Or perhaps what you need to recognize is that you can play at all these qualities—that all the goddesses are inside you, some of them manifesting outwardly while others act in your subtle inner world, the world of your spiritual life.

Embodying a Goddess

When you feel that it's time to become more present to the energy of a goddess, or when you want to engage her help, you can use the core techniques of deity meditation to bring her into your energy body for a few hours.

Begin by deciding which Goddess energy you want to explore, or which energy you need at this moment.

Using one of the practices in the book, imagine yourself drawing the goddess into your body. Feel her energy filling your field. Notice how the energy feels: Light? Solid? Soft? Sharp?

Now imagine your body being filled with the signature quality of the goddess. For Lakshmi, it would be the feeling of abundance; for Durga, protective strength; for Sundari, queenly beauty; for Bhuvaneshwari, encompassing compassion. You don't necessarily need to put words to the quality of a goddess's energy. In fact, it can be more powerful to simply invoke her by name or through her mantra or visualization and feel your way into her presence.

PART ONE: WALKING AROUND AS THE GODDESS
Imagine how the goddess would hold herself. How does she walk? How does she interact with others? How does she eat? What clothes does she like? Where does she like to hang out? In short, how does this goddess experience herself as you? You are seeding her Shakti into your own field. Continue to sense just how the goddess's Shakti moves through you, how it feels to allow yourself to be the goddess.

Is this feeling familiar to you? Does it feel new? Notice how the energy sits within your body. Where do you feel it most strongly? Where does it seem not to reach?

Spend a couple of hours, if possible, walking around as the goddess. Start while you are alone, then try taking yourself out for a walk *as* the goddess.

Notice how your practice of embodying the goddess affects the way you are with others and the way they are with you.

PART TWO: LETTING GO AND CLOSING YOUR PRACTICE

When you are ready to let go of the practice, do a conscious closing. In Indian ritual practice, this is called "dismissing the deity." It's a heartfelt, respectful practice for returning your attention to your ordinary human state. In Tantric traditions, there's an innate understanding that the transpersonal energy of the deity should not be allowed to crowd out our individual, human selves for too long. When you know how to consciously invite the goddess in and then bid her goodbye after a time, you develop a balanced relationship between these powerful deity energies and your personal self-sense. This is what it means to dance with the goddesses, to allow their power, their wisdom, and their unique love to infuse you gradually, mingling with your mundane, unique personal self, so that the goddesses' qualities grace your being without overwhelming or—to use C. G. Jung's word—"inflating" you.

So, when you are done with your practice of "being" the deity, thank the goddess you are working with for being present with you, and say goodbye to her. With a long inhalation, imagine that energy from the earth rises up through your feet, sweeps up the center of your body, and out your crown. Exhaling, imagine that light energy from the sun sweeps down through your crown and out your feet.

Now, ground yourself in the body by feeling your feet on the ground, and take your attention through your body from the soles of your feet to your crown, using your breath to help you feel each part of your body. Inhaling, imagine that the breath fills your feet, your legs, your abdomen, your chest, your shoulders, arms and neck, and finally your head. Sit for a moment with the sense of being fully inside your body. And then, trusting that the energy of the divine feminine is alive and expressing herself in you as you, go about your day.

THE GODDESS LIVES AS YOU

The energy of each goddess will show up for you in a uniquely calibrated way. The more you can recognize the particular flavor of the goddess in you, the more you can dance with her, and the more of her gifts you will be able to embody. If there is a goddess Shakti you feel shy of, or whom you resist, let her be for now. There will come a time when a goddess who now seems too big or too intense or too beautiful will become accessible. Playing with the goddesses, and integrating their energies in your life, is a life-long process. But each time you turn to the goddess, inwardly or in the natural world, you will discover another flavor of her fluidity and her strength, her fierceness and her compassion, her exquisite love, and her incisive transformative power.

Finally, let me mention one of the most important aspects of the goddesses. They give boons—all kinds of boons. For centuries, people have been asking the Goddess for help in all sorts of matters. They've invoked different aspects of the feminine for health, for having children, for gaining wealth, skill, love, a good mate, a better job. You can do this, too. The Goddess *is* the world, and her energy is present in your desires and needs, as well as in the ways they get fulfilled. Whether you invoke the Goddess through petitionary prayer or through a more contemporary practice like affirmation, she is not averse to answering prayers for mundane things.

You can connect to any one of the goddesses through petitionary prayer and ask for what you need. You'll probably receive it—perhaps not immediately, and perhaps not in the exact form you expect, but in time. Above all, though, the Goddess gives spiritual gifts—the capacity to meditate deeply, to heal, and, if it's what you really want, *self-realization.* The form of enlightenment you receive from the goddess is an awareness so open that you can know everything that exists to be a part of your own consciousness. She can lift, in a moment, the illusions of ego and show herself to you inside your body and the world.

Here's the inner secret: as you really get to know the Goddess, you come to know that just being in her presence can fill you with sweetness. The Goddess is love. That's her nature. At times, her love will require you to let go of some piece of your false-self ego before you can see her blissful essence. Sometimes she inspires humility. At other times, self-confidence. At others, play. At all times, she invites you to pay attention to the energy playing inside and around you. The more you "see" her in the energies at play in the world, the more naturally worshipful you become.

The Shakti of the Goddess, even in her fierceness, is both adorable and adoring. The more you honor her, the more you'll relish her paradoxes. Adore her for her sweetness, and be grateful for the sharp edges of her sword. Open to her nurturing love and trust her ruthless dispassion. As you do, you'll realize how intensely the Shakti of the universe adores you. Those who know the Goddess come to realize that every particle of this world is pregnant with her presence. That's why, since the beginning of human time, lovers of the sacred feminine have lived with a secret current of sweetness that never really goes away.

May the light and ecstasy of the divine feminine awaken your life. May her sword of compassion free you from all obstacles. May you know the depths of her love, which is your own love. May you realize the Goddess living within you fully, joyfully as your body, your mind, and your inner self. And may your life, through her grace, be of benefit to all!

The Goddess Families and Their Consorts

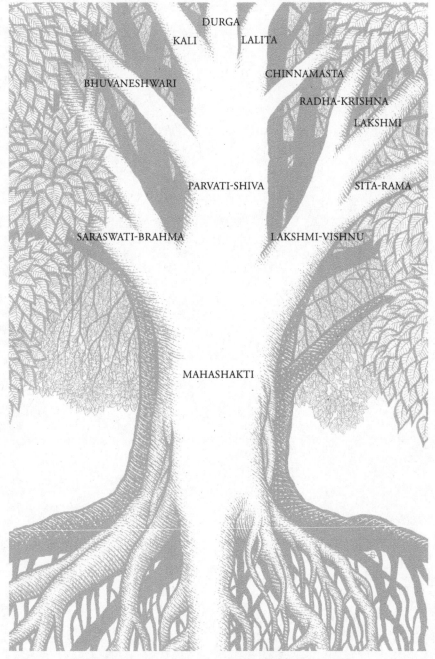

DURGA
KALI   LALITA

CHINNAMASTA

BHUVANESHWARI

RADHA-KRISHNA

LAKSHMI

PARVATI-SHIVA   SITA-RAMA

SARASWATI-BRAHMA   LAKSHMI-VISHNU

MAHASHAKTI

FIGURE 20: THE GOD AND GODDESS FAMILY TREE

Calling Out the Power in Mantra

Overview and Pronunciation Guide

In the Tantric view, mantra is the subtlest, the most powerful, and the most essential of the three forms (image, mantra, and yantra). That's because the process of manifestation takes place through vibration, or sound. Mantras are inherently creative, because at their heart is the *spanda,* the vibratory essence of the primordial Shakti. Spanda (creative vibration) *is* the creative power itself. So in Tantra, the teaching that "In the beginning was the word" is not a metaphor, but a core mystical truth. The subtle vibrations that emanate from the primordial creative vibration take articulated form as the *bija mantras.* Bija is usually translated as "seed." Just as a tiny uranium atom releases vast energy when we split it, so too when you concentrate deeply on the seed mantra form of the Goddess; it releases energy through your body and mind. The bija mantras—hrim, (pronounced *hreem*), aim (pronounced *aye-eem*), krim (pronounced *kreem*), shrim (pronounced *shreem*), hum (pronounced *hoom*) and others—*are* the Goddess in sound form. So, by reciting the mantra, you are revealing, making manifest, the deity herself. To get the full benefit of a mantra, it needs to be activated or "awakened." This is traditionally done by a process of initiation, but you can also awaken a mantra through your own mindful repetition, as we'll be doing here.

One secret of tapping into the hidden energy in a mantra is to pay very close attention to the energetic touch of the mantra as you repeat it. Focus on the way the syllables "feel" in your mind, whether you are thinking them, letting them flow with the breath, or paying attention to how the mantra vibrates in one of the inner centers of the body. See if you can practice with the feeling that you "touch" or "taste" the goddess energy with your tongue and speech. When you repeat the mantra with awareness of its energetic "feel," it doesn't take long to awaken it, though you should expect to repeat it several thousand times before you fully experience its power.[1]

PRONUNCIATION

In Sanskrit, vowels can be either short or long. In the original Devanagari script, they are written as different letters.

Throughout this book I've offered pronunciation guides for Sanskrit names, mantras, and seed syllables. I have rendered the vowels as follows:

Short "a" is rendered as *uh*

Long "a" as *ah*

Short "u" as *u*

Long "u" as *oo*

Short "i" is rendered as *i* (as in "bit")

Long "i" as *ee*

The vowel "e" (as in the Sanskrit word *devi*) is pronounced *ay* as in "day" and has been rendered as *ey*.

The diphthong "ai" is pronounced like "eye" and "sky."

The Sanskrit "c" is always pronounced *ch*. I have rendered it as *ch* throughout.

All this aside, people who love the Goddess will often simply call out to her as Ma. That simple syllable, the word for mother in nearly every Indo-European language, can be sounded as a sigh, a call for help, an expression of love, a simple invocation. You'll hear singers crying out "Maaaa!" in ecstasy when their chanting reaches its climax. As you lose your inhibitions about invoking her, you may find yourself crying out to Ma with unexpected intensity in all sorts of moments!

Quiz: Goddess Power in Action

I f one of the goddesses in this book met a mugger on the street, how would she handle it?

1. Command him to leave (and he would).
2. Point out that she has nothing worth stealing, then lay a curse on him.
3. Pull a knife and leave him bleeding on the street.
4. Give him a karate kick to make him run away.
5. Give him all her money, then call the cops and have him busted.
6. Give him her money, then charm him into giving it back.
7. Make herself disappear.
8. Explain rationally why he should let her go, then analyze how she could have let this happen to her.
9. Repeat powerful mantras that stop him cold.
10. Look at him with complete disbelief, melting him with her smile, then walk away.

Answer Key:

1. Lalita Tripura Sundari; 2. Dhumavati; 3. Kali; 4. Durga; 5. Sita; 6. Lakshmi; 7. Chinnamasta; 8. Saraswati; 9. Parvati; 10. Radha

Which Goddesses Are You?

Most of us hold the energies of several different goddesses. But often, one or two of them predominate. Below, you'll find some revealing questions that might help you recognize your goddess affinities and which ones tend to predominate in your personality.

Please approach this questionnaire playfully! The more playful you are with it, the more you are likely to discover about your connection to each goddess. Certain goddesses will undoubtedly resonate with you more recognizably than others, but look for yourself in all of the goddesses. All of them are within you.

Durga
- Do you have a strong desire to protect others?
- Do you feel acutely the wrongness of social injustice?
- Are you impatient and sometimes hot tempered?
- Do your friends and family sometimes call you bossy?
- Are you often the person others turn to to head the committee or lead the campaign?
- Are you a natural fighter?
- Do you like to be in charge?
- Do you believe that you're usually right?
- Are you capable of doing several things at once?
- Are you the head of a large family, company, or circle of friends?
- Are you a leader?

Lakshmi

- Are you very physically attractive?
- Do people fall in love with you easily?
- Do you have a strong interest in fashion, decoration, and design?
- Are you good at spotting trends?
- Do you prefer the people in your life to be outstanding in some way?
- Does money tend to fall into your hands?
- Do you have an almost physical need to have beauty around you?
- Do you prefer to avoid anything unpleasant?
- Do you love a good time?
- Do you secretly believe that you can never be too rich?
- Do people around you feel more joyous because you are there?
- Are you supremely confident that you'll be taken care of because you deserve the abundance of life?
- Are you generous?
- Do you surround yourself with beautiful things?
- Do you feel negatively impacted by any form of disharmony?
- Are you a gifted business coach?
- Do you have a natural talent for making money?
- Do you have a green thumb?
- Have your friends and lovers noticed that their material lives improve when you're with them?
- Do you prefer being around good-looking, successful, and refined people?
- Are you kind?
- Do you pride yourself on your taste?

Kali

- Do you sometimes feel that there is a battle cry wanting to get out?
- Is your sexuality wild? Does it sometimes feel out of control?
- Do you sometimes frighten people (or yourself) with your intensity?
- Do you have so much raw power that you can accomplish anything you set your mind to?
- Have you ever felt so repressed that you turned your energy on yourself?
- Do you love fiercely?
- Do you have more energy than anyone you know?

- Do you sometimes wonder if you are a rage-aholic?
- Are you decisive?
- Do people ever tell you that since you've come into their lives they feel transformed?
- Do you often feel you have to hold back?
- Do you identify with outsiders and outlaws?

Parvati

- Are you in a powerful yet combative relationship in which there is a strong drive for equality?
- Are you in a creative partnership of some kind in which your partner is in a leadership role and you handle the relationships?
- Are you an athlete or dancer?
- Do you practice intense yoga or meditation?
- Are you a loving but relaxed mother?
- Are you quirky, independent, and able to stand up to any sort of opposition?
- Are you a man's woman, who has had important male mentors?
- Have you ever set your sights on a lover or a career goal and stopped at nothing to attain it?

Saraswati

- As a child, did you tend to fall in love with words?
- Do you forget about the outside world when you're reading or problem solving?
- Do you have a gift for eloquence, even if you're naturally introverted?
- Are you a gifted communicator?
- Are you a *compulsive* communicator?
- Do people tell you that you talk too much?
- Can you sway people with words?
- Are you picky about the words you use?
- Are you careful and detail oriented in your work?
- Is clarity particularly important to you?
- Are you a nitpicker?
- Are you musically gifted?
- Do you naturally understand technology?

- Do ideas and inspirations come to you out of the blue?
- Do you have a beautiful voice?

Sita

- Do you tend to be loyal and self-sacrificing?
- Are you in grieving over a recent loss?
- Has your husband or lover left you?
- Do you feel that your role in life is to support others?
- Do you tend to be a caretaker?
- Are you pregnant?
- Are you a devoted wife or lover, or do you tend to become consumed by the people close to you?
- Are you able to endure a lot of physical pain or misfortune without complaint?
- Do you have quiet moral force?
- Are you the center of your family?
- Have you ever been raped or sexually abused?

Dhumavati

- Do you generally feel somewhat alienated from the social order?
- Are you reclusive?
- Do you have great empathy for the poor, the marginalized, and the aged?
- Are you elderly, frail, or sick?
- Do you have a chronic condition that keeps you from ordinary functioning?
- Are you lonely or depressed?
- Have you been out of work for a while?

Radha

- Are you in love and passionate about your lover?
- Do you enjoy flirtation, playful lovemaking?
- If you are not in love, do you long for it?
- Are you a romantic?
- Do you still hold onto the thought of a lost high school lover?
- Are you the girlfriend of a man who is irresistible to other women—but loves you best?

- Are you passionately devoted to the divine?
- Are you a married person in love with someone who is not your husband?

Chinnamasta

- Do you tend to be radically experimental?
- Are you a cutting-edge teacher, therapist, or workshop leader?
- Are you deeply committed to truthfulness, even at the expense of keeping friends?
- Do you like to push the edge?
- Have you ever self-mutilated?
- Are you able to turn your own wounds into ways to help others?
- Are you easily able to let go of your egoic self?
- Do the people close to you tend to turn to you for support?
- Are people energized by being in your presence?
- Are you committed to democratic enlightenment and willing to give your own energy for the sake of a group?
- Do you regularly spend time in a thought-free meditative state?

Lalita Tripura Sundari

- Does every man who meets you fall in love with you?
- Are you beautiful?
- Do you love sex?
- Are you deeply happy with yourself? Are you confident in your own feminine power?
- Do you have an unusually good relationship with your husband or partner?
- Do you tend to be easily successful at most things you undertake?
- Do you gravitate toward circles of power?
- Are you comfortable with power?

Bhuvaneshwari

- Do you have a natural capacity to create welcoming energy or hold space for others?
- Do people want to congregate in your home?
- Do you have a green thumb?
- Are you the favorite hostess, mom, or teacher in your circle?

- Do you remain friends with everyone you ever knew, including ex-lovers and ex-spouses, because you don't let anyone out of your heart?
- Do people naturally gravitate toward you because everyone around you seems to flourish?
- Are you a therapist, yoga studio manager, or dedicated mentor or coach?
- Do you seem to have a natural healing energy?
- Is your love somewhat impersonal?

Reader's Group Guide

There are many ways to work with *Awakening Shakti* in a group. My suggestion is that you use the group as a platform for discussing the book and the issues it raises, and also as an opportunity to practice together with some of the meditations and contemplations.

You can use the following questions as the basis for discussion about each of the goddesses. You can also work with any of the exercises in the book in a group setting.

If you are reading this book over a period of weeks, you might want to read one chapter each week, practice individually with that goddess, then come back together to discuss the chapter and do some of the exercises together.

Opening Questions

Name a few qualities that you would call specifically feminine.
Consider your image of the divine feminine. How were you brought up to think about the divine feminine? About feminine power?
Do you feel that there is a type of creativity that is specifically feminine? How does that show up in you or in the people you know?

Durga: Warrior Goddess of Protection and Inner Strength

Describe some of the qualities of Durga that you see in yourself or in people you know. What do you like about these Durga qualities? What do you not like about Durga in yourself and others?

Who are some famous Durga women? How do you recognize Durga in others?

How does your inner Durga manifest at work? In relationships?

In your life, how do you recognize the divine Durga impulse to stand up for truth? To protect others? How do you feel that you have succeeded in acting as a protector to yourself or others?

How is the Durga quality in the feminine seen in our society? What aspects of Durga are appreciated? What aspects are denied or seen as unfeminine?

Group Exercise

Choose someone to read the instructions.
Everyone should have paper and pen handy.

Close your eyes, sit comfortably upright, and spend a few minutes focusing your attention on the natural rhythm of your breath. Silently say, "I invoke the presence of the Goddess in the form of Durga."

Feel the presence of the Durga Shakti as a shimmering energy around you. You can visualize her lion, or simply intuit her presence. Imagine her with dark hair streaming over her shoulders, with a golden crown, a scarlet silk sari, and golden necklaces, rings, and bracelets.

See her magnificent arms, strong and bristling with weapons: the bow, the sword, the trident, the mace, the discus. See the lotus she carries.

She is watching you with an intent gaze. Her eyes are large and dark.

Silently offer your salutations to her.

Ask her, "What is the major inner obstacle I have to face now? What do I need to let go of? What should I pay more attention to?"

Close your eyes and turn to your heart. Ask the questions in your heart.

Begin to write. Let the writing come naturally, without thought. Keep writing until you feel that there is no more to say.

Look over what you have written.

Now, close your eyes and imagine yourself turning all these obstacles over to the universal power of grace. Offer the obstacles to Durga, saying, "I offer all this to the Durga Shakti, asking that your grace dissolve all obstacles, inner and outer."

Afterward, share what you experienced.

Lakshmi: Goddess of Abundance and Good Fortune

Describe your secret feelings about the goddess Lakshmi as described in this chapter.

What is the role of beauty in your life? How do you feel about your own beauty? How could contemplation of Lakshmi change your relationship to your own body?

What are your Lakshmi-like qualities? How do you avoid Lakshmi? What do you do to honor or attract Lakshmi?

What areas of your life feel abundant? Where do you feel a lack?

Group Meditation

With pen and paper handy, close your eyes and recite nine times "Om shrim maha lakshmyai namaha" *(ohm shreem muh-hah luhk-shmyai nuh-muh-huh).*

Ask, "What do I need to know about abundance in my life?"

When you are ready, begin to write, feeling that Lakshmi is writing.

Kali: Goddess of Revolution

Are you comfortable with the fierce feminine as embodied in Kali? How do you express fierceness? What is your reaction to fierceness in others?

What do you see as the shadow Kali in yourself, in the people you know, in our society?

How has Kali been suppressed?

Group Meditation

With pen and paper handy, close your eyes and repeat "Om krim hum hrim" *(ohm kreem hoom hreem)* nine times, feeling the mantra resonate in your heart.

Ask: "How would Kali like to express herself now?" Then write down what comes up.

Now, ask for a physical expression of Kali to flow through you. It could be a strong "Ahh." It could be sticking out your tongue. It could be a dance.

Share with the group—either what you write, or the gesture that expresses Kali.

Parvati: Goddess of the Sacred Marriage

How does Parvati achieve her goals? How have you used inner intention combined with practice to achieve desired outcomes in your work or relationships?

How can Parvati's story suggest ways to achieve balance in work, partnership, and practice?

What in the Parvati stories resonates with your own ideal of partnership?

How does the Shiva-Parvati marriage echo contemporary marriages or partnerships you know of or live in?

What do you see as the difference between Parvati and Durga?

Group Meditation: Parvati and Shiva as the Two Halves of Your Body (Finding the Masculine and Feminine within Your Own Body)

Find a comfortable seated position for this meditation, and be sure to have your journal and something to write with. Read aloud the introduction to the exercise and then practice the meditation.

This meditation can surprise you because it allows you to tune into the presence of the divine masculine and feminine within yourself. As mentioned earlier, the interdependence of spirit and matter, masculine and feminine, intellect and feeling, is epitomized by the figure of Ardhanarishvara, God as Half Man-Half Woman. The right side of this androgynous being wears a tiger skin, has matted locks, and carries a trident. The left side has a bared breast and a delicate skirt; her hands dance in mudras. In the tradition, the left side of the body is considered feminine, while the right side is masculine. (Refer to figure 8 on page 153 for a representation of this figure.)

Begin by making a list of the qualities and behaviors in yourself that you consider feminine. Then, list the qualities you consider masculine.

Now list the qualities of the divine that you consider feminine and the qualities you consider masculine.

Now, imagine that the left half of your body is filled by the divine feminine as the goddess Parvati. Sense the qualities of the goddess in that half of your body: beauty, devotion, playfulness, charm, sweetness, nourishing love, erotic tenderness, gracefulness, feminine strength.

Imagine that the right side of your body is occupied by the divine masculine in the form of Shiva. Feel his energy in your body. Sense his qualities: stability, steadiness, penetrating intellect, clarity of vision, peace, vastness, ruthless swiftness, masculine strength.

Let your attention move from the feminine side of your body to the masculine side of your body. Notice the differences. Feel these two sides of the divine nature held within you. Sense them held in balance in your own body.

Afterwards, journal and share your experience.

Saraswati: Goddess Who Flows as Language, Insight, and Sound

Before you begin, the facilitator can ask everyone to close their eyes and decide that, for the next five minutes, you'll speak with the feeling that the goddess Saraswati is sitting on your tongue. Then, each of you can inwardly ask her to speak through you. Do you notice a difference in the way your words come out?

As you discuss the first question, see if you can notice how the words come out when you've invoked the goddess.

Discuss the ways you experience flow and intuition flowing through your own words. Have you ever felt that you were channeling? That intuition was arising from elsewhere?

Do you use words cautiously or freely? Does your speech feel blocked, or do people tell you you talk too much?

What negative effects have you noticed in your own life from negative gossip or harsh speech?

How do you experience flow and rhythm in music and dance?

Group Writing Exercise

With pen and paper handy, spend a few minutes
with closed eyes, focusing on the breath.

Repeat together nine times "Om aim saraswatyai namaha" *(ohm aye-eem sa-ra-swah-tyai nuh-muh-huh)*.

Sit for a moment or two, asking the goddess of speech and wisdom to write through your pen.

Starting with the sentence, "The goddess dances as . . ." write a short paragraph about the goddess of wisdom, speech, and music as you experience her in your life.

Sita: Goddess of Devotion and Mystical Submission

Have you ever been in a relationship where you felt submissive or protected? Would you like to be?

How have you reacted when unjustly treated?

Have you ever felt trapped or captive in a situation?

What do you feel about the Sita story?

How did it affect you emotionally?

Have you known women like this?

Group Meditation: Feeling the Sorrow of the Earth

This is a powerful meditation that can bring up grief as well as compassion. Give yourself at least half an hour to do it; leave enough time to share and discuss what arose for you as you did the contemplation.

Sitting quietly, breathe in and out through your heart as if there were a nose in your chest wall. Let the breath touch your heart center and soften any hardness or armor around your heart.

Imagine yourself in a forest. You are sitting on a bed of moss, breathing in the scents of the trees and flowers. Breathing in, take in the feeling of Sita's love. Feel that you absorb her sweet, encompassing love through your heart.

Now imagine that around you are some of the creatures of the forest and streams, creatures whose survival as a species is threatened, species who are disappearing or have disappeared from the earth. Each of you might call to mind a different type of animal or bird. Sense their presence, and let yourself feel the uniqueness of all of them.

Perhaps you might find yourself in the presence of the gray wolf, the leopard, the ocelot, the brown bear, the tiger, the chimpanzee, the Indian elephant, or another of the species of animals and birds that are endangered or have already disappeared.

Now consider the places on earth where there has been damage due to human carelessness or exploitation. Consider the oil on the sea floor of the Gulf of Mexico, the melting polar ice caps, the droughts across the American West, the trees and plants no longer living.

What emotions come up when you consider these things? Rather than trying to name the emotion as anger, fear, or grief, notice where you feel it in your body. What is the emotion saying to you?

Now, feel the presence of Sita in those feelings. Ask her to speak to you through the feelings in your body. How can you hold the pain unfolding daily in this world, with love, without despair? How can Sita reveal to you the mystery of loving acceptance of what is, the "full catastrophe" of life, and your response to it? Stay with the feelings and the question as long as you need to.

Imagine all this being embraced by the vast, compassionate, sorrowing heart of the goddess Sita. Feel the vast spaciousness of her love and her understanding encompass your grief and feeling of having been abandoned. Feel the grace that comes to you through this.

When you are done, share and discuss what came up for you.

Dhumavati: Crone Goddess of Disappointment and Letting Go

How do you feel about elderly people? About your own aging process? What happens inside you when you face homeless or other street people? How have you experienced growth through disappointment? What disappointments or apparent failures have you had to process recently? How have you done it? How can the way in which you let go help you process the inevitable disappointments of life? Is it easy for you to let go? If not, what do you think is in the way?

Group Practice: Meditation on Letting Go

Sit quietly for meditation.
Focus on the breath.

Breathing in, let your attention flow into the heart.

Breathing out, have the thought, "Let Go." Your entire intention is to let go. Softly, let the breath become relaxed through the thought, "Let go." Let go of worries, thoughts, or whatever else arises through the breath.

Recognize that the capacity to let go of thoughts and ideas is one of the gifts of the Dhumavati Shakti. Tune in to the inner spaciousness that arises when you let go.

Breathe with the feeling that you are breathing in peacefulness and breathing out peacefulness.

Radha: Goddess of Romantic Longing

Can you identify with Radha's passionate love and longing? Have you ever felt this way about another person?

What are some modern examples of the Radha-Krishna love affair? Have there been moments in your life when you felt romantic devotion for another person? Have you ever passionately longed for the divine or for another person? How did that passion affect you?

How has longing functioned in your life? What, if anything, do you long for now?

What do you feel when you read descriptions of devotion or of bliss?

Group Practice: Invoking Radha

One person can read the meditation out loud, while the others practice.

Sit comfortably. You are going to invoke Radha and ask for her help to bring more love to a particular area of your life. Consider what it will be. Do you want help with a romance? Do you want to invoke more or deeper love with a partner, a parent, or a friend? Do you want to understand divine love itself?

Gather your intention, and write down your needs, desires, and requests. Place your journal before you.

Together, repeat the following mantra five times: "Jai shri Radhe namaha" *(jai shree rad-hey nu-muh-huh)*, which means "Hail, O auspicious Radha! Reverence!"

With your eyes closed, imagine yourself seated in a garden on a warm, scented night. A sweet breeze blows, caressing your skin. There is a bright moon overhead.

Ask that Radha, beloved of Krishna, be present with you.

Now, imagine that she walks into the garden. She is golden skinned, with the face of a fourteen-year-old girl. She has long, wavy hair bound with fragrant white flowers, and she wears a short blouse that bares her midriff and a long skirt. Her breasts are lush. Her rosy toes, with silver toe rings, peek out from beneath her skirt. She is smiling playfully—half girl, half woman. She seats herself on the grass in front of you, and gazes into your eyes.

Looking into Radha's eyes, you see them overflowing with love and mischief. She looks at you questioningly, inviting you to speak to her.

Now, begin to pour out your heart to Radha. Ask her for help in finding love, in finding joy. Ask her to untie a knot in your relationship. Ask her for whatever you seek in love. As you speak to her, feel that your requests are received.

If it feels right, ask her that your human relationships be touched with her divine love. Ask that you find the divine through your human loves.

Rest in the knowledge that you have received Radha's blessing.

Afterwards, discuss what you have experienced.

Chinnamasta: Goddess of Radical Self-Transcendence

In this session, we'll begin with a group practice to get in touch with the feeling of headlessness. Then, see if you can have the conversation from the place of "headlessness." Notice how it feels to look out at the room with the sense that you have no head. Do you feel more free? Are there fewer thoughts? What other effects do you notice?

Group Practice: Meditation on Headlessness

With your eyes closed, imagine yourself with no head. Sit for a while with your eyes closed, then open them and look around at the room and each other, as if you had no head. What is the difference in how you see the world?

Try to have a conversation, speaking from the place of headlessness.

How do you feel when you contemplate the image or description of
this goddess?
What inner spiritual state does the image of headlessness suggest?
How do you experience Chinnamasta's energy?
Contemplate the times in your life when you have channeled energy
or given energy to others. What part of that felt healthy and satisfying?
What part felt like you were being drained?
What in yourself have you cut off that now needs to be restored?
What would you say is the main gift that someone might experience
by meditating on this goddess?

Throughout the conversation, periodically stop and refresh your feeling of headlessness. Share the insights or emotions that come up for you as a result.

Lalita Tripura Sundari: Goddess of Erotic Spirituality

Are you comfortable with women who exhibit great power combined
with sexual charm? How do you feel about your own sexual power?
In what way does the Goddess Lalita express your own fantasies about
beauty and power?
Have you had experiences of deep pleasure or bliss in meditation? In
creative activities? In other parts of your life? Where and how?
In what parts of your life do you express Lalita's energy? Decide
together which action each of you might perform this week that
would express Lalita within your own lives.

Group Practice: Channeling Lalita's Heart Energy with a Partner

Sit in pairs, and close your eyes for a few moments.

Each of you, place your attention in the heart. You can place your right hand
over the center of the chest. Feel the warmth of your hand against your chest.
Breathe into the inner body behind your breastbone.

With each in-breath, have the thought "I offer blessings." With each exhalation have the thought, "I receive blessings."

Open your eyes and gaze into the other person's left eye. Keep your
center in the heart, and with each breath offer and receive blessing. Sense

the thread of energy running between you both. Stay with this for at least three minutes.

Afterward, share your experience with the other person and with the group.

Bhuvaneshwari: Goddess of Infinite Space, She Whose Body Is the World

What is your felt sense of the Goddess Bhuvaneshwari? Do you experience her energy as compassionate?

What happens to your view of the world when you contemplate the fact that we are all part of the goddess's body?

How do you understand the concept of "holding space"? Based on the chapter in the book, discuss how you have held space for others and/ or how others have held space for you.

Group Practice: Meditation on Bhuvaneshwari

Have one person read the following paragraph, then follow the instructions and contemplate together.

We are all made of the same elements as the stars, the rocks, and the plants and animals. All these elements, and our own bodies and minds, are held within the body of the goddess.

Close your eyes and consider an issue that is of concern to you, either in your personal life or the world at large. Then, together chant the mantra "hrim" *(hreem)* and summon the energy of Bhuvaneshwari as a space that holds you and your question. Feel what it is like to hold this issue in the space of the goddess. Ask this question: How can my life change if I consider that everything I see and do is happening within the goddess?

Now, take pen and paper and write any insight that arises about the issue you chose.

Share and discuss the experience and insight that arose through the contemplation.

Notes

Chapter 1—A Crown of Feminine Design: The Goddess Incarnates

1. I am indebted to Heinrich Zimmer for this version of the story, which comes originally from the *Kalika Purana*. His delicious retelling appears in the chapter called "The Romance of the Goddess," in Joseph Campbell, ed. *The King and the Corpse: Tales of the Soul's Conquest of Evil*, (Princeton: Princeton/Bollengen, 1973).

2. Told by poet and teacher David Whyte in his CD set, *What to Remember When Waking: The Disciplines of Everyday Life* (Boulder, CO: Sounds True, 2010).

3. See Riane Eisler, *The Chalice and the Blade: Our History, Our Future* (New York: HarperCollins, 1987); Andrew Harvey, *The Return of the Mother* (New York: Tarcher/Putnam, 2001); and Llewellyn Vaughan-Lee, *The Divine Feminine and the World Soul* (Inverness, CA: The Golden Sufi Center, 2009).

4. Cited in Harvey, *The Return of the Mother.*

5. Neil Gaiman's *American Gods* (New York: William Morrow, 2001) is a dark adventure featuring gods of several traditions, including Norse deities Odin and Loki, as well as Hinduism's Ganesha.

Chapter 2—The Grand Tantric Narrative: Gods, Goddesses, and Worlds

1. The recognition that there is such a thing as an active feminine power has slowly gained some ground in the West partly through

the works of three Jungian psychologists: Erich Neumann's *The Great Mother,* Genia Pauli Haddon's *Uniting Sex, Self, and Spirit: Let the Body Be Your Guide to New Consciousness and Deeper Spirituality in a Changing Age,* and Gareth Hill's *Masculine and Feminine: The Natural Flow of Opposites in the Psyche.* Genia Haddon points out that our bodies naturally contain these two poles. In the masculine, the yang energy is embodied in the phallus, with its power of thrusting, penetrating, and dominating. The yin energy is embodied in the testicles, which contain and store the sperm, and which embody the masculine aspects of patience and containment.

In the physical body, the yin pole of the feminine is the womb, which embodies the passive feminine attributes of nurturance and patient submission. The yang pole of the feminine is the powerful outward thrust of the birthing process, which pushes actively out from the body's center and brings forth life from within itself. Haddon points out that just as the phallus often seems to have an independent life apart from a man's will, masculine assertion tends to be outer directed and ejaculative. The assertion of the feminine, however, explodes from a deep center. So, the creative thrust of the active feminine has a quality of bringing something forth from within, of transformation, while the active masculine has the quality of acting upon the external world. The West has tended to ignore both the yin quality of the masculine and the yang quality of the feminine. That has meant, as Haddon points out, that when men want to tune in to their own capacity for passive containment and stability, they think of it as turning to their own feminine side. In the same way, women will tend to regard their active, dynamic energy as intrinsically masculine. A passive man will tend to feel unmasculine; an active woman unfeminine.

Though in social and psychological terms, Indian society is no more likely to be fully comfortable with the passive masculine or the active feminine, the goddess traditions of Tantra allow us to access these inner dynamics through ritual and meditation.

2. Kshemaraja, a tenth-century Kashmiri adept who commented on many of the primary texts of Kashmir Shaivism, wrote in his commentary on Shiva-stotravali by Utpaladeva, "Shakti, thrown up by delight lets herself go forth into manifestation." Quoted by Jaidev Singh in his introduction to Kshemaraja, *Pratyabhijnahrydayam* (New Delhi: Motilal Banarasidas, 1977).

3. Brian Swimme, *The Universe Is a Green Dragon: A Cosmic Creation Story* (Rochester, VT: Bear & Company, 1984).

Chapter 3—Durga: Warrior Goddess of Protection and Inner Strength

1. See David Kinsley's essay on the birth of Durga in *Hindu Goddesses* (Berkeley: University of California Press, 1986), for several versions of how the devas gifted her with their own powers. Thomas Coburn, in his essay in *Devi: Goddesses of India* (Los Angeles: University of California Press, 1996), points out that though it seems that the goddess is being "created" by the gods, in fact, the text never loses sight of the fact that Devi is preeminent as a primal power in the world. He writes, "Devi is the primary reality, and her agency is the only effective one."

2. In Indian tradition, the practice of austere yogic endurance is known as *tapas,* meaning "heat." Tapas performed with dedication and ardor is regarded as the force behind all creative endeavor as well as of yogic self-transformation. (See *The Yoga Sutras of Patanjali,* II-1 for the foundational yogic definition of tapas as spiritual heat.) From Vedic times on, it was understood that to make anything happen, you needed to create heat and energy within your own body. Scholar Raimondo Pannikar writes in *Mantra Manjari: The Vedic Experience* (New Delhi: Motilal Banarasidas, 2001) that "tapas or cosmic ardor, ascetic fire, arduous penance, concentration, which here amounts to an ontic condensation, is said . . . to be the energy giving birth to cosmic order and to truths. The three major concepts of Indian wisdom and of man's awareness are tapas, rta, and satya: ardor, order, and truth" (p. 59). The effectiveness of tapas has everything to do with the ardor with which it's performed. The Indian tradition is full of stories about human beings, gods, and demons who train like Olympic athletes, and the implication is that anyone with that much dedication can perform tapas and gain their goal.

3. Sri Aurobindo, *The Mother* (Sri Aurobindo Ashram: Pondicherry, 1996).

4. The lectures published in Swami Chidananda's *God as Mother*, (Divine Life Society, Shivanandanagar, 1991) exemplify the traditional view of Durga's battles as stages of the "battle" with ego. I am indebted to the author for his insight into the nine days of the Navaratri Festival as the framework for describing how each of the three great goddesses presides over a stage of spiritual transformation.

5. W. H. Murray, *The Scottish Himalayan Expedition* (London: Dent, 1951).

6. The *Pratyabhijnahrdayam* is the CliffsNotes for the central teaching of the Recognition School of Kashmir Shaivism, which describes the process by which consciousness becomes matter and then recognizes itself once again. This text explains that both the involution and the evolution of consciousness are part of an unbroken continuum of action "performed" by ChitShakti (the power of consciousness), whom it calls Chiti (the feminine form of pure consciousness.) The text begins with a sutra "Supreme consciousness in total freedom is the cause of the manifestation of the universe. She manifests it upon her own screen." In twenty succinct aphorisms and commentaries, the text describes how Shakti contracts to become the human being, then awakens herself as kundalini. Sutra 12 describes how the primordial Shakti acts through the nervous system, the brain, and the senses to give us an experience of being trapped in duality and suffering, but how these same faculties can give us the experience of nonduality when the liberating face of the Shakti is activated.

7. See Christopher Isherwood, *Ramakrishna and his Disciples* (Hollywood, CA: Vedanta Press, 1965).

Chapter 4—Lakshmi: Goddess of Abundance and Good Fortune

1. "The Secret Heart of Lakshmi," v. 88, quoted in Constantina Rhodes *Invoking Lakshmi* (Albany: SUNY Press, 2010).

2. Aurobindo, *The Mother.*

3. See lyricstime.com/johnny-cash-a-satisfied-mind-lyrics.html for a full version of the lyrics from this famous country song, which was recorded by Johnny Cash, its author, and many other singers.

4. Aurobindo, *The Mother.*

5. Jonathan Kozol, *Amazing Grace: The Lives of Children and the Conscience of a Nation* (New York: Crown Books, 1995).

Chapter 5—Kali: Goddess of Revolution

1. *Rama Prasad's Devotional Songs: The Cult of Shakti,* trans. Jadunath Sinha (Calcutta: Sinha Publishing House, 1966) no. 6, p. 3, as quoted in David R. Kinsley *The Sword and the Flute: Kali and Krishna, Dark Visions of the Terrible and the Sublime in Hindu Mythology* (Berkeley: University of California, 2000).

2. Sister Nivedita, *The Master as I Saw Him,* 9th edition (Calcutta: Udbodhan Office, 1963) p. 178, as quoted in Kinsley, *The Sword and the Flute.*

3. Aurobindo, *The Mother.*

4. Kinsley, *The Sword and the Flute.*

5. This story was told to me by a young woman journalist during a class I taught in 2000.

6. Lykke Li, "The Only" YouTube video, posted by "joshuRAWRRvideos," February 22, 2011, youtube.com/watch?v=rorfUVmTnGs.

7. "All Things yOni," accessed July 31, 2012, yoni.com/bitch.shtml.

8. Rachel Fell McDermott, "Kali's New Frontiers," in Rachel Fell McDermott and Jeffrey Kripal eds., *Encountering Kali: In the Margins, at the Center, in the West,* (Berkeley and Los Angeles: University of California Press, 2003).

9. *Kularnava Tantra* rendered by M. P. Pandit from the Sanskrit (Delhi: Motilal Banarasidas, 1983).

Chapter 6—Parvati: Goddess of the Sacred Marriage

1. The human archetype of the detached male, losing himself in meditation and disdaining worldly life, persists into the twenty-first century. Psychotherapist and author Mariana Caplan, in a 2002 article in *Tricycle Magazine,* "The Problem with Zen Boyfriends," expressed a contemporary woman's frustration with the classically detached yogic masculine. She describes her partnerships with certain types of "spiritual" men who refuse to engage in the messiness of intimacy, while claiming a "Shivaic" detachment from emotion. http://www.realspirituality.com/pages/pdf/zen_men.pdf.

2. Miranda Shaw, *Passionate Enlightenment: Women in Tantric Buddhism* (Princeton: Princeton University Press, 1994)

3. Paraphrased from Heinrich Zimmer's stellar retelling of the myth of Shiva and the Goddess, from *The King and the Corpse,* 264–265.

4. Ibid.

5. Ibid.

6. Anne Roiphe, in her memoir *Art and Madness: A Memoir of Lust Without Reason* (New York: Doubleday, 2011)

7. Daniel Liebert, trans. *Rumi: Fragments, Ecstasies* (New Lebanon, NY: Omega Publications, 1981).

8. Shaw, *Passionate Enlightenment*.

9. Daniel Odier, *Tantric Quest: An Encounter with Absolute Love* (Rochester, NY: Inner Traditions, 1997).

10. In the 1970s, a friend of mine, while studying with his Tibetan guru in Kathmandu, decided he wanted to explore Tantric sexual practice. He was thinking of it as something he would do with his girlfriend, as part of their erotic repertoire. He approached his guru and asked how he should go about it. The guru thought for a moment and said, "You should go live with [the wife of a particular lama] in her cave for three months, and she'll instruct you." My friend, who had never realized that sex could involve practicing austerities, decided to forget the whole thing. When he saw my friend's reaction, the guru burst out laughing.

11. Shaw, *Passionate Enlightenment*.

12. Jaideva Singh, trans. *The Yoga of Delight, Wonder, and Astonishment: A translation of the Vijnana-Bhairava.* (NY: SUNY Press edition, 1991).

13. Shaw, *Passionate Enlightenment*.

14. Odier, *Tantric Quest*.

15. David Kinsley, *Hindu Goddesses* (Berkeley and Los Angeles: University of California Press, 1988).

16. This meditation is based on a similar one that appears in Rudolph Ballentine's book, *Kali Rising: Foundational Principles of Tantra for a Transforming Planet* (Ballentine, SC: Tantrikster Press, 2010).

17. Robert A. Johnson, *We: Understanding the Psychology of Romantic Love* (San Francisco: HarperSanFrancisco, 1983).

Chapter 7—Saraswati: Goddess Who Flows as Language, Insight, and Sound

1. John, 1:1. (English Standard Bible)

2. Abhinavagupta, *Saraswatistotra*, from Sir John Woodroffe, *Hymns to the Goddess* (Madras: Ganesha and Co., 1913).

3. Ibid.

4. Ibid.

5. Kinsley, *Hindu Goddesses.*

6. From the *Devisukta*, Rg Veda, *Mandala X Sukta 725*, quoted in Woodroffe, *Hymns to the Goddess.*

7. Reported by author Elizabeth Gilbert in an interview on NPR's Radio Lab, March 8, 2011, radiolab.org/2011/mar/08/ me-myself-and-muse/.

8. Scott McDowell, "Creative Practice Tips from Brian Eno," Think Jar Collective, accessed July 31, 2012, thinkjarcollective. com/2012/06/creative-practice-tips-brian-eno.

9. Ibid.

Chapter 8—Sita: Goddess of Devotion and Mystical Submission

1. Kinsley, *Hindu Goddesses*, 66.

2. Makhanlal Sen. *The Ramayana of Valmiki* (New Delhi: Munshiram Manoharlal, 2003) book 2, 29.

3. Quoted in Kinsley, *Hindu Goddesses*, 70.

4. See Jean Houston's introduction to *The Mythic Path: Discovering the Guiding Stories of Your Past—Creating a Vision for Your Future* by David Feinstein and Stanley Krippner (New York: Tarcher-Putnam, 1997).

5. Carol Gilligan's *In a Different Voice: Psychological Theory and Women's Development* (Cambridge, MA: Harvard University Press, 1982, 1993) is one of the groundbreaking books on this aspect of feminine psychology.

6. This "teaching tale" is recounted in Marc Gafni, *Soul Prints: Your Path to Fulfillment* (New York: Atria, 2001).

7. This meditation owes a debt to the work of Joanna Macy. See the bibliography for information on her book *World as Lover, World as Self.*

Chapter 9—Dhumavati: Crone Goddess of Disappointment and Letting Go

1. Quoted in David Kinsley, *Tantric Visions of the Divine Feminine: The Ten Mahavidyas* (Berkeley, CA: University of California Press, 1997).

2. Ibid.

3. Ibid.

4. "Lily Tomlin, Katie Couric, Shirley MacLaine, and even Gloria Steinem all admit to having a bag lady in their anxiety closet." From a column by Jay McDonald, *Money* magazine, 2006.

5. For one of many accounts of occasions when Robert Kennedy quoted this poem, see NPR's *Morning Edition,* April 4, 2008, in a story on Kennedy delivering news of Martin Luther King's death. Kennedy misquoted the poem, changing the original translation of the words "in our own despite" to "in our own despair."

6. Eckhart Tolle, *The Power of Now: A Guide to Spiritual Enlightenment* (Novato, CA: New World Library, 1999).

7. Byron Katie, *Loving What Is: Four Questions That Can Change Your Life* (NY: Three Rivers Press, 2002).

8. James Fowler, *Stages of Faith: The Psychology of Human Development and the Quest for Meaning* (NY: HarperCollins, 1981).

9. Burton Watson, trans. *Chuang Tzu: Basic Writings* (NY: Columbia University Press, 2004).

Chapter 10—Radha: Goddess of Romantic Longing

1. Nikhilananda, trans. *The Gospel of Shri Ramakrishna.*

2. Chandidas, *Love Songs of Chandidas*, Deben Bhattacharya, trans. (London: George Allen and Unwin, 1963) quoted in Kinsley, *Hindu Goddesses.*

3. Ibid.

4. From *Vidagdhamaadhava* by the Sanskrit playwright Rupa, quoted in John Stratton Hawley and Donna Marie Wulff, *Devi: Goddesses of India* (Berkeley, CA: University of California, 1996).

5. Vidyaspati, quoted by Kinsley in *The Sword and the Flute.*

6. Johnson, *We.*

7. Vidyaspati, quoted by Kinsley in *The Sword and the Flute.*

8. St. John of the Cross, "The Living Flame of Love," from *Twenty Poems* (Radford, VA: Wilder Publications, 2008).

9. Leibert, *Rumi: Fragments, Ecstasies.*

10. Doris Lessing, *Love, Again* (New York: Harper Collins, 1996).

11. Robert Bly, trans. *The Kabir Book* (Boston: Beacon Press, 1977).

Chapter 11—Chinnamasta: Goddess of Radical Self-Transcendence

1. Kabir, *Songs of Kabir*, Rabindranath Tagore, trans. (New York: Samuel Weiser, 1981).

2. Randal C. Archibold, "In Latin America, Prisons Condemned to Crisis" *New York Times*, March 13, 2012.

3. Abhinavagupta quote from *Tantraloka*, translation paraphrased from Lilian Silburn, *Kundalini: Energy of the Depths* (Albany, NY: SUNY Press, 1988).

4. Douglas Harding, *On Having No Head: Zen and the Rediscovery of the Obvious* (Carlesbad, CA: Inner Directions, 2002).

5. John, 10:10 (English Standard Bible).

6. Ram Alexander, ed. *Death Must Die: The Diary of Atmananda* (Varanasi: Indica Books, 2000).

7. In the Tantric traditions, there were a number of formal and informal initiation ceremonies, called *diksha* (*deek-shah*). The *Kularnava Tantra* (chapter ten) mentions seven basic types of diksha, including diksha through ritual, though the letters of a mantra, through "special emanation," through touch, through speech, through sight, and through thought. Diksha is also categorized by the level of empowerment it offers and by the type of ritual undergone. Commonly, a basic initiation, *samaya diksha* (*suhmuhyah deek-shah*), was given to entry-level disciples and entitled them to study with the teacher and read sacred texts. The most advanced, *nirvana diksha* (*ner-vah-nah deek-shah*), was given to samayins who had proven their commitment. It removed karmic obstructions, so that a keen disciple could, through effort, attain enlightenment. In a ritual setting, the guru laid his hands on the disciple and transmitted a mantra imbued with his or her own realization, directly from his heart to the heart of the disciple. This was supposed to confer the energy that would stay with the disciple lifetime after lifetime, until the disciple became fully enlightened. However, the *Kularnava* also states that initiation can take place without formal ritual, and can be equally effective and transformative. See Arthur Avalon, *Kularnava Tantra* (Delhi, India: Motilal Banarasidas Publishers, 1965, 1984, 1999, 2000, 2007).

8. Alex Smith, "Dating a Yoga Goddess," *Elephant Journal,* August 4, 2010, www.elephantjournal.com.

9. E. L. James, *Fifty Shades of Grey* (New York: Vintage Books, 2012).

10. Marion Woodman and Elinor Dickson, *Dancing in the Flames: The Dark Goddess and the Energy of Transformation* (Boston: Shambhala Publications, 1996).

11. Mark F. Schwartz and Leigh Cohen, ed., *Sexual Abuse and Eating Disorders* (New York: Brunner-Routledge, 1996).

12. Woodman and Dickson, *Dancing in the Flames.*

Chapter 12—Lalita Tripura Sundari: Goddess of Erotic Spirituality

1. In any case, the more we meditate on these goddesses, the more we recognize their individuality as well as the qualities they have in common. Looked at from a historical and anthropological perspective, we could explain this by pointing out that India is a large country with many regional versions of its core myths. Looked at from an inner perspective, we could say that the subtle world has many parallel realities, in which the Goddess takes on different forms, personalities, and guises.

2. Shankaracharya, *Ananda Lahari*, v.14. Rendered by me from the Vedanta Spiritual Library edition, translated by P. R. Ramachander.

3. Douglas Renfrew Brooks, *Auspicious Wisdom* (Albany, NY: SUNY Press, 1992).

4. Ibid.

5. Marc Gafni, *The Mystery of Love* (New York: Atria Books, 2003).

6. Adyashanti, *Spontaneous Enlightenment* CD program (Boulder, CO: Sounds True, 2003).

7. Kinsley, *Tantric Visions of the Divine Feminine.*

8. Merilyn Tunneshende, *Don Juan and the Sexual Energy* (Burlington, VT: Bear & Company, 2001).

9. Christopher Wallis, *Tantra Illuminated: The Philosophy, History and Practice of a Timeless Tradition* (The Woodlands, TX: Anusara Press, 2012).

Chapter 13—Bhuvaneshwari: Goddess of Infinite Space, She Whose Body Is the World

1. From *Mantramahaarnava*, quoted in Kinsley, *Tantric Visions of the Divine Feminine.*

2. Chandogya Upanishad 1–3 (My rendering, from RadhaKrishnan, *The Ten Principle Upanishads*)

3. Bly, *The Kabir Book.*

4. Joanna Macy, *World as Lover, World as Self: Courage for Global Justice and Ecological Renewal* (Berkeley, CA: Parallax Press, 1991).

5. For the imagery of light and color at the start of this version of tonglen practice, I am indebted to Pema Chödrön, who describes it in several of her books, including *Start Where You Are* (Boston, MA: Shambhala Classics, 2001).

Epilogue—Dialoguing with the Goddesses

1. Gafni, Marc. *Your Unique Self* (Tucson: Integral Publishers, 2012).

2. Mrinal Pande, *Devi: Tales of the Goddess in Our Time* (New Delhi: Penguin Books, 1996).

3. Jean Shinoda Bolen, *Goddesses in Everywoman* (New York: Harper and Row, 1984).

Appendix II—Calling Out the Power in Mantra: Overview and Pronouncation Guide

1. For a longer explanation of bija mantras and their power to manifest, see Sir John Woodroffe's *The Garland of Letters: Studies in the Mantra-Sastra* (Madras: Ganesh & Co., 2004) much of which consists of translations of Sanskrit texts about mantra from the Tantras. The Vedic and Tantric traditions, like the Jewish tradition of Kabbalah, were founded on language mysticism, in which sounds, properly pronounced and properly enlivened, had the power to manifest the corresponding realities in the physical and subtle worlds. Even today, in India, there are priests reputed to have the power to kindle fire by reciting the seed mantra for fire, "ram" (pronounced *ruhm*—unlike the Hindi name for the god Rama, which is pronounced *rahm*). According to the *Shiva Sutras*, (2/7), the true mantra is the Shakti within it, and the nature of mantra is the light of consciousness. In short, though the mantra associated with a deity is considered the actual sound-embodiment of the deity, in order for the mantra to be effective, the power (shakti) within it needs to be awakened—either through initiation, intense personal practice, or both.

Annotated Bibliography
for Further Reading

Aurobindo, Sri. *The Mother*. Pondicherry, India: Sri Aurobindo Ashram, 1928. A passionate tribute to the Goddess as the force of evolutionary transformation.

Ballentine, Rudolph. *Kali Rising: Foundational Principles of Tantra for a Transforming Planet*. Ballentine, SC: Tantrikster Press, 2010. A doctor and contemporary Western teacher delves into the concepts of Shiva/Shakti tantra, in accessible dialogue form.

Baring, Anne, and Jules Cashford. *The Myth of the Goddess: Evolution of an Image*. London: Arkana, 1993. Tracing the history of the Western goddesses, from Isis to Sophia.

Bhairavan, Amarananda. *Kali's Odiyya: A Shaman's True Story of Initiation*. York Beach, ME: Nicolas-Hays, 2000. Memoir of a South Indian boy initiated as a practitioner of Kali rites.

Bolen, Jean Shinoda. *Goddesses in Everywoman*. New York: Harper and Row, 1984. A Jungian psychologist's classic book on the Greek goddesses as archetypes in the feminine psyche.

Brooks, Douglas Renfrew. *Auspicious Wisdom*. Albany, New York: SUNY Press, 1991. A scholar-practitioner unpacks the tradition and text of Shri Vidya worship in South India.

Caldwell, Sarah. *Oh Terrifying Mother*. New Delhi: Oxford University Press, 1999. An anthropologist's account of a village Bhadrakali cult in South India.

Chidananda, Swami, *God as Mother*. Shivanandanagar, India: Divine Life Society, 1991. Lectures from a traditional teacher on the meaning of Navaratri (the Nine Nights Festival dedicated to the Goddess Durga).

Coburn, Thomas. *Encountering the Goddess*. Albany, NY: SUNY Press, 1991. A scholar's translation and commentary on the Devi Mahatmya (Triumph of the Goddess), the 700-verse cycle that describes the goddess's triumph over dark forces.

Coomaraswamy, Ananda and Sister Nivedita. *Classic Indian Tales*. Mumbai: Jaico Publishing House, 2008. Well-told versions of myths from the Hindu and Buddhist traditions.

Dyczkowski, Mark S. G. *The Doctrine of Vibration*. Albany, NY: State University of New York Press, 1987. An inspired scholarly work on the Spanda tradition of Kashmir Shaivite Tantra.

Eisler, Riane. *The Chalice and the Blade*. New York: HarperCollins, 1988. A feminist scholar describes the clash between "partnership" culture of the goddess civilizations in Europe and the "dominator" culture that came in with the Aryan warriors.

Frawley, David. *Inner Tantric Yoga: Working with the Universal Shakti: Secrets of Mantras, Deities, and Meditation*. Twin Lakes, WI: Lotus Press, 2008. Yogic lore from the Indian tradition of Shakti.

———. *Tantric Yoga and the Wisdom Goddesses: Spiritual Secrets of Ayurveda*. Twin Lakes, WI: Lotus, 2003. A useful and accessible guide to the ten esoteric yoga goddesses, the Mahavidya.

Feuerstein, Georg. *Tantra: The Path of Ecstasy*. Boston: Shambhala Publications, 1998. A yoga scholar's accessible and wide-ranging survey of the major aspects of Tantric religion in India.

Gafni, Marc. *The Mystery of Love*. New York: Atria, 2003. Eros and the divine feminine explored from a Kabbalistic perspective.

Gafni, Marc. *Your Unique Self*. Tucson: Integral Publishers, 2012. Teachings on the postenlightened individual self.

Gimbutas, Marija. *The Civilization of the Goddess*. San Francisco, CA: HarperSanFrancisco: 1991. An archeologist traces the cultures of Neolithic era goddess worship in Europe through art and other remains.

Goswami, Shyam Sunar. *Laya Yoga*. Rochester, VT: Inner Traditions, 1999. Translations and commentaries on several key Tantric texts describing kundalini, the chakras, and the practices that relate to them.

Haddon, Pauli Genia. *Uniting Sex, Self, and Spirit*. Scotland, CT: PLUS Publications, 1993. A groundbreaking look at the yin and yang elements in men and women, which Haddon argues are carried in different ways in the bodies of men and women as well as in their psychological makeup.

Harvey, Andrew. *The Return of the Mother*. New York: J.P. Tarcher/ Putnam, 2001. A passionate survey of how the feminine manifests through different sacred traditions and figures, mixed with social and personal advocacy for appreciating the need for recognizing the divine feminine in religion and society.

Hawley, John Stratton and Donna Marie Wulff, eds. *Devi: Goddesses of India*. Berkeley: University of California, 1996. Essays on different aspects of the Hindu goddesses by several contemporary scholars.

Hill, Gareth S. *Masculine/Feminine: The Natural Flow of Opposites in the Psyche*. Boston: Shambhala Publications, 1992. A Jungian psychologist's exploration of the yin/yang feminine and the yang/ yin masculine.

Ironbiter, Barbara. *Devi: Mother of My Mind*. Ahmenabad, India: MapinLit, 2006. A scholar-poet offers us her radical take on the Goddess Durga, in a contemporary interpretation of the goddess cycle from the Devi Mahatmya.

Isherwood, Christopher. *Ramakrishna and His Disciples*. Hollywood, CA: Vedanta Press, 1965. The most accessible biography of the iconic saint whose disciples helped bring Hinduism into the Western world.

Johari, Harish. *Tools for Tantra*. Rochester, VT: Destiny, 1986. An illustrated guide to the mantras and yantras with explanations of key rituals in Tantric practice.

Kali, Devadatta. *In Praise of the Goddess: The Devimahatmya and Its Meaning*. Berwick, ME: Nicolas-Hays, Inc., 2003. A lively translation, transliteration, and commentary on the verses of the goddess cycle.

Kidd, Sue Monk. *The Dance of the Dissident Daughter*. New York: HarperCollins, 1996. A Christian novelist discovers the feminine face of God.

Kinsley, David R. *Hindu Goddesses: Visions of the Divine Feminine in the Hindu Religious Tradition*. Berkeley: University of California, 1986. A scholar's studies on the major and minor Indian goddesses.

———. *Tantric Visions of the Divine Feminine: The Ten Mahavidyas*. Berkeley: University of California, 1997. Definitive essays on ten goddess figures of India.

———. *The Sword and the Flute: Kali and Krishna, Dark Visions of the Terrible and the Sublime in Hindu Mythology*. Berkeley: University of

California, 2000. A study comparing the dark goddess Kali and the dark god Krishna.

Macy, Joanna. *World as Lover, World as Self.* Berkeley, CA: Parallax Press, 1991. A deep look at what it means to love and protect the earth in a time of ecological crisis.

McDermott, Rachel Fell and Jeffrey J. Kripal. *Encountering Kali: In the Margins, at the Center, in the West.* Berkeley: University of California, 2003. Essays on Goddess Kali by contemporary scholars.

Mookerjee, Ajit. *Kali: The Feminine Force.* New York: Destiny, 1988. The mythology and iconography of Kali unveiled.

———. *Kundalini.* Third Ed. Rochester, VT: Destiny, 1986. A guide to kundalini and the chakras, beautifully illustrated, from core texts of Tantra.

Muktananda, Swami. *Kundalini.* South Fallsburg, NY: SYDA Publications, 1978. A master yogi's description of how kundalini works in the human body and spirit.

———. *The Play of Consciousness.* South Fallsburg, NY: SYDA Publications, 1978. The spiritual autobiography of a lover of the Goddess, describing his personal experience of awakening and enlightenment through the rising of kundalini.

Odier, Daniel. *Tantric Quest: An Encounter with Absolute Love,* trans. by Jody Gladding. Rochester, VT: Inner Traditions, 1996. A compelling tale of the author's initiation by a Himalayan yogini.

Pandit, M. P. *Kularnava Tantra.* Madras: Ganesh & Company, 1973. Translation of one of the definitive texts of the Kaula Tantric tradition.

Pande, Mrinal. *Devi: Tales of the Goddess in Our Time.* New Delhi: Penguin, 1996. An Indian journalist tells true stories about women in her life who incarnate the goddess archetypes in contemporary India.

Pattanaik, Devdutt. *The Mother-Goddess: An Introduction.* Mumbai: Bimal Mehta, 2000. Key myths of the Goddess in accessible, bite-size form.

Radhakrishnan, S. *The Principal Upanishads.* New York: Harper, 1953. Foundational texts of Indian philosophy.

Ramakrishna. *The Gospel of Sri Ramakrishna.* Translated into English with an Introduction by Swami Nikhilananda. Mylapore, Madras, India: Sri Ramakrishna Math.

Ramaprasada, Sena, Leonard Nathan, and Clinton B. Seely. *Grace and Mercy in Her Wild Hair: Selected Poems to the Mother Goddess*. Prescott, AZ: Hohm, 1999. Poems of ecstasy and longing by a Bengali devotee of Kali.

Rhodes, Constantina Eleni. *Invoking Lakshmi: The Goddess of Wealth in Song and Ceremony*. Albany, NY: State University of New York, 2010. A scholar's poetic and accessible translation and commentary of a group of ritual texts on the goddess Lakshmi, including an overview of Tantra and the role of this goddess.

Sen, Makhanlal. *The Ramayana of Valmiki*. New Delhi: Munshiram Manoharlal, 2003. Translation of the Indian epic tale.

Shankarananda, Swami. *Consciousness Is Everything*. Melbourne, Australia: Shaktipat Press, 2003. An American spiritual teacher's explication of the principles and practices of Kashmir Shaivism.

Shankaranarayan, S. *The Ten Great Cosmic Powers*. Chennai: Samata Books, 1972. A practitioner's unpacking of the meaning of the ten Mahavidyas, by a member of the Aurobindo community.

Shaw, Miranda. *Buddhist Goddesses of India*. Princeton, NJ: Princeton University Press, 2006. The iconography, history, and meaning of a group of deities of the Tibetan Tantric tradition.

———. *Passionate Enlightenment: Women in Tantric Buddhism*. Princeton, NJ: Princeton University Press, 1994. A scholarly work on Tantric female practitioners in the Himalayan regions.

Singh, Jaideva, trans. *The Yoga of Delight, Wonder, and Astonishment: A Translation of the Vijnana Bhairava*. Albany, NY: SUNY Press, 1991. A foundational text of Tantric meditation, containing 112 verses on practice.

———. *Shiva Sutras: The Yoga of Supreme Identity*. New Delhi, India: Motilal Banarasidas, 1979. A foundational text of Kashmir Shaiva philosophy, revered in the Tantric traditions of India.

———. *Spanda Karikas: The Divine Creative Pulsation*. New Delhi, India: Motilal Banarasidas, 2005. Translation and commentary on this core text on Shakti by an Indian scholar. A companion piece to the *Shiva Sutras*, describing reality from the point of view of Shakti.

Srimad Devi Bhagavatam, Books 1–12. Translated by Swami Vijnananda, alias Hari Prasanna Chatterji. New York: AMS Press, 1974. A core text of traditional goddess worship in India, containing myths, cosmology, and much more.

Terry, Lynda. *The Eleven Intentions: Invoking the Sacred Feminine as a Path to Inner Peace.* Santa Rose, CA: Vessels of Peace, 2005. Contemplations on goddesses of several traditions as doorways into world peace.

Urban, Hugh. *Tantra.* Berkeley and Los Angeles: University of California Press, 2003. A contemporary religious scholar traces the history of Tantra's encounter with the West.

Vaughan-Lee, Llewellyn. *The Divine Feminine and the World Soul.* Inverness, CA: The Golden Sufi Center, 2009. A Sufi teacher's lectures on the feminine as the "soul" of the earth and related subjects.

Wallis, Christopher. *Tantra Illuminated: The Philosophy, History, and Practice of a Timeless Tradition.* The Woodlands, TX: Anusara Press, 2012. A scholar-practitioner's clear and accessible guide to nondual tantric teachings and the different tantric schools of thought. A go-to book for modern practitioners.

Wilber, Ken. *Integral Spirituality.* Boston: Integral Books, 2006. A perspective on spirituality that integrates the spiritual-practice traditions with developmental psychology and more.

———. *No Boundary.* Boston: Shambhala Publications, 1979, 2001. Exploring the practice and goal of the nondual spiritual traditions from a full spectrum psychospiritual perspective.

———. *The Simple Feeling of Being.* Boston: Shambhala Publications, 2004. Writings on the self, taken from the traditions of Vedanta and Buddhism as well as the author's experience.

Woodman, Marion and Elinor Dickson. *Dancing in the Flames: The Dark Goddess in the Transformation of Consciousness.* Boston: Shambhala, 1997. A nuanced exploration by two Jungian psychologists of the different aspects of the "dark" feminine.

Woodroffe, John George. *Hymns to the Goddess.* Delhi: Shivalik Prakashan, 2009. Traditional praise songs from the Shakta tradition.

Zimmer, Heinrich Robert and Joseph Campbell. *The King and the Corpse: Tales of the Soul's Conquest of Evil.* Princeton, NJ: Princeton University Press, 1971. A brilliant mythologist retells and comments on a group of classic Indian tales, including the cycle of the Goddess from the Kalika Purana, a work of the Shakta tradition.

About the Author

S ally Kempton (1943–2023) studied and taught the wisdom of yoga for 40 years. A highly regarded teacher of meditation and spiritual philosophy, she wrote the popular *Yoga Journal* column Wisdom. Known for her gift of making yogic wisdom relevant to daily life and for transmitting deep states of meditation, she taught retreats and teleclasses internationally.

About the Illustrator

Ekabhumi Charles Ellik is a poet, artist, husband, student, and teacher of classical Tantric Hatha Yoga. He holds a fine arts degree from California State University, Long Beach with an emphasis on figurative art, yet his creativity is expressed in many ways. He is the youth programs director for Yoga Mandala in Berkeley, where he also teaches adult yoga asana classes and displays paintings. A former options broker, he quit finance to produce poetry events full time in 1999, when his team of poets won the National Poetry Slam. Cofounder of the Berzerkeley Poetry Slam, poets he coached have won numerous national and regional titles. In 2007, he became the national Head 2 Head Haiku champion, and in 2009 he chaired the home city committee of the Individual World Poetry Slam.

With the encouragement of his guru, Dharma Bodhi, he retired from producing poetry events in 2010 to focus on sacred art and teaching. At that time, he also became a regular student of Nepalese master painter Dinesh Charan, who is teaching him the traditional Newar style of *tankha* and *paubha* painting. In 2011, he took a trip to India to study Yantra and the painting of Devas in the lineage of Harish Johari. In 2012, he was featured artist at the Wanderlust Festival in Tahoe and illustrated Christopher Wallis' seminal book *Tantra Illuminated*. When not writing, painting, or practicing yoga, he can be found in his garden learning directly from nature.

About Sounds True

Sounds True is a multimedia publisher whose mission is to inspire and support personal transformation and spiritual awakening. Founded in 1985 and located in Boulder, Colorado, we work with many of the leading spiritual teachers, thinkers, healers, and visionary artists of our time. We strive with every title to preserve the essential "living wisdom" of the author or artist. It is our goal to create products that not only provide information to a reader or listener, but that also embody the quality of a wisdom transmission.

For those seeking genuine transformation, Sounds True is your trusted partner. At SoundsTrue.com you will find a wealth of free resources to support your journey, including exclusive weekly audio interviews, free downloads, interactive learning tools, and other special savings on all our titles.

To listen to a podcast interview with Sounds True publisher Tami Simon and author Sally Kempton, please visit SoundsTrue.com/awakeningshakti.

SOUNDS TRUE
many voices, one journey